Sisters of the Screen

Sisters of the Screen

Women of Africa on Film, Video, and Television

Beti Ellerson

Africa World Press, Inc.

P.O. Box 1892
Trenton, NJ 08607

P.O. Box 48
Asmara, ERITREA

Africa World Press, Inc.

P.O. Box 1892
Trenton, NJ 08607

P.O. Box 48
Asmara, ERITREA

Copyright © 2000 Beti Ellerson

First printing 2000

Book design: Wanjikũ Ngũgĩ
Cover design: Jonathan Gullery

Library of Congress Cataloging-in-Publication Data

Sisters of the screen : women of Africa on film, video, & television /
  [interviewed] by Beti Ellerson
        p.   cm.
    Filmography: p.
    ISBN 0-86543-712-2. -- ISBN 0-86543-713-0 (pbk.)
    1. Women in the motion picture industry--Africa. 2. Women in
  television broadcasting--Africa. 3. Women motion picutre producers
  and directors--Africa--Interviews. 4. Women television producers
  and directors--Africa--Interviews.   I. Ellerson, Beti.
  PN1995.9.W6S47   1998
  791.4'082'-096--dc21

98-44144
CIP

CONTENTS

ACKNOWLEDGEMENTS

I would like to express my sincere appreciation first to those sisters of the screen who are included in the collection, as well as those who gave their voices but from whom I was not able to secure permission to use their conversations in this volume; those who agreed to be a part of the project, but for various reasons we were not able to make it happen, as well as the many, many other sisters of the screen everywhere who have, by the act of making, thinking about, writing about images, contributed to my interests, ideas, thoughts, and evolution in this project. I would also like to note the true sense of commitment and sisterhood that so many of the women showed as they spread the word about this project and made contacts with other women.

I would like to acknowledge the Center for the Study of Culture and Development in Africa (1994-1997), housed in the African Studies Department at Howard University, and its Program Director, Mbye Cham. I would also like to thank Mbye for his support and also for believing in this project. As a recipient of a Rockefeller Humanities Fellowship, administered by the Center, I was able to realize a significant part of this project during the 1996-97 fellowship year.

Grateful acknowledgement is hereby tendered to the many institutions that gave me access to their collections or provided me with helpful information: the Moorland Spingarn Research Center, Howard University (Washington, DC); Audecam (Paris); Atria (Paris) with a very special thanks to Andrée Davanture, Annabel Thomas and Claude le Gallou; Amina Magazine (Paris) especially acknowledging Assiatou Bah Diallo; FEPACI (Ouagadougou), a special thanks to Gaston Kaboré; Ecrans d'Afrique, a thank you to Clément Tapsoba (Ouagadougou) and Alessandra Speciale (Milan); FESPACO (Ouagadougou) thanks to Regine Yoda; and Zimmedia (Zimbabwe).

A sincere thanks goes to my friends and colleagues who assisted me in editing and proofreading the text: Lisa Fanning-Diene, Glenda Johnson, Yvonne Poser, Ruth Rhone and Maria Roof. I would also like to acknowledge the many people, too numerous to mention all by name, who assisted me in contacting the "sisters" who I needed to get in touch with to secure permission to use their conversations in the book. Although I was not able to contact or secure permission from some, I sincerely appreciate the tireless effort of so many who assisted me in the search; I would like to mention, in particular, Isaac Mabhikwa of the Southern African Film Festival.

Special thanks to Robert R. Edgar, Professor in the African Studies Department at Howard University, and a friend and colleague. I thank Bob for his inspiration, patience, and thoughtfulness as well as his invaluable experience, which he offered throughout. Other friends and colleagues who have been supportive and encouraging are Mtembezi Inniss, Mueni Muiu, Guy Martin, and Susan Andrade.

I would also like to thank Africa World Press publisher, Kassahun Checole, who believed in this project and who was the catalyst to its being conceived as a written work.

I definitely must mention the Ellerson family, my mother Vera, my sister Audrey, and my brother Anthony—all of whom watched excerpts of the filmed version of this project and gave lively and enthusiastic comments and who are now anxiously waiting to read the book. I must also add my niece, Tracey, who has been an avid cheerleader.

I am indebted to my partner Christophe Poulenc, without whom this project would not have been possible. He has been a constant companion throughout this effort. Initially conceived as a documentary project, in the capacity of director of photography (etc.), most of the conversations were filmed by Christophe, in Ouagadougou, Montreal, Washington, DC, and Paris. As I took on the task of translating the conversations from French, which constituted more than half, Christophe, with infinite patience, listened to the audiotapes and proofread the translated copy.

FOREWORD

The publication of this book is a most welcome development in the short history of studies on African cinema and screen practices. To date, scholarship, criticism and general commentaries on African cinema and video have focussed disproportionately on the films made by men and, among other topics, the various roles, images and portraitures of women in these works. Reasons advanced for this slant include the perennial lament about the general absence of women filmmakers and films by women in Africa, with the exception of pioneers like Safi Faye and Thérèse Sita Bella. Few, however, have bothered to probe beneath the surface of this absence to explore, explain and interrogate the complex of reasons and factors which account for this absence. Even fewer have actually made it a task and a priority to *look for* these female filmmakers and videographers, as well as other modes of female presence and practice in the arena of African cinema and visual media. *Sisters of the Screen* accomplishes these two seminal tasks. Enough of the cry and whining about absence.

Presence, albeit emergent, however, does not spell absence or disappearance of the structures, practices and factors that are responsible for the continuing imbalance between male and female screen practitioners in Africa. The responses and commentaries that Beti Ellerson's questions and queries elicit from the female filmmakers, videographers, actresses, producers, writers, and film scholars whom she sought out and followed in numerous places in three continents over time, testify to the staying power of these structures and practices. More significantly, they reveal African female will and agency, for they speak to the challenges and need to dismantle those structures and practices that want to inhibit or retard a more forceful and equitable presence of women in all aspects of African cinema, media and society, in general.

Sisters of the Screen is a statement about the creative process for women screen artists in Africa, as well as the Diaspora. *How* and *why* African women screen artists create and work, their challenges, difficulties, traditional restrictions, their background, their aspirations and numerous other factors covering a wide spectrum of women's experiences in domains—artistic as well as social—usually figured as male—these constitute the thread that runs through the conversations Ellerson assembles in this ground-breaking anthology. Equally pronounced in this anthology is the range of subject matter and concerns of the work of African female screen artists and practitioners, their conflation of the personal and the public, and the place of their work in African cinema and media, in general.

The women presented in *Sisters of the Screen* illustrate the range and variety of female involvement and practices in African cinema and visual media. The anthology is a bold assertion of presence and significance in the midst of laments of absence. *Sisters of the Screen* is a significant contribution to more wholesome and better descriptions and understandings of African screen practices.

—Mbye Cham
Washington, DC
June 2, 1999

Preface and Methodology

Sisters of the Screen emerged out of my research on African women in visual culture, my desire to find a paradigm for reading images of and by African women, and my own work in videography and as a performance artist. I undertook this project on a Rockefeller Humanities Fellowship during the 1996-97 academic year at the Center for the Study of Culture and Development in Africa administered by the African Studies Department at Howard University. As a fellow, my objective was to make a critical inventory of the works, thoughts, and practices of African women in the various areas of the cinema and present it in the form of a documentary.

Nineteen ninety-seven proved to be an exceptional year for encountering African women in the cinema. Three events took place where thirty-four of forty-one interviews were conducted. The 15th edition of FESPACO (Pan-African Festival of Cinema and Television of Ouagadougou) presented the highest entry ever of films of all categories by women. There was the rare appearance of Safi Faye (Senegal), who presented her feature film *Mossane*. Though Tsitsi Dangarembga (Zimbabwe) was not present, her debut film *Everyone's Child* was screened. A week after the closing of FESPACO, a film screening of works by women, Films de femmes pour le développement/Women's Films for Development, was held in Ouagadougou on March 8th and 9th in commemoration of the International Day of the Woman. (A commemorative event is held every year.) This event provided another occasion to meet women whom I had not encountered during the actual festival, as well as view films that were not part of the FESPACO screenings. It also allowed me to meet some of the filmmakers who were still in Ouagadougou within another context. Less than two months later, the 1997 African Literature Association Conference, hosted by Michigan State University at East Lansing, Michigan, devoted its entire platform to African cinema. Dangarembga was the keynote speaker of the Women's Caucus Luncheon. Also at the conference were Ngozi Onwurah (Nigeria) and Salem Mekuria (Ethiopia) who spoke on the ALA panel "Women and Cinema" which was also to include Flora M'mbugu-Schelling (Tanzania) who was not present. Another highlight of the conference was the screening of Assia Djebar's

1978 film, *La Nouba des Femmes du Mont Chenoua*, and her passionate discussion of how the film was made and the response to it at that time. Diasporan filmmaker Gloria Rolando (Cuba), who had previously toured the United States with her films in 1996, talked about her film *Oggun* during the discussion after the screening. While many of the women who attended the 1997 Vues d'Afrique were also present at FESPACO, there were several that only attended the Montreal festival.

The same year, the Paris-based cinema house Images d'Ailleurs organized a film forum titled "Cri du coeur des femmes" at which many of the films that were viewed at other festivals throughout the year were also screened. Also, during 1997, the book *With Open Eyes: Women and African Cinema*, edited by Kenneth Harrow, was published. In addition, in 1998, the Festival international de film de femmes/International Women's Film Festival at Créteil had an impressive platform devoted to women of Africa. These various events give evidence of the growing interest and visibility of African women in the cinema.

During the fellowship year 1996-97, while talking with Kassahun Checole, I mentioned that as my fellowship project I was working on a documentary on African women in the cinema and that I had already filmed conversations with more than twenty women and was hoping to have as many as forty. Kassahun suggested that it would be a great idea to publish these conversations, since a collection of voices of African women in the cinema was in itself an original idea. We talked more in depth about the project and he told me to send him a proposal. The book *Sisters of the Screen* was conceived.

As the material for the documentary became larger, and the footage grew into hours and hours, I began to worry about how I would be able to present all the wonderful and important information that the women were revealing. I thought that perhaps in addition to an initial work of 90 to 120 minutes, I could later do several volumes presented thematically to somehow include the more than 20 hours of conversations. When there was the possibility of having the conversations compiled as a written collection, I realized immediately that it would be an ideal way of allowing the women to have their say, to allow them to speak for themselves and elaborate their experiences.

I feel it is very important to present the conversations in an interview format so that the reader may follow the context in which the points were made. In some cases, the women wanted specific questions to guide their thoughts; in other cases the women took the lead and revealed things about themselves and their experiences that I would never have dared to ask. While I had certain questions that I wanted to ask in order to get certain views from as many women as possible—regarding, for instance, the notion of a women's sensibility, attitudes about African women and the image, women organizing, etc.—I was careful not to impose a "feminist agenda," but rather to elicit an African woman's perspective.

Methodologically, there have been certain adjustments that have had to be made since the project was not originally conceived as a written collection of conversations. Since the original goal was to edit the women's voices together as a conversation in a documentary, questions were posed differently than they would have been during a face-to-face, audiotaped conversation or other non-visual interview methods. The presence of a camera and cameraperson, or in the few instances when I was both cameraperson and interviewer, presented a different dynamic. While a conversation in the absence of a camera could take place in an isolated, exclusive setting, the filmed interview required special lighting and audio, as well as specific locations conducive to the requirements for filming.

When the possibility of a written collection emerged, I solicited interviews from women with whom I was not able to arrange a filmed conversation: by telephone, e-mail, in person by audiotape, or by letter. In order to obtain the same level of conversational spontaneity in all the voices, I exercised a certain degree of editorial license. Also, in some instances I was in touch with women after our initial conversation and was able to get current information about the status of their projects or even more in-depth information that had not come out during the interview. In several instances, I was able to have pre-interviews or a series of interviews over a period of time. Thus, some conversations are more evolved, while in others women expressed their thoughts, feelings, and reflections in the spirit and energy of a film festival or conference. This often produced more specific information, usually about the film that was being screened at the festival.

Conversations that took place off-camera outside of the context of an organized event tended to be longer and the women had more time to deliberate on what they wanted to say, since I often gave them questions beforehand or when we had switched off the tape recorder. In addition, there was not the pressure of having to have a visual presence before the camera, or the concern about saying all the right things. In other words, the *errrs* and *umms* or the search for words was not a concern during an audiotaped interview since they would be edited out. In many instances, women asked to review a transcript of the interview, which allowed them to add or delete information and make corrections as they saw fit. It was also in these instances that I lost several of the participants, who perhaps got too busy to return the revised interview along with the permission to include it. I had one entire conversation by telephone and another by electronic mail. Mbye Cham announced—to my delight—that he had conducted two interviews for this collection in Zimbabwe at the Southern African Film Festival in October 1998. Since Cham has been close to the project from the beginning, he was aware of my objectives and asked questions that related the spirit of the project.

One significant adjustment that had to be made in preparing the filmed conversations for written publication was the need to obtain the permission of the women to allow their conversations to be transcribed and published in a book collection, a requirement of international copyright laws. I must note that it was because of the three events during 1997 that I was able to meet so many women in the cinema in such a short time. (In the time span of three months I interviewed thirty-one women). The book permission requirement meant that I had to get in touch with thirty women spread across the world. Unfortunately, due to an assortment of reasons, I was not able to secure the permission of all the women involved to have their voices included in this collection. These women had so much to say, so many important ideas to express and share: Safi Faye (Senegal), Tsitsi Dangarembga (Zimbabwe), Anne Mungai (Kenya), Zeinabu irene Davis (USA), Gyasiwa Ansah (Ghana), Horria Saïhi (Algeria). Their inclusion would have contributed much to the conversation. Safi Faye as a pioneer; Tsitsi Dangarembga who as a writer has added filmmaking to her list of talents; Anne Mungai, who gave an overview of filmmaking and organizing as an African woman; Gyasiwa Ansah as the daughter of a filmmaker takes the baton; Zeinabu irene Davis talked about African/African diasporan connections, problems, and experiences in filmmaking; and Horria Saïhi, journalist/filmmaker, spoke of the perils of being an artist and documenting artists at a time when integrationist terrorists are prohibiting cultural life in Algeria.

I had made arrangements to interview other women, but, due to conflicts in schedules, inability to make mutual arrangements, or being downright too busy, since often times these interviews had to take place at organized events where time was a factor, some other wonderful women are not present in this collection: Nadia El Fani (Morocco), Bridget Pickering (Namibia), Werewere Liking (Cameroon/Cote d'Ivoire), Flora M'mbugu-Schelling (Tanzania), Assia Djebar (Algeria). Of course, there are the many, many other women who were not in attendance at the events that I attended or with whom, for various reasons, I was not able to make contact.

I felt the reality of the dilemma that Anne Mungai brought out in her conversation with me as I attempted to re-connect with women by e-mail, fax, telephone, post, or by "tam-tam" throughout the world. She talked about the problems around organizing and the awesome challenge of communication, follow-up, and networking outside of the boundaries of festivals and conferences, when women go back to their respective countries. Women are scattered throughout the world, perhaps attending a workshop, shooting a film, in the editing room, visiting a potential financier, or simply attending to the roles of mother, spouse, partner, friend. It becomes a formidable task to make connections and follow-up contacts.

While the majority of the women in the collection are from Africa south of the Sahara, the scope of my project extended to women throughout the continent. While only one North African woman, Najwa Tlili (Tunisia), is included in the book, I interviewed Horria Saïhi and had attempted to interview two other North African women. I had also contacted several North African women who resided in Paris, but was not able to arrange my own schedule to connect with them during my visit.

It is important to detail these methodological choices and their consequences because there is not a clear delineation marking the space that North Africa holds within African cinema. In other words, in some contexts North Africa is included within African cinema discourse and in other instances it is defined within the sphere of Arab cinema. In still other instances it is simultaneously presented as African and Arab cinema.

Another theoretical discussion in defining who is African in African cinema is the question of Africans of European descent. Which raises the question of my choice not to interview Ingrid Sinclair of Zimbabwe for this collection although she was among the FESPACO 1997 participants on the same list of feature films in competition as Safi Faye from Senegal, Tsitsi Dangarembga also from Zimbabwe, and Nadia Fares Anliker from Tunisia.

Perhaps still another theoretical discussion relates to my choice of including four African diasporans (Zeinabu irene Davis was also interviewed), which has to do with my own positionality as an African diasporan. I would like to revisit Keyan Tomaselli's question as a point of departure for the above "debate":

> Questions not easily resolved on the issue of what is African cinema concern, for example, what constitutes Africa. Is Arab film and South African production part of African cinema? Is 'Black' cinema necessarily 'African' in origin? Is there such an identity as 'the African personality'? Should African cinema necessarily be linked to its Black diasporic equivalents in the United States, France and England?[1]

Have I denied Ingrid Sinclair an identity as African, yet defined Arab women within an African identity as well as linked African diasporans to African cinema as Tomaselli states in his essay?

My interest in including African diasporan women is directly related to the FESPACO 1991 Women's Workshop during which time women of the African Diaspora were excluded. My interest in bringing up the event during the conversations with diasporan women as well as the African organizers of the workshop was to resurface a dialogue, or rather to bring about a dialogue between the two that never took place.

While I have attempted to present a "conversation" among women in the cinema, I am not suggesting that there is a synthesis, that there is one voice. Although many of the women know each other, know about each other, have seen each other's work, or have been in each other's company at conferences, festivals, and workshops, it is extremely difficult to have a concerted dialogue in order to share the complexities of experiences, ideas, interests, and attitudes regarding the diversity of issues in the cinema arena. Perhaps, in a way, this is my own projection of a sisterhood. Sarah Maldoror (Guadeloupe), when she read the title of the book (which I had translated literally in French "Les soeurs de l'écran"), suggested to me, "But we are not sisters, really, we are each in our own isolation making films." She did not like the title, though I assured her that it works much better in English, and I promised her that if it is published in French I would not use that title. In many ways, Sarah Maldoror was stating that, in essence, there was not a sisterhood in African cinema, at least not yet.

On the other hand, the phrase "sisters of the screen," to me, elicits a kindred spirit among women where the screen is their ultimate point of convergence. It is there, where their images are read, whether it is on a movie screen, television screen, or video screen. As directors, producers, film festival organizers, actors, and critics—those who have constructed these images, played the characters in these images, interpreted these images, found money so these images could be made, or organized so that these images may be projected—that space, the screen, is the ultimate site from which the moving image is viewed, interpreted, understood.

There is a growing body of work on the image of African women in cinema as well as an emergence of theoretical studies on "African women filmmaking." However, the purpose of this project was to document the voices, experiences, and thoughts of African women as a collective body in order to hear their voices, to allow them to speak about how they interpret their image and African cinema in general. This project extends the work that *Amina* magazine[2] has been doing for over a decade: profiling African women in the cinema. Some of the distinct differences are that the text is in English, the women are from all regions of Africa rather than mainly francophone areas, and there is an attempt to weave the voices together and make an analysis of trends, themes, and processes. I am indebted to *Amina*, which in many ways exposed me to the world of African women in the cinema as far back as 1983, when nine-year-old Rosine Yanogo was featured in the June issue for the role she played in Gaston Kabore's *Wend Kuuni*. I commend the work of Aïssatou Bah Diallo, editor-in chief of *Amina*, with whom I had a long conversation about this project and received a great deal of encouragement and some assistance in developing contacts.

Ecrans d'Afrique/African Screen[3] has also been an important source on African women in the cinema. From the first issue in 1992, which covered the 1991 Women's Workshop at FESPACO, and profiled certain women, there has been a high visibility of women and an impressive effort to make their voices heard. Faces of women in the cinema have also been well represented on the covers. Vues d'Afrique, the annual African and Creole film festival of Montreal, has been on the landscape of women in the cinema since 1989, when it held an important colloquium on women in the cinema. The prize Images de femmes, established by ACCT (Agence de Coopération Culturelle et Technique), was first presented at Vues d'Afrique in 1992. An index of women filmmakers, titled *Femmes d'Images de l'Afrique francophone*, compiled by Najwa Tlili (Tunisia), was born from this 1989 colloquium. For me it has been a helpful guide to names, contacts, and films by women in francophone regions of Africa.

I deliberately sought out film students in order to document their feelings and experiences at the beginning of their filmmaking process. While a few, such as Wabei Siyolwe (Zambia) and Zanele Mthembu (South Africa), had returned to school to learn another aspect of cinema, Lucy Gebre-Egziabher (Ethiopia) entered film school after a decision to change careers and realize a dream she had had since childhood.

I began a series of conversations with Lucy Gebre-Egziabher in the summer of 1996 and had the occasion to document on video her third and fourth student film productions. In an interview during the shooting of her most recent film, *Weti's Poem*, she stated that, cinematically, she had reached a higher level. And indeed she had, for this film has given her high visibility locally and has launched her name in film circles beyond the Washington, DC region as she has won several awards and has been invited to festivals. When I talked to her recently, she felt that while her words presented in this collection are still her thoughts, at the same time, she has seen a great deal of growth and evolution during the past three years. Then, there is Gyasiwa Ansah (Ghana), who, while also a film student, has a special experience. She grew up in the world of cinema, as the daughter of Kwaw Ansah. Her choice of a career in film came as a natural process.

African women filmmaking practices come full circle, from those who are beginning as makers to those who entered at the start of African cinema itself. A young woman who acted in her first film talks about the fascination of that experience while a veteran actor talks about her experience acting in a film by the elder of African cinema. In addition to conversations with those behind the camera and those in front, there is a range of discussions with other representatives in the domain of cinema: a film festival organizer, a film scholar and critic, and film producers. I have also included a bibliography of relevant literature as well as a filmography of films, videos, and programs for television.

How is African cinema visualized, described, experienced, theorized, and interpreted by the women who circulate, navigate, negotiate in the diverse areas of this world? Is there a woman's sensibility, a female imaginary, a woman's visual text, a female gaze? Who are their models, their references? What are the specificities of their experiences in cinema? What are their struggles, accomplishments, goals, and objectives? What are African representations of female subjectivity? These are the questions whose answers I set out to find.

Notes

1. Keyan G. Tomaselli, "'African' Cinema: Theoretical Perspectives on Some Unresolved Questions," *African Experiences of Cinema*, ed., Imruh Bakari and Mbye Cham (London: British Film Institute, 1996), p. 165.
2. *Amina* is a Paris-based magazine published in French that focuses on black women.
3. *Ecrans d'Afrique/African Screen* is an international bilingual review of African cinema.

Introduction

The Evolution of African Women of the Image

"African women in the cinema" is a concept that must be analyzed within the context of social, political, and cultural structures in Africa. It must be discussed within the specific conventions of cinematic practices that have emerged in Africa since the inception of what has come to be called African cinema. The concept "African women in cinema" encompasses the diverse mediums of television, video, and film, which include the narrative, short, documentary, and tele-film. Whatever the genre or format, the films often focus on the social, political, and cultural realities of African society. As more African women work and live outside of the continent, they also deal with issues relating to immigration and the specific situations that they encounter in their host countries. As in African films in general, it is rare to find a film for the sake of entertainment.

The dominant idea of cinema as the feature film projected on a large screen viewed by large audiences in cinema houses does not portray the reality of African cinema in general, and even less the cinema of African women. Perhaps more appropriately, African women in the cinema have chosen the concept "African women of the image," which, as a concept, encompasses the diverse means and processes that comprehend their film practices.

While one may now speak of the development of an "African women in the cinema movement," in fact, the emergence of African women as film/video practitioners has been gradual and sporadic. The visibility of African women as "makers" may be described as an evolving process. The beginning coincides with the emergence of African cinema in the 1960s and 1970s as a body of African films was forming and an African filmmaking practice was taking shape.

Safi Faye (Senegal) as a film student made her short film *La passante* in 1972. It was because she was the first African woman to make a film, Faye believes, that her film became a curiosity in the film circuit of Paris at that time. There were, however, other African women who arrived in the world of cinema even before most of the filmmakers that are recognized today as pioneers. Journalist Thérèse Sita-Bella (Cameroon) made a 30-minute documentary in 1963, entitled *Tam Tam à Paris*. The film documented the National Dance Company of Cameroon during its tour in Paris. *Tam Tam à Paris* was featured at the first FESPACO (at the time called the Week of African Cinema) in February 1969, along with the films of Mustapha Alassane (Niger), Ousmane Sembene (Senegal), Ababacar Samb (Senegal), Urbain N'Dia (Cameroon), Paulin Vieyra (Senegal), and Momar Thiam (Senegal).[1] Thérèse Sita-Bella has had a long, productive career in the area of radio and print journalism. During a 1989 interview she indicated that she has many scripts that she would like to put to film and, "since cineastes are ageless," upon her retirement she hopes to be able to do so.[2]

In 1967, Efua Sutherland (Ghana) produced *Arabia: The Village Story*, a major documentary film made by ABC, a national U.S. television network. The documentary records the success of one of her most important projects, the Atwia Experimental Community Theatre Project. It has been internationally recognized as a "pioneering model for the now popular theater for development."[3] Her career focus was as a dramatist and writer, for which she is well known and admired.

Guadeloupian Sarah Maldoror of the African Diaspora is often accorded Angolan nationality[4] and, "because of her work and dedication to the cause of Africa," she is "commonly given a privileged place in comprehensive analysis of Black African cinema."[5] Her presence as a filmmaker in Africa dates from as early as the 1960s. While her important contributions to African cinema cannot be denied, her positionality continues to be debated. This unresolved status was brought out during a meeting among African women in the cinema in 1991. Nonetheless, she holds an important place as a filmmaker of the African world.

Sarah Maldoror's *Monangambee* was included in the second FESPACO in 1970 under the country Angola. Her film *Sambizanga* was included in the Carthage Film Festival (Tunisia) in 1972, where it was awarded first prize, the Tanit d'Or. Both events, among a long list of other accomplishments and experiences in Africa and filmmaking in Africa, demonstrate that Maldoror's place in African cinema has been firmly recognized and visible since its inception.

The filmmaking experiences of these four women are indicative of the filmmaking practices of African women who have come later. The entry of Safe Faye and Sarah Maldoror into filmmaking was the beginning of a sustained career, with the intention of evolving in the area of cinema. On the other hand, Thérèse Sita-Bella and Efua Sutherland continued in their chosen fields of journalism and drama, having never made a second film, although Sita-Bella still has plans to do so. In other words, some women have entered filmmaking as an intended career, while others have wedded careers in communication, journalism, literature, information work, human rights advocacy, and education with filmmaking and use it as a medium of expression in their work. Thus, there is fluidity in the use of the term filmmaker and in the boundaries of filmmaking practices. An important sector of the audio-visual medium that is generally included in the definition of "African cinema" is television. Film festivals that include African films also program films from this category, which gives a great deal of visibility to women television directors.

Only a handful of films was made during the beginning period of the 1960s and 1970s. However, film/video/television productions more than quadrupled in the 1980s and continued to increase in the 1990s.[6] While the few film productions in the early period were represented in only a few countries, by the 1980s most regions of the continent were represented, and by the 1990s production had doubled from the preceding decade. While the beginning period of an African woman filmmaking practice was sporadic, during the last two decades there has been a steady increase and proliferation of film production. Thus, African women now have a visible presence on the landscape of cinema.

African Women in the Cinema Movement

"African women in the cinema" as an organized movement emerged at the end of the 1980s and the beginning of the 1990s as African women in the visual media began to concretize their desire to come together as a larger force in order to make their interests and needs known. 25-27 February 1991 marked a historical moment for African women in the visual media. The genesis of an organized movement of African women in the image industry, as it was later named, may be traced to the 12th edition of FESPACO in 1991. A part of the festival platform was organized under the title "Women, Cinema, Television and Video in Africa."

The meeting brought together fifty women from more than fifteen countries. It was chaired by Annette M'Baye d'Erneville (Senegal), a veteran in the field of communications in Africa, founder of RECIDAK (Rencontres Cinématographiques de Dakar) and director of Consortium de communications audiovisuelles en Afrique (CCA) in Senegal. Annette M'Baye d'Erneville opened the meeting, laying down the objectives of the workshop: 1) to provide a forum for women to exchange and share their experiences; 2) to adopt propositions that will help ensure women their rightful place, particularly in the areas of training and production;

3) to devise a follow-up structure for dialogue and common action; 4) to identify the frustrations of women professionals and produce images that consciously reflect women's realities, social contexts, cultures, and histories; and 5) to disseminate that perspective.[7]

During the workshop, women filmmakers, producers, actors, technicians, and others in visual media production put forth the fundamentals of a solid organization to defend their interests. Five of the main goals that resulted from the meeting were as follows: 1) to develop an index of African women visual media producers and their films; 2) to promote their work across a wide range of networks internationally; 3) to establish an itinerant training workshop composed of a group of trainers who circulate throughout Africa; 4) to train instructors in the various spheres of visual media production; 5) to seek funding so that women may attend and participate regularly at film festivals.[8]

The events of this meeting set in motion the groundwork for what would become the visual media network called L'Association des femmes africaines professionnelles du cinéma, de la télévision et de la vidéo/The Association of Professional African Women in Cinema, Television and Video (AFAPTV). It was reorganized in 1995 under the name, The Pan-African Union of Women in the Image Industry/L'Union panafricaine des femmes de l'image (UPAFI).

In April 1989, two years before the FESPACO workshop, the Montreal-based film festival Vues d'Afrique organized a special section devoted to African women in the visual media. The program consisted of: 1) a screening of short and feature length films, television shows, and video programs produced and directed by African women; 2) a discussion of the on-screen image of women and the influence of the media; 3) a colloquium on the role of African women in the audiovisual media which included a survey of the participants' assessment of the current situation and their recommendations.

The colloquium addressed needs and interests similar to those expressed at the FESPACO workshop. The objectives of the colloquium were: 1) to plan specific projects for exchanges, training programs, and professional cooperation with African women to develop in the film, television, and audio-visual sectors; 2) to have an ongoing discussion between Canadian officials at the Office of Canadian Film and Television and African women film directors, technicians, and actors regarding the ways that the Office can meet the women's professional needs; 3) to discuss with representatives of governmental and non-governmental international cooperation agencies the ways that women's level of participation in the audio-visual production sectors in Africa may be raised.

Femmes d'images de l'Afrique francophone, compiled by Najwa Tlili (Tunisia), was one of the direct results of this 1989 meeting. The index brings together the biography and filmography of women in the cinema from "francophone" Africa, as well as a listing of other relevant contacts. Another initiative that came from the meeting was the creation of the "Images de femmes" (Images of Women) project, from which emerged the prize "Images de femmes" offered by ACCT and presented during the annual Vues d'Afrique.

Since the African Women in the Cinema Movement began in 1991, regional bureaus and national associations have sprung up throughout the continent. African Women in Film and Video (AWIFAV) was created in November 1992, of which African Women in Film and Video—Kenya Section, created in 1993, is an affiliate. A Gabonese national bureau of the Pan-African Union of Women in the Image Industry was created in 1995, while the Association of Women Filmmakers of Zimbabwe was formed in September 1996.

One of the results of the restructuring of the pan-African organization of women in the cinema was the creation of regional bureaus, including Diaspora sections in London and Paris. There is a general coordinator for the continent and there are coordinators for the various regions in and outside of Africa: Northern Africa Region, Western Africa Region, Southern Africa Region, Central Africa Region, Eastern Africa Region, Diaspora France, and Diaspora Great Britain.

Anne Mungai (Kenya)[9] brought out some of the problems that come with trying to organize within such a large scope, notably language barriers and traveling. Even to come together regionally, among women in Eastern Africa, has been a formidable task. Some of the obstacles are related to allotting limited funding for making films, maintaining a household, and keeping contact with other women in the region. Often the latter is the lowest priority. Despite the problems and difficulties of organizing among women in the cinema, the emergence of the movement has allowed women of the image to better know each other and attain higher visibility.

Towards a Woman-Defined Criticism

Is there an African woman-defined critique of the image, of filmmaking practices, of cinema in general? What are the tenets, what are the canons? While there is no formal infrastructure in terms of a specialized group of women who name their work or discourse as film criticism, each woman in this collection, as well as the many other women in the diverse areas of the visual media in Africa, has distinctive impressions about women and

5

the image and their role as maker, interpreter, cultural producer and reader in general, so that critiquing the image is integrated in their filmmaking practices or in their interpretation of a character as an actor.

On the other hand, there have been other instances where the broad issues of African women in the media as well as the visual representation of African women have been addressed. As early as 1978, research was conducted on African women in the media during a study visit by journalists Elma Lititia Anani (Sierra Leone), Alkaly Miriama Keita (Niger), and Awatef Abdel Rahman (Egypt), held at the United Nations Economic Commission for Africa at Addis Ababa, Ethiopia, 24–30 September 1978.[10] The purpose and goals of the study were as follows:

> To date, virtually no research has been carried out on women and the mass media in Africa; this study is the first to analyze women's image in the media. It also documents the small number of women in policy-making positions in the African media, which necessarily affects the media's portrayal of women. Since the mass media in Africa are in their infancy, it is hoped that the implications of women's current media image will be carefully considered by media policy makers, with a view to establishing future media policies which will foster women's participation in the development of Africa.

While women in the visual media have made great strides in the 1980s and 1990s, the issues brought out in the 1978 study continue to be relevant. They echo the sentiments of a majority of women in the cinema regarding their role as image-makers and visual journalists and the contributions that they want to make:

> Women have an especially important role to play in the development of Africa. By its portrayal of women, the mass media can either impede or foster women's integration in the development process. If women are portrayed only in traditional roles in the media, society's attitudes and women's expectations for themselves will necessarily be confined to these roles. On the other hand, if the media's image of women reflects the full range of contributions women are capable of making to society, societal attitudes towards women will be correspondingly broadened.[11]

In many ways these past reflections, which often mirror the present, are indicative of the tremendous power that visual media has had and continues to have on African societies, rather than the lack of progress towards reaching the objectives set forth.

On the other hand, while there has been improvement in the visual representation of women, there continues to be stereotypical, negative, and harmful portrayals of women that have worsened in some cases. Sarah Maldoror, veteran filmmaker, who came to cinema in the late sixties, laments the gratuitous portrayal of nude African women in today's films. At the same time, African actresses addressing this issue almost a decade ago questioned the use of nudity, specifically in the film *Visages de femmes* by Désiré Ecaré.[12]

In contrast to those male filmmakers who have used the woman's body for mere objectification and nudity for the sake of nudity, Safi Faye (Senegal) and Fanta Nacro (Burkina Faso) are, they insist, presenting a realistic image of women's sensuality and sexual expression. Safi Faye states that her portrayal of women's sensuality in *Mossane* echoes her own experiences:

> I more or less experienced that with my childhood girlfriends in Senegal and I wanted to tell it as such. This film that I have made, is for me, a song to women. The things that I find so beautiful, the things that I have lived, that I have experienced or that I have been told. And then, I made these images according to my vision...My sexual education was more or less like that. We always had an older girlfriend who was married before us and it was she who explained to the others what went on. One does not go into marriage naive and unaware. No, one knows, but without having actually experienced it.[13]

Fanta Nacro felt that not to show the sensually explicit scene in *Puk Nini* would be hypocritical to herself and her audience. Zara Mahamat Yacoub was condemned by the Islamic Council of Chad for having shown the genitals of a young girl during an excision operation in her film *Dilemme au féminine*. Her response was,

> If excision had not existed, I would not have shown this part of the body. I did not show the female body for the pleasure of showing it, but within a specific context. There is an important distinction.[14]

These experiences of makers and actors reveal that they are fully aware of the implications of the presentation of certain images and how the viewer will perceive them. In certain instances they take risks and experience the consequences of their choice to reveal the reality and gravity of a situation. In the varying and diverse experiences that women have had with the image, there is a consensus, that women's experiences and their perceptions of reality are essential.

African women in all areas of the visual media are addressing the issue of the visual representation of women and are asking themselves what role they play in the projection of positive images. Like most of her colleagues in the cinema, Anne Mungai feels that her role is to present realistic images of women:

> When I finally started going to the cinemas and watching television programs in Kenya, each time an African woman appeared she played a very weak character. She was always a cook, a servant to somebody, a mistress to somebody, a slave, she's crying, she's pregnant. So the images that I saw on the screen and on television were always of an African woman in trouble. I said yes, but how does she overcome these problems? That was never shown...I think that is what motivated me. I've seen my mother, I've seen her in trouble, I've watched my father die, there was my mother with six children. We are all grown up and I admire the way she did it. I then started wishing that I saw more films with strong African women characters; and that is the role I want to play. And that is why I say that there is that gap, and I want to fill it in my films.[15]

Wanjiru Kinyanjui (Kenya) feels that in taking part in film criticism, African women "can correct images of themselves and even their surroundings." She likes to see an African woman portrayed as a person of independent mind, not passive and submissive. As a filmmaker, she is interested in giving her the chance to define her own place.

Actresses are also taking the lead in insisting on positive, interesting, and strong characters to interpret. Aï Keita-Yara (Burkina Faso) expressed a special affinity with her character, the legendary Queen Sarraounia. While M'Bissine Thérèse Diop (Senegal) has been generally pleased with her roles, she also suggests that male filmmakers present important characters for black women to play and not always the small, insignificant ones. Alexandra Duah (Ghana) a veteran actor, has come to feel like "Ghana's international actress who has found herself redundant." Despite her disappointments, she emphasizes how important it is for her to accept scripts that are educative and not demeaning or demoralizing to women. Naky Sy Savane (Ivory Coast) asserts that actresses should even go to the point that they actually suggest certain roles to filmmakers, perhaps even roles that they themselves create.

Masepeke Sekhukhuni (South Africa) suggests that because the process of filmmaking itself has been defined by men, women must adequately learn how to express their womanhood within this medium. One important step in this process is to demystify filmmaking, which she thinks has also been mystified by men. As director of the Newtown Film and Television School, Sekhukhuni encounters many women who are intimidated by the filmmaking environment, including heavy cameras and other equipment. Her response to the women is to remember those heavy buckets and other objects that women carry on their heads and are able to manage. In applying this idea to the filmmaking environment, they will know that "they have the energy, they have the power!" Applying their specific experiences as women in their filmmaking, and as actors, African women as makers, interpreters, and readers of the image are also shaping a woman-defined criticism.

Women of Africa and the Diaspora: A Meeting Place

The events of the FESPACO 1991 meeting of African women are revisited by several women as it relates to the diasporan women who attended but were later asked to leave. It was an emotionally charged experience,[16] which has yet to be resolved. In other words, there has never been an attempt to work out the differences that this meeting so apparently revealed nor has there been an official meeting between women makers of Africa and the Diaspora.

While Sarah Maldoror (Guadeloupe) and Shirikiana Aina (USA) expressed severe disappointment about the events that took place, Zeinabu irene Davis (USA)[17] said that though it was a painful experience, in retrospect she understood the importance of African women meeting among themselves. She brought out some important points regarding the differences and similarities between women of Africa and the African Diaspora in cinema.

On the other hand, while Aina agrees that there are differences that distinguish the needs of diasporan and African women, she feels that the unification of women of African descent should have been a priority at that moment:

> yes, it is important for continental women to meet, very critical.
> But what is the urgency that requires the de-unification of what
> we have here?

Aminata Ouedraogo (Burkina Faso) and Chantal Bagilishya (Rwanda) discuss the events leading to the misunderstanding and attempt to explain the decision to ask the diasporan women to leave. They both describe the importance of having African women meet together among themselves first before inviting others, since this was the first time they had ever met as a group. They felt that because of the difference between Africans and diasporans it was necessary to work through their own agenda as African women on the continent.

Some of the differences that Zeinabu irene Davis pointed out were the issues around access to equipment and training. She stated the obvious possibility of going to film schools, which is rare or non-existent in most African countries. She also suggested the availability of low-cost equipment use and training at public access stations in the United States. On the other hand, Davis finds that African women have more power in the area of television broadcasting than do diasporans in the United States. Women from the United States as producers and directors in television are rare, while there is an increasing number of women in those positions in Africa.

Aminata Ouedraogo focuses the differences between women of Africa and the Diaspora on issues and themes. She felt that while diasporan women may focus on issues of aesthetics, body image and corporeality, African women in the cinema must deal with issues around education, health, housing, and nutrition. In general, Aminata Ouedraogo emphasized the importance of African women coming together to get to know each other and express their interests and needs. Mahen Bonetti, executive director of African Film Festival, Inc. based in New York City, notes distinctions as well:

> I find that the subjects that the African women deal with are different from those of African-American women's films, much less Hollywood. Here in the States, one doesn't expect to see things like polygamy, female genital mutilation, or about women in Tanzania crushing stones.

Shirikiana Aina agrees with Davis that African Americans do not have an organized film body within the African festival circuit where they can promote their films and voice their interests and concerns. Aina notes that while there is a prize for the African Diaspora at FESPACO, the Paul Robeson Prize, it is not Diaspora groups that pay for it, which points to the lack of real power. Davis voiced the need for a film advocacy body within the filmmaking arena that acts as a support network for independent African and Diaspora cinema. Aina, who works with her filmmaker/husband Haile Gerima from Ethiopia, corroborates Davis' emphasis on the importance of a film advocacy network.

The filmmaking experiences of African diasporan Gloria Rolando from Cuba are much closer to those of women on the continent than to those of diasporans from the United States. While she shares the common diasporan desire to reflect African roots in her work, the conditions for filmmaking in Cuba make her task particularly formidable. She expresses many of the same obstacles that African women indicate, such as the lack of funding and equipment, among others.

Diasporan Françoise Pfaff (Guadeloupe/France) is well known among anglophone readers of African cinema history and criticism especially. However, in the collection she presents perhaps a less known aspect of herself. Of mixed-raced heritage, she came to the United States to find roots in the black community in the United States and emerged as an important scholar of African cinema, a place where she also went in search of her roots.

As Africans from the continent traverse frontiers and migrate to extra-African locations, issues of the "Diaspora" have become larger. Mahen Bonetti (Sierra Leone) brings out this point in her discussion about first-generation-born "hybrids." While there has been much more focus on Africans migrating to European metropoles in order to work and function as filmmakers, they are also migrating to North America, both to Canada and the United States. In this collection, there is a number of women who are based in North America, particularly in the United States: Mahen Bonetti (Sierra Leone), Lucy Gebre-Egziabher (Ethiopia), Salem Mekuria (Ethiopia), Thembi Mtshali (South Africa), Zanele Mthembu (South Africa), and Wabei Siyolwe (Zambia); and in Canada: Cilia Sawadogo (Burkina Faso) and Najwa Tlili (Tunisia). Gyasiwa Ansah (Ghana) was also a film student in New York. Some other women who studied in the United States are Bridget Pickering (Namibia) and Palesa Letlaka-Ngozi (South Africa). Presently, Flora M'mbugu-Schelling (Tanzania) is also based in the United States, as well as Assia Djebar (Algeria). Ngozi Onwurah recently spent time at a U.S. university as a visiting filmmaker-in-residence. The conversations will reveal other women who have visited the United States or have had other contacts with U.S. diasporans. They realize that the communities of people of African descent in the United States are eager to embrace Africa and connect. Mahen Bonetti was aware of this as she created the African Film Festival based in New York. Cornelius Moore of California Newsreel realized this as the Library of African Cinema was added to the collection. Certainly, Haile Gerima and Shirikiana Aina realized this as they began the successful commercial run of *Sankofa*.

Diasporan Sarah Maldoror, an exemplary model of African/Diasporan interconnecting in filmmaking, started the tradition at the inception of African cinema. Others are continuing the process: Safi Faye, *Elsie Haas, femme peintre et cineaste d'Haiti*, 1985, a portrait of Haitian filmmaker Elsie Haas; Salem Mekuria, *As I Remember It: A Portrait of Dorothy West*, 1985, a portrait of Harlem Renaissance writer; Euzhan Palcy (Martinique), *A Dry White Season*, 1989, set in Zimbabwe; Shirikiana Aina, *Through the Door of No Return*, 1997, set in Ghana. Coming full circle while continuing the tradition, more than thirty years after Sarah Maldoror began her film-making journey in Africa, Anne-Laure Folly (Togo) saw the importance of tracing the footsteps of her life and work, in *Sarah Maldoror ou la nostalgie de l'utopie*, 1998.

Boundaries are blurring, borders are extending, and—as Ngozi Onwurah asserts—there must be differences made between African women working in and out of Africa. While there was a great deal of focus on African/Diasporan differences in 1991, perhaps now, almost a decade later, the conversation extends its frontiers to comprehend the many places, spaces, and practices of women of Africa and the image.

Through African Women's Eyes

Twenty-one years after writing her first novel, Assia Djebar (Algeria) made her first film, *La Nouba des femmes du mont Chenoua* in 1978, and four years later her second film *La Zerda ou les chants de l'oubli*, in 1982. When asked why she made films, Djebar said:

> I realized that woman was forbidden any relationship to the image: While her image cannot be taken, she does not own it either. Since she is shut away, she looks on the inside. She can only look at the outside if she is veiled, and then, only with one eye. I decided then, that I would make of my camera this eye of the veiled woman.[18]

Visualizing through the lens of women's experiences, feelings, and histories, Djebar lifted the veil that obscured their vision, also allowing others to see through women's eyes. At the beginning of Anne-Laure Folly's (Togo) film, journalist Monique Ilboudo cites a poem by a Burkinabé woman that says: A respectable woman should learn from her husband. She should not read. She should not have her eyes open. Folly titles her film *Women with Open Eyes*, thus opening to view the diverse conditions of women in various African societies. While some women remain blinded by the traditions that oppress them, other women move forward with open eyes to improve their lives and that of their societies. Fanta Nacro's film, *Puk Nini*, which means «open your eyes, be vigilant» in Moré, attempts to encourage women to go forward and move ahead toward finding a solution to their problem rather than stand immobilized and be pessimistic.

What, then, is an African woman's vision, her gaze, her way of seeing and visualizing? As the camera becomes her eye, as the lens becomes the vehicle for expressing woman/women's experiences and showing her vision of the world, many African women transcend geographies and locations, boundaries are blurred, their positionality goes beyond nationality and country. The themes and subjects of their films reflect personal experiences, the search for identity, the demands of financiers, as well as the self-imposed duty to teach, to reveal injustices, and to construct positive images of women and African society in general. The voices in this collection provide an "alternative discourse" to the many issues of cinema in general as well as African filmmaking practices that have been discussed and theorized. In multiple voices, *Sisters of the Screen* begins the conversation.

Notes

1. It is also significant to note that one of the founding members of FESPACO—and the president of the organizing committee of the first festival in 1969—was Burkinabé Alimata Salembéré, who at the time was a television director at the Burkinabé television, Radiodiffusion Télévision Voltaique (RTV). She also served as General Secretary of FESPACO from 1982 to 1984, thus overseeing the 8th FESPACO in 1983.
2. André-Marie Pouya, " Thérèse Sita-Bella parle de la presse et de l'élégance," *Amina*, September 1989, p. 44.
3. ALA Bulletin (African Literature Association), Summer 1996, p. 10.
4. Her companion of many years was Angolan writer Mario de Andrade, one of the leaders of the Popular Movement for the Liberation of Angola (MPLA).
5. Françoise Pfaff, *Twenty-five Black African Filmmakers*. (Westport: Greenwood Press, 1988), p. 205.
6. While my statistics are based on a filmography that is not exhaustive, they may be used to suggest tendencies and the evolution of African women filmmaking practice.
7. Claire Andrade-Watkins, "African Women Directors at Fespaco," in *Cinemas of the Black Diaspora*, ed., Michael T. Martin (Detroit: Wayne State University Press, 1995), p. 150.
8. Assiatou Bah Diallo, "Les femmes à la recherche d'un nouveau souffle," *Amina*,

May 1991.

9. Interview by author not included in collection.

10. *Women and the Mass Media in Africa: Cases Studies of Sierra Leone, the Niger and Egypt* by Elma Lititia Anani, Alkaly Miriama Keita, Awatef Abdel Rahman. The United Nations Economic Commission for Africa, Addis Ababa, 1981. Research Series, African Training and Research Centre for Women/Voluntary Fund for the United Nations Decade for Women. Other studies include: Association des professionnelles africaines de la communication (APAC), *Femmes, développement, communication: quelles perspectives pour Nairobi 1985?* (Proceedings from the seminar organized by BREDA, Dakar, Senegal), 1-10 October 1984; and Association of African Women for Research and Development (AAWORD), *Women and the Media in Africa*, Occasional Paper Series, No. 6, Dakar, 1992.

11. *Women and the Mass Media in Africa: Cases Studies of Sierra Leone, the Niger and Egypt* by Elma Lititia Anani, Alkaly Miriama Keita, Awatef Abdel Rahman. The United Nations Economic Commission for Africa, Addis Ababa, 1981. Research Series, African Training and Research Centre for Women/Voluntary Fund for the United Nations Decade for Women.

12. See "Quand la nudité chasse le beau" (When nudity chases away beauty), *Amina*, May 1991.

13. Interview by author not included in collection.

14. *Amina*, September 1996. Interview with Zara Mahamat Yacoub, p. 49.

15. Interview by author not included in collection.

16. See Claire Andrade-Watkins, "African Women Directors at Fespaco," *Cinemas of the Black Diaspora* ed. Mark T. Martin, 1995 and Assiatou Bah Diallo, "Les femmes à la recherche d'un nouveau souffle," *Amina*, May 1991.

17. Interview by author not included in collection.

18. *Je me suis dit que la femme était interdite d'image: on ne peut pas lui prendre son image, mais elle n'en est pas propriétaire non plus. Du fait qu'elle est cloitrée, elle regarde l'intérieur, mais elle ne peut pas regarder l'exterieur, ou seulement si elle est voilée et qu'elle ne regarde que d'un oeil. Je me suis donc dit que j'allais faire de ma caméra cet oeil de la femme voilée.* Cited in *Littérature et cinéma en Afrique francophone, Ousmane Sembene et Assia Djebar*, edited by Sada Niang (Paris: Harmattan, 1996), from Ghila Benesty-Sroka, "La Langue et l'exil", *La Parole métèque*, 21 (1992): 24.

Aïssatou Adamou

Niger

Interview held during the Vues d'Afrique Festival in April 1997, Montreal, Quebec. Translated from French.

Aïssatou, you are a pioneer in the area of visual communications in Niger. Could you talk a bit about yourself, and how you evolved into the area of film and television?

I am from Niger. I am thirty-five years old. I initially worked in print journalism, but I began working in television immediately after completing my studies when I heard about an opening at the national television. My goal had always been to work in television and radio. Of course, when I heard about the opening, I quickly presented my application and was immediately accepted. I began working as television announcer, a position I held for the next three years.

I later realized that, though being an announcer was a good thing, I still needed to advance my career. So I completed an examination and was accepted at the Institut de formation au technique de l'information et de la communication (IFTIC). After completing a three-year program, I returned to the television station as a director.

Since 1982, I have directed programs relating to women's issues. The programs are aired weekly on Nigerien television. I have also focused on health issues relating to women and children. I make documentaries, and though I do not always have the means to make fiction films, I have made some as well. In fact, I have a variety of tasks at the National Television of Niger. Presently, I am production manager.

In another conversation, you stated that you work in 3/4 format. Do you have the opportunity to work in film as well?

For the most part, we work in 3/4 format at the National Television of Niger. Although recently, thanks to the support of certain Western countries, we were able to acquire Betacam equipment, and we have now begun to film on Betacam. However, we still use the 3/4 format for short programs that are geared towards sensitizing people on certain issues as well as for animation shows, or vignettes. We reserve Betacam for larger, more competitive productions.

Is there a school or location in Niger where people can study 16mm and 35mm filmmaking?

We have filmmakers in Niger who work in 16mm, but because of our present economic situation, they do not always have the means to work in film. Not only is film stock expensive, but developing the film is also. Unfortunately, even our internationally known filmmakers such as Mustapha Diop and Djingareye Maiga can no longer make the number of films today that they did in the beginning. It is a pity, we regret this, but that is the situation now.

In another conversation, we talked about Mariama Hima, who is also a pioneering woman in the media in Niger. Could you talk about women in the area of television and cinema?

The National Television of Niger was established in 1978, as an educational television. At the time, only experimental programs were shown. I was the first woman to work as television announcer. I had many problems at the beginning, because a woman presented on television speaking to the public was not highly regarded. Initially, the public was critical of my public image on television. However, this did not discourage me, because I had the encouragement of my parents and friends to persevere. Gradually, people realized that women could work in the television industry just as well as men. They realized that there is no difference.

Because of this gradual change in attitude, as the years passed, more women became interested in television. More schools are directing their students, both women and men, to the Institut de formation au technique de l'information et la communication, the professional school here in Niger. Today there are women directors and journalists—not one, not two, nor three, but we are, in fact, quite numerous. There are more than seven women directors and eight women journalists at the National Television of Niger. Moreover, I can tell you it will not stop there. The school continues to exist and each time women complete their studies we encourage them to work in these areas.

Could you talk about the programs that you have produced and the films that you have made? What themes do you focus on?

In fact, I address diverse themes. I deal with ethnographic themes with a cultural context, such as the film *Gossi* that was screened here in Montreal. I also address social themes such as pre- and post-natal health issues regarding women and children. Women in the process of national development is a general theme on which there is a great deal of focus. This includes women from both rural and urban sectors. I also touch on issues concerning children, because it is necessary to focus on children. An example would be the education of the young girl, which is a prevailing theme today.

I directed three programs, one in French, one in the national language Zarma, and the third in Hausa. The public appreciates these programs a great deal. Because I have the advantage of speaking the three most widely spoken languages in Niger—French, Zarma, and Hausa—the programs that I produce are always presented in two or three versions. Of course, I think that the language question is very important.

You also produce programs that focus on life in the village, such as your film **Gossi.** *Could you describe your experiences during these film productions?*

We do have the means to go to the villages to film. In order to do a program we must first do a location survey of the village. To develop the script, sometimes we spend three to four days in the villages in order to live the reality of the people and the environment. We return to the studio, write the script, and then choose the necessary equipment. We are then ready to go back to the location to film.

Sometimes we run into problems because many of the people are very careful about what they say. When they see a woman come in with a camera, or even a man for that matter, it is not easy for them to convey to us certain issues that we are trying to explore.

When shooting the film *Gossi,* I had to spend two months in the small village with only water from the pond to drink, often eating non-hygienic food. Of course, we wanted to live among the people in order to integrate into the village to be able to obtain certain secrets, certain practices of the village. When we broadcast the program afterwards it was viewed by the people in the village and they appreciated it very much. We solicited their comments and learned that they were very happy with the results.

What were some of the specific responses that they made regarding the film?

They were delighted to see their village on film. They were pleased to see one of their own representing their population. For example, a brother or a father spoke in front of the camera, and talked about their needs— revealing, perhaps, that the village does not have a school. This was possibly a call to the government to take action, to build a school in their village. They also spoke about their need for a community clinic and the importance of the government's intervention to do something for the people and the children of the village. There was, in fact, a variety of responses to these needs from different people. Some actually took the steps to find ways to meet the various needs that the people expressed. In the end, these are the kinds of programs that gradually bring results into the villages. The people are pleased with the programs that we do because the outcome is generally satisfactory.

Do you choose the subject matter of your programs?

We generally have the freedom to choose our themes and ideas. However, it must reflect a certain reality of the region. If not, these programs will never see the light of day. We do have this freedom and are, therefore, able to do many productions. We have the freedom to choose and deal with the subject that is in the interest of the population. On the other hand, when the government recognizes certain trouble spots, we are called to focus on these issues. Of course, the goal is to get the attention of those who can make decisions *vis-à-vis* the various areas of concern. I think it is very important that we have this freedom.

Have you ever been commissioned to do or have an interest in doing films for international agencies?

The National Television of Niger works in collaboration with certain institutions such as UNICEF, UNDP, and UNFPA,[1] with whom we work on a regular basis. Presently, we have signed agreements with UNICEF and are in the planning stages. UNICEF also assists us financially. We do not always have the financial means to produce our programs entirely, and therefore, we must seek funding from outside institutions in order to work more effectively. UNICEF and UNFPA often give us videocassettes or various equipment and materials that we may not have.

Have these programs only been aired on television or is there the possibility to screen them elsewhere? Have they reached the diverse sectors throughout Niger?

The national television is a public television as well as a state television. The programs are broadcast in cities and rural areas. Even in the smallest villages in Niger, there are television sets. In the village, people gather around the television set to watch the programs aired by the national television. The programs that I produce are broadcast in almost all the households in Niger. Since we produce programs for the national television, we cannot show these documentaries and fiction films in the cinema houses.

While the audiences for these films are generally Nigeriens, do these films also have an international audience?

For the time being, we only have FESPACO, which is an African film festival where we bring our films to show. More recently, we have developed a relationship with Vues d'Afrique. The festival has been a great medium for Africans to show their work. When we show our work it is not only the director's work that is being seen, the country is also being represented. I think this is very important. FESPACO and Vues d'Afrique are the two institutions to which we send our films for competition.
Unfortunately, there is a certain reservation on our part to get more information. Perhaps we are not always open to learning more about the institutions or outlets where we may present our work, and this is our problem.

You have stated that you focus mainly on ethnographic and consciousness-raising films; are these films also fictionalized or are they mainly informational and educational in content, or a combination of both?

The great majority are documentary films, but we do fiction films as well. However, making a fiction film requires a great deal of money. The actors must be paid. There must be retakes, as well as shots from different angles; thus, if there is not a certain amount of financial support, it cannot be done. Nonetheless, with the little that we have, we have tried to do fiction. For example, before the devaluation of the CFA, I was able to do a program in fiction form. It required only a small budget and it was well received. We do fiction films, but we must have certain institutions that can co-produce with us or assist us in co-production arrangements.

What role do you want to play as a woman in the media?

I am a woman, I am a mother, I am a wife, and I work in the media. So one of the roles that I have to take on is to transmit my knowledge to my sisters who perhaps have not had the chance to go to school. The fact that I work in television is in no way an impediment, in terms of the role that I have to play in my household.

I have my work to do on the public level and I have a role to fulfill regarding my husband and my children. I am able to combine them without a problem. I am most happy to say that I have children who are very understanding, and I also have a husband who encourages me. If I am here today in Montreal, it is because of my husband. He encouraged me to come; he insisted that I must come.

Many of your films have focused on women in various situations and in diverse sectors of Niger. Would you say that, as a woman, you bring something particular to your work in film and television?

Yes, absolutely. I think women are in a better position than men to speak about the problems of women. Women are in a better position than men to speak about how to care for a sick child. As mother and communicator, I think that I have the better advantage to go in the direction of my sisters, without any difficulty. Reciprocally, my sisters also encourage me. They encourage us during the production of each program, often by letter, often by telephone calls, and just as often at work or at home. They come to tell me that the treatment of a certain subject was well presented. They encourage us to continue the good work.

I think that women are the only ones who can truly touch their sisters; because there are certain things that a woman cannot talk about to a man, such as the problems around polygamy. A man may perceive it in a certain way, while a woman, as woman, perceives it in her way. We as women can present themes without the problem of vexing either men or women.

Could you also talk about the position of women in other sectors of the Nigerien society? Are women also visible?

My country is a democratic country. In terms of raising the consciousness of women and sensitizing the population about the conditions of women, we have institutions that have done their best to change old attitudes regarding women. We have women's organizations, we have legal organizations whose goal is to sensitize women about the role that they must play. On the administrative level, we have many women who occupy positions of high-level responsibility.

On the governmental level, we have women officials, though they are not very numerous. Women constitute fifty-two percent of the population; however, we have a disproportional small number of women in the government. We have three or four women officials; but, in relationship to their actual number in the population, we think that the government can do more. In the parliament, we have women, women who are fighters. I would say that gradually the attitudes are beginning to evolve. People now have a much better understanding of the role of women. They realize that there can be no development without the participation of women. Nigeriens have understood this and I think things are advancing. Any project without the participation of women is doomed to fail.

Notes

1. (UNICEF) United Nations Children's Fund, (UNDP) United Nations Development Fund, (UNFPA) United Nations Fund for Population Activities.

Shirikiana Aina

United States

Three interviews were held between November 1996 and June 1997. The November 1996 conversation, which was published *in Ecrans d'Afrique/African Screen* (3rd Quarter, 1997 Nos. 21-22), was transcribed from a televised interview which is part of *Reels of Colour*, a talk show series aired locally in Washington, DC, produced and hosted by the author.

Could you talk about your film **Through the Door of No Return** *and your process in the making of the film?*

In this film, I go on a personal journey. It is a documentary, but I would probably call it something closer to a docu-journey because it really is a personal journey back to the continent. I use my father's experience as sort of a bridge to get me there, as a child of Africa in the Diaspora looking for her roots or a re-connect.

My father traveled to Africa when I was about seventeen and apparently was trying to move to Ghana. Unfortunately, he contracted malaria. It was fatal, and when he came back, he died. I was a budding adult, but we never had a chance to synthesize or pass on some of the things he gained by himself going on that journey.

He was the child of a sharecropper. He moved to the North and was involved in whatever industry was available to him. And for him to make that leap to Africa in his lifetime was quite significant. So, I used that as an opportunity for me to re-link to the continent.

You narrate the film as your story. Could you talk about the importance of your voice in telling the story?

Well, from the very beginning, I say exactly what I am doing and you hear me going across the ocean. I wanted to go back at night the same way that we came. I wanted to go back across the water the same way that we came. I wanted to go back through that same door that you see in our other film, *Sankofa*.

If you've seen that film, you've seen the dungeons and the slave forts on the coast of Ghana. In the so-called Elmina Castle, there is a very small door, so small that only one person could fit through it at a time. You almost have to go sideways to get through this door and that is how we were exited out of that dungeon at night because the slave-traders figured that it would be the best way to sneak us out. The surrounding residents know something is going on, they know about slavery of course, but just to keep it low key we were sent out at night. We were sent down in these little boats and these boats would take us to the bigger ships. By that time we had waited in these dungeons for months and months, we had watched many of our family members and other people die right next to us. Food was almost non-existent, of course; the conditions were horrible: we were packed, no blankets. We lived in these hellholes. We were stored, actually, and the purpose of that storage was to wait until our numbers got high enough while waiting for the ships to come. The ships would come once a year or however often and then they were filled up with two or three hundred of us packed even tighter. So for me it was very significant to go back through that door because for me that was the point of departure, and it had to be the point of return, because it was the reason, it was the threshold.

So as a docu-journey, it is your journey in your father's footsteps, but it is also the journey of your ancestors, a journey of present diasporans. In the film, you document African diasporans during their journey so it encompasses all the journeys and all the footsteps of past and present that Africans and African diasporans have taken.

At the beginning in the voice-over there is a poem that says: *I follow the voices of my ancestors who are calling me back; they are calling me back as they did him, as they did my father.* So the idea is that those people who have not been paid tribute to, the bones of these millions and millions of people that carpet the bottom of the ocean are calling us back. So it is a very symbolic trip at the beginning. We watch the water; we hear them calling. The poem in the film continues: *We reach up to carry across in the cradle of our palms, the children, the carpenters, the artists, we call you back, come home.* So it is the way that the film is set off to do exactly what you said, which is to look at the number of people from the Diaspora who have begun to try to reconnect with the continent through the slave forts which happen to be in Ghana, or a majority of them.

Through the door of no return!

Through the door, camera in hand, and I followed the journey of my own father who went through this similar process, and that helped me to make this link in finding other people's footprints, and symbolically I found his. So that helped me to make a particular link and that was enough for me. In the film I ask the question: "Was my father standing on this coastline, was he watching, looking at this ocean the way that I am looking at it?" He took a Super 8 camera there. When I was investigating all these connections it felt really interesting and symbolically important for me, his child, having taken up the profession of filmmaking, now to go back with my own camera to really pick up where he left off. What I try to do in the film is to multiply his image with all the people I find going to Ghana who are basically doing the same thing, trying to reconnect, trying to sew back this terrible tear that history has caused between Africans in the Diaspora and Africans on the continent.

The film goes on from this point to see to what extent we remember, because, as infantile as it really might be to think, "Do they remember us?" this is the horrible fact of history: it lasted four hundred years and there are concrete questions of economics, of rewriting history, that are confronting us now. So how can we say, "Do they remember us?" It feels like such an infantile question, but it really is at the root of a lot of our psyches, I think.

*In the last scene of the film **Sankofa**, we see diasporans at the final exit as they wait to welcome others to return to the point where their ancestors exited before crossing the Middle Passage. Could you talk about the links and connections with **Sankofa** and African/African Diaspora relationships that you talk about in the film?*

In fact *Through the Door of No Return*, which was inspired entirely by my experience with *Sankofa*, and the film that is going to come after that, were both a result of that experience in Ghana. I spent a lot of time over there before the crew came, and even the year before we shot I spent a lot of time, compared to the actual production time, I should say. I think that the presence of pan-African work, the presence of people of the Diaspora in Ghana during the time of Kwame Nkrumah, for example, is what really just catapulted this whole project. I couldn't talk about W.E.B. Du Bois' influence in Ghana and the subsequent influence of independence on the continent, without talking about slavery. I just found that it was impossible.

So the challenge that I faced with this camera and crew was to break down, sort of travel through this understanding. Du Bois asked to be buried at the foot of the castle, facing the ocean, the foot of a slave fort. He died in 1963, he was beyond his time; and that symbolism for the whole world is striking. I had to sort of do what he did. He was at the foot of the castle, through the slave fort dungeons facing back, so he was making this human. And I had to do something similar—to look at how somebody like Kwame Nkrumah, a country boy who went to Europe to study, hooked up with George Padmore, studied Du Bois, studied Marcus Garvey, and then this group of people having the nerve to come back to Africa to liberate the whole damn place.

To look at that I had to see how these men and women had the capacity to see themselves on equal planes. Hadn't history divided them? Hadn't history thrown them asunder? Hadn't history said that now they were totally different kinds of human beings? They were apparently able to cross that divide and I had to cross that divide myself. It was very important for me to do the same thing.

As a filmmaker at the Elmina Castle, what was it like? Describe your emotions, your own feelings. How were you able to continue to tell a story through filming, keeping a certain vision, a certain perspective, and at the same time experience a very deep, emotional journey?

That part was probably the hardest for me to come to terms with. In the editing room, I figured out a way to sort of begin to represent some of the feelings, in one of the poems. It happens after the song of Abbey Lincoln's scream. *After passing through the door, passing through the dungeon and almost coming out to the water to be cleansed, you almost feel like it is a boiling water, sterilizing water, but a relief, not a leaving water.* I try to say in that poem, and I don't know if it comes across effectively; it is a very, very difficult thing to say, but for me I had my experience in that dungeon. And you know, you experienced it yourself.

I had the opportunity, and I think this is important in filmmaking, to sort of decide at what point you are going to turn on the camera. How I would have shot if I had turned the camera on when I first went in there is one thing. How I would shoot a while after having begun to process the emotion, to try to come to terms with myself, to come to terms with that reality, is another stage, and both are very legitimate. The stage that I shot at was not the first stage, it was the second stage, and I tried to recreate the journey—I went from the first stage to the second stage in the film. That is basically what the film is trying to recreate: that journey to come to grips with someone who has been ejected out of a continent returning back home to say, "Where is my mom, do you still remember me?" When you find the answer, what do you do about it? I tried to recreate that process of that kind of confrontation.

In one part of the film there is that remembering, there is a conversation with a woman who you met in Ghana who actually is a storyteller and she recounts a kidnapping that took place long ago. She has continued this story that has been passed on from generation to generation.

You're speaking about the woman who sings a lullaby. When Haile looks at her, he says, "This could have been Billie Holiday." She was a woman who was almost shipped out because her ancestors were captured from the interior of the country and were marched down on this horrible month-long trek to the coast which was also a time when many people were killed or died. Those that made it to the coast were going to be shipped out. Her family was bought by someone in Africa, by an African actually, and that person eventually became a part of that family. So other Africans apparently bought a number of people like that. When we see these huge families around this part of Ghana, it's because people were bought at one stage or another and were absorbed into the family.

This particular woman's son has gone back and traced this heritage. Now she tells the story of how her ancestor was stolen. She sings a lullaby to children telling the story of a woman who had been tricked to go on a slave ship. Some people came to her and some other people in the village and said that if she came on the ship and entertained she would be paid. So she told her mother that she wanted to go on the ship and gave the baby to her to hold until she got back. She goes on the ship with the others and, of course, the ship steals them off. The lullaby tells the story that whenever the baby cries, the grandmother takes the baby to the shore and looks out onto the ocean and sings: "Your mother has been taken on a ship with no wings but the door is always open for her to return."

Did you discover as you were researching deeper, or during the actual filming, that you found more information for which you will have to do more research, for then another film?

It is so vast, Beti, because you know what happens in this process is that you want to make more movies. I am talking about things now that are touched on in the film, but they really have to be investigated more. One thing that is asked in the film is: "Where is the evidence?" Where is the evidence? You cannot tell me this whole period got lost!

I found more questions. My experience in making *Sankofa* is what launched me into this whole investigation, because people didn't know. One brother on my film crew from Ghana did not know that black people from Jamaica came from Africa.

Those African diasporans who took the journey with you, who you documented during your journey in Ghana, what was it like for them to be in Ghana, perhaps some for the first time?

The film interviews them a bit, they are our vehicle for going around Ghana and they go through an interesting process too. There is one young man who says that before he went to Ghana he thought that those slave dungeons should be torn down, that we should forget about it and go forward. After having visited the dungeons he says now, he feels that they have to be kept there, because they are like a monument to the way we are now.

For a black man to say that is so very important. Given the era we are in now, where the value of a black man is just meaningless in this country, for him to be able to assert that the situation we are in now has a direct link to those dungeons is very important for other black people to see. So it was that kind of process. There was also a linking process because these people went to the villages and in the villages people had varying images of what a black American looked like, or what we were doing, or what we were about and things like that. It was a moment of contact that people are not used to.

Most of the people that you documented came from the United States, but there were those expatriates who actually live in Ghana and have been there for some time. You document them and their experiences as well. What was it like to have this triangular process, African diasporans coming to the continent, those who live in Ghana, among which are those who came with the call of Kwame Nkrumah, and Africans on the continent? So you have all these pieces that were brought together in the film.

In fact, what happened was that we ended up putting the film into two parts because we found that the reuniting process was so fascinating. The pan-Africanism concept in effect was so fascinating that it really warranted a separate film. And Part I was going to be about the Holocaust, the confrontation. In Part II we go more in depth with the people who actually moved there, not only with the people who have recently repatriated to Ghana but also with people who have been there as you say, since the time of Kwame Nkrumah. Because we realize that there was an era from 1960 to 1966 when African people from the Diaspora went to Ghana to live in a free place, for them they were in a sort of laboratory. W.E.B. Du Bois, of course, was there, and so many other people from the Diaspora put their mark on Africa through Ghana.

You and Haile have forged an important institution in independent filmmaking as well as within the local film culture of Washington, DC. Could you talk about Mypheduh Films, Inc. and your more recent addition, Sankofa Video and Bookstore?

I think it is important to emphasize that it was the vehicle that made it possible to distribute *Sankofa*. *Sankofa* was Haile's seventh film, but because of its content and the other contradictions having to do with racism in the institution of filmmaking, *Sankofa* was never going to be seen by anybody but our friends. Once we completed the film after nine years, it was just not going to be seen because the larger distribution industry in this country was not going to distribute it. As you know, it is a film about slavery, it was written from the point of view of us, the captives in slavery. And we tried pretty much to portray in that film black people as human beings, as three-dimensional. Like in any society, there are people who give in easily; there are people who don't give in ever. As in any society, there are people who evolve. So we depicted all those kinds of characters in *Sankofa* and that was not something Hollywood was interested in seeing.

*What was Mypheduh's role in the production of **Sankofa**?*

Mypheduh had the charge of going from a distribution company that had been distributing our films and other films by African and African American filmmakers in a non-theatrical market and now suddenly becoming a theatrical distributor. In other words, the non-theatrical market includes distributing films to universities, to film festivals, and maybe even art houses, but we had never opened a film commercially. It is a whole different field.

29

What is Mypheduh, what does it mean, the symbolism? We notice that the logo is red, black, and green and there is a woman and a man walking together with a shield. Could you give a little background of the word Mypheduh—it is from the Amharic language?

Mypheduh is actually from the language that my husband speaks, Amharic. It is actually from the language that predates Amharic, Gez. Gez is very, very ancient; it is not spoken today except in the church. It means "protector of culture." And the symbol that we use, which Haile basically designed, is a picture of a man and a woman who together are forging something forward. You see coming from them this strip of film, or culture, or heritage, that they are preparing for the next generation, preparing and protecting.

And that is the objective of Mypheduh, to forge or protect culture, or to present it and protect it?

Yes, more so every day. With this most recent experience of *Sankofa*, this is exactly what we find ourselves doing, fighting to say that nobody has the right to say that black culture is not valid and cannot sustain itself. If we could be left alone to create our own institutions, it would perpetuate itself. So we are definitely in the process of fighting obstacles that continue to denounce the validity of our culture.

Could you talk about the present location and the myriad activities that take place at this expanded space, perhaps what I could call a culture center?

Because of the process of distributing *Sankofa*, we were able to move from our basement, where we had been since 1982, to a multi-office location that we rented and eventually we were able to buy a building. So we are developing programs that we have had in mind for a long time. One of the most visible is the video/bookstore and the most wonderful thing about that is that it is a place where black movies can be seen on video. You can come and get a variety of black titles—from Martinique, from Senegal, from California, from New York—that you would not be able to find otherwise. So when people ask how can we see more films like *Sankofa*, or how can we see more black films in general, we can say that there happens to be a black video store around where we can go see these kinds of movies. We rent and sell videos. Haile's idea is to put film on the same high plane as literature. Instead of thinking about film as something that is only entertainment, something that is expendable, something that you can just play with and put any images that you like, he is putting it on the level of literature, which we generally think of with respect.

We want to begin a film culture, a reading of film culture. We want to develop an audience that is able to read film in a way that film requires, so that we no longer have to put up with films that are less than high quality. By putting film and literature in the same environment, we hope that audiences will really begin to see this idea of film as something that you actually read, as something that you critique and analyze, as something that was conceived by a human being as opposed to something that represents real life as it is—as opposed to swallowing it without analysis, without saying, "wait a minute something is wrong with this, life isn't like this, or why didn't the filmmaker say this, or a better way to do this is to have this character do this." So that we stop swallowing, wholesale these stereotypical, destructive images that don't represent world history. So that is one idea of the video/bookstore.

A number of years ago, some of us merged together at Howard University—Haile, myself, and other professors and filmmakers and students. I would really like to recreate here this same kind of film forum activity where you look at a video. You bring in artists, community organizers, and others who can prepare their view of the movie and we can begin the process of reading it together. What does this mean? Why did the filmmaker choose a black dress for the villain? Was that intentional? Why did the filmmaker choose a light-skinned protagonist? What was the subtlety of it being a black hand that delivered the drugs? Why was the police officer Hispanic? These all are important things that pass by us otherwise. In the case of watching black videos, are we repeating stereotypes? Is the filmmaker using a new way of expressing a certain idea? Is the filmmaker challenging stereotypes? In that way, we hope this will be an opportunity to strengthen the viewer.

Other programs that we have been able to develop in that space are post-production facilities. We have acquired some equipment that will allow filmmakers to be able to afford to finish their films. One of the hardest stages of filmmaking is post-production. We get enough money to shoot the film and maybe to pay the lab. But then what do you do to complete it? We think that we are offering a very important service by offering low-cost post-production services, editing services—on film and on video. We feel that we are able to realize a few dreams. One encouraging thing is that emerging filmmakers have been seeing the facility as a base. So it is kind of a place where film culture thrives. To people from this country, from Africa, it feels like a center, a thriving center for thought and art. It makes people think that it is possible. Though they have not been able to have a script published in the last ten years, maybe there is another way that they can do it. Maybe if they take our camera and make a deal with a few filmmakers in that circle, maybe they can shoot the film and then go step-by-step rather than just sitting wasting away as an artist. Maybe they can figure out a way to put these pieces together to produce their own film.

Now it has become even more a meeting place for people who are interested in making films work more to control our images. So when people from Africa come by, people from different parts of this country come by, we can support them in showing their films when they come to this city. Generally, we find that because of our experiences with the theaters here and other places around the country, we can be very useful to filmmakers who are trying in some way to access these theaters. Most people don't realize that the reason they don't see more films by black filmmakers in theaters is because there is a barrier between black filmmakers and theaters. It has nothing to do with the availability or the existence of black films; there *are* black films, as you know.

You attend FESPACO often, and you and Haile were involved in the activities that brought about an African diasporan presence at the festival. These efforts highlight your commitment to making transatlantic links, which are reflected, in the films **Sankofa** *and* **Through the Door of No Return**. *You talked to me in another conversation about the 1991 FESPACO, where you attended the African Women in the Cinema workshop and about your disappointment in the failed attempts at making connections among women in Africa and the Diaspora.*

The only value that comes out of talking about what happened that year in FESPACO with the women's group is to understand the implications it has for pan-Africanism in the future. There is really no point in discussing in-family disputes for the sake of drama and gossip and who said what and how angry whoever was. But I think that the value in looking back at that incident is that there were some elements involved there that we should be aware of. So that when we go to have these efforts at unity again, we will be more aware and less naive.

I think that for me it was a very awakening experience, because I had been there a number of times, and Haile and I have been trying to make these links through our films and through organizing filmmakers and artists across the water, and FESPACO has already represented this attempt at pan-Africanism. That is what the term "Pan-African Festival of Cinema and Television of Ouagadougou" means, across the continent— and, in more recent years, across the ocean. So we thought that it was wonderful that FEPACI [Pan-African Federation of Filmmakers], finally saw at this time the importance of playing a role in seeing to it that African women filmmakers were part of this pan-African linking.

We were invited to this meeting, we came early, women were coming out of the woodwork to make sure that they could unite with other women. They had their own ideas and the enthusiasm was pretty incredible. I got there a few days early before the conference started, and even before the film festival, and as people came in it got more and more bubbly about what to anticipate, what things could come out of it, and ideas for the structure. We had not heard yet about how it was going to be structured. The makeup of the organizing committee was great because there was a sister from Great Britain, June Givanni, and there was a sister from Ouagadougou, Aminata Ouedraogo, who were key organizers. They had been working on this for a long time and we were all waiting for the word to come down about how it was going to be structured. I think it was scheduled to start on a Sunday or Monday and we were told that there was going to be an opening session. We all went to the opening session; I had spoken to June, who was the diasporan representative on the organizing committee, and this was what she told us was going to happen. So when we got there that morning we were waiting for it to begin. It was a wonderful mix of people from the Caribbean, from Europe, from the United States, Canada, Africa. It was a wonderful mix of black women interested in film or video. They had the microphones in place, the translator in place.

The first thing we heard when the meeting opened was a request for non-African women to leave. We looked around, there were a few brothers in the room, and they said, "Okay, you saw us, we couldn't get away with that." So the brothers left and we looked around and said okay we are ready to start. The next announcement comes—now all of this is in French—"Please, all non-African women please leave the room." We looked around to see whom else they were talking about; I think all the men were gone by that time. They said it a few more times in French and we were still waiting; we assumed they saw someone that we didn't see, and we were waiting for them to leave.

Then Sarah Maldoror stood up and spoke in French. She was just incensed and just spewed off this reprimand in French that I could not understand. I asked the woman next to me what she was saying. She answered that she is angry because they asked her to leave. I said, well she must not have understood they were asking all non-African women to leave. She can sit down, she is from Guadeloupe, and clearly an African woman. And clearly because of her personal track record, is to be em-

33

braced by Africa because she has even been honored with the title of the first African woman filmmaker because of her contribution to African cinema. So I was sure that she misunderstood. So I waited, and it continued and they kept repeating this.

Finally, it got through my head that there was a request for women that were not born on the continent to leave. I suppose this dawned on a number of women in there that this is what they were asking us to do. It was an incredibly emotional moment. It was ripping to shreds not only the purpose that we came there for, but also the identity that these women had spent years and years putting in place, reconstructing from a racist environment that denied them this identity all this time. And all of a sudden, people who were the ones, who could recognize this, affirm it, and embrace it, were rejecting it. So you can imagine the pandemonium. Finally the translator was worn out, he could not work it anymore, the confusion was too much.

The importance of elaborating is to take time to say that, that horrible moment in history had the potential of shaking foundations that had taken a long time to put in place, historical foundations, and more foundations to be laid. I later found out that it was not a simple act. Why would something like that happen? Why would sisters all of a sudden wake up the next morning—and the sister on the planning committee, June, had no idea that this was going to take place, that this is what they were going to ask us to do, so she was also thrown off—what thing from Mars was inserted all of a sudden in the mentality of these women to decide just moments before or perhaps the night before that they were going to have to divide the women like this and disrupt this delicate unity? I understood later after I left FESPACO that this was something that was not new to FESPACO or to pan-African efforts around the world. I later understood that Europeans have historically inserted themselves in insidious ways in pan-African efforts and a number of the women who were part of the organizing were very linked to French interests, French partnerships. And it was then when I got back home that I said, okay now that makes sense, if the French did not want this to happen apparently it was not going to happen.

I then began to hear of a number of other instances within FEPACI and FESPACO where there was this invisible presence that was able to cut us like a cake into as many pieces as they wanted us to be cut into, and it reflected our own weakness. I think that damaged what took a long time to overcome and if we have that in the back of our minds we will understand future attempts to work together. It is very important to understand that there was a French presence. I think that, had more women understood that, more women would have refused to leave. The only reason that I left was because they said, "Okay Shirikiana, you can stay because your husband is an African filmmaker." That is when I left. But had I had that knowledge in the back of my head I would have said, "No, I am staying on the basis of my own African-ness." But I was too disgusted.

You said that you felt that there were women who were linked to French interests, which is why diasporan women were asked to leave. Then what about the anglophone and lusophone African women—what were their reactions?

They were incensed. They were shocked. Of course, the most passion was coming from people from the Diaspora. One woman from the Caribbean, I don't know what country, said, "You are not taking me out of this room, my ancestors paved the way for me to be here, their blood is enough for me to be here." I think they did reorganize another meeting. I don't think that the simple presence of a language difference is a barrier. I really don't. I think that when language becomes an issue for the purpose of division, it is very easy for that to be used. It happens in Africa all the time, anglophone Africa, francophone Africa. I think that outside interests do use that as a barrier.

If you want to look at language differences look at the continent before Europe. People spoke three, four, five different languages and still do today. And you don't find conflicts based on language, you don't find disagreements that have far-reaching effects based on language. Europeans will exploit that forever, and have historically and will continue until we stop allowing it. I did not have a problem one-on-one, we had a wonderful time; there are translators. You try to learn French, they try to learn English, whatever; but again that third party comes in, that often invisible third party.

One thing that we did state very clearly, and which I think was everyone's point of view, was that there are points of divergence, there are issues on the continent that have to be dealt with by continental Africans. But I tried to make this point at the moment because I was naive enough to think that there was a sincerity there that could hear it: that, yes, it is important for continental women to meet, very critical. But what is the urgency that requires the de-unification of what we have here? Schedule that meeting, have that meeting, but don't call us to an African women's meeting and then say that we are not African! Everyone agreed with its importance. There were many hours in the day, have that meeting at two o'clock!

But there have been efforts in the past to bring a diasporan component to the pan-African concept of African cinema. Was there resistance in these efforts, such as the establishing of the Paul Robeson prize for the best film from the Diaspora at FESPACO?

You would need to talk directly to Haile, I know he had some incredible experiences. Again this colonial mentality sneaks in, this invisible white hand in the minds of people, because he has incredible stories about early days of FEPACI and the challenges that people would make to the legitimate African.

When I heard these stories, then I really understood where this nonsense was coming from in this other discussion with African women. Haile could tell you stories about when his own African-ness was challenged, here an Ethiopian country boy was being questioned by people who thought they were more African! I mean, these same African filmmakers who were questioning him are operating for the most part in the Diaspora, because the unfortunate reality is the difficulty of operating in film in the continent. So a majority of them operate outside the continent. One of the main women who got caught in this trick bag of "real African women" is based in Paris. It is a mind circus.

I don't think that Haile would say that there was an incredible opposition to diasporan presence. He and I went there to organize the first delegation of diasporans in FEPACI; it was a matter of putting it on the floor, and it was accepted right away, as non-voting members or something equivalent. The weakness is that we in the Diaspora are not organized. We can't say that there is a U.S. delegation. Africans in this country have failed over and over again in every attempt at organizing ourselves into a filmmaking body that can be represented at FEPACI, that can be represented at PBS [Public Broadcasting Service], that can be represented anywhere. So that has been the main weakness in that link. FESPACO pays for the Paul Robeson award that represents the Diaspora. Other awards, for example, from other interest groups are paid for by that particular interest group. We propose the award, but we don't even pay for it!

Could you talk about you and Haile Gerima as filmmaking partners? You are married to each other, you have children together, and you are both filmmakers. Haile is from the African continent; you are from the Diaspora. You have a pan-African vision, a vision of a viable independent film movement by black people.

I think it would be very hard to be a filmmaker with a partner who does not know film. Maybe that changes when your income reaches a certain

36

level, but at this level if I had a partner who did not understand filmmaking it would be very difficult to sustain a family or even a relationship. Not knowing the pressures of production, the pressures of deadlines, the pressures of raising money for every stage, the pressures of being able to express yourself within an arena that doesn't give a damn, basically, and keep that creative element in your expression while you are trying to oppose the commercialism of that environment—there are real hard elements. It is easier having someone who is facing that same pressure.

In the first place, in my own situation, Haile was my filmmaking teacher. So much of my training in filmmaking was influenced by him. Now the way we work together is mutually exploring and sort of discovering ways and means and ideas in filmmaking, and that is an exciting element. The problem comes when we try to raise kids in between, and he may be totally consumed in editing, or if we have to travel. So I think that is a challenge because both of us understand the challenge posed by filmmaking, we don't have unrealistic expectations in terms of, "You are not being a real dad" or "You are not being a real mom." But we are still facing the challenge of, "How do we be real parents and be filmmakers at the same time?" I don't know what grades we would get on a day-to-day basis for both of those efforts, but it is a constant effort, and we do the best we can. I guess the problems are particular problems.

The other interesting element is, of course, the cultural chasm that we are constantly trying to reach across. Those are issues that face us on a daily basis. And that is the challenge, isn't it? When editing my film, Haile says that we are trying to make up for lost beats. In fact, Haile is the editor of my film, and we are constantly discussing this and that, and one thing that he suggested for one part in the voiceover was that "we are making up for lost beats over time." And I think that we are, he and I also, and it is not easy. I don't think it is easy at all.

Could you describe what you mean by "making up for lost beats"?

Well, you know, I was supposed to be on the continent somewhere. I should have been born there. There were a lot of things that we missed over time and the development of the cultures within our own continent—you miss a lot when that gets interrupted, and if you are away so long from each other, how do you catch up? And how do you recreate, resynthesize? So that is the challenge. Haile brings new things to the table, I bring new things to the table, we are not the creatures we used to be.

37

But here we are, what can we do with it? And that is what we are facing. And it is not easy.

I understand the duality of African/diasporan experiences, relationships and feelings. While in Africa doing research I remember that I sometimes felt in a position as insider/outsider.

There was an interesting thing and perhaps it relates to the question you asked about Haile and I being of different birthplaces. A woman in my film—and it was so good to hear her say this—lives in Ghana now and is raising her family there. She is from some place in the United States and she says now we have to start all over again. We are insiders/outsiders and now we just have to sit down and figure out where we go from here, and not think: We are going to go back to where we were. I mean to "go back to where we were" is to find what? You are not going to find the people that you left in terms of where they were culturally. We are going to find a neo-colonized Africa. We won't find the African cultures that we left. All of us have to go through some kind of journey, and I don't mean just people from the Diaspora. It is very important for people on the continent to see themselves as having to go through this journey with us because there is a certain naivete that I ran into often.

Not understanding the importance of the moment at this time, not understanding our relationships, not understanding us, means that they don't understand themselves. And there is a need for them to understand. For example: Why would we feel like an insider/outsider? Why would we have this compelling need to reconnect? Maybe there is something that they better take a look at. It is like in the voiceover, "Oh, that's who you are?" I think that is symbolically very important to realize. "If I forgot about you that means I forgot about a whole era that I went through and this place went through, that shaped me and I don't even know about it." So, when we go back, I think there has to be that kind of determination and steadfastness. We are not going to go back and beg anybody for anything. Any lack of understanding of us has to be understood as a lack of understanding of themselves.

In this country I don't mind any day of the week clarifying to someone who doesn't know what I am, who I am, because it doesn't represent an insecurity on my part. I am not mixed for example, I am an African American, my heritage has all kinds of salt and pepper in it just like everyone else's. But this society doesn't understand this; it is *their* weakness. And it is up to us to be able to say: "Maybe you need to come up to par. Do you understand history? I represent a fact that cannot be changed.

I represent a part of your memory that you'd better go back and look at."

I think that it is that kind of firmness that we have to take with us when we leave this country and go to Africa and be able to stand steadfast: "Don't forget, if you don't remember me there is something amiss here; go back and check it out." And as we go through this emotional reconnecting, I think we have to feel free to do that. That, if anybody understands it or not, we have to feel free to do it. If people who are born on the continent can't understand it, it is an educational process that they have to go through. If we are ever going to become a pan-African people, they have to go through it with us. And they are. So that is why I think the journey I take in this film is important, because I don't get hurt by it anymore.

Chantal Bagilishya

Rwanda

Interviews held at the 15th FESPACO in February 1997 in Ouagadougou, Burkina Faso, and in Paris, France in August 1998. Translated from French.

Chantal, could you talk about how you came into the world of cinema? What were your experiences as a young girl? Did the idea develop as early as your childhood?

No one in my family has worked in this milieu. It was a dream like all other dreams. One never actually knows whether it will become a reality. As it turns out, my dream has become a reality and I am quite satisfied.

I remember exactly when I became aware that I was attracted to the world of cinema. It was the first time I saw the cinematic image, I was just about ten years old. I was completely fascinated by this image. I was watching the TV for the first time. I thought to myself, "How is it possible? How can people actually be behind the television image?" I don't know how it happened exactly. I did not consciously decide to work in the area of cinema. I know that I was very fascinated with the people and later, thirty years later, here I am inside of this world.

You entered having already met people in cinema?

No, not at all. Since it was an area in which I was quite interested, when I went to university I studied communication with a specialization in the audiovisual. In the audiovisual area, I already began to focus on production. While I definitely wanted to work in cinema, I preferred to stay behind the scenes, thus in production.

You have never been interested in actually being a filmmaker?

No, I have never been interested in being a filmmaker or doing any of the artistic aspects. I have always been interested in the area of financing, organization, and the structure around the production. I like the idea of being at the head of the production line.

Did you study cinema production management as part of your course work?

No I did not; actually, there were no formal courses in which one could specialize directly. It took personal motivation and then, of course, the interest in wanting to focus on this aspect. For instance, during my studies, each time that I could pursue a subject or theme individually, I would work on the financial aspects of production, while my colleagues would focus on a certain filmmaker, and so on. The majority of the colleagues in my class became journalists. Out of thirty students, only two of us went in the direction of cinema. I went in the direction of film production, and another colleague is a camera operator for FR3.

After your studies, how did you evolve into cinema in general and cinema production in particular?

I went to the cinema five or so times a week. I had many subscriptions to film journals and I read everything concerning cinema. Gradually, I met people who in turn introduced me to others. Eventually I found myself on the inside.

As a producer, could you talk about your profession, and what you do?

The work of a producer consists of going from a project, an idea, and finding the means to materialize it. To materialize an idea, unfortunately, costs a great deal of money. That is, in summary, what I do.

Do you produce mostly African films?

Actually no, for a long time I worked in a French production company where we made documentaries. I have a passion for documentary films, and I am interested in this genre in general. For a long time, I have wanted to work in African cinema, on African film projects. I have lived a great deal of time outside of Africa and, since I do not live on the continent, I feel that to work on a project about Africa provides me with a connection with Africa. The most direct way to have this connection is to work on a film project that takes place in Africa, which gives me the impression of living with Africa.

Have you had the opportunity to be the producer for an African film yet?

Yes, for the first time I had the opportunity to be chosen as executive producer of an African film by Cheick Oumar Sissoko of Mali. I was doubly proud. First, because I would be working on an African film and, secondly, in my opinion Cheick Oumar Sissoko is the best. We have completed the shooting of *Genesis* and are beginning post-production. It has gone well so far because Sissoko is very good; he is a real artist, and so we speak the same language.

*Could you talk a bit about **Genesis** and the post-production process?*

I am now organizing the people and materials needed, which include a technician, editor, mixer, and others who will participate, as well as finding editing and mixing facilities. In addition, I must negotiate prices. Because the costs are very high and it is rare that payments can be made entirely up front, there is always the role of negotiating installment payments.

How did you and Cheick Oumar Sissoko come together in a director/producer relationship?

I was looking for work, he was looking for someone to organize his production, and I was available. Since we all know each other or about each other in this area—we knew each other as colleagues, we knew who was who—we both agreed. I, of course, read the script, and then we discussed how the production would be organized and what was necessary to bring it to fruition.

You are located in Paris and Sissoko is in Mali—is the distance an impediment to the process?

We communicate a great deal by telephone and fax, but also he passes through Europe quite often. Of course, it would be much easier if we were in the same place.

Do you have your own company?

Actually no, I am executive producer and I work independently, in a free-lance context. Companies call me to work on a particular project and when it is over I go to the next one.

In terms of the production of African films, do you think that African filmmakers find it especially difficult to find a producer? Is there a lack of producers who are interested in African films?

No, there is not a lack; in fact, I think that a good idea always finds a producer. Of course, I am exaggerating somewhat. There are many great ideas that, unfortunately, never see the light of day. However, it is as difficult for an African filmmaker debuting in cinema to find a producer as it is for any other artist in the world. Because a producer is someone who, above all, believes in *your* idea. It is not just any idea, but one that is of interest to the producer. It is also the filmmaker as a human being that interests the producer. To be able to combine both is not always easy. A producer is not a machine; an artist is not a machine. It must be understood that to make a film takes a minimum of two years; it can take five years. Therefore, for two years, five years, we will be together. We work together in difficult conditions. We do not know if the film is going to be made, there is no money. We really have to be motivated and supportive of each other.

If there is a certain compassion and sympathy in the relationship, the work will be easy. You can have one of the most magnificent projects in the world, that is also well-financed, but if I find that on the human level we do not have the same values I will never work with you.

Someone who comes with an idea wants me to find five million, ten million francs to produce it. There is a great deal of ambition on the part of the artist and a great deal of megalomania on the part of the producer to imagine that from an idea she or he will find five million francs; and this is a minimum. Of course, if you are talking about an American film we are talking about millions and millions. On the one hand, there is a certain "absurdness" that goes with this work, and this excitement or extravagance must be managed efficiently. There is a great deal of money that is at stake and everyone is expecting to get something out of it. It takes a special kind of profession to imagine that "your vision" of the world is worth all these millions!

What role do you play once the film has been produced? Do you have any connections with the distribution and exhibition of the film that you produce?

First of all, there is a difference between the production of the fiction film and the documentary. When I worked on documentaries in France, it was handled in a certain way. For instance, either you were an "heir to Ford"— where you could finance your own film—or you had to go through several stages. For example, there must be a television company that is connected to your project and interested in financing it, after which you may get funding from other state institutions, such as the Centre National du Cinéma. Of course, I am simplifying the process. Your film is then contracted to be broadcast by the television company. It is the television company that finances the funding of the film production. In this case, distribution becomes less of a problem. Of course, it is up to the producer to find other companies around the world if you want to reach a larger audience.

On the other hand, the fiction film is more difficult. Financing through a television company only is not sufficient because the cost is often much higher, and the television company cannot assume the cost alone. Then you will still need to find a movie distributor, and that is also difficult.

There are many films that are financed but are never screened in the cinema houses. For example, in France there are some two hundred films that are made each year with a lot of state funding, and there are perhaps only eighty percent of them that are actually shown. Imagine all the people involved in making the film: the producer, the filmmaker, and others who have participated for some time. The family has suffered, and then no one sees it! It is dramatic, but, in fact, it happens often.

Would you say that it occurs twice as much with African films?

Yes, I would say twice as much, but not because they are African films. I do not think that African films are censored. If one can define African films, I would say that they are viewed as art films. Moreover, art films throughout the world have difficulty finding producers. Because quite simply, they do not bring in much money. And this is the case, whether it is a French filmmaker who does not enter in commercial cinema, as we know it, or any other filmmaker across the globe. Even within independent cinema in the United States, filmmakers are in the same situation, although it is America with all the film networks. I think it is a false problem to say that African films are treated differently because they are African films. All films that are different have a limited audience.

45

What do you see as the future of African cinema?

A cinema cannot exist without the support of the state. So much is determined by it; financial support, for example, and there is a whole legislative structure that must be established. It is not the filmmaker or even FEPACI (Pan-African Federation of Filmmakers) that can do it. It must be the state that takes the lead. And for the moment, African states have no interest at all in this area, or in culture in general. I can even say that there is no interest in anything that has nothing to do with weapons or defense. As long as African governments do not take culture as a right, as a basic element that is essential, as important as any other domain, our cinema will always be nonexistent.

Every cinema in the world—except the United States, which exports its cinema and is doing quite well—the cinema in all the European countries, apart from France, is almost dead. France has been able to preserve a cinema because the state is involved on a daily basis, on all levels. It supports a national cinema; it is an example. Our countries do not do this because, first, culture is not a priority for our governments and, secondly, even if they were financially motivated, they do not understand that cinema is also a source of revenue. For Americans, for instance, U.S. cinema exports rank second in foreign revenues. Support of African cinema does not exist in Africa. Therefore we are obliged to look to the outside for funding. The majority of the funding of African films comes from Europe, from foundations such as the Ministry of Cooperation. While it comes from outside of Africa, it is very generous on their part, because otherwise African films would not exist.

It is rather troubling to realize that without outside support our cinema would be zero, it would not exist. Not because there are no artists—there are many—but because we do not provide the means. There are a few countries in Africa—I know the francophone countries better—that attempt to do something, notably Burkina Faso. We must pay homage to them, we are very thankful. Burkina Faso is a country that is not financially wealthy, but it has given culture the importance it deserves in everyday life. It has done a great deal for cinema and for African cinema in general. There have been many inter-African co-productions initiated by Burkina Faso. Each time that assistance is asked of the state of Burkina Faso, support is given.

At the 1991 FESPACO, there was a focus on African women in the image industry and you played a role in the organization of the platform. During the workshop, tensions arose between women from Africa and the African Diaspora, which if I may suggest, have not yet been resolved. Could you talk about the African/African Diaspora relationship during this event? What were some of the problems and how can they be resolved, though it is already six years later?

In 1991 at the 12th FESPACO, there was an event that was very dramatic for me. We decided, as African women, to create an association to get a better sense of what we could do to support each other. Initially, we merely wanted to get together because we did not know each other. Anyone who knew an African woman who worked in the domain of cinema would put her name on the list to be given to FESPACO. At the time of the festival, I was astounded to find hundreds of names that, since my career in the field of cinema, were unknown to me.

There was quite a large number of us in attendance; we did not yet know each other. We began by becoming acquainted with each other. We were from Chad, Eritrea, Libya, and so on; it was very moving. There were filmmakers and producers. We decided to organize workshops to find out our interests and thoughts.

On the day of the opening of the workshops there were others who came, among them women from the African Diaspora, the majority of which were black Americans. We told them that these workshops were a place where women from the continent could come together because they do not know each other. That we from the continent must first organize, after which, when we have a better sense of what we want to do, we can then meet those who have other experiences.

We operated on the principle that though we are all black, we do not have the same experiences. There are many things that separate us. There are many things that unite us, but there are as many differences. I do not believe much in absolute mimesis among black people. We kindly stated to the diasporans, that this is a workspace, but tomorrow we will have a meeting when we will meet each other. We would like very much to work together and to exchange our experiences. They did not want to cooperate. They refused to leave the room. It was very dramatic. There was also the television press, whom we also told not to film the workshop; usually it is never filmed. They refused to leave. There were also French women; they also refused to leave. It was unbelievable.

Politically I was troubled by this. In spite of the affinity that I naturally feel towards my sisters, it was dramatic. At one point it was surrealist to see the response of the women after asking them to leave and stating "that tomorrow we will have an open session where we may all meet, but for the moment we do not know each other, and before we can work together with others we must meet among ourselves." This event was something that really hurt me. It was a pity that we could not come to an understanding.

They come for the initial meeting. We ask them to wait until tomorrow, and then, they shun us, and that was painful. It was a difficult decision to make, yet the following day it was equally troubling to realize that there was an actual rupture between us as a result of this incident.

Was there a gesture on the part of the diasporan women to attempt to reconcile the misunderstanding?

None at all.

It has now been six years, has there been any contact between African and African diasporan women in this context?

Since this "missed opportunity," I do not know of any other attempts that have been made in this context. Nevertheless, I remain persuaded that our diverse experiences—whether there is a commonalty or not—can only mutually enrich us.

However, there have been significant strides within the infrastructure of African cinema to make connections between Africa and the Diaspora. So there are things that bring the two together.

We do have many things that we can do together. However, behind the myth that we are sisters and brothers, there are many things that separate us. We have a tendency to simplify the things that actually distinguish us. Yes, there are things that unite us, but we must also recognize the important differences. The myth, unfortunately, does not bring out the reality, those very tangible differences. It works on an ideal level, but how is it concretely translated?

Do you know many African American filmmakers?

No.

Would you like to have more contact with diasporan women?

I would say that I am interested in having contacts with interesting people throughout the world. However, I will not act differently simply because they are "black." Otherwise, I will gladly meet and get to know them.

Do you think that it may be a question of language that may cause misunderstanding and misinformation?

If we really want to talk to someone, we can always find a way. There are anglophone women in our organization that is forming. Yes, we have difficulty understanding each other, but we are able to communicate. This communication happens when we relate on a human level.

Do you feel that there is a chasm between—if I may use an expression that is also ambivalent—anglophone and francophone African women?

Yes, it does exist. I think in general, it is a question of language. This comes from the colonial legacy. It is true that the rapport we may have is not as close because we are not always able to communicate with each other. Another problem we have coming together is the difficulty of inter-African travel. It definitely complicates our being able to network. It is more costly and harder to come together throughout Africa than, I would say, to go to Paris and Europe in general. There are many things that render communication difficult.

Therefore, in order to facilitate the contact between us, we must think about other ways of communicating. The current method is simply not working. In the group that we are in the process of forming there are women from Kenya, Ghana, Burkina Faso, and other countries, we have all the will and determination in the world to make things happen, but it is very difficult.

There is something wrong here, at a time when there is a tendency around the world for people to broaden their scope. Take the example of the European Union: it takes time, but gradually the countries are coming together, but we have not been able to achieve this. It seems that we are not able to work together. Nevertheless, we must learn to work and fight together to get what we want.

To go back to the problem with the women of the Diaspora in the United States, you have other experiences, whereas language separates us. We realize that there are things that we just do not talk about, and as long as we do not talk about them, we cannot resolve them. We will continue living the myth of "Africa United"..."Black people as brothers" where there are many obstacles. It is important that we talk about this from time to time.

Marie-Clémence Blanc-Paes

Madagascar

Interview held during FESPACO 1997, Ouagadougou, Burkina Faso, in February 1997. Translated from French.

Could you talk about your background, yourself in general, and how you became interested in cinema?

I was born in Madagascar of a Malagasy mother and a French father. I just saw a film and I remember a phrase in it that I liked a lot: "I was born of a colonial orgasm." And the more I think about it the more it's true. Well, actually, throughout my entire childhood in Madagascar the question of being of mixed race was a real problem. All my Malagasy cousins would always say to me: "Anyway, you will never understand anything because you are white, you can never understand." And for a long, long time I wished I could go live in France. I thought that once I was in France all of this would be over. As an adolescent I went to live in France, and on the first day of school I was told: "Hummm, you are not quite French, where are you from?" And there it began again. Adolescence is already a period that is particularly difficult, one does not always feel comfortable in one's body or with the experiences during that time, so that being of mixed race was truly a problem for me.

When I met my husband, Cesar Paes, who is Brazilian, we went to live in Brazil. Never again did anyone ask me was I French, Malagasy, or what I was. Right away everyone saw me as Brazilian. That experience was a great discovery for me. It was, in fact, in Brazil that I learned that to be of mixed race was not a handicap but a blessing. It allowed me to live just as well inside water as outside of it. To know many things was not a handicap but wealth, a richness.

Cesar and I quickly decided to make films in order to talk about this experience. He is Brazilian, from another continent and another culture. We wanted to talk about countries of the South in another way than what we had seen, what we had lived. We lived in Brazil, but shortly afterwards we left for Paris. Paris was the compromise between Brazil and Madagascar, it was at the midpoint. The idea was to go in the South and see the things that we could bring out in a new light regarding its reality. We wanted to make films other than about economic problems, droughts, underdevelopment, children of the streets. We wanted to go look for the riches of the South, to bring out the things that we had lost in the countries of the North.

How did you evolve into filmmaking and film production, having the desire to visualize the cultures of people of the Southern Hemisphere?

In 1988, we began to think about doing a film in Madagascar about the Malagasy richness that does not exist elsewhere. And the richness that we found was orality, oral literature. We created a production company and that is how we began. It seemed to me to be much easier to devote my energy to convincing a financier, than trying to convince a producer.

It was our first film and we were completely unknown, so we started a company that we call Laterit Production, like the red earth which is found everywhere in the South. We left for Madagascar, taking enormous risks which I think that I would no longer do today. We did a kamikaze production, taking on all the debt for the entire production. We met a man who leased film equipment, and said to him "Okay, we want the equipment for three and a half months to do a film." He wrote us a budget and asked, "Okay, when are you going to start paying me?" We paid him back for years and years and today, this man has been paid. The film is finally paid for.

After this kamikaze film was finished we had the extraordinary chance that this first film, *Angano Angano*, was awarded prizes in very important festivals in Europe, after which we succeeded in selling it. I think that as of today there are eighteen television channels around the world that have aired the film—which is quite an accomplishment, since it is a film that is spoken entirely in Malagasy, because we never accepted voice dubbing. Since it was a film that was presented in the form of storytelling, to dub what the people were relating would be awkward and some of the value of the story would be lost.

I found **Angano Angano** *to be especially rich in its visual documentation of Malagasy tales and myths. Your second film,* **Aux guerriers de silence,** *follows this approach. When did you begin to think about a second film?*

Through the many years that have followed the production of *Angano,* I am still quite happy with the work that we did on the film. As I already said, the production company was established to make this film, it was a tool. But very soon after the film was finished we had to continue. We have a particular way of working, since we are married partners, because we are in the same boat all the time. We began quickly to work on the second film, which was a continuation of the first. At the end of *Angano Angano* a man says: "Take this history with you, carry it beyond the sea, because the oral tradition should not stay only among us. Others must hear it, and maybe they can get something from it." We took this idea and decided that we would make a new film about oral traditions, which means to show that life cannot only be led by the written word. We live in societies today where written civilization is dominant.

The following film, *Aux guerriers de silence (Songs and Tears of Nature),* was about the relationship between oral and written cultures. We chose two geographical locations that were total opposites. Brazil in the south and Lapland in the north. In both of these regions of the world there are indigenous people who are of oral cultures. The Indians of Brazil were dominated for five centuries by a Portuguese majority, followed by Brazilians. In Lapland we went to see the Sami, who are more commonly called the Lapps. They, too, experienced the same problem with Europeans. In Europe, there is much discussion about the Indians of North America, the Indians of Amazonia, but there are also Indians in Europe.

Has the reception of this film been as favorable as **Angano Angano***?*

Well, the film, *Aux guerriers de silence* had very successful reviews and we also won prizes. However, it has been much more difficult to distribute commercially and to be picked up by television, because it is a film that is not easy to label. Since it takes place in the North *and* in the South, bringing together people from totally different cultures, it is not easy to classify—neither in the field of ethnology, nor as a film from the Third World, nor as a travel film. I am not discouraged; one day this film will have its place on the audiovisual landscape.

How were you able to finance the production of the film?

In terms of production, *Aux guerriers de silence* was very difficult. We were quite known after *Angano*; however, the television channels that bought it, other than the Belgium television, did not want to take the risks on *Guerriers*. We were still crazy enough at that time to say, "No, we will still do it and see what happens." On the other hand, as of today this film has not been paid for. Actually we have never been paid a salary, and there are many more sales to be made before the debts will be paid off.

Your latest film is in competition here at FESPACO. How soon after **Guerriers** *did you begin filming it?*

Between *Guerriers* and the most recent film, I produced a series of short programs for Sandra Kogut, a woman from Brazil. It was co-produced with a video company in France. The series was well done and well received. However, a co-production is not at all the same thing as being in a production where one takes all the risks. As the executive producer, one signs all the contracts, giving one's word, in fact, to others: "I commit myself to the completion of this film, for a certain sum of money, for a certain amount of time."

Cesar and I have just finished our film *Le Bouillon d'Awara (Awara Soup)*, a production on Super 16 blown up to 35mm which I co-produced with ARTE. I actually went from a two horse-power to a limousine in terms of production. We were basically making ends meet when we first started. The problem with the limousine is that it consumes a lot of energy. I had many associates to manage. There was ARTE on the French side, there was the Belgium television, there was ORSTOM (L'Institut français de recherche scientifique pour le développement en coopération), a French research institution. I had an independent co-producer like myself from Belgium who was terrific.

Because it was shot on film it was a much larger budget. Since we wanted to have the same level of quality in terms of shooting conditions, I did not want to do the film in a rushed manner. I wanted this project to have the same plan of action that we had used up until then. During a shooting we generally take the time that is necessary. We spend enough time so that the people who we want to meet and put on film can feel at ease and be willing and actually want to come our way. A film is—before anything else—an encounter, and our endeavor is to put on film the relationship that we have with people.

We completed this film with a great deal of time devoted to coming to an agreement, convincing associates that the film was easy enough to understand on its own without having to edit or narrate it. None of our films have ever been narrated; the people themselves construct the story, and the editing is done in such a way that commentary is not needed. The images speak for themselves.

Where do you situate your films in relationship to African cinema? Would you locate them in the African Diaspora, in the world of the people of the Southern Hemisphere, in the multicultural world?

The best response is to tell you about—and I don't know if it is pertinent to the question—the idea of the last film, *Le Bouillon d'Awara.* We decided to make a film about a place in the world, a kind of little laboratory in the world, where people from very different cultures and races live in one location. It is a tiny place, a microscopic area, which is why we like to say laboratory. We went to shoot a film in a little village in Guyana where there are 1,500 inhabitants, and among these 1,500 people there are thirteen languages spoken. Over the last twenty years, sixty percent of the population of this city is made up of recent immigrants. They come from the Antilles, Brazil, China, Laos, France—from where there has been a presence for a long time—and, of course, there were Amerindians from the beginning, and there are also Lebanese. Actually, there are people from all of the continents who are in this little place together, and who intermix. We wanted to show that, despite the increase of nationalism everywhere, in the world there exists a glimmer of hope. In this little place the people are able to live together despite all the different languages, cultures, colors, and customs.

How do I situate myself in the context of the subject of this film? I am mixed-race, Cesar is Brazilian, we have children together and we live in Paris. I don't feel that I have the right to claim my negritude. I don't feel that it is mine to claim and I don't want to. Because of my multiple identity, I am more interested in an identity that creates, an identity in movement. I am very afraid of identities that block this movement, that refuse the other, that reject all the contributions of others. This film refuses this as well.

I was fascinated by how the story is told using the actual making of the soup itself. The mixture of ingredients was the thread that weaves the cultures and the experiences of the people together.

Yes, the history of the *metissage* and cultural mélange in *Bouillon* is actually told through the preparation of a dish called Awara soup. It is a metaphor because it is a dish whose ingredients normally are not cooked together. Pork is not cooked with shrimp nor are cucumbers mixed with eggplant; these are not what normally blend together in a dish.

There is a legend behind this Awara soup. In Guyana it is said that when one eats it, one will never leave Guyana. One becomes Guyanese, one becomes Créole. There was another story that was not in the film that I found very interesting. When invited to eat Awara soup, the mistress of the house never obliges anyone to eat everything. She comes to ask you what you want to eat. The person who wants to eat only shrimp may do so; the person who wants to eat only fish may do so. The person who wants to eat everything may do so. But she never says, "Here taste this." No, it really is about fishing about in the soup to find the consistency, or the color, or the odor that appeals to you.

In many ways my culture is similar. My husband is South American, I take a lot of things from Latin America. I am very Malagasy, and the older I get I recognize in my manner, in my values, things that are deeply Malagasy. I am French, I cannot deny that. I was educated in a French school, I learned "my ancestors the Gaulois" before learning who the Malagasy king was. Besides, I don't think that I ever learned it in school, it was much later when I began reading books on my own that I learned about Malagasy history. So Diaspora, yes, I would say; but more nomad than Diaspora, which is also implied in the latter term. It's true that the films that I have done up until now, and I intend to do others, have been to fight against this rise of nationalism which concerns me a great deal at the moment.

In future films that you and Cesar do, will the division of work continue to be allocated in such a way that you are the producer and Cesar is the director, or does it change according to the needs of the film?

When we first began, we did everything together. We wrote *Angano* together. However, I never do the cinematography, Cesar has always done the shooting; in fact, that is how he started. We go on location together and we direct the interviews together. We have always edited together. I would say that with *Bouillon* there was a division of tasks that was such that I was dealing more and more with the production aspect, while he dealt with the direction. We have a tacit agreement together, which is; when we are not in agreement, and this comes from my producer side— sometimes we discuss a great deal, sometimes for days—but when we do not agree, he has the last word. I know he is the director, and as the producer I don't want to lose money or time. Time flies by and when we are using film, with each second that passes there are lots of dollars that are spent. Thus it is agreed between us. I feel that the *écriture* of a film, the sensibilities that come from both of us are very much visible in the film. We complement each other very much. But more and more as time goes by, the production, financial, and administrative aspects, are my responsibility.

Mahen Sophia Bonetti

Sierra Leone

Interview held by telephone between Washington, DC and New York, November 1998.

Mahen, you are Executive Director of African Film Festival, Inc., an important institution that you established and which has steadily grown since 1990. Could you tell us about Mahen Bonetti?

I am a Sierra Leonean who has lived in the United States for the past twenty-five years. I reside in New York with my husband and daughter. After completing my studies, I worked in advertising and later for *Weekly News Magazine*. I developed more of an interest in the arts when I met my then future husband, Luca, who is now my present husband and hopefully my last [laughter]. He is an arts conservator. As a result of this union, naturally I became aware of and interested in African art and culture. Basically, you take things for granted because you grow up with these things all around you. Besides being an arts conservator, Luca grew up in a family where, for them, art was like food. His mother, who is now retired, headed the Swiss Arts Antiques Conservation Committee. When I met his mother, I realized how important African art was to her discourse. This led me to the realization of how great Africa's influence and contribution had been, and still is, on universal arts and culture.

My family had been active in Sierra Leone's post- independence government, and when that government was overthrown my parents were jailed for a period of time. Shortly thereafter, I left Sierra Leone and traveled to Liberia where I lived for about a year as a ward of an uncle, who was also active in the government there. Eventually I came to the States. After meeting my husband, I then embarked on an art restoration apprenticeship of sorts. I assisted my husband at a very elementary level and also did some public relations work for art-related projects. So over time my interest and involvement increased, I was growing steadily. So in a larger sense, that is the story of how the film festival began.

In 1980, when I was able to return home, for the first time since leaving in the early seventies, I visited Sierra Leone. I was truly inspired and also felt a sense of rejuvenation which sparked an awareness in me of the misunderstanding which existed between Africa and the United States, where basically the images of Africa that were most seen or known to Americans were those of starving children, despots, natural calamities. It seemed like Africa was just one disaster zone. Yes indeed those things exist, but there are also many positive things which include the rich culture, which is so entrenched in American popular culture, as far as I am concerned. These are things that people take for granted.

Feeling helpless, I thought, in my lifetime I had to find a way to make a contribution, to correct some of these misconceptions, about Africa, her people. Then, on the other hand, I felt that I had no tools available to do this. There was something forming in my head but I did not know how to execute it or make it become a reality.

Could you talk about some of the images that you grew up with of Africa?

I'll start off with the women in my life. When I came here, and you get more involved in different discussions with people, and of course, there is this whole issue of female genital mutilation and these stories. There is always this poor, suffering African woman. Where I grew up—and this makes me the person I am today—the women were such a force in my childhood. To me they were always liberated, they were the first people that I would address or think about when there was a problem or when I had to say something. They just seemed to be bigger than life. So that for me the women in Africa have this silent power that really is the backbone that sustains Africa. So those images are never really transported in the minds of people elsewhere. Moreover, the fact that I grew up in a society where there was, you may call it, a very advanced society where social issues were addressed, are the values you grew up with.

I am not saying what people imagine Africa to be is not true, because, mainly, in the last twenty years, there has been a sort of breakdown of society and morals in Africa. Basically, corruption has a lot to do with that. However, here is a scramble for Africa and there is this redistribution of territories and all those things that people don't hear. There seems only to be that, "this Africa cannot get it together or cannot handle things." That is what frustrated me a lot. Even today, you try to book a ticket to

Rwanda for Christmas, every seat is taken. What people do not realize, despite the fact of what we are reading or hearing, everyone goes home for Christmas because it is really rejuvenating. It is like going back to get new cells to come back and cope. Of course, there is a brain drain in Africa because of the corruption and the breakdown of the infrastructure. Most people cannot find a job or cannot live there, but if really those societies could sort of get it together, and hold their own, a lot of people would go back. Because every African in their hearts wants to live on the continent, I really believe that.

So, in fact what propelled you to create the African Film Festival, Inc. is your interest in presenting the reality of Africa, through film, to people in the United States.

Yes, reality through African eyes. There were several other factors, but yes, to show that, culturally, Africa's contribution to the world—and what black people brought to the Americas as slaves, as immigrants, and so on—was culture.

So what was the seed that got it started?

In fact, the unlikely forerunner, let's say, to the film festival was an "African Nights" concept that I developed for a Manhattan nightclub in 1988, believe it or not. Some of my friends were involved in the nightclub. These were people who saw how the hip hop scene was becoming more mainstream, they had the Spike Lees, there was this sort of rush of films made by African American directors, which were showing in theaters. That was also the time when the name African American became official. All around the late 1980s.

To return to the "African Nights" concept, it was really a special kind of gathering and all types of people would come together and create such an incredible energy that was truly African in spirit. However, I felt like I could never stay in a nightclub all my life. I also wanted to crystallize all of these energies and thoughts and to get all these people to begin to think beyond a nightclub.

So you screened films in the nightclub?

No, we played music. I was trying to describe how this was the forerunner to the film festival. It was the idea. As I was saying, I felt that I had no tools, I did not know what to do. And I wanted to contribute something. You stay here all your life, you go back home and what do you take back? You have the security here, you try to get a pension, you go back and you become a bourgeois, you have your house, and you put on blinders, but then what do you offer? You are never really safe. Because all of a sudden, sporadically, a war can erupt and you do not know where it is coming from, but it is festooning all this time, people sweep over it and act as if it does not exist. When you have these child soldiers who are carrying guns, who are maiming and opening up pregnant women's stomachs, who get drugged by leaders, they just don't jump from the sky. They are a product of their environment, and that is what we as Africans have to address. Why has our society gone down to this point? It is not in our psyche to perform such heinous acts.

So for me, I don't have the tools, I don't have a professional degree in medicine or law, nor do I have a lot of money. So, what do I do? So I started this concept. A lot of African musicians were coming here, and the concerts would sell out. Youssou N'dour, Ismail Lo, Toure Kunda, and others, you would go to a concert and it was packed, people from Asia, South America, Australia, you had everyone there. So, in terms of modernity this is where Africa had paved a way, through music. So, I started with that, I started "African Nights" concerts where I would bring in a local band which played African-inspired music, and drummers at times. It was incredible. It was a dance party, but it was also a *soirée* sort of thing, with reception. It was a lot of work to pull together; well, perhaps not compared to the festival. So, working in a nightclub was not what I saw myself doing at forty-five, especially if I wanted to have a child.

That same year, 1988, I visited my in-laws in Lugano in Switzerland and next door, there is the Locarno Festival that goes on every year, it is the fourth largest festival in Europe. I went to open-air film screenings. I was leafing through the brochure, I came across a "thirty year retrospective of African cinema," and I was just blown away. I am looking around and I am thinking, "Who is interested in this?" I am looking around and I see it is basically a European town, a European audience. They were showing so many films, there were lectures, symposia, catalogues, translations in several languages, and the audiences revered African culture and art.

Returning to the United States (and, like I said before, the name African-American became the official term), simultaneously African-American filmmakers were making waves. I found in cinema a powerful and immediate medium for promoting awareness and understanding. I thought that we could ride on the coat-tails of these events. Yet, what was really the driving force of this idea was what I saw in Locarno. I thought that this was something that could be done here. Next to Africa, you have the largest number of people of African descent living in the Americas. So you really had a ready-made audience in a way, and I think at that point in time there was really a sincere interest. Normally there was a trend or fashion that would die in time; we had the dashiki and Afro. I thought there is a whole generation coming up, and also there were a lot of hybrids. You have these first-generation kids born here from the Caribbean or Africa, mixed-race and mixed-culture. So there was a whole other mindset formulated here. I felt that the medium of film, that cinema was really the tool to promote an awareness and understanding of African culture in the Americas and I really believe the time was right.

How were you introduced to African films?

There was one film distributor here, Dan Talbert, who was the one and only, the sole distributor. He brought Truffaut, he created the New Wave, Cinema Nova in the sixties in America, he is a real film purist. He is the one who brought Ousmane Sembene's films to America for the first time. So, intermittently from 1979 through 1988, every two or three years an African film would come. Many of the Sembene's films, then he started bringing Idrissa Ouedraogo, and they would appear in the New York Film Festival. Then they brought Henri Duparc's *Dancing in the Dust* [*Bal Poussière*]. Talbert also had an affiliation with Lincoln Plaza Cinemas, which were commercial theaters. We were clued in and knew that these screenings were happening; and the review would be in the *Times*. When you went to the theater you would see that ninety percent of the audience was white and European, eight percent African, two percent the rest of the world. By the time that you got out word to people that you knew, "that you have to go, you have to see this film," the film had come and gone, because it was not reaching into the grassroots community. At least I was not aware of it, and I am sure that I am right, because most of the people in those communities that are culturally rooted to this, and who should know, were not aware. Also, information filters into those communities in a different way, they patronize different types of publications.

So what were your impressions of the first African films that you saw?

You know Clyde Taylor describes it in a really great way and I always like to use his quote. He says, "It is like you go to a river and the water is flowing, one season you go and it feels a certain way when you stick your toes in there. Then maybe you go a few years later and you stick your toes in there and it really feels differently, and maybe you want to stick your whole foot in then." And that is how I felt. Because the first time that I saw an African film, to be honest, was here. I had seen things as a child growing up, but mainly theater. Because of the British, we had many theaters, like British Council stage plays, or Yoruba film shorts for TV, but it was a play that was shot, so the camera is stationary and you are watching a play really.

One of the first African films that I saw was in the United States in 1979. I remember it was one of Sembene's films. To be honest with you, I did not digest it because I think I felt...it seemed something so surreal. I felt numb almost because *Ceddo* is also dealing with religion, dealing with slavery. So I saw Sembene's films initially, then I started seeing Idrissa Ouedraogo's films. I would think about it. It's like leaving Africa when you go on holidays and when you come back the smell is still in your nose and in your hair. You have this smell around you all the time. So that is what I felt when I saw the film, and it was in the winter, I remember! I kept saying there is this smell. I kept thinking, "My, how Sembene tells this story!" He tells the African story like no one else. There might be others who are even more gifted, creatively, but he really goes and grabs it, he really understands his people. So in a way I was happy that was my introduction, because it was really a good way to enter. He gives you the training of how to view it.

So the period from 1979 to 1988 was the gestation period to the film festival concept?

Yes, we were popular in New York. We were part of the art scene. And, as I said before, there were many things going on in terms of music, in African-American culture, and so things were ripe. However, I noticed that while there were many African influences, any time that Africa is discussed it is always someone else speaking. There is never really an African voice in all these discussions. Here we are in the late eighties and here is someone speaking for us. I think that is why it is so hard for Africans to be accepted in a contemporary sense, especially in the arts. In primitive art you have some of the best collections. Some of the most respected art collectors and dealers have incredible pieces of African art but then it stops there. Because as far as that period goes, there is someone else who is an authority, who has that information, and who can explain what it was all about, how the African felt when he was doing this art and the argument is that it was never signed. However, most do not realize that it was done for the community, so no one signs things, it functions as everyday life in Africa. A stool is carved and everyone is going to sit on that stool. So that the art form exists within.

Would you say that there are similar distinctions made in African film, where those that look African, in other words, are in so-called African settings, are viewed as African films as opposed to those which are not presented in "familiar" African contexts?

This is what is so great about Sembene, like what I said, being a story-teller he takes you on a guided tour from the urban to the rural. Africa, in all its complexity, there is no one set picture of Africa. Just like the arts, it's timeless, what goes on in urban or rural settings is always sort of dependent on each other.

In your experience as an organizer, would you say that African films teach the viewers the realities of Africa and dispel myths and stereotypes that they may have?

Absolutely, that is the whole point! As I said I was frustrated, I felt that I wanted to show the Africa I knew, but I wanted to educate not only Americans but Africans living here. Because throughout the continent we don't have this. You know you can travel from Washington to New York easily; at one time, for me to call Senegal from Sierra Leone, I had to go through England, England had to go through France to connect me to Senegal. So even for Africans here, the films are a milestone. Because we get to know each other through film. Because you can read all you want—and we have great writers—and you can envision something, but it is another thing when you really see it. You can also look at it another way, that people are more inspired after seeing the film to go read about how they fit in, how their footprint works on that cultural landscape.

Could you talk about the goals and objectives of African Film Festival, Inc.?

We started in 1990. The idea started in 1988, and in 1990 we became officially an African Film Festival organization with no office, no money, a typewriter that ate ribbons. In 1993 when we did the major festival in collaboration with the Film Society of the Lincoln Center and the Brooklyn Museum of Art, we broke all records in Lincoln Center so far, at the Walter Reade Center.

My main purpose for doing it was twofold: to show images and to educate people. Ultimately our goal is to promote an awareness and understanding, and to increase knowledge of African culture using the cinematic medium. At the same time, we are committed to developing an international audience for African cinema and to expand the opportunities for the distribution of African film in the U.S. We have the festival in New York, we have a traveling series, which introduces African cinema and culture to new venues, widens the audience of African film on the national level, which is also audience development. For future productions, you must sustain the interest. The festival is the showcase. We are presenting works and that is important because those works get seen and maybe they get picked up. Even if they get picked up by other festivals, it is still good; it is still activity that is going on.

The educational and outreach program is twofold. First, to appeal directly to American and African-American youth and adults with images of Africa, in narrative film structure format. And secondly, to make African cinema more accessible to various communities that are significantly rooted, like public and cultural institutions, such as what we do at the Schomburg in Harlem, and going into Brooklyn.

I think that the Lincoln Center in any case is neutral, because the Lincoln Center is the bastion of, or the institution for culture in America. And that was another problem, some people asked, "Why did you have to start there, why not in Harlem?" I felt that we were going to go to community centers anyway. I felt that this culture is the greatest gift to the world and she should be seen in a place where you have to think of the technical and creative projection of it.

Especially in New York, which is an international city, the exposure is phenomenal, I am sure...

Sure, the best state-of-the-art theater was built there, and the best sound system. That was where we had to be, that is all I knew.

Could you detail the inner workings of organizing a film festival?

When we did this festival, not to pat ourselves on the back, but we did a lot of hard work getting there. I think it was the time, because a lot of people tried before us. So it is not that we came with something really new. We were persistent. I had to be persistent because initially my husband helped me a bit and I kept thinking, "All those phone bills he had to pay and all that money he gave me to travel; if it doesn't work he is going to kill me, it has to work." I went to see people who were in high positions in the black community who said "We have tried" or "People are not really interested in Africa" or "How about *Roots*" or "Why don't you bring in a Brazilian slant, that would bring in more recognition" or "People are not going to go to see African films." We wrote so many proposals, I thought at least we would get an "A" for effort because we did such a good presentation with a supplement. The proposal was so well written, we thought, at least people will look at it. I wrote to so many institutions, they really felt for me. I wrote to the Public Theater, I wrote to the Lincoln Center, I wrote to the Brooklyn Museum. And everyone said, "We are really with you, we have tried before, but now it is hard to get this work out, much less about Africa."

The best response I got was from Richard Pena of the Film Society of Lincoln Center. At the time, he told me that they were building the Walter Reade Theater and their purpose was also to promote international and independent works. So, I thought that if they would be willing to join forces with our organization...we came with a brilliant idea to them and we said, how about if you join forces with us. They said, "Well, yes, but we have nineteen programs like this, we cannot specifically sponsor one of them and ignore the rest." He said, "What we do is that we have enough money for bare bones," where if you run the films they put it on and they send information out to their forty thousand-plus membership and people come. Nothing else is done because they do not need to do any more promotion than that. They said that "You are talking about something major here, there is not much money right now, if you find the money, we are on." I thought, "Well, this is the first step." I thought, "With all these corporations doing business in Africa..." We went to the foundations, but then each time the envelopes arrived, after you received ten of these rejection letters, or where people think it is great and they wish you well but they are supporting this or that already or it is not the time of year right now, write us back next year. I kept thinking, no, I cannot give up. I did have inroads to some important people, mind you. I was relentless; I would speak about it even at night in my sleep. Everyone I met, because that is how it works in New York—someone who may have a lead to a funder, or who may know how to get the films here without paying for shipping, or who might write me a letter of support, or who may have an affiliation with a newspaper, anything—so I spoke about it all the time. In that sense we had lots of leads and were able to cut a lot of red tape and went directly to the top of some of these corporations. They would seem very enthusiastic and we thought that this was definitely coming through and then we would get a letter a few weeks later saying, "Well, we thought about it...." Everyone is skeptical about touching Africa, even if they are making tons and millions out of there. I think a lot of them want to be clandestine and they do not want the attention. Remember the Shell story and the scandal that happened? Well, that year they sponsored FESPACO.

Speaking of FESPACO, how do you link with other African film festivals and film festivals in general?

I would say that we are the premier showcase, we really are, because also our focus is strictly on sub-Sahara Africa for now. I think that Diaspora festivals are wonderful, but I personally do not have the sensibility for all those works. One of the best programmers that I saw who could do that is Cameron Bailey at the Toronto Film Festival. Because if you do not have the sensibility and really do not do clever programming, someone is compromised, and in most cases it is Africa because people come to see what they are familiar with, the names, or titles or something in English. So, you really have to do something genial to get people to see all the works and not only come for those they feel comfortable or familiar with.

Eventually, of course, I would like to branch out where we do parallels between Brazil and lusophone Africa in a modern context, to see, for example, what has been the influence of the conquistadors, if there are any influences.

You stated that in 1993, at the first festival, there was a record-breaking turnout. Could you talk about the general responses to the festival?

Initially, I would have to say that, to a lot of the African filmmakers who came out of francophone Africa I was suspect. They thought, "Who is she, first of all. She is not a filmmaker, she is not an academic. What did you say she did? What country is she from? Do they really show films in her country?" So they were really hard with me, they were not kind, to put it that way. There is a very good friend of ours, who has helped us so much and is a board member. He is from Senegal. He knows a lot of filmmakers, he works here, he runs the France 2 office in New York. He would get many calls from them asking, "Who is this person, what does she want?" "Someone else trying to use us? Are you sure she is even from Africa?"

The first year, Sembene was here. We showed thirty-seven films for a whole month. Two o'clock screenings on a Monday were sold out. That blew their minds. Sembene gave his blessings right away. We opened with *Guelwaar*, it had just come out. It had not been shown anywhere. We were scared. Everyone around us was skeptical. They gave us an "A" for effort, for trying. Then we found the money. Then they thought, "Oh my God, she found the money!" Then they said, "She found a lot of money." Well, certainly a lot for a festival, and the first time. We sent out flyers, we got an activist to go out to the communities. We did an extensive grassroots effort. Of course, when the festival opened and you had screenings on a Monday afternoon that were sold out, everyone was sort of swallowing their tongues, they did not know what to make of it.

It was scary, Beti. I was green, I didn't know one camera from the other. It was something phenomenal. Then everyone jumps on you, all the sharks come out. When I think what the other two women and I went through to make this festival, and then everyone comes afterward, sucking our blood and riding the wave of this success, and never mentioning us. It was amazing! I could have acted ugly like they did, but I think that is the beauty of Africa, also. She is like the breast that never dries up and everyone wants to suck from it but she just keeps giving milk. You have to be very careful. You have to say to yourself, Why am I doing it? Because it is not really a money-making venture. Eventually, of course, you are able to pay your phone bill, it can lead to other possibilities, and we are not-for-profit, by the way. If you go for profit and you want to produce, maybe you can make something, but your initial purpose cannot be to make money. What also blew people's minds is that I raised the money, and most of the time you are expected to shave off your salary right away. However, for me, I am fortunate also. Not that we are rich, but my husband has been very supportive. Friends have been extremely supportive. I think that it is very important to do a first-rate festival. We are expected to be mediocre, to be kind of slack. I am proud of it and that is how it should be: let us at least give her that honor, Africa, she deserves it.

After the initial first two festivals the filmmakers started getting rentals here, some come here just to pick up checks and we do this technical brochure, even if it is a simple one, where we put all the contacts. It is like a bible for programmers. I send them out. Before, people would want to program an African film, maybe within a world cinema or something, and think, "My where do you even start looking for this film?" What we do is list the contacts, the distributor, the credits, bibliography, so that programmers or even community centers that have the facility can call or send a fax to a distributor in Europe, Africa, or here and do it on her or his own.

It is very active. I am proud to say that there are people who were before us, but I think it was timing and diligent hard work that made this happen. It has to be the timing, because it has not stopped. Everyday I'm hearing that someone is doing a new festival or doing a retrospective or including a centerpiece of African films within a framework of a larger film festival.

What role do you see film festivals playing in the promotion and dissemination of African cinema and culture? And particularly African Film Festival, Inc.?

You know it troubles me when I hear this, and not only from African filmmakers, who say, "You know, we are tired of film festivals." Listen, Woody Allen's *Celebrity* opened the New York Film Festival. It is not necessarily that he had a distributor ready, but it is a showcase and especially a high-profile showcase of stature. Naturally, distributors are going to see our audiences because they are sitting there. Producers are going to see how audiences react to a certain film: whether the theater is crowded, how popular the film is.

Every filmmaker's dream is to have a theatrical release right away. But if people don't know who you are, or you don't have the possibility of getting as many distributors to watch your film when you screen it one time, a festival is so important as a showcase. Because distributors, producers, film critics, film writers are aware that a festival happens at a certain time of the year. Before the festival, weeks or months ahead, the public is already being informed, they get the schedule, they prepare, they come to see your work. They see that it is in the setting of an audience. Other programmers hear about it. It is critical, especially to African filmmakers.

Television is another medium that people should start considering, or cable; that is what we are also working on, to try to get some people to FESPACO [1999] this year from HBO and places like this. I think it is so important for them, if these festivals were not in place for African cinema, believe you me a lot of these films would not be in circulation and people would not even hear of them.

During the festival, are you directly involved with distributors who are interested in distributing films that are being shown?

Yes, some incredible deals have happened during our festival. There are also other results as well. A guy here has been writing a script. He has been here two years and he is getting a salary. Another one is working with some people on the West Coast. Wanjiru Kinyanjui, from Kenya, got a really nice review which was reprinted in the local paper in Nairobi. She is making commercials, she is making educational information films, and she has found some money for her next film project. We are proud of these things. There is one filmmaker, Jean-Marie Teno, every time he comes here someone gives him money, maybe if it is only a check for $500. He says it never happens to him at a festival. Not a corporation or foundation, but someone in the audience who feels so moved by his work that they always give him money. Every time that he has attended our festival, three times, and this time we did a little retrospective of his work, someone gives him money.

How does your being a woman reflect in your work as organizer?

It is a very good question to ask. First of all, as I was saying to you before, I did not come with a background. Of course when I see what one really considers to be a background, I do not have a complex because I think that I am in tune and I know a lot more than a lot of others. I can talk all day and have a discussion among elitist colleagues about film. But if these same people do not have us, because we are the ones who disseminate the work, we get it out there. Someone who writes about cinema and culture can write all they want, but putting the films out to the larger public is what a festival does, because that also spills over into the literary and other disciplines of art related to Africa and the Diaspora. It is twofold. Primarily, our purpose is to educate and to help the filmmakers, but it is helping every other art form in a way, because the films depict that also.

As a woman, well, it is a very male-dominated scene and the thing is—and I don't think that I am challenging personal confrontations—but, at times, you say enough is enough. Some of the filmmakers, because they are dealing with me, think they have to behave a certain way. It is a cultural thing. They see I am a woman—and they wonder, I am not a European woman, I am not African-American, and I am an African working in America and in New York of all places—it was something that was very odd for a lot of people, too. They were trying to put their finger on it, yet it is no big mystery. I am just someone who lives here, who happens to do it. One filmmaker actually—I won't name him—was in Carthage and he told this person, "Yeah, she is Richard Pena's assistant," and the woman said, "No, she the director of African Film Festival, the founder and the director." She said, "It is her idea and they do it in collaboration." And he said, "Oh no, then she must be his mistress." So, that sums it up for you. This is a big, intelligent, African filmmaker, who does not want to believe in his mind that I have anything to do with this, so I must be sleeping with Richard. The younger guys are great. This is what is nice about the emerging group. Some of them are difficult, but it is so nice. Even with someone like Sembene, it is nice to have his support. To my back, they will praise me, but in front of me, they really work me. The guys in my country will tell me, "You married a European because none of us wanted you." When they see Luca they say, "You know you got a good one, so you'd better hold her well."

Do you envision organizing an African women film screening as a component of one of the festivals?

Definitely, starting next year we are going on an annual basis. The main festival will always be the even years and it will be major, something like two weeks. During the odd years we will do perhaps four- or five-day weekend festivals. We will start out like that and build it up. Perhaps I will start out with the lusophone regions the next time, or perhaps the 2000 festival will focus on women.

In another conversation, you talked about your role as a mother and your interest in exposing you daughter to African images. Could you talk about that in the context of your work?

We started this work, and obviously we are not going to change the face of Africa or save it today, but at least we are setting an example. Going back to my childhood, this is the quality of traditional and formal education that I had. That is why people of my generation are really so in tune with our culture and there is a lot of pride in that. It makes you who you are. For all black people, our past is so connected with our present. That is why in certain parts of the Diaspora, people are still in a state of searching, because you need to do something. I think these hybrids, this first-generation-born group, who thinks, "Oh no, African food today," who look down on it, or who could not stand this or that, or African music. They want Burger King or they want to go to rap parties. Then when these children are in their late teens, early twenties, and they are curious about Africa, they are so upset with their parents, that they never taught them their language. Maybe this generation of African kids is not as passionate as we are, and on the one hand, they do not have that tribalism baggage and other baggage that we have. The way that they lack the passion, they shrug their shoulders, but maybe we need that sort of complacency right now in Africa, this kind of muteness, to sort of clean things up.

So I feel, for me, that it is very important that we catch our young people, even if they are complaining and they hate it when they are young. Later in life, they will appreciate it because I know that there are some things that I hated as a child. And today I am so happy that my parents were insistent on sending me upcountry during the holidays, of making me eat certain foods, or listen to certain stories. I am post-independence, so the first schools I attended were with English kids, and I was ashamed of the beads on my waist because I took swimming courses and the English kids would asked, "what is that," or I had *mor mor*, the gold earrings that are twisted in your ears and I was ashamed of those things. I wish I could find those earrings, or those beads.

My daughter really wants to know. Maybe it is Mariama's unique personality, but she likes to be known as an African *and* a Swiss child. She likes all those unique things about Africa. She likes to show off with her friends. I think that it is important.

In another conversation, you said that though there are not many African women filmmakers, you do attempt as much as possible to profile African women filmmakers, that you actually seek out their work. As a woman, do you feel that you have a sensibility towards African women's works?

Could you talk about the visual image of African women and the representation of African women in the film industry and also share your impressions on films by African women, the sensibility, themes, tendencies?

I think Africa is a woman and everything that is working in Africa is because women are behind it. They also have a sensitivity and the rhythm. Women are more three-dimensional, they are deeper, and in Africa, that complexity comes from a woman. I find that the subjects that the African women deal with are different from those of African-American women's films, much less Hollywood. Here in the States, one doesn't expect to see things like polygamy, female genital mutilation, or women in Tanzania crushing stone. You feel their passion, you feel their confusion, you share it with them. Safi Faye's film *Mossane* is a beautiful film; there you have three generations of women. I also felt lucky; she let me show it this year. I love the relationship between the grandmother and the granddaughter.

No aspect of African cinema is more miraculous than the most unbidden emergence of female filmmakers on the continent. What makes film the most immediate, the most direct of all art forms is its ability to transport, to place one instantaneously in someone else's situation. Their films sometimes focus on the challenges of adjustment and this is why audiences can identify. Whether they are depicting upheavals or celebrating life, they show "little people" trying to "do the right thing."

I believe the female African filmmaker has a defined perception of her world and because of this her films translate. It can move from one language into others. They have tenacity, resourcefulness, and buoyancy. Their situation requires all these qualities.

I also believe that, in using the cinematic medium, we find that in their films, women are best able to recapture, help define the true essence of African culture and African people. They address issues in a sense that are taken away from imposed colonial values or colonial distortions and point of view.

Maïmouna Hélène Diarra

Mali

Interview held at FESPACO 1997, Ouagadougou, Burkina Faso; includes written correspondence during May 1998. Translated from French.

Maïmouna, could you talk about yourself and your background?

My name is Maïmouna Hélène Diarra. I was born in Segou, Mali. I have a DEF (Diplôme d'Etudes Fondamentales) and a Diplome d'Etudes Theatrales after four years of study at the Institut National des Arts, in the dramatic art section. I am an actor by profession and I am host and producer at the ORTM, Office de Radio et Télé-diffusion du Mali.

You have an impressive background in the theater. How did you become interested?

I do not know quite how to explain how this all came about. I remember I was still in primary school when one day I was fascinated by the theatrical representations of the Groupe Dramatique National du Mali that was touring throughout the various regions of Mali.

You stated that you did formal studies in theater. Did you first study theater and then join the group?

Yes, after receiving a diploma in theater at the Institut National d'Art of Mali I spent ten years on stage with the National Drama Group commonly called the "Koteba of Mali."

How did you come to join the drama group?

After I completed my DEF exams I indicated that I wanted to study at the INA in the Dramatic Arts section. It was during my studies at the INA that this same group, the Groupe Dramatique National du Mali, discovered me while working on our play "Gouverneur de la Rosée by Armand Dreyfus, my professor of theater at the time. I was in my second year when the group requested that I come to work with them after I completed my studies.

Unfortunately, I was not able to complete my studies at the scheduled time because of a strike followed by the suspension of the students. The entire establishment was closed until further notice. However, the group was very anxious to have me and requested that I sign a contract, so I worked with them for two years. After the student suspension period was over I received my diploma and officially became part of the drama group.

The Koteba theater is a well-known theatrical genre in Mali. Could you talk about it a bit?

Koteba is a traditional form of theatrical expression in Mali. It is adapted to all kinds of stages but most particularly to the "round stage." In Koteba theater, everybody can be simultaneously spectator and actor.

In fact, it is a way to expose the defects and various conduct of the leaders. This theatrical form has worked so well for the drama group that the public has dubbed the group, "Koteba".

As I said earlier, I played in the "Gouverneur de la Rosée" in the role of the old Délira Délivrance when I was a student. However, I also realized that there were other problems and demands arose.

I suppose your evolution from the theater to the cinema was a natural process. How did it come about?

My entry into cinema was quite by chance. I played my first role as an extra in 1981, in Souleymane Cisse's *Finye*. My second step into this world of film as actor came about when I played in *Nyamanton*, by Cheick Oumar Sissoko, followed by *Finzan*, also by Sissoko. It was at that time that I got a taste of this "thing" and I decided to give my all. Thus far, I have played in six feature films, in both principal and secondary roles. I have also played in five short films and one téléfilm.

You have acted in films by the most important filmmakers in Mali. You have also played important roles in the theater. What connections do you make between the theater and the cinema?

I do realize that my performance is much appreciated by filmmakers and that I am, in all modesty, one of the most sought after actors in Mali today. At the same time, I also recognize that my first profession, the theater, assisted me a great deal. If the theater taught me how to move with ease in front of an audience that was in communion with me, the cinema, in turn, forced me to concentrate all the intensity of my actions at the same time that I am totally aware of the camera and the demands of the director. This work is as demanding as it is passionate, because it is here that the actor, shot by shot, scene by scene, must embody a character.

In the films in which you have acted, could you talk about the roles that you have played?

I have often played the role of mama or the grandmother in the films in which I have acted. I have also played the role of wife.

Do you feel a certain affinity with your character in these roles?

I feel that I have a certain gift. The personality of the character comes naturally to me. When I am asked to play a certain character, I look in my environment and I reflect on what could resemble this character. It often comes spontaneously. I do not have any difficulty in embodying the character.

*You acted in the film **Guimba** by Cheick Oumar Sissoko, which was awarded the Etalon de Yennenga at FESPACO 1995. **Guimba** is a period piece with wonderful scenery and costuming. Could you talk a bit about the film and your experiences during the production of it?*

Guimba is a film that dealt with the subject of power. You know, in Africa, these kinds of situations actually take place, the question of power, of tyranny, and there was much drama right until the end.

As an actor, what are your general impressions of the image of African women in the cinema?

At the beginning of African cinema, people did not understand the role of women, nor did they accept them, but people are now beginning to understand their importance. They now see that, in the roles in which we are playing, we are actually communicating something, and they now understand. At one time people thought that actresses were women of loose morals, but now they realize that we are not that at all. They see that we are showing and exposing problems that actually exist. They are beginning to realize the true value of African women in the cinema.

Do you think that you are now being taken more seriously as an actor and in the role that you play in society in general?

Yes, I believe people are taking us more seriously.

Have you only acted in films by Malian filmmakers, or do you also act in films by directors from other countries as well?

I did act in two other non-Malian films, a film by David Pierre Fila of Congo and *Macadam Tribu* by José Laplaine of Zaïre (now Democratic Republic of the Congo); however, they were shot in Mali. I would also like to act in other films outside of Mali, but unfortunately I have not yet gotten a contract.

As a veteran actor, what do you say to other actors who follow you?

If I have advice to give from my modest experience, I would say that an actor must never take herself or himself for a star. To the contrary, she or he must be open to criticism and let the public judge as they see fit.

I would not want to finish without putting a particular accent on the importance of discipline in the actor's work; it is essential and paramount.

In what capacity do you work at the Office de Radio et Télé-diffusion de Mali?

At the radio station I work with "Magazine Expression," a program on culture, cinema, theater, sculpture, painting, and other art. At the television station, I do commercial spots and public service announcements. I also did an inter-Africa theatrical play presented on RFI (Radio France International). In addition, I was chosen to play in the Mande Theatre Troupe initiated by Sotigui Kouyate and Jean-Louis Duvauroux for the piece *Antigone*. I also received a National Merit Award by the president of the Republic of Mali in 1996.

M'Bissine Thérèse Diop

Senegal

Interview conducted in Paris, France during the Racines Noires [Black Roots] Festival held in July 1998. During the festival M'Bissine Thérèse Diop was profiled as a pioneer African actress. Translated from French.

M'Bissine Thérèse Diop, your place as an actor is very important in the history of African cinema. During your career you played the role of Diouana in the film **La noire de...** *by Ousmane Sembene. This film marks the first feature film of African cinema. Before this film, made in 1966, African cinema did not actually exist. Could you talk about this period? What was it like to be an actor in Africa at that time?*

In general, the milieu of cinema is very difficult. It was very difficult for me at that time. Oh, if I could have come in contact with someone then who could have assisted me...but no, there was no one! Even in the neighborhood where I lived, to see a black woman in the cinema! As I said, it was very difficult for me. After the film *La Noire de...*, when I passed by mothers in the neighborhood where I lived, they would turn the other way. Some people were also very critical of me. This period in my life coincided with the 66-68 period in France. Having just returned from France, I wore traditional clothing as well as clothing designed with the "Mao collar." Of course, that did not help matters, for there were people who said that I had communist ideas, something which I did not even understand. There were those who also said that an African woman who acted in the cinema was a loose woman. Others loved the film, but I was highly criticized. People talked all around me saying, "That girl who acted in *La noire de...* is Sembene's woman, they are going to get married." They did not understand at all! In other words, having acted in the film people saw me as belonging to Sembene. It was difficult for me to understand this reaction. Even my own mother—normally a mother supports her child when the latter is in difficulty. However, in my own family, I did not get this, I was not given support. No one encouraged me. There were months that passed when my mother did not speak to me because of the film.

*Could you talk about how you came to act in the film **La Noire de...**? How did you meet Ousmane Sembene? Did you do acting before your role in **La Noire de...**?*

No, but I already had the idea. While I was in France attending tailoring classes, I told a friend that I wanted to join the army to be a parachutist. So, you see, I already had the idea that I wanted to do something different, and it evolved from that. My friend said, "I don't see you either as a seamstress or as a parachutist, but rather as an actor." I said, "Actor?" She said, "Yes, I see you as an artist." Everything evolved from that moment. We contacted Josephine Baker. We wrote to her and she responded, I remember that very well. She sent me one of her photographs. She invited me to come to visit her, but I did not have money to do so nor anybody to help me get some. So at that time I could not really realize my dream. I could not accept any of the invitations that I received.

However, this dream stayed with me; and when I returned to Africa, I enrolled in the Ecole des Arts de Dakar. After my sewing classes, I attended classes at the art school in the evening, from 5 p.m. to 9:30 p.m. I had a friend, Mariam Dembele from the Ivory Coast, who knew a photographer who worked at the *Actualités Sénégalaises*. He took pictures of both of us, and everything evolved from there. Ousmane Sembene saw my photograph and contacted me and then I began to work with him. Each time that I think about *La Noire de...*, I realize the impact that this period had on me. I think that if I had to do it again I would think more carefully.

Do you mean that you would reconsider your role in the film or as an actor?

No actually, in the film I see my true character. My gestures, movements are actually reflected in the film. The manner in which I see things. I attempted to imagine what the camera sees.

Ousmane Sembene talked to you about the film, his intentions and message, the inner and outer character of Diouana. What were your impressions of the character Diouana?

Sembene gave me the script and I read it carefully. I said nothing to him about it, even until this day. In some ways, I connected the story of Diouana with my own problems. I did not suffer to the same extent as Diouana, who committed suicide, but I know suffering in other ways. Something attracted me to Diouana. Diouana went away to succeed in her life, but yet she committed suicide. I wondered if it was really a suicide or if she was eliminated. Those were the thoughts that I entertained. Though I did not go to France to seek employment, I suffered here in Senegal. One can stay right here at home and suffer in the same way that one can leave one's home and suffer. Suffering is universal. Perhaps this is what made me accept this role.

You knew the French actor Robert Fontaine before playing in the film **La Noire de...**?

Yes, he was actually my teacher at the Ecole des Arts de Dakar. I liked Robert Fontaine a great deal because his class was very interesting. He explained everything very well and I asked him questions continually. I remember his telling me, "M'Bissine Thérèse Diop, you must always look at children at play. Their movements are innocent. They are very interesting to observe. This will help you in your work." And in fact, it was true. Each time I look at children, I get so much pleasure. Children's behavior differs from that of adults. What they say and do comes from the heart. While adults attempt to hide things, children hide nothing. Adults have gestures that are hard, while the gestures of children are tender, as if touching cotton. These are the things that Robert wanted me to understand. To act in cinema or in theater, one must work at it. I would say that even now, what I really want to do or be in cinema, I have not yet attained. I have not yet reached this goal. I hope it will happen one day before I am old [laughter].

What could that be?

I don't know actually. I am musing. The role that I would really like is difficult on one hand. I am not political but I would like to play the role of the spouse of a head of state. I would also like to play the role of a warrior. Actually, it would be interesting to see the two roles in order to compare the difference between them. Certainly the spouse of a head of state has a role, but it is not the same as the role of a warrior. There are several roles that I would like to play. However, these roles have not yet been written. Scripts for which African women artists may act are rare, very rare. They are given only small roles; either you accept them or you don't. Scriptwriters don't seem to be able to define or seize the beauty of African women.

You also acted in Ousmane Sembene's **Emitai** *(1969), a film that showed the effectiveness of the silent rebellion of women.*

I like *Emitai* very much because of the role of the women. I think about that period when all of those women rebelled. Women have had to rebel when things were not right. When things are not right and men act contrary to what is expected of them, if women are not able to obtain peace and calm, to educate and feed their children as they want, they are obliged to "show their claws" and say "we have had enough." One thinks that women do not have anything to say. On the contrary, women have as much to say as men. But the difference between us has been so well emphasized that some women think they have nothing to say. However, as the film reveals, we often do not even need to rebel, some things can be said and done calmly, in silence.

After **Emitai** *you played the role of the spouse of Patrice Lumumba in the film* **Soleil noir** *by Alexi Pechniev (1970). It was a film made in the ex-Soviet Union. How were you chosen for this role? Could you talk about your experiences with this film?*

The filmmaker chose me to play the role. I was in Dakar, he wrote to the Minister of Culture, and he also sent the script. There were those who were opposed to his choice. I was required to get the permission of a spouse, when I didn't even have a boyfriend! I felt that these requirements were made to set up obstacles for me. There was only one person I have to thank, and each time I think of him I say, "May God help him in all his endeavors because he helped me enormously." Thanks to him, I was able to go to the Soviet Union to work on this film.

Who was he?

I am no longer in touch with him. He worked at the Ministry, he has now retired, he was a teacher. To this day I thank him. I had to obtain signed authorization from the Minister of Culture before going to the Minister of Interior. If I were involved in politics, I could understand this demand. But I am not in politics, I am an artist. Because Sembene was political, I was put in a similar category, I suppose, I don't know why. I always had this problem, each time I wanted to leave Senegal I had to go first to the Minister of Culture before going to the Minister of Interior for authorization to travel.

And you are not sure why you were associated with the leftist politics of Ousmane Sembene?

I remember once when I was in Kaolack [Senegal]. I was with Sembene, in fact. He asked me to go with him to Ziguinchor, but I told him I would stay in Kaolack with one of my cousins. The next day my cousin came to tell me that there was someone who wanted to see me. I wondered who it was. I remember that day, with my cousin next to me, I was called a communist. Afterwards I wondered whether or not these people really paid attention to the film. I did not make a big fuss but simply said that I was neither communist nor capitalist. I was not interested in these kinds of things.

*Let's return to your experiences with the film **Soleil noir**.*

Yes. *Soleil noir* is the story of Patrice Lumumba and the events that took place in his life. Of course, it touches certain people who were involved in politics in Zaïre during his time. I interpreted the role of the wife of Patrice Lumumba, how she and her children were saved.

But, you see, the actor plays the role that she is given. That is the role of a true actor. However, others are not convinced that this is only the movies. They consider the actor even more dangerous than they consider the others, as if the ideas expressed by the character are actually those of the person who interprets them.

Thus, they imagine that we really want to take the place of the characters in the film. In reality I am not interested in these events. One cannot be interested in everything. I am merely interested in art: tailoring, pottery, weaving.

*You later acted in the films, **Borom Xam Xam** (1974) and **Cap Manuel** (1986), made by your husband Maurice Dorès, who is both a psychiatrist and ethnologist. Could you talk about your experiences working together?*

Oh, it has not been easy. With the film *Cap Manuel,* it was the second time that I had worked with him. I pouted a bit because it is not always easy to work with one's husband. He paid attention to everyone else except me. One of the camera operators dared to tell him about this. I even said to my husband, "This is the second time and the last time that I am working with you" [laughter]. The role that I played was that of a well-to-do woman who moved about in the *haut-bourgeois* Senegalese society. She traveled everywhere, everything was easy for her. She had all the money and possessions she wanted. Towards the end of her life, she had some understanding of "black magic" and its powers. She settled at the lakeside and became, well, she was called "crazy," but in fact it was not madness. Actually, at the end of the film many of those who came to the seashore to fish would go to her to make wishes or receive her blessings. This is a double-layered film; there is one side of it that is ethnological and one side that is cinematic. The film also has an aspect that focuses on this mental illness.

Could you talk about some of your experiences while interpreting this character?

While playing this character my only hope was that I would not end up like her later in my life. When playing a character, whether it is the main character or a secondary role, I do not want to incorporate it too deeply within me. I tell myself that it is a dress that I am wearing today. As soon as I come home, I take it off. I attempt to behave like everyone else, leaving behind the character that I played on the set. I lay it aside and live as everyone else.

During your career as actor you have not played in many films, especially African films. However, you were one of the first actors to play in an African film!

This has not been my decision. I remember there were two filmmakers who came to see me, right here at my home. They asked me to act in their film. However, at the last minute they changed their minds, without having even informed me, not a telephone call, not even a letter. Of course, that was their decision, I was not bothered by it.

In your opinion, what do African filmmakers look for in their female characters, their female actors?

I don't know if I could really answer that question properly. I think that certain filmmakers give roles to black actors that I would say are not even fit to play. Certain filmmakers, who write scripts, even if they are not important roles, should create interesting characters. I would like to think that from time to time the black woman as actor could play important characters, not always the small, insignificant ones. If our filmmakers themselves do not make the effort to give us work, other filmmakers will not be encouraged to do so. If I were to work on a film today, I would have the means to do so. I would not mind at all going to the United States, Kenya or the Ivory Coast. I heard about a woman in the Ivory Coast with whom I would like to work. Unfortunately, I don't know her name. It would be with great pleasure to work on a film with her one day.

I am often asked why I am no longer seen on the screens. I can only say that it is not my choice. I don't really regret this, that is the way things turned out. Of course, I have been interested in many things and I like to do many different things. Well, I just hope that everybody who wants to work in cinema will be able to find work, that they will find the means. It does not mean that since I do not have roles to play that others will not.

Currently you are working as an artist using textiles. How did you develop an interest in this area?

I make tapestries and I love it! This interest actually began at the same time that I entered in the cinema. I had hoped to study tapestry in Thies [Senegal], but I was not able to make the connections there. Afterwards, when I came to France, the first thing I thought about was to do tapestry. I told my husband that whether it was acting in films or doing something else, I have always worked. Rather than crying over my predicament— which I don't do and never have—I looked for someone to teach me tapestry-making. I found a woman who lived in the 13th *arrondissement* in Paris. It was at that moment that I began doing tapestry work. I adore this work. It has helped me both physically and morally.

You also have a daughter; I met her at the opening night of the Racines Noires Festival. What does she think about your experiences in cinema?

You know, it was only this past year that Zara saw my films. Once when returning from the cinema she looked at me and said, "Oh mama, you were so beautiful, and you still are." Later, when we went to Senegal, she saw *La noire de...* a second time in Dakar. We were together when she saw *Emitai.*

During the festival [Racines Noires], many people asked me if I would mind if my daughter worked in the cinema. I laughed, but when I think about all the problems that I had, I would not want my daughter to be subjected to the same thing, or anyone else for that matter. I remember once she met a photographer who wanted to make photographs of her for casting, but I objected. She is like me in that she likes to do many things. It would be her choice to work in cinema. I want her to complete her studies first. However, it certainly depends on Zara. I will not be the one to tell her to do so. She reads and hears about what is going on.

You have had many interesting experiences from **La noire de...** *to the present. Could you give a summary? What does African cinema mean to you?*

What I hope is that African cinema continues to evolve. In African cinema, you find it evolving in some countries more than others. Even in Senegal, where it has evolved more than in other countries, it should be more advanced. There is not only Sembene, Djibril or Johnson [Traoré]. There should be more.

Alexandra Duah

Ghana

Interview held at FESPACO 1997, Ouagadougou, Burkina Faso, February 1997; combined with a short written correspondence, December 1998.

Could you talk about your acting background and how you came to cinema in general?

I initially trained in cinematography and qualified as a film editor. People say that I am not very easy to live with because any time I go out of a place and return I am able to detect that a chair has been moved; that a flower has been touched. My children know how I am and they have begun calling me "Radio Ghana" because I query every thing that I see. I got my actor training from an old actress named Jean P. Martin in London.

I have, over the years, taken acting seriously. Every little word, every little statement, I make sure that I conduct enough research to be able to know the bearing my statement has on the entire script or story and my relationship to the other actors. I think about costuming and everything. When I am on location, I am not just an actress, I am more like a mother who tries to solve problems between artists and producer, but then, having done all these things, I am satisfied with having my name only as actress in the credits.

However, since I acted in *Sankofa*, where I played the role of Nunu, no producer has offered me any script, no one has hired me. I now consider myself Ghana's international actress who has found herself redundant. As an actress, I think that I have been let down miserably. I have now decided to try to go back into what I learned in film school.

When you say producer, do you also mean film director?

Yes, the producer often does it all. But yes, I am talking about the director.

You have acted in some highly acclaimed films. Could you discuss your experiences in these films and other roles that you have played throughout your career?

I managed to land on *Sankofa* in 1989, when *Heritage Africa*, a movie produced by Kwaw Ansah, was premiered here at FESPACO. It also won the Grand Prize the Etalon de Yennenga at the time. It was then that some friends from America saw me and said to Haile Gerima, "Go to Ghana—you will find your woman there." And that is how I got the job. In *Heritage Africa*, I had a role symbolic of "Mother Africa." Usually Africa is seen as miserable, illiterate, an old lady, but she is full of wisdom and that is how I portrayed this woman in *Heritage Africa*. The director had a special perception of who this special woman was and he created her as someone who was deep, full of wisdom, clean, smartly dressed, and highly traditional.

Sometimes I expressed myself in a loud manner, and whenever the director saw me going off the beat he found a way of bring me back by saying "Alexandra, this woman is a cool woman." I think that this is what we need of directors: they should not leave the actor to do what she or he wants because she is a good actor. This is what I always tell the film students at NAFTI, the school for film and television production in Ghana. Most of the students fear approaching seasoned actors like me for their graduate productions. I tell them that they need to have the courage or, otherwise, when they come out they will end up using mediocre actors and their films will never get anywhere.

After *Heritage Africa*, I played the role of a spiritual leader in *Ama*, a film by the Ghanaian filmmaker Kwesi Owusu. In one scene, she was in the church singing "Hallelujah" and then in the next scene she was on the back of a horse dancing the traditional war dance. Although I played well, I feel that I did not have enough time to digest the role. That is one of those things: I can't be good in all cases, but I did my best under the circumstances.

Because of the huge cost involved, it is very difficult to make a proper movie on celluloid in Ghana. So over the last ten years producers/directors have tried to content themselves with producing features on video.

Have you also acted in these video films?

Yes, I have acted in several of these video films. In one video film I played the role of a woman who, though satisfied and well taken care of, sometimes needed the warm embrace of a man, but her husband was too busy. I thought to myself, "You have been playing roles as "Mother Africa," what will the public say if your character makes herself that cheap by sleeping with her daughter's boyfriend?" I developed a very sympathetic character that appeared quite decent and responsible. She showed that money isn't everything and once in a while, a woman, no matter how old she is, needs a warm embrace. It is through this identification with the spectator that I managed to survive that role by not disgracing women.

I played in another video film called *Youngblood*. This was a film portraying a woman who wanted to make money at all costs, so it was about integrity. The woman was married and had a little shop. She observed that her counterparts were swimming in affluence; however, she did not know how they made their money. She advises her husband to retire so that his severance pay could be used to expand the shop. The husband retired and she expanded the shop, yet her friend kept insisting that there was a lot more she could do. The friend told her that she would take her to a friend who would give her a handkerchief, nothing more. Each day there was still another thing to do and it got to the point where she could not come out of the house because she had tied herself completely up in knots and in the end she died a shameful death.

I think the film taught our women that we must be content with who we are, and strive harder and make money through honest work. There is no point in using *juju* or preparing special foods to eat, from which some have actually died. I accept scripts that are educative, nothing that demeans or demoralizes women.

What were your experiences during the shooting of **Sankofa***? What were your impressions of your character Nunu?*

I will always give a big Thank-you to Haile for giving me the chance to play Nunu in *Sankofa*. I actually learned a lot and maybe this is the reason that I am still alive. My experiences with this film made me realize that I don't need anything. I am just thankful that I wake up in the morning and can breathe free natural air and move about freely in my own country.

As for the role of Nunu, I see very much myself in the character. I am a princess, my father is a king, my whole paternal family came from royalty, and we are a big family, at least three thousand. Our family includes intellectuals, the moderators of the Presbyterian Church, a chief priestess, a woman medical doctor, teachers. The first black woman to be sent to Switzerland by the Basel Mission to help translate the Bible into our language comes from my home.

We have everything and yet we are greatly persecuted politically, because we despise oppression. We have the ability to see beyond and to read between the lines, and thus sometimes we clash with authorities. This made me start secondary school, barefooted. My father had been forced into political exile in 1958, and I started secondary school in 1959. I did pass the common entrance exam, and had an interview at a prestigious secondary school, but my father could not afford to pay the fees. So I had to go to another secondary school in my hometown as a day student. A princess going to school as a day student!

In those days, education was very disciplined. We had brown shoes for school and black shoes for church. I did not have any brown shoes, so I wore black shoes and I got punished all the time; though I just wanted to go to school! So one day I took off those black shoes and went to school barefooted and I got caned and then sent home. It was a terrible situation and if my parents did not put the fear of God in me and did not raise me with good morals, I might have ended up in some irresponsible man's bed. Maybe my child would have been forty years old by now.

So these experiences growing up prepared you for the role of Nunu?

Nunu's parents were persecuted...her father was a warrior and her mother was a medicine woman...they had already prepared their daughter and she was tough....Yes, I see myself much like Nunu.

What were your feelings about the character Joe, who actually, disowned and despised his mother Nunu?

Joe? Well, I think that it would be very difficult for a mother to accept such a situation because as a mother you care so much. Imagine your children are playing, the moment you hear a car screeching outside your heart jumps into your hands: "Is it my child?" The scream you hear, you automatically ask, "Is my son screaming?" You care so much for your child. So, for a child that you care so much for to turn his back on you, it is devastating. Nunu was a mother. I am a mother.

Could you talk about your experiences working with African diasporans from the United States and Jamaica during the shooting?

I used to be scared stiff of Rastafarians. My father always had a clean-shaven head. He would shave all the hairs in his nose and on his chest. He had a clean-shaven body. There I was in the midst of all this big hair. That is when I went for the rehearsals in Washington, DC in 1989. In Jamaica, I shared a room with Hasinatou, who played the role of Juma. I asked her what should I do, there were Rastafarians everywhere and then there was Mutabaruka who played the role of Shango. I had to pray hard and find a way to understand them. And sooner or later, I realized that we were all human beings and that is their way of presenting themselves.

The first day we were to shoot on location in Jamaica I had said that we should pour libation. We forgot the gin and I said it does not matter, we could use pure spring water. There was a Rastafarian man with one bunch of hair, which was three yards wide, very long, all the way to the floor. When I got the courage I went to him and I asked him, "Please, sir, is this tap water?" he said, "No, this is pure spring water." I then asked him, could we have a little to poor libation? and he said, sure and poured the water. I took a picture with him and we made friends, and that was how I began to accept Rastafarians.

*What are some of the projects that you have undertaken since **Sankofa**?*

Well, as I stated before, I trained in cinematography from 1970 to 1972 in Ghana, and I specialized in film editing. I also learned directing, writing, as well as other aspects of filmmaking. In 1992, I tried to put my writing to the test. I managed to write, produce, and direct four children's movies for Ghana Television. I actually developed the juvenile participation in the program. I know that children relate better to each other. If children are involved in acting in plays with other children, they will learn quickly. This principle comes from folklore, which our forefathers and ancestors used to mold the moral upbringing of the children.

So you actually teach acting to children? What are some of the things you teach?

Before teaching them acting I think it is important to take their welfare into consideration. As I have said, I have been considerably let down. Producers do not care about the welfare of the artist, they do not help to promote the interest of the artist, the fee they pay is so small and the actors are not fed well. In many cases, they take it for granted that the actors will provide their own costumes. In the end, the actor's attention is divided. It takes very strong and dedicated artists to continue to present a role in a way that it could be acceptable.

When I was working with the children, I realized that it was going to be very expensive. For a child you need a chaperon, you need to lecture or counsel the child about what it takes to be an actor. You need to talk to the parents so that they may encourage the child as well. Otherwise, if they don't get the encouragement to continue, they will drop by the wayside. On the other hand, I had to tell the children that they need a good education to be a good actor; acting is not for dropouts.

I think this 15th edition of FESPACO with the theme, "Childhood, Youth and Cinema," is good. Children need to know about Africa. Children need to be taught. Children need to be helped to develop as Africans. But then, we will need to use children artists in films. My question is "Are producers prepared to use African children in their movies? Are they just going to waste them like they have wasted our generation of actors?" They will only succeed if they have a future for these children. FESPACO should be encouraged because this is a location where artists are spotted.

*You stated that since you played in **Sankofa** you found it difficult to find work. Why is this?*

Sankofa was released in 1993, but to date no producer or director has approached me or hired me for work. I don't know—maybe they are not able to identify me when they see me in person. People are surprised to see me so small because they say that in *Sankofa* I appeared so huge and strong. Even though cinema has been with us for years, sometimes people think the character you play is really you, that you are playing yourself on the screen. Sometimes they think that I am a very strong spiritualist and they are afraid to approach me.

I would very much like to play in another film like *Sankofa*, or play a character like Nunu. Because of lack of work, I have tried my hand in producing my own shows. Of course, it is not easy, either, to raise as much as 40,000 dollars to produce a video. I am working on a program that has a strong message about issues regarding women. I have written a script on rape and the trauma and haunting that a woman experiences afterwards for the rest of her life. The woman fights to shed this trauma and tries to live a somewhat normal life. It is kind of a tragedy-comedy. Another script I have is about a filmmaker who waits for a long time for a producer in order to make a successful film and, meanwhile, he ends up making eight babies instead. I have some nice programs that I would like to produce.

Could you talk about some of the activities that you have done since we last met at FESPACO in February 1997?

I am teaching film-acting techniques and poise at the Academy of Film Acting. This is the first film acting training school in Ghana, which a colleague producer/director and I established in January 1998. We have so far trained thirty-six would-be actors, actresses, and those already in the system. We plan to offer training for other disciplines in the film industry.

Anne-Laure Folly

Togo

Interview and Press Conference held at the 15th FESPACO, February 1997, Ouagadougou, Burkina Faso. Translated from French.

You came on the cinema scene in 1992 and have made several films since then. Could you talk about your evolution into cinema?

I am not really a filmmaker, in conventional terms I mean. I began several years ago. I am an international lawyer. I was sent on a mission to my country. I was very happy to get a chance to see my grandmother. She died when I was there, and I attended the funeral. I observed the treatment of the dead, their relationship with the cosmos and the world, and their basic values.

It occurred to me that the West has a particularly thorough understanding of Asia, of Asian philosophy, but I found it curious that there is not this understanding about Africa. I thought about how necessary it is that we express ourselves. Since I work in an international milieu, I know that power comes from those who say things. There is a widespread attitude that if you do not express yourself, if you have nothing to say, then you do not exist. The problem is that, culturally speaking, Africa does not say things. We think that what is important is not told, or is expressed discreetly, or is told only to one another, by word-of-mouth. Our attitude is that a culture that exposes itself disintegrates. I think that in some ways it is true, the idea of total diffusion of something—when you diffuse everything—you lose something of your essence.

I think the change in the Western world is because the West produces and diffuses, because once you diffuse things they are modified, they change. These notions and values are told to someone else, that person receives them, then modifies and changes them, and so on, and the values themselves evolve. Whereas in African society, the values that you are told once, you keep and apply all of your life. The societies are very fixed, and they are much more solid. Though this is not only in African societies, there are many closed societies in the world. The Japanese society, for example, at the same time fascinating, is also apparently very diffused. It is a society whose economy is known everywhere, but no one knows a fourteenth-century Japanese poet. It is somewhat like the African societies, but the only difference is that the Japanese culture went through a cultural mutation and had other things in exchange. It could diffuse its economic conscience, its economic philosophy. We have not had this. I think that we are a bit lost in our international discourse. We no longer exist. Now we must say something.

I started with culture. I made a film called *Le gardien des forces*, on so-called magic, which is not magic at all, rather a belief that we practice in my village. It was a film about my neighbor, who is a fetishist, and his practices. I was not very experienced in film at the time, so I simply filmed this remarkable practice that had been in existence since I was born. The film was presented at the Margaret Mead Society in the United States. I was invited to the Society—where the people were very formal—and was asked to explain the events, since they did not know about this practice. In the film, people killed with their voices, with words. However, the people at the Society could not believe it.

Why didn't they believe what they were seeing in the film?

It is cultural. You cannot comprehend Africa with a Western cultural perceptive. Because your investigation into things speaks of your understanding and inner explorations. We do not have this same internal inquiry. That is what culture is! All cultures have equal worth, but they are different. If you were to ask someone to show you how to kill other than with a gun, you would be told that there are other ways, which are not necessarily negative, but perhaps are more impressive.

When the film was screened, I thought, what is curious is that when we see something, we do not believe it merely because we have seen it. We are not like St. Thomas in the Bible, "I believe what I see"; we believe what we understand. In addition, what we do not comprehend by intelligence is not grasped. So from then on, I decided to do socio-political films, and I have always been interested in women's discourse, because I think it is an alternative discourse. I have always treated my themes from the perspective of women.

Your latest film, **Les oubliées** *is being shown here at FESPACO and women are your point of departure. Could you talk about the film and why you chose this theme?*

Initially the idea was to talk about war, to make a plea for peace. In analyzing situations of extreme war, I had a choice because there are many extreme situations throughout the world. I chose one of the longest wars of the century, the war in Angola. It has lasted thirty years. For the last thirty years, the people have been fighting. The purpose was to have an alternative discourse, one that was not simply based on the reasons for war—which always seem to be legitimate; nor one that is filled with dates or simple facts.

I tried rather to treat the problem of war from the women's perspectives. Their perspective does not simply analyze things; they live them. That is what I proposed as my initial premise, and it was filmed along that line. In fact, the women that I encountered told me things about the history of the country that had nothing at all to do with what we know of the history of their country.

Earlier you talked about wanting to show an alternative discourse. Do you think that African cinema in general provides this? What does the notion of an African cinema represent for you?

It is an endeavor to restore its values within a thought system that exists, but can no longer survive here at the end of the twentieth century unless it is mediatized. This is necessary. I do not have this naive vision that all cultures must be expressed, though I think it is true. Beyond that, we share the same world and we have alternative values, and that is important. It is interesting to know how others perceive the world, what they consider most essential, because this is how we exchange. The world is evolving in such a way that we will interchange with each other no matter what. Everything is interconnected, and if we express our culture, the logic of the system is such that it will be shared elsewhere as well.

What do you envision when one says "the image of the African woman in cinema"? What does that represent for you?

The African woman is woman, quite simply. I am trying to reflect on the question because I have never filmed any other women. I think it is a discourse on values, of other values than those that have been advanced. It is the essential testimony of fifty-two percent of humanity, or fifty-two percent of the people that I address.

As a maker of the image, do you feel that you have a role to show a certain representation of the African woman?

The image has never had as much importance on a moral level, in educating people, as it does today. Before, it was only accessible to a minority of people, whereas now it is available to everyone, and it has become the cultural norm. I think this applies to everyone, to have a moral duty regarding what we do. I present the values that I consider positive. Absolutely, I think the image must be treated seriously.

In film criticism discourse there is much discussion and debate about aesthetics. Do you think that a feminine aesthetic exists?

If aesthetic means a sensibility, emotional sentiments, then yes, I think so.

And how is this presented?

By having a certain understanding, perception, and awareness of practices beyond the accepted standards, the familiar views and references. I do not know if I would say that they are necessarily feminine, because there are men who share this perspective. I think that at this moment in the evolution of humanity, certain human beings, notably women, sense those things that are important and express them, and these things are different from what has been previously communicated. There is a sensibility that is expressed that is different, and that is how things change. I do not know if one can say that it is exclusively feminine.

Where have your films been shown? Could you talk about the exhibition and distribution of your films?

I distribute some of my films in the United States. I do not know how it is done in this country of yours! There is an audience; there is a general interest in Africa among black Americans. However, I do not know who renders the image of Africa in the United States. Because there is very little chance that the films made by Africans are bought by American distributors. I do not understand how a [black American] community that searches, politically, for its roots in Africa and draws its inspiration from Africa, actually nourishes itself culturally. I do not understand who actually makes these images of Africa!

Do you...

It is a question that I am posing to you!

We will talk afterwards [laughter].

Afterwards! [laughter].

Do you think that the distribution of African films is very different in Europe and in Africa than in the United States?

No. You are absolutely right. However, not for the same reasons. The BBC has always done the best documentaries in the world. An Englishman goes to Thailand and states, "Well this is how the Thai live." He has no problem examining this affirmation within himself, nor does he question it. He never presents his remarks with hesitation. He simply states "I come from England and I think that these people live this way." That is the view that becomes exclusive, the center, Europe.

The West gives you an image of the world based on a European cultural framework. This is done for economic reasons as well. In a television station, the program director will assign the production of a documentary to a friend, because there is unemployment, or a friend is looking for work, etc. On the other hand, it may be assigned for political reasons: because certain views may be seen as subversive, these opinions are not readily acceptable and thus are kept away from the public.

The image of Africa in Europe has been in existence for three hundred years, and there is not a readiness for change. The attitude is: even if Africa does evolve, it must do so slowly. In addition, while Africans have been voicing their own thoughts, it is viewed that Europe has contributed to these thoughts. What interests Europe is what it has taught us about Africa. When other perspectives are presented, they are not accepted.

I remember, during preparation for a French television program on African women, I was invited to come because my film was included. I was told that the women in my film were not really African women because they were modern. I made the film, *Femmes aux yeux ouverts*, here in Burkina Faso, about women, all illiterate, who fought against excision. They were considered too modern, because the *écriture* was modern. They did not think that these women, or people anywhere in the world who submit to exploitation, are conscious of their exploitation. The people who are exploited are not stupid. It was a perspective that was very difficult for them to grasp.

So how would you compare this to attitudes of black people in the United States?

Perhaps you have the same reasons in the United States, but I think that, culturally speaking, it should not exist there. There is not a black community in Europe important enough to create a market for African films, whereas there is a black community in the United States. And that has always amazed me. I do not want black Americans to have a fantasy view of Africa. There is a real culture, a philosophy, a world-view. Many a thesis or dissertation may be made on this. However, because it has not been written about as much, it is not known. It is beyond the popular images of customs, rituals, gestures, and movements. It has nothing to do with these things, it is about the way of thinking, about the individual in the universe, and it is as serious as Plato or Aristotle.

And the image of Africa in Africa? You have talked about the image of Africa in the United States and in Europe. What are your thoughts about African images of Africa?

That is the question! However, everyone here is connected to her or his satellite dish, that is the problem. I am not as concerned in Africa, because culture is very real in Africa. An African may overtly adapt to Western culture, but, culturally speaking, she or he will not change. You may be animist and go to your fetishist in the morning, and afterwards go to church. There is not the substitution of one mode of thinking for another. That is the intellectual politics of the West, where modernity means that if you become Baptist you are no longer what you once were. You become what you have decided to be, you are reborn.

Whereas Africans accumulate, being all at one time. Because what is important is not what one is, but what one can get as knowledge. What is also important to us are the thoughts of others; it is knowledge, above all. There is an apparent cultural detachment, but I am not sure that it is profound. An African knows she or he is African, and may not want to change, and perhaps cannot change.

Could you talk a bit about the association of African women in the cinema that was established at FESPACO in 1991?

Yes, there was a movement that started, but African cinema itself is too young and has too little means. You know, in order to organize as a group there must be something in common to uphold. In order to have an organizing spirit, there must be a culture that develops this, which we do not have. There must be a means to support ourselves, and we have very little means to do so. When we do come together, it is from a demand to do a documentary made by women. Because we as filmmakers are not the ones who initiate projects; it is the television network or distributor. In addition, the distance inter-continentally makes it difficult, we are too far from each other. We do not have the means to come together. We are not always interconnected, and perhaps we do not have a sufficiently elevated political consciousness to do so.

But you do come together when you are at FESPACO?

Yes, but FESPACO takes place only every other year.

And during the interval?

We meet at other festivals. Each woman knows where she wants to go and what she wants to say and she does it.

What format do you generally shoot in, film or video?

I like Betacam. Everyone tells me that I should work in film. Betacam, it works, its simple for me. I am not a great cook, so I try to do simple things with it. I like the digital Beta.

Lucy Gebre-Egziabher,[1] an Ethiopian film student from Howard University was invited to participate in this interview. She had the following questions for Anne-Laure Folly.

Ousmane Sembene said that it is easier to show his films in Paris than in Senegal. My question, thus, is: For whom does the African filmmaker make films? If we cannot show our films in Africa, in our own countries, for whom do we make films?

I make films for me first, to materialize my thoughts, to make sure they are clear and communicable. And then, to make sense out of what sur-rounds me. My problem is to possess this sense, but I cannot impose my vision of the world on someone. I make a product and if it is good I will put it on the market. The system is such that, eventually, what happens will happen. We have already discussed political and economic reasons, but my problem as a filmmaker is to do what I must do as best as possible.

What can you say to younger and emerging filmmakers? There are some of us Africans who live outside of Africa and are studying film.

Good for you!

Really! Why do you feel this way?

I think it is good because cinema is a tool that is not inherent to African culture. We must be mediums. When we speak of culture to the rest of the world we must be capable ourselves of knowing both sides, we must travel beyond our boundaries. That is the reason why a great many African filmmakers have not crossed the oceans, because those who utilize cinema, though it is good, can only use it in their own communities, because they have only regional or continental references.

It is normal to go elsewhere and be a medium for your own culture, there is no problem. You have the tools, you have the culture, you mix it together, and you do your own cooking.

I have lived in the United States for seventeen years and I realized that I am a bit detached from my culture because I am not there.

You are not detached from your culture, you are part of an evolving world. We are in a world that is globally interconnected and you are a product of the end of the twentieth century. You are not out of context. You are a product of the world. Unfortunately, it is sad to say, but it will be the others who will find difficulty in keeping in touch in this world, whether in Ethiopia or in the middle of Kansas.

What can you say to those who are beginning in the world of African cinema?

"Just do it" [stated in English]. You know I did not study film, I did not consciously come to it. I came by chance, because one day I had an idea. I would never have thought that I would be doing films, never in my life! Besides, I was not convinced at first that it was even useful. Now I know it is worthwhile and effective. And then, it is also simple, but necessary. There is no other means that is as efficient. There will be no other means to unify the world. It will not be CNN that will do the job.

Excerpts from the Press Conference of *Les oubliées*, FESPACO 1997. Questions are from various panel members and audience members.

A few years ago you were here with the documentary film, **Femmes aux yeux ouverts**, *you are back with another film,* **Les oubliées** *which deals with the consequences of the civil war on women and children in Angola. Why did you take this direction?*

We must all try to touch the reality of the situation. My interest is reality, even in fiction.

The film, **Femmes aux yeux ouverts** *touched on the problems of the emancipation of women,* **Les oubliées** *focuses also on the problems of women and of children...*

It is not only about women, it is a plea for peace, and I treated war not through the ordinary perspective that we have about the facts and events, the battles and territorial gains, but rather from a perspective that is specific. Women have a different perspective about this history, especially of a war that has lasted more than thirty years. They experienced the war based on personal suffering, having lost people they know, and sensing the impossibility of being able to provide a future. They live this history from another point of reference and I found this interesting.

I decided to not approach this plea for peace from an intellectual level, because we are all for peace. I wanted to hear it from people who spoke from the guts about their fears. We respond more radically for peace, but within the reflection, "really this violence has to stop." The film comes more so from the guts, reason should not be the basis for bringing up the problems of the world, because reason is not sufficient to change things.

There are many wars going on in Africa, why did you choose the war in Angola as the subject of your most recent film?

It is an exemplary war, not only for Africa but also for the world. It is nearly the longest war of the century; it has lasted for the last thirty years. There is an entire generation, which only knows extreme violence. There are people who live in a world where morals do not exist, where in the absence of morals the only rule is: To survive you must kill.

I also find it interesting because it was a war that took all forms. Initially it was a war to end colonization and then an East-West conflict involving Cuba and South Africa, and afterwards a civil war. Perhaps there were several motives for the war but, nonetheless, it continued to be one group fighting against another, which leads one to believe that the motive had only one interest at stake, which was war itself.

It is certainly one of the richest countries in Africa. There have been colossal stakes, to the extent that the war has allowed the maintenance of a considerably profitable economy of war.

It is also a way of exposing war. You also go beyond the francophone sphere to enter the lusophone in posing the problematic of Angola. Perhaps the next film could be the equally long war in Eritrea?

I was very happy when I came to FESPACO and saw the poster with the little black boy and white boy, it was the first actual expression that we have had here of a very multi-racial continent. The strength of Africa has always been its multi-raciality, whether it appears so or not, whereas other continents have not had this. I think that it is interesting to present a country that is very different from our region in West Africa....

You have always used women as the vehicle to express yourself, to show what you are thinking. Is that your choice? Why?

I think that they bring another discourse, I am not saying that women view the world differently, but they do not have the same social function in society. The women in the countries where there is war are all victims. They participate in the war to assist in the survival of their children, sons, and husbands, but that is all, and then they lose them. Yet, they do not actually participate. In the film, there was a woman who said, "One day I was in the war zone and I saw the Cubans coming." This was an amazing image of a woman who did not know what was going on. She has been wandering around the country for the past ten years. I think these perspectives bring about another appreciation of the world, of values, and I am always for another discourse.

At the end of the film, the women made a call to the international community. Have you gotten responses?

I was fascinated when the woman took the microphone and began to speak, saying, "Look how we live, we live like dogs. Go tell the others." Because when you live in those camps it is really like being at the other end of the world. You must take a plane to get there, you must have authorization, no one goes there. What is happening is that at the moment they are in the process of making a peace treaty. So I hope that this war will end—and there are others—I hope with all my heart that it will end.

To return to the discussion about international responsibility, you are right to say that in Angola there are economic stakes for "the international powers." I will remind you that there was a summit in Brussels where financiers decided to invest a million dollars to remobilize this ravaged Angola, and at the same time mines which are manufactured by those same foreign countries continue to kill. What message would you like to show regarding this problem?

I am not sending a message, but I want to say that no one has obliged me to make a film, I chose this subject. What made me change to this theme was that, before, I had an intellectual relationship with all that was war, and now I have the impression that because of globalization we are coming to one single way of thinking and there will no longer be an ideology. There will no longer be a reason to oppose one another. I think there is good reason to continue to revolt, those reasons are simply for human values. What is actually positioning itself is a sort of rigid liberalism with no thought about the economic consequences, which is very dangerous. In fact, with this liberalism there will be no need for individuals. There can be an economy and business without anyone now. I think that it is interesting that people are now fighting for their values, but we are at a point in history where we will fight simply for the right to exist.

Do you think that Africa can contribute, if nothing else, to bringing positive values in the world?

You know, no one actually understands African thought; even Hegel asked if Africans actually think. In my society, as here and elsewhere in Africa, when you are born, you are given life. Intellectually, that means that when you are given something, the person who gave it to you exists, and possesses the thing. Thus, to live is to give something, and to be alive for an African is to give something; whereas, in the West, principles and philosophies are based on the economy and money. Moreover, money, in principle, is not given away: by definition when one has it one keeps it. It is a vision that is totally opposed to what we have *vis-à-vis* the Western world. There are many things that differentiate us, and to diffuse these things permits others to have other conceptual tools.

At this point, Sarah Maldoror[2] spoke from the audience:

Sarah Maldoror: *The first point that I want to make to Anne-Laure Folly is that your film is outstanding, it is fantastic. Because you are a woman, you have the respect for life, because you have courage. You could have been blown up a* *hundred times in those mines, but you were not, thank God. I think that you had courage to do this film. And it is very well done, and it gives one something to think about. And that these women who fight and suffer, who are hungry, could actually do a theatrical play, I find extraordinary. I regret that there are not more women who can be here to participate in this peace effort. Because if we women do not do it, it will not be the other African filmmakers, who, alas, are not at this conference. There are very few people here, which I find regrettable.*

However, what I am not in agreement with is your impression of this FESPACO poster. This poster is terrible. If you look closely, there is a black boy and white boy—I agree that there are no borders, that Africa is multi-racial—but, if you look closely at this poster, you have a little white boy who looks very well fed who puts his hand on the shoulder of a little skinny black boy. That is the symbol of FESPACO, the only thing that counts now is not the African filmmakers, it is the others who count. Of course, we need others, but this poster is horrible.

Anne-Laure Folly: I would like first to thank Sarah, she inspired me to do this film. She did a film called *Sambizanga*, which in my opinion is one of the masterpieces of African cinema. When I saw it, I had a desire to make a film thirty years later, about Angola. She cleared the way by showing the Angolan war interpreted from the perspective of a woman. Mine is not a pioneering approach; she has already done that.

Coming back to the poster, I accept that de Klerk received the Nobel Peace Prize and I think that it is symbolic. And this poster, I also see as symbolic. It is true that the little white boy is a little plump, but I did not read it that way. I read it otherwise, because six years ago we would never have seen it, and I think it gives a history of the continent.

Panel Member: *Your film was intended to focus on children and women but I think that you did not give the voice to the children. The women were able to express themselves, but I did not feel the presence of the children.*

Anne-Laure Folly: I did not interview the children simply because there was a language problem. I shot in a lusophone country. It was difficult for me, but it was not just that, I wanted a discourse on the situation. I wanted it to be somewhat conceptualized, thus I chose people who could conceptualize the problem. Secondly, the level of chaos in this country means that there is no longer an educational system. If you find a fifteen-year-old in front of you, he does not know what a pen is. In the schools, a child at one level teaches the child at the level below.

What concerns me about this country is that this whole class of young people is not in a suitable position for development. They are not in a position to provide this country with the energy to develop and, thus, I had very few interlocutors, among which there were no children at all. And I am not sure, if I had asked them questions, that they would have been able to answer them within the problematic that I posed.

Panel Member: *What were some of the obstacles that you had when doing the film in Angola?*

Anne-Laure Folly: First, there were psychological obstacles. I have never made a film where everyday I felt that I wanted to stop, that everyday I wanted to leave, simply because the ugliness of this country is unimaginable. This is not even depicted in the film. Half of the population lives in filth. We cannot imagine this when we come from here [Ouagadougou]: Here it is an Eldorado. And I couldn't adapt to being there. In addition— and I do not want to go into all the details—since everything is mined, if you go in to film you must have an airplane. You perhaps can obtain one through an international organization, which requires a great deal of permits. What happened to me one day, we were about to start filming and I was told repeatedly that there was going to be a delay. Of course, there was no airplane, nor the hope of getting one soon, perhaps for three weeks, and we were in a remote area. That was the first time during a production that I had to call for an airplane to take a crew back home. Imagine. For a producer, it was a disaster.

Sarah Maldoror: *I want to respond to the woman who asked the question about children. It is an important question. [Anne-Laure Folly] did not interview children, but you, here in Burkina Faso, how many children come to the theaters? Why don't the filmmakers go to the schools, to the universities, to show them other films? No, she did not interview them, but what have you done? What do you do for children here, where the children should be? They are not here!*

Panel Member: *As you certainly have seen, there has been a great deal done for children throughout the city. However, I think that they should not necessarily be at this debate. I still had the right to pose the question regarding the film.*

Sarah Maldoror: *You have every right, we are in a free country. But, I also have the right to answer. I am asking why you do not ask us filmmakers to present our films in your schools, in your high schools, in your universities, to give them other things to see? You observed that children were not interviewed in Anne-Laure's film, I simply noted that they are not around, it is in the theaters that I would have wanted to see them, and university students here at this conference participating in these discussions.*

*Audience Member: I just want to say that when I went to see the film **Macadam Tribu** there were many children present. I also want to talk about the poster. I see it as sending a message. I see the children converging toward something, and that is enough for me; I do not need to go into the smallest detail to know why about this or that. I think that one must aim at what is essential, go forward towards that which is important.*

Panel Member: To revisit the discussion regarding the mines, there was a bomb disposal expert at the end of the film who said that mines will continue to kill up until 2050....

Anne-Laure Folly: It happens in Angola, in Cambodia, and elsewhere. He explains very well that all these mines are constructed by the West. He has a sense of humor when saying, "I think that those who construct the mines must utilize them." There is an absurd logic, which is very interesting. There is a lesson that I learned from making this film. I could have rallied against the war. However, I also thought that one must die for her or his ideas, and have the courage to do it. From what I saw there are several ways of dying. For me the only thing that is important is to no longer engage in warfare. I am of a generation that has not yet seen war and I hope never to experience it. I am ready to fight to find other means to defend ideas, but not by violent means. I am capable of losing on the side of values in order to be in a world where there is no violence. Before this film, I did not feel this way.

Notes

1. Conversation with Lucy Gebre-Egziabher included in this collection.
2. Conversation with Sarah Maldoror included in this collection.

Lucy Gebre-Egziabher

Ethiopia

Interviews were held on several occasions during 1997, in Washington, DC and at FESPACO, Ouagadougou, Burkina Faso. One of the conversations was transcribed from a televised interview, which is part of *Reels of Colour*, a talk show series aired locally in Washington, DC, produced and hosted by the author.

Lucy, could you talk about your journey from Ethiopia to the United States and perhaps in between? You also have Egyptian heritage. How do you identify yourself?

When people ask me where I'm from I say Ethiopia. Technically, I was born in Egypt, my mother is Egyptian, and my father is Ethiopian. I moved from Egypt when I was six, I moved to Ethiopia during the Israeli-Egyptian War. I stayed until I was almost eighteen. I pretty much grew up in Ethiopia and I consider it my home: I am familiar with the language, the people.

Do you feel that you have a dual identity?

Absolutely! I associate my Egyptian-ness with my mother and I hold on to that because I have a great love for my mother. As for my identity, in recent years, when I started questioning myself—"Who am I? What is my mission in life?" and other numerous questions—the question of identity arose in the process, and it's a very important question!

How about your identity as African in the West?

That's part of it, my position as an African in the West is what began the questioning process.

Could you talk about your process and how you became interested in cinema?

Let's talk about why I wanted to be a filmmaker, aside from having the passion for cinema as a visual art that came a long time ago when I was still in Ethiopia, though I dismissed it. Maybe it was a manifestation of the mis-education of myself, my heritage, my history. While I was in Ethiopia—and I am sure any African could tell you this story—on the screen all we saw were white faces. The images that we saw on the screen made us want to come to America, to live the American dream, to wear the clothes and so on.

Realizing how powerful this medium is and how destructive it could be, at first I jumped into it almost idealistically: "I want to educate my people!" Why don't we show *our* faces on the screen? Why don't we show the wealth of our history? Why don't we ever see a film about the battle of Adwa? Why do we have to celebrate the British soldiers by the river battling the Japanese?[1] Why can't we see our own soldiers battling the Italians, defeating the Italians with spears and shields?

So it was in Ethiopia that you began to ask these questions?

No, it was much later. As a kid in Ethiopia, having consumed so many Hollywood movies, we were influenced by them to the point where we decided to name a place near my house "Chicago." It was a very natural place with waterfalls, trees, and rocks, nothing like Chicago.

Of course, you had not been to Chicago before?

Never. Through the films that we saw and consumed there was always a notion of America, and everybody wanted to go to America to the point that we were totally immersed in those images. That was all that we wanted and all we saw.

Have you been to Chicago since?

Yes, and I remember when I went, I just laughed and I couldn't wait to take pictures to send back to my friends. That shows you the power of images!

So, you went from consumer of images to a maker of images....

Once I started to pursue filmmaking—and, by the way, I don't consider it a career, it is a passion—I started studying what it takes to make a film: the initial idea, the script development, the production, post-production. And with this comes the realization that it starts with a thought and it can evolve into a film that is displayed and screened for millions of people. To me film is the most powerful medium in the world. It could be used for good or bad; a lot of people form images based on it, good or bad. What is most important is who is showing these images, and what the consequences are of screening those images, what it does to our psyche.

Recently, I wanted to buy a Bible for Alexia, the daughter of a friend of mine. I looked all over and all the Bibles that I saw had pictures of white figures and icons. Africans, African-Americans, children of color in general, look at white images and associate them with the Bible. I started questioning a lot: "What does that do to them while they are growing up?" Again, film is another means.

Could you talk about how you relate identity to your filmmaking?

Well, asking the questions, "Who am I? What defines my Ethiopian-ness?" began the awakening stage. Then, from asking the question of "What is my Ethiopian-ness?", I further explored my bi-culture identity, my Egyptian part, and then the larger question of my African part. So, what evolved from the questions was the realization that I had a big void to fill, and if I ever was going to fill this void I would have to do so myself. The schools that I have been to did not teach me. I have to do it myself. I have to read more books. Then I went through the stage where I realized that I have to be careful what books I read and by whom, because they could also do just as much damage. And I am still a student, I am still learning.

As a filmmaker today, I am rethinking: when I first came to film school I wanted to make films about my people, about our history, to educate my people so they could feel proud of who they are, instead of always looking at James Bond and others as a reference. So we could feel proud and celebrate our heritage. That was the idealistic stage, that was the first.

Now I am at a stage where I say, if I ever dare do a film about Ethiopians, first I have to fill my own void. I have been away from Ethiopia for seventeen years. Whether I like it or not I am a stranger to my own country, and to my own people. A lot has happened in seventeen years. I've never been back. How dare I think about going and making a film about my people when I don't even know the realities that my people face today!

When did you make the deliberate decision to study film?

Time became important to me after my mother passed away in 1993. With that came the realization that life was too short and I had to follow my passion. I feel like it is a gift that she gave me before she left. That is when I made the decision to go to film school and pursue my dreams—all my life my mom gave me the utmost support and made me believe that I could do whatever I wanted. Both my parents were very supportive. My father was very big on education and my mother is the one who gave me the strength and independence in being.

I decided to go back to school and study film because up until then it was only a fantasy, a dream that I wanted to pursue, but I didn't think it was practical. Time became very valuable. I realized that it could not be taken for granted and that you have to do what you want to do in this lifetime and that we all have a mission that we have to pursue on a bigger level, that is beyond our little world, that we are obliged to do. Sometimes we don't even know. I don't know what my mission is, to be honest with you, but I know that there is a strong sense inside of me that I am doing something that I need to be doing.

With the passing of my mother, time became alive. Up until then, it was just another factor in life. It didn't have that much importance. Time and faith became very strong, not necessarily in that order.

Why did you choose the film school at Howard University?

I chose Howard University because I wanted to be in a black institution, and I needed to be in a black institution. The program teaches you to learn everything; granted you have to do a lot of the learning yourself, you have to teach yourself a lot. The program is designed in such a way that you can be a scriptwriter, a director, a DP [Director of Photography], an editor. You are exposed to all the aspects.

Could you talk about your first film, and your evolution as a filmmaker through this film?

Each piece that I've done is a reflection of where I was at that particular time. *Emancipation,* is my baby because it was the first film I made, so it was the beginning of the de-mystification process.

Once we talked about Frantz Fanon's theory on liberation. And I said something to the effect that as Ethiopians we have not experienced physical colonization so I didn't think that the theory necessarily applied to us, that it has never happened in the sense of Frantz Fanon's stages and the notion of assimilation and remembrance.

My Ethiopian-ness has always been an inner feeling that has been a force; it's like a foundation. Though we never took time to learn about our history, the one thing we did learn and heard over and over is that our forefathers won against the Italians in Adwa. That gave us something, the ability to stand in front of a white person or anyone else, and say "I am." It was a source of strength, but I never questioned it. On the other hand, I think there is a duality among Ethiopians as it relates to Frantz Fanon's theory. Whether physically colonized or not, we have in some way been colonized in some form, whether psychological or physical. A lot of damage has been done.

During the time of my first film, I was dealing with the issue of identity, which is by the way a recurring theme in my pieces. Being in a different world away from home, trying to assimilate and at the same time trying to hold on to our national identity as a people in voluntary exile, is a very hard balance to maintain. So, in our homes, a lot of times we surround ourselves with Ethiopian icons, our music, the way we dress, and so on. So *Emancipation* was to me a way of maintaining that balance when it is sometimes impossible.

In the film, I used a symbolic way of maintaining it. The protagonist rips up all his Western clothes and puts them on the floor. Then you see him barefoot, dressed in his national attire staring at the camera. For the audio effect I used the static on the radio in the car, all this information, commercials, news, etc. I also used the television, as the remote control flipped images from one channel to the next. It is a representation of all the information one is bombarded with every single day. The bills are there before you get home. They have invaded your home.

So, you have the visual representation of identity and then the notion of consumption, of having things....

That is on the surface. Do you know of the notion of wax and gold called *Sem-enna-worq*? *Sem* means wax, *worq* means gold. In Amharic, there is a style where you may say a sentence on the surface and then there is the sub-text. So, with that style someone says one thing, but only afterwards does the subtext sink in.

That has been one style of the language that has always fascinated me. I try to use that in my films. The bills, television, the radio, are the wax. The gold is the psyche, of how much that information becomes an entrapment. This information becomes a form of slavery. Some of us are here in voluntary exile, as I will call it; whether we want to admit it or not, we are enslaved by the system, by this way of life.

Are these themes indicative of being in exile, or would you say that these themes are also treated in Ethiopia?

When I showed *Emancipation* at the Biograph,[2] a lot of my friends came to see it. They said that they thought that they were seeing their lives on the screen, they could relate to a lot of the symbolism. A friend who came to visit from Ethiopia suggested that I send it to Ethiopia and have it shown on Ethiopian television. Another friend who lives here in the U.S. said that it might do just the opposite of my intentions.

He explained that if you think about it, the [protagonist in the film] has a television set, is dressed in a three-piece suit, has a big car, drives on the freeway to a nice building, and returns to a nice house. Ethiopians in Ethiopia would look at these things and say, "Wow! What a life he has!" Because those who are there, and have stayed there, do not want to hear it when you say, "America is not what you think it is, you're better off staying here. Do something else with your life."

Were you describing your experiences in this film?

Yes. I had come to a point when I had finished my undergraduate education in 1984 and got a job in the field of international education. I got to a point in my career where I said I will not take a job unless it is related to Africa in some form. I don't know how to explain it. I feel despair when I think of us as Africans in the United States, on the continent, and elsewhere in terms of the power that will never be allowed us. The more I read and learn about Africa, the more I realize how much I don't know. Any African with a consciousness, who has lived and looked at the truth about life and ourselves, must incorporate this in her or his work. Hollywood filmmakers are entertainers, period. European filmmakers consider themselves more artistic. They see it as an art. An African filmmaker, in my opinion, is a political activist, is a social worker, is a educator, is an entertainer, and has to be all of these. I am sure there are some who consider themselves just filmmakers. We have so far to go that we cannot consider ourselves as just artists or just entertainers, because, if we truly want to do something for our people and for the continent, we cannot make that mistake.

*And your next film **Bag-Age**?*

I still get choked up when I see *Bag-Age*, because to me it was at a time when I had just lost a good friend who passed away and then two months later I lost my sister. To me it was the manifestation of my own spiritual growth, coming face to face with death and looking at life as a full circle. *Bag-Age* leads you from birth into life and the last stage in life before we go on to the next stage.

*And your film **Tchebelew** continues the theme of identity....*

Yes. My next film, *Tchebelew*, has to do again with identity. It is a story about a couple that is struggling to maintain a relationship that has gone bad, but is their only sense of security. Again, they live outside of Ethiopia, and they are hanging on to the security of each other: even though it is bad, it is their security blanket. Identity comes up again.

Being a foreigner in this country, the question of identity always comes up, whether as a foreign national or as a black person, that notion of identity is always played out and you are always reminded of it. This is good, I think we need to look more into it. Because I was not aware of my Ethiopian-ness when I was home. I became more Ethiopian here, more of an African here in this country. I became more aware. I started reading a lot, and felt the void we talked about earlier—about my Ethiopian-ness and African-ness. I am just now filling that void by reading about my history, knowing my culture. So, it is a lot of work.

You will find in many African films this search for identity, this showing of the clashes, the ways that there are tensions between the West, the U.S., European, and African culture....

Well, I think, in terms of identity, if you are an African with any type of awareness, you cannot help but explore this issue. It is what Frantz Fanon describes in the three stages of development of the decolonization process and it is the same with film and it is the same with everything. First assimilation—thus, naming our neighborhood "Chicago": you identify with the colonizer. Then you go into a stage of melancholy about your own. And the third stage is when you really start being one with yourself and your culture.

The fighting stage!

Yeah, it is a fight in the literal sense, it is a psychological fight, which is the most dangerous kind, versus the physical kind. Adwa—it's an African victory against the Italians, but, in a way, an easy fight. I am not trying to simplify an important African victory. But, relatively speaking, at that time you were on a set battlefield, you knew who your enemy was. Here, when you are engaged in a cultural fight, you don't know or see your enemy, you don't see a set battlefield, it is everywhere. So you use whatever means you have to contribute to the process of developing your mind. That starts, I think, by beginning to feel good about ourselves, who we are and where we come from.

There is no reason why the BBC goes anywhere into Africa and does documentaries about African treasures. Why not us? We have to start doing that because it will never be seen or portrayed in the same way. It is not even about us-against-them, it is not even that. It is about us taking charge of our own resources, our own treasures, our own God-given riches.

How do you bring your culture, African culture, Ethiopian culture into your work?

It is a part of me as a filmmaker, I am a human being first and, as a filmmaker, my being will manifest itself in my work. And all the work that I do, my vision. An added step that I try to take is to ask, "What messages do I want to project to whomever is going to see it?"

Culture is an essential component of filmmaking, especially for African filmmakers. Because we are engaged in a cultural battle, whether we acknowledge it or not. We have to take the initiative as filmmakers, as artists, to promote our culture. And that in turn will hopefully give us our self-worth that has been taken away from us. Maybe then we will start feeling good about who we are, and what we are, and treasure our history and culture.

For whom do African filmmakers make films? Who is your audience?

The question that you are asking is the big dilemma. Remember, the last time we talked I told you that before I even attempt to make a film about Ethiopians today, in Ethiopia, I would have to go back first and get reacquainted with the culture and re-immerse myself back into my culture before I can even attempt to do something? At this point, the only thing that I would be comfortable documenting are themes, issues that pertain to Ethiopians here. Because I have lived that reality, I am living that reality. That is what I think I can do, be true to that without being presumptuous. So if I make a film about Ethiopians here, the issues that we face here, I know it will have the effect of my film *Emancipation*. Ethiopians here related to it, they appreciated it.

One thing I'll tell you is this. If I make a film and I want it to be shown in Ethiopia, if it is about us here in the U.S., I'd have to do it in such a way that I know they would understand what I am saying. Some things here you don't have to spell out in order for those who live your reality to understand. They will get it. In *Emancipation* I showed some envelopes, they knew they were bills, but that is not clear to Ethiopians there, they may think letters. So, I would have to do it differently.

So what are your films about, then? What does an exiled African do? What are her films about?

I think Africans in the Diaspora, or I know for me, the three films that I have done, have identity as their major theme, and that is a manifestation of my own sentiments and my own struggle to preserve my identity. I notice this recurring theme, identity. I wrote a script called "The Tractor"; in Amharic it's called *Ye Neket Ewket*, which, literally translated, means "knowledge of condescension." The main character, Daniel, truly fits in Fanon's three stages of liberation. The residents of a farm village in the countryside get together to collect money to send him to the city to go to school so that he comes back and hopefully changes their lives. He goes to the United States on a scholarship to study agriculture and comes back home with his diploma, wearing a three-piece suit.

The moral of the story is that we cannot transplant the knowledge that we have gathered from elsewhere and come back and impose it on the people. We have a lot of knowledge to begin with that we have to value; then we take this other knowledge, but filter it first through what applies to our reality, or can help us, but most importantly can co-exist with our own knowledge and values. When I did that script I was very happy and I thought it was an original idea. But then, the more I started reading and talking to other people, I realized that they had the same story: we share something in common—the search for identity.

Do you find that there are issues that are specific to you as an African woman?

I'll speak as an African woman living away from home, first. I cannot speak about women living on the continent. When I first came to the States, I embraced feminism; I was on the bandwagon for women's equality. Then during the awakening stage, that was another thing that I started questioning. In the name of feminism a lot of damage is being done back home. It is a very tricky question. Yes, women endure a lot in Africa; they go through a lot more hardships than men. But I don't think Western feminism is the answer.

Just like many other things, such as the political situations where it is either capitalism or communism, either the East or West. So it would end up being African women who follow Western feminism. Whether it be our economic system or our political system, we have to start creating solutions for ourselves that match our reality. The same issue goes for the issue of women.

The other day, after seeing Safi Faye in the film *Ouaga*, I began to realize that it is important to pose the question: "As an African woman filmmaker what do you think?" I think it should be celebrated, because to be an African woman filmmaker, in Africa or away, is not easy. To begin with, you have to realize that film is not taken seriously. Of course, I am not going to speak for the whole continent, but for Ethiopia. In addition, being a woman, it is not an easy thing. So, I feel being a woman should be emphasized. When I heard Safi Faye say, "As a woman filmmaker," I felt a sense of pride because I know how hard it has been for her.

What role do you see African women filmmakers playing in African cinema?

I see African women filmmakers as warriors: they face a lot of obstacles. African filmmakers in general face a lot of obstacles. On another level, African women filmmakers face a lot more obstacles. I remember seeing a picture of a Kenyan filmmaker, and I feel ashamed not to remember her name, she was behind the camera, she had her baby behind her on her back and she was directing. That was a most powerful image, it has stayed with me. To me that is an African woman filmmaker. They don't have the luxury to disengage their role as a wife or a mother and then become a filmmaker, they have to incorporate everything into that. So to me they are warriors.

Do you think there is, or there need be a woman's aesthetic that is distinctive in her films?

I think your style as a filmmaker, your aesthetics, comes from your experience as a human being and even if you happen to be a woman, you are still a human being first. So your experiences through life will come through and that's how your aesthetics or your cinematic signature, I'll say, comes through. I remember having a discussion in class, while looking at a scene and studying the camera movements. They were described as very soft and smooth. Someone said, "That must be a woman cinematographer because she was in tune with the movements and there was a sense of gentleness." I thought, "Wait a minute I know men who are more sensitive than me!" Why do we need to label? I have always resisted categorizing. And it's the same, as it relates to the discussion of women. "A woman is gentler therefore, her camera movements will be gentler"—is that how you are going to know a woman cinematographer from a man? I don't think so! I think we are so busy in the West categorizing everything that we miss the experiences. The essence of a filmmaker, whether it's a woman or a man, is her or his life experience; that is what will come out in the work.

Do you feel that as a woman you have a duty to present images of women? Though in your few short films you don't focus on women, per se, you do relay your experiences. Is that what you mean?

It is my duty as a human being, as a decent human being. And therefore, my films will reflect that. I will tell you this, and maybe you will have to play this tape for me years from now, but I will never show a rape scene. And if there is a rape scene, there is a way of showing that, or implying that. I will never present my female characters in sex scenes just for the sake of it. So, I will do justice by my gender in that sense, not out of a sense of duty, but because I feel that is the right way to treat a human being: with dignity.

You said that you have not seen Ethiopian films from Ethiopia, but how about African films in general?

It was only when I came to Howard University that I saw my first African film, and at the beginning I only saw the films of Ousmane Sembene. I remember when I heard about FESPACO, I said I am going to FESPACO to see Ousmane Sembene. I have seen most of his films.

Who are the models for an African filmmaker? What informs her film language, her film aesthetic?

I don't believe that you create your own signature by watching others. There are African filmmakers that I respect very highly, but I think that in order to have one's own signature you have to be true and honest with

119

yourself. It has to come from within. It cannot be based on looking at someone else's work. I'll give you a very good example; one of the characteristics of African films is the much slower pacing. My films, without consciously making a decision, are very slow in pace. It's reflective of our way of being.

Well, could you talk about the notion of time in the context of African film?

When I think about making a film, I want to present things as they are naturally. African films present that style that I have been talking about. I remember the scene in *Harvest 3000 Years*. The camera sits in place and the farmer climbs from the bottom to the top of the hill. We see the whole trajectory. I love that scene. It's long and we only see him walking. We are conditioned by Hollywood to think that it should be cut. No! We should see the whole process. I was tired by the time he reached the top; I was tired for him. African films that I have seen so far, they show the time and space in reality, in the present.

Do you see it as important to see Africans as cultural readers, to get the African audience's response?

Here in the United States the gauge of whether people like a film or not is the dollar sign, the box office. But you are asking a question where the circumstances are that African filmmakers cannot even show their own films in their own countries, let alone think about how the audience is receiving it. If I am having such a hard time opening the door, I cannot think about where I am going yet. I am concentrating on opening the door.

If you imagine the struggle of African filmmakers who make films in Africa, about Africans, for Africans, and they cannot even show their films in their country, then it becomes a luxury to ask what is the audience's reaction, do they or don't they like it. But that is why I am saying that the African filmmaker is not just an entertainer. That is an important thing to keep in mind. When you are thinking about the social welfare of the people, the political situation, education, health issues, all of that, it's part of you when you create your piece. It's not just thinking, "Let me put a comedy together and make them laugh." The first step is to get your film shown.

But if there is going to be an evolution in African cinema, a development, a growth, what will it be based on? What will be the point of reference?

Cinema is not separate from other aspects of life. It's a valid point. First of all, it's important that the governments intervene. Can we count on this? That's not sure. It has to be part of the infrastructure. Those who have a monopoly on distribution are not Africans. When cinema is seen by African societies as part of the culture, versus a foreign thing, I think things will change. Things are not in our hands.

Ghanaian president Jerry Rawlings recounted a situation that rings so true. Ghana exports bananas. The price of the bananas was dictated to them and they did not accept it. Crates and crates were left at the port and all the bananas were rotten. So they lost a large amount of the crop because Westerners, the buyers, said, "Forget it, we are not buying at that price." Rawlings said, "If I want to buy a Land Rover I have to pay the price that you tell me. I don't have a say. So basically, I don't have a say in what I produce, I don't have a say in what I buy." When I heard that I said, "This is our reality!"

So what happens to the vision?

You don't give up. My source of strength, one of the reasons that I have a tremendous amount of respect for Ousmane Sembene, is that he could have lived in Paris, anywhere in Europe. But he stayed in Senegal, he made films. And when he said, "My films are much more easily shown in France than in Senegal," I could feel the pain in that sentence. But in spite of it all he stuck it out. He stayed there and we need to learn from him.

So do you see it as a mission? It's not like you are going to make a lot of money out of it?

Yes, an obligation, a duty, if I can at all contribute to that. I don't see any other choices, I don't have any other choices. Money has never been the important factor. Yes, its important in getting the film done, but that has never been my motivation, otherwise, I would be trying to knock on Hollywood's door.

You make your films under the name Teret Productions....

Teret means "story" in Amharic; it represents an image I envision of little children sitting around an old person who is telling a story. The old person would say *teret, teret* and the kids would say *yelam beret* and that is how the storytelling process starts. So, to me, perhaps, it is the feeling of wanting to be a storyteller.

*I noticed at the end of the film **Emancipation** you sign off as director/story-teller and I was struck by that.*

I would not dare put myself next to the African storytellers, the griots and the real storytellers. I aspire to be that someday.

FESPACO, Ouagadougou, Burkina Faso, February 1997

Here we are at FESPACO, give me your impressions, tell me some of your feelings.

I feel blessed to be here, period. It is my first time at FESPACO. I didn't know what to expect because I had never been here, but, from what I see, it is just good to be here and see African films, African faces on the screen, made by African filmmakers, to be around so many African filmmakers. The highlight of my trip was seeing Ousmane Sembene. You know, I told you how excited I was to meet him.

Having been at FESPACO, do you have a more definitive idea about what African cinema is? Have your attitudes been confirmed? Have they changed?

To me African cinema is life, and life is African cinema; it is about our life, about our reality. I noticed a lot of African films are based on day-to-day situations, whether traditional or modern, or about Africans who are living in the Western hemisphere. It's about reality. It's not covered up or painted, but life "as is." And it's the interpretation of the artist, the film-maker, and it's a reflection of their realities. I am more convinced that African cinema is African life.

As a film student, where do you go from here? What impact has FESPACO had on you?

Actually, what this has done for me—not only as a film student but as an African film student—it has validated my existence, really, in the true sense of the word. I had a lot of conflicts, if you can remember in previous conversations. Here I am, an African living in the West and I wanted to do films about African reality and yet I don't live in Africa—so how do I reconcile those two?

Anne-Laure Folly, one of the women filmmakers that I talked to, kind of validated my being in the U.S. and the need for me to utilize the knowledge and education I can get there, to help me in my future plans. She kind of removed the guilt factor, because there was a lot of guilt and a hesitancy: "How dare I live in the U.S. and just because I have a film degree go back and make a film about my people. When in reality I have been gone for so long I no longer know their reality!"

Another thing that it has accomplished is that it has made me decide to go and live in Ethiopia and spend some time, living, getting acquainted with the people, the life and all. Being in Burkina, which is very close to life in Ethiopia, it took me back home. And it made me realize, of course, home is always there. The notion of home.

Is there something about this experience that will have an influence on how you make films or the subjects that you choose?

Yes, I was very intense that African films have to be about messages, issues, struggles, and I still believe that; but I also feel that there is room for comedy, there is room for all kinds of emotions. To make people laugh—that is an accomplishment by itself.

I saw *Taafe Fanga* yesterday and it was beautiful, it was funny. The beauty I find in African cinema is the use of metaphors; it's part of our culture, and we use it on the screen. It is a comedy, but the issues were still there. It made me a little bit—not less serious, I am still serious about addressing the issues—but it made me realize that there is room for all types of films within the African cinema context.

You are here with film students from Howard University, largely made up of African diasporans from the United States. What importance do you see for African diasporan film students to attend FESPACO?

It depends on the individual, but if I could give my advice, I would reiterate something that was said recently. We just had an interview with Ben Beye from Senegal. And I asked him did he have any advice for African American film students and he said: "Number One, I advise them to come to Africa, they are always welcome."

Because for African Americans in the States, I believe, who have not experienced Africa, it is just a picture in their minds, and who knows what that picture is. That picture is not drawn by Africans; it is drawn by the West. It is very important, especially as a filmmaker, so that the stereotypes about Africa and Africans are shed, it is so important to come to Africa and experience it.

So, I think this is a very important trip. But I go back to what I said at first; it depends on the individual. If someone is not open to it, someone can come to Africa and stay ten years; it won't make a difference. So there must be an openness and a willingness to know and seek new worlds, and tolerance.

Excerpt from interview during the shooting of *Weti's Poem*, May 1997, Washington, DC.

*We are actually on location during the shooting of your fourth short film, **Weti's Poem**. Could you talk about this film?*

This piece means a lot to me on different levels. One, it was inspired by a poem called "Sadness" written by Weti Enkenelesh Solomon; she is twelve-years old. The moment that I heard the words I had no choice but to do something; they are very powerful, very deep, the words. Also my sentiments are that with children we have a tendency to dismiss them or not to take them seriously, but they have some very powerful ways of expressing themselves, whether it be through writing, or art, etc., and they must be given a chance to excel in that. On a second level, cinematically I feel like I just reached a higher level: I am really starting to dare.

After eighteen years, Lucy went home to Ethiopia, from mid-October 1997 to the end of December 1997:

> My visit home
> ...I went back to Ethiopia
> after being away for 18 years
> I went home to visit my country, my people, my family
> I went back to visit my home
> little did I know
> I went back to revisit myself
> > *Lucy Gebre-Egziabher*
> > *(July 6, 1998)*

Notes

1. In reference to the film *Bridge Over the River Kwai* by David Lean.
2. The Biograph was an art cinema house in Washington, DC, which was in existence from 1967 until its closing in 1996.

Valerie Kaboré

Burkina Faso

Interview held at the 15th FESPACO, February-March 1997, Ouagadougou, Burkina Faso. Translated from French.

We are here at Media 2000; I am impressed with what looks to be the result of a lot of hard work and dedication. Could you talk about the company, your background, and how you came to cinema?

I am producer/filmmaker and general manager of Media 2000, a company that I created after finishing my studies in 1991. I did my studies in cinema, then a Master's degree, followed by a DEA (Diplome d'études approfondies). I am now preparing to defend my doctoral thesis; it is somewhat difficult with all the work that is to be done here.

Media 2000 is a production company for film and video as well as communication consulting for advertising. We do technical consulting for business publicity. On the production side, we do a television magazine for the National Television of Burkina Faso as well as television reports and other magazines for TV5 Afrique. In addition, we do fiction films and commissioned institutional films. We work with the United Nations systems, such as UNDP, UNESCO, and UNICEF. When they ask for our assistance, we attempt to meet their needs.

What is the topic of your doctoral research?

I am working on the subject of media and development. Because you know in our country we have not yet achieved a certain level of development, which means there are many questions left to be resolved in the area of health, AIDS, and education in particular. I am doing my research on the media as it relates to development. How can we Africans, who have several languages—you know in Burkina we have some sixty dialects—how can we use the media support to transmit information and to communicate so that the people can acquire knowledge in all spheres of development?

When speaking about sustainable human development, I think that the media can contribute a great deal in this context. You know this is a concern of women in general. All the films that were screened yesterday [March 8, the International Day of the Woman] were like a collective call, they were films that were very *engagé*, and they all focused on development. Though we think that commercial cinema is a good thing, we also think that a cinema for development can be a complementary source, if we want the country to go forward. That is, therefore, the objective of my research.

As you stated, yesterday [March 8th], and today, a colloquium was held to commemorate the International Day of the Woman. This event gave me an opportunity to see films by women that were not presented during FESPACO, as well as to participate in the forum that dealt with women in cinema and their contribution to women and development through the use of the media. What do you see as the role of women in the cinema?

I think, generally speaking, that African women have much to bring to the development of our continent. It is for this reason that we fight more and more so that women may be trained and educated and have at least a minimum amount of instruction. Because to put a woman in school is to teach her how to open the door to life. Even if she does not go to school for a long period of time, she can at least acquire a minimum amount of knowledge to be able to manage her household and communicate values to her children for their future. In general, the development of Africa depends on what we will do for women of our generation and those of the future.

If we extend this philosophy in the context of cinema, we, with a woman's sensibility, can bring a great deal to this continent. While the number of women who go to school is not very high, the number in the area of the media and cinema is even less. Though we are only a few in this field, if each of us would aim her camera towards the area of awareness-building—or even in commercial filmmaking—she may contribute in her own way to the development of the continent.

I think that a complementarity is necessary between genders in the audio-visual area in general. Because we have our perception that is particular to us, we have our way of seeing. Moreover, we women have always taken on the role of organizer of the household. Though we speak about images contributing to the general deterioration of morals, I don't think that women filmmakers will contribute to this deterioration of morals. Thus, we have our brick to add to the construction. I think that encouraging women to become producers or directors in the cinema is to open another style of expression to this half of Africa, which has a great deal to give and much to say.

Are there workshops or training sessions that are organized either here at Media 2000 or in other structures in Burkina Faso for women to be able to train in this area?

The school, INAFEC (Institut Africain d'Education Cinématographique), where we received training in Burkina, no longer exists. We had people like Filippe Sawadogo, the outgoing Secretary General of FESPACO, filmmaker Idrissa Ouedraogo, Ardiouma Soma of the Cinémathèque, Souleymane Ouedraogo who is the assistant to Baba Hama, the Secretary General of FESPACO, and others. They as well as others were products of this school. It was a school where filmmakers were trained throughout Africa.

Burkina Faso found itself alone in administering the school and was forced to close it because of the difficulty in trying to manage it alone. Since then, the training for filmmakers has taken place outside. This means that the possibility of getting training has been reduced. I think that FEPACI (The Pan-African Federation of Filmmakers) is now working on a project to revive it.

During the colloquium in commemoration of the International Day of the Woman, it was encouraging to see the many films and videos by women. At FESPACO, also, there were many short films and videos and documentaries as well as several feature films. What can be done to encourage more women to go into cinema?

To encourage women to go into cinema would not be a bad thing. Unfortunately, it is an area where training is expensive, which means that it is not necessarily a priority. However, it is absolutely necessary that there be more women trained in this area in order to have a complementarity between women and men. Beyond the problem of training, perhaps, it is women themselves who do not venture into cinema. I think this is because working in the media is considered a profession occupied by people who are not very serious, who frequent too many people, who go out a lot. And for an African woman this is not particularly encouraging. As long as this attitude persists, women will continue to rebuff the possibility to go into this area.

I think that more and more, however, especially in our country that organizes and houses FESPACO, people understand that a woman in the cinema is not vulgar, nor is she someone who is not serious. I think that the mentality is changing. People of the younger generation come when we have screenings. Afterwards we meet many high school students who express an interest in going into the cinema like us, and I think it is very encouraging for the future.

FEPACI wants to initiate a project in this sense, but with a focus more on video. Because, you know, video is a means that is much more accessible, at the present time, simply because it is more manageable. The technology has evolved in terms of the quality of the image, and in terms of the level of production costs it is more reasonable to work in video than in film. Even in the context of the United Nations system, there are funds that are no longer allocated to our countries. Our countries are very much in debt. Thus, the cinema may be seen as a luxury if it continues to be so costly. Whereas video is more practical and we are able to work as simply as possible.

I know that there is a big debate between film technology and video/television technology. But I think that people are beginning to realize themselves, that aside from the conservation—the durability of celluloid versus the video-cassette, where there is no comparison—that in the future there will be no choice but to work in the video/television format.

Unfortunately, the reality is there, and it is advancing rapidly, so I think people should reconsider. Of course, films will still be made, but there has to be a credible endorsement, such as with the work of Gaston Kaboré and Idrissa Ouedraogo, in order to gain the confidence of investors. On the level of funding, we are increasingly realizing that people are not putting money in African cinema because it is not considered to be profitable. It is also a fact that we do not have the means, and so people are going more and more to video/television technology.

You are producing a film series called **Naitre fille en Afrique** *(To Be Born a Girl in Africa) and you have already done two films for this series. Could you talk about these films and the reception they have received?*

This series was my first work with fiction film. The film that you saw this morning is called *Kado ou la bonne à tout faire*, which received Second Place for the best fiction film in video at this edition of FESPACO. I also made the film that you saw yesterday called *Les vrais faux jumeaux*.

These were actually the first two public screenings that I have had. But for the first release, I have to thank the public because the responses were favorable. Since these are *engagé* films, whose purpose is to fight for

128

the right of education for girls, it is not always easy to find such favorable responses in all situations.

On the other hand, I have done many commissioned institutional films, and advertisements. This has been limiting to some degree, because if one only does advertisements or institutional films, one cannot really measure one's capacity as a director. Since these are orders with precise terms and references, we must do the work according to these specifications. With these last two films, I was free to write and create the script, and I am satisfied. I would not have minded if I could have worked a bit more because, when looking at the film again today, I felt that perhaps I could have developed the script differently. Because one always learns, even from one's own work.

For the public who do not have access to the cinema houses such as those who live in the villages and rural areas, how does Media 2000 assist in making the cinema available to a larger, non-urban public?

We do have plans to have itinerant screenings, which means going to the villages with video-mobile vans and having public screenings in the marketplace areas and under the palaver trees and discussing the themes of the films with the people.

We have made films whose objective is to sensitize the public on certain issues. Because we are a private company, we are waiting for backing from the NGOs and it is up to them to purchase these films to use for specific audiences. At any rate, we are prepared to do the itinerant screenings. It has in fact already begun: people have screened videos, even in the city, and afterwards they discuss it.

You completed your film studies at INAFEC, and you have established a media company. It seems that you have a commitment to a viable cinema in Africa. Could you talk about African cinema in general, your impressions, thoughts?

Actually this is a question that has brought about a great deal of debate at the present, because some African filmmakers prefer that one speak of their cinema as simply cinema, rather than the term "African cinema." They also say that there really is no African cinema. However, I think that this is not totally true, because our cinema does not always have a large budget, thus our films cannot be as competitive in the international arena.

We have the skills; we have all been trained in schools in Europe or here with well-known professors. We have the technical expertise, but

129

you know cinema is not only technique, it is more of a problem of having a large enough budget. It is also a problem of actors, to have known talent. For a long time a lot of the filmmakers have worked like us in the area of consciousness-raising, which means that this cinema has been usually known as a "cinema of consciousness."

We are increasingly seeing that films such as *Buud Yam* [by Gaston Kaboré] and *Kini and Adams* [by Idrissa Ouedraogo] are definitely commercially viable. These are films that can be viewed in the large cinema houses in Paris and that can hold their own anywhere. Thus, there becomes less of a distinction, apart from the fact that the actors are Africans, between a film from Africa and any other film. The level of professionalism is such that financiers have confidence in certain filmmakers and they are doing quite well. However, for the younger generation of filmmakers it might not be as easy.

What are some of the future plans for Media 2000?

Some of the future goals for Media 2000 are to do television series for African television stations and international networks. We have already done a treatment and plan to develop it using a professional scriptwriter. In addition, there are also plans for animation films, because there is a paucity of programs for children and youth.

The programs that are broadcast on African televisions come from the outside, while we have our own culture. We have our own stories that we can tell to our people. Thus, our ambition is to initiate an African series, which may permit us to be less dependent on the exterior and to consume locally. We are also interested in developing a type of partnership with television networks or independent companies interested in buying footage from the image bank that we are developing.

I am optimistic about the future of African cinema because, as I said earlier, it is a question of having the means and a general policy. For instance, our country is not known in the context of music. Outside of the country, it is rare to hear about Burkinabé music. On the other hand, when one talks about cinema in Africa, everyone looks toward Burkina because we have a cultural policy that has always encouraged cinema. In addition, I think that this cinema will be very profitable one day and there will not be a question about investing in it. What is lacking, perhaps, is a leader who will tap the pointer on the table and say, "We have had enough, this or that has to happen." Things are happening. I think that the European Economic Community (EEC) wants to support Burkina in developing its cinematic infrastructure.

We are seeing a true emergence of a national cinema with the centralization of diverse components, which perhaps means that this is a good indication for African cinema in general and for Burkinabé cinema in particular. There is a consciousness among filmmakers and a political awareness in general. These two forces united may bring much in the area of productivity and creativity. What perhaps is lacking is the means for exhibition, and with the emerging significance of satellite, we may find the means for exhibiting our work, if it is sufficiently competitive.

In an earlier conversation, you told me about your experiences with people from the Africa Diaspora during your stay in the United States. Could you talk about your encounters and your impressions?

Before going to the United States, I had somewhat of a preconceived idea about black Americans who lived there. I was able to visit the country in 1994, in Atlanta, as well as New York. I realized that they were a people who were on a perpetual quest for their identity. As soon as it is known that you come from the continent, you are immediately adopted by them. They wanted to know everything about the continent.

I actually gave this small detail in order to say that we are very proud when we have such a warm meeting. I noticed that when living in France, one could live ten years in an apartment building without knowing the people who live there, and in the streets no one will greet you. However, in Atlanta, I actually wondered if I was dreaming. In the elevator, everyone says hello. They live a bit like in Africa and it was very touching to find this contact, which was very warm and particular to the black world, because we are not a people who are immediately cautious and apprehensive. We are always open; we always open our doors; although later, there have been consequences.

In terms of the diasporan participation at FESPACO, for sometime FESPACO has opened up to all of its black Diaspora, in the United States and other areas of the world. We have observed an increasingly great passion that this world has for Africa, for Burkina. There has always been a great deal of emotion when they come, when we meet. We have realized that there remains a certain resemblance, despite the differences, and that is something that is very strong that we share. It brings about a chain of friendships.

In the film school where I was in Atlanta, we worked with Haile Gerima, who is a professor at Howard University. He came with a group of young black students who wanted to do research on African cinema. Since then, we continue to maintain contact.

Black Americans, in fact, have been the ones to make FESPACO known in the United States. I find it great that they have always come to the source to learn, understand, and meet other people, and vice versa. It is true that it is a festival, but it is a film festival. We converge in Ouagadougou because there is this magical image, the cinema, that attracts people. The media may be the source of a union and the source of the discovery of oneself and others.

We speak of awareness films or information films in general, if through your stay in Burkina you return to the United States to show what you have seen here, there is not a better thing on which to speak about it than the audio-visual medium.[1] In my opinion, the aspect of image and sound is very strong. If you were only to do a written report when you return and it is filed in the library, perhaps one day someone will come across it and read it. However, it is not the same effect as the audio-visual.

On the other hand, if you distribute your videocassette, thousands or even millions of people can see it at the same time around the world. Therefore, the magic of the image and sound remains irreplaceable. I cannot imagine a medium that will be able to extend this medium. The media remains the most important means by which people may come together.

Notes

1. The interview was filmed to be included in a documetary on African women in the cinema.

Wajuhi Kamau

Kenya

Interview conducted by Mbye Cham for the African Women in the Cinema Project, October 1998 at the Southern African Film Festival (SAFF) in Harare, Zimbabwe.

Wajuhi, you directed the video feature film entitled **Mine Boy** *that was screened here at the festival. Could you begin by talking a bit about your background, how you came into cinema, what interested you to take up the camera and begin working in this area? Also, what are some of the previous works you have done prior to* **Mine Boy**, *which came out in 1997?*

I would say that I was attracted to film as early as eight years old, when in grade four I was made the leading actor in a film. At that time, for whatever reason, I was made to play the role of a man. I do remember some of the lines because I played King Kamut. This was the story of King Kamut and the Sea. King Kamut had been praised by his henchmen; they told him that he was great, that everything obeyed him, the sun obeyed him, the sea obeyed him. What I remember the most was when King Kamut goes to the sea and the waves are coming in and he is telling the sea to go away and the sea just would not go away. I remember my excitement and the excitement of the crowd when we put this show on. I was a little girl and I threw the crown into the crowd saying, "I will never wear this crown again because now as King Kamut the sea has refused to obey."

I dreamed on: even when I went to high school I was recruited by the drama teacher for stage; I believe again he spotted talent. And that time they needed a little girl. I played a little girl in the play that we were putting on for the year's drama festival. From then on I stayed in drama throughout high school. I was in charge of drama in college. On and on I dreamed about being an actress, the big screen. Of course, at that time, we did not have any African cinema, but they would bring in occasionally films like *Sound of Music*. While looking at outside films, I had been seeing myself and seeing my starting role in it, where at that time we did not have anything going for film.

After high school, I met one of our leading drama teachers. He had not taught me, but his wife was our drama teacher in high school. By that time he had left classroom teaching, he was working with the Educational Media Service with the Minister of Education in the Film Production Department. He asked me, "Are you still acting?" I said, "Why not?" He said, "After college, come over and I will let them know about your talent." That is how I ended up at the Educational Media Service. After that, I was trained in film production, documentary film production, and 16mm.

I did a number of documentaries. Eventually we had to shift to video production because the cost of 16mm was just impossible. In the process, again, the teacher who I would say was my mentor was in charge of TV drama production.

Is he a Kenyan?

Yes, he is Kenyan, but right now he is working in Namibia in the same line. He was in charge of television drama production at the institute. I was picked to be his production assistant as part of my training package, that was before I went to formal media training. Eventually, the man left the institute and I took over the production of the drama festival. I have being doing that since. I have been working in drama production and documentary production, I would say that I have excelled in both.

Did you go elsewhere outside of Kenya for formal training?

Yes I did, I have been trained in Japan, especially for educational television production. I have also been trained in Britain in the same area. In Japan, we were attached to NHK for a month and then we had formal training at their training institute.

Could you talk about the documentary films that you did on 16mm?

I did a film in 16mm on prenatal conditions and how they affect the health of the unborn. In this film, we followed a lady at home; this was in rural Kenya, because that is where the majority of the Kenyans live. We saw her day-to-day activities and we were able to get background information from doctors and psychologists on how diseases, for example, that a pregnant woman gets will affect the unborn's health, and also how the diet of the mother relates to the unborn's health. Again, like I said, because I am working in the educational institution, our target audience usually would look for that kind of material, especially trainees, because they have to understand the students that they are teaching. Therefore, we were able to relate that information to the learner in class.

*Was **Mine Boy** your first feature film?*

I would say not, because, like I have said, previously I have done quite a number of drama productions. In Kenya every year, we have our annual drama festival where college students, high school students and primary students also come and compete. We pick the best script out of that, work with the film students and, using one camera, we shoot the programs. So, the difference between that and *Mine Boy* is that *Mine Boy* is longer, because the plays coming from the drama festival would be, at best, fifty minutes, but *Mine Boy* certainly is longer than that.

So these are basically plays that you shoot on video?

Yes, these are the dramas, although we do now write the screenplay and so on.

*What pushed you towards **Mine Boy,** which, of course, is a novel by Peter Abrahams from South Africa? What were some of the things that attracted you personally?*

The choice of *Mine Boy* was not my decision alone. We have *Mine Boy* as one of the texts that has being studied in high school for the last three years. Over the years we found it very useful to produce plays for television, because what has been happening is, especially for the city of Nairobi, free-lance theater artists would put up the place and students would come into the theater and watch. But then, that only caters for about five percent of our students. So, as a ministry, we had the responsibility of making similar information or similar resources available to schools. So we designed a system whereby we, on an annual basis now, take up the textbooks for English literature and Kiswahili, because those are the two national languages. We dramatize and put the films on tape, then we send them to the schools. Either the schools will buy the cassettes or we have mobile vans that go to different locations in the country and we show these films. We found that by using this method, performance in literature has improved dramatically in the schools. That was the major reason for choosing to put *Mine Boy* on video.

*So the audience for **Mine Boy** is basically the school age children who are going through the process of exams?*

That is our main target audience, but what we found out is that there is a thirst for people to see themselves on the screen, regardless. And although our intended audience is the high school students we have found that a lot of other people out of school do not hesitate to buy the same tapes and watch them for their own entertainment.

*Has **Mine Boy** run on Kenyan national television?*

Mine Boy has not been screened on our Kenyan Broadcasting Station, which is a public station. Unfortunately, the station wears two hats: it is public and it is commercial. To be able to put up such a film on our television you have to pay. We find it more cost-effective to use the same money...you would be paying something to the rate of maybe half a million Kenyan shillings for one show, because we are charged at the rate of about a hundred and thirty-five thousand Kenyan shillings for a half an hour. We find it is more cost effective and we will reach a greater audience. Again, when you are showing the films in the schools, or when we give them the tapes, they are watching it under a controlled situation. Therefore, they can stop it and discuss and watch again, or they can watch several times. So we find it more cost effective to take the programs to the people rather than putting it once, for the same amount of money, on the national broadcasting station.

You stated that you work primarily on video now rather than 16mm?

Oh yes, we cannot afford 16mm anymore, especially the cost of the raw stock and the processing. You know, you take more time with film than with video, so that is where we are.

Could you talk about the Kenyan Institute of Education where you are? Is it a government department? What is the structure and how is it funded?

The Kenyan Institute of Education is a department within the Ministry of Education. It is the major curriculum development center for the country, and the Educational Media Service where I work, where we produce educational materials, is now a department within the Kenyan Institute of Education. Originally, programs of a school were housed under the Ministry of Information. In 1965, we were doing broadcasting for radio and television programs. However, what they realized was that since programs done as educational resources are to support the curriculum, then the Educational Media Service was better placed under the Ministry of Education and housed at the Kenyan Institute of Education. Because then we are able to work hand-in-hand in consultation with curriculum development on a day-to-day basis.

You have other women filmmakers in Kenya; what is your relationship with them, have you seen their work? What has been the influence of their work on your own perception of cinema?

The most interesting thing about the Kenyan women filmmakers is that we went to the same college at the same time. Anne Mungai and I did quite a few student productions together. She was originally trained as an editor; I was trained as a producer. We have other producers like Dommie Yambo; her program was also showing at this festival. She is also quite heavy in terms of documentary productions and, right now, she is also going into a feature production, her script is ready. We went to college together, except for Jane Murago-Munen, who was a year ahead of us. By then, eventually, because it is a small industry, we ended up working together. I worked with Jane; again, she was an editor at the Kenyan Institute of Education. We have edited programs together. Right now, we are in the same film organization. We have a Kenyan National Film Association where Jane is the secretary and I am member. We are working together. What we have been able to do now as an association and as colleagues in the profession is that, we keep probing each other, or challenging each other. So that if I do something that Jane thinks is not very well done, she would not hesitate to ask me, "What do you think you are doing?"

Like we have been saying all along, this is a male-dominated area and therefore people would be faster to spot a fault in a production done by a woman. If a similar fault is in a production done by a man, they may choose to overlook it. Let me give you an illustration from one experience that I had. We had a new team of young men that was recruited in my institute around 1990. That team had just acquired an outside broadcasting or outside production unit with three cameras and the whole shoot. I was sent out on an assignment. I had a man who did not have any experience in production as my assistant. So I have a lot of new guys on my crew, they don't know me, I don't know them, their first attitude was, "Couldn't they get a producer? Why are they sending us out with this little girl?" We spent a week; this was a national festival of music and drama. We spent a week with them, came out with very good material.

As you know, with every production there is always a hiccup here and there. Then on the final day we had, not a major problem, but nevertheless, they made it sound like, if it were not a woman in charge of this production maybe this problem would not have occurred. So we had a bit of tension. I was the only female producer in the department. Then a year and a half later, the guys came to me and said, "Why are we not busy?" I said, "What do you want to do? All of the male producers are there, why don't you challenge them?" They said, "We are sorry, we didn't know that you were the best." They said, "We did not know who we were dealing with at the time," and they actually apologized. Not so loudly—no man would apologize so loudly—but in their own way and on an individual level they would say, "We didn't know what you were talking about," because I was able to prove myself to them. So those are just some of the challenges that one has to face.

Do you face similar challenges when it comes to seeking funding? Have you ever had to go out on your own to secure independent sources of funding for other than government mandated programs?

As an institute, we do believe in cost sharing or even going out to seek an extra coin here and there. I have not found it much of a problem. Because, in the first place, when you are searching funds from whomever, the first thing they ask for is not just a CV on paper, they want to see a program that you have done. You prove yourself that way, they come over or they ask you for a tape and they see your program. They like it; they give you a job. I would not say that I have felt discriminated against as a woman, because I have got my work to support my application.

Are you thinking about doing anything in 16mm or 35mm in fiction, feature, outside of the Kenyan Institute of Education, in the near future?

I have been working on a script for some time now. I went to FESPACO in 1991 and I saw what the West African filmmakers are doing. You know, now you are looking at this and you start writing you own script. In the process, again, you realize that it is not easy to get funds. So, what I did was I started out writing a script and then I thought maybe I could make it a book. So, I am working on a book, and I am hoping that I should be able to sell a screenplay on the same book. Yes, it is in my dreams that one day I should be able to make a film outside the Educational Media Service mandate, to put my statements on the screen.

Is the book you are working on a novel or a play?

It's a novel.

Are you in any way influenced by the writings of some of the women writers in Kenya, let's say, Micere Mugo and Grace Ogot or other African women writers, at all?

Yes, in a way, I am. Of course, I agree with some of their views and some of them I don't. There are quite a number of short stories that Grace Ogot wrote, some of them based on oral narrative; when you read some of them now, the way of thinking has changed somewhat, towards looking at whether they were gender sensitive. We say that the women are the traditional storytellers. What kinds of stories have we been perpetuating?

In another workshop, we were looking at quite a lot of stories that have been told by men and women, but largely by women. What you realize is that, although we are saying that the society is male dominated and therefore a lot of stuff is seen from male eyes, but when women tell the stories, the characters that they are painting, are not female heroes. So when one looks at those stories, some even picked from oral literature, one wonders how relevant they are. Is it a story that you want to perpetuate? Or, is it a story that you want to put on paper and put question marks around? Because quite honestly, in a lot of our oral stories, they call the woman the woman, but they name the man in the story, they name the boy in the story. They talk of the mother of Kamau, they talk of the wife of Kamau. So we are saying at this time in life, we need to have women who have a name in the stories, as much as I respect the older writers.

So that in any project that you do, you believe that there is a female sensitivity that comes through and that critically engages some of the established conventions already in place? So that the way that you as a woman see things is different from the way that maybe a man will see them created.

Maybe, not because I am a woman. I have followed the gender debate, and I have, maybe, been influenced now to start looking at things the way they should be and the way society portrays them. As an example, when you watch the soap operas that we have from America and elsewhere, what we have is the wife who is shorter than the husband, which means she always has to look up to him. Is this done deliberately? Do we do it consciously? Or, is that the way life is? The wives are shorter than the husbands? Why is it that the woman has to earn less? So that, again, she is a dependent. When you are casting, either for the stage or even in a book, that is the kind of character you are putting up. Therefore, you don't know whether that is the way it is. But you know that there are some wives who are taller; again, when you put up such a scenario, you are almost telling those who are not married, if you are looking for a wife you've got to look beneath yourself, she's got to earn less, she's got to be shorter, she's got to be whatever you are not. So that the man is always up there and the woman is down here. So these are some of the subtle messages that one has to think about consciously when you are writing, or even when you are putting up a show on stage or bringing it to film.

You mentioned that you were in Ouagadougou in 1991. As you remember, there was a meeting of African women video/filmmakers. I don't know if you attended the workshop.

I remember it very well. What happened with me in Ouagadougou, I had gone as an UNICEF delegate and at that time UNICEF was running a parallel workshop on films supporting children to the other workshops at Ouagadougou. Because I had done quite a number of films about children with children as central character, I was involved more with the UNICEF workshop. Nevertheless, I was able to interact with the women from Africa and the Diaspora.

As a woman, how would you define your role as a filmmaker?

I would say that filmmakers are storytellers and as a filmmaker, part of my responsibility is to make sure that I am telling the right story and in the right way. Not just for Kenya, but I believe for Africa and for the whole world.

Do you see a political or socially oriented role that filmmakers should play in contemporary society? Given the kinds of challenges that face African peoples in general, and Kenyans in particular, what role do you see film playing in terms of engaging those challenges? And also, maybe perhaps provoking some kind of thought and action towards transforming it?

I believe film can be used effectively as an information medium. It can also be used effectively for education and, in fact, we have been using it for both. Other departments, including my department, have been doing programs on video about subjects like AIDS and family planning. Some projects in Kenya work on video within a certain district so that you are not bringing information from outside the region. The team would go there, spend two weeks, talk with the people, shoot, have discussions, have community theater, go back to Nairobi and edit the material; we then bring it back to them. In that way we have been able to use it effectively to entertain them and to educate them; and, also, for their own reflection. When you are seeing yourself, you are seeing your situation, then it is easy to remember and to change to a certain extent both attitudes and behavior.

Aï Keita-Yara

Burkina Faso

Interview held at FESPACO 1997, Ouagadougou, Burkina Faso, February 1997. Translated from French.

The place African actors hold in African cinema is increasingly visible in the context of film criticism and African film history. There is a genuine interest to know their feelings about the characters they interpret, and their impressions of cinema in general. What do you feel is your role as an African actor in African cinema?

In African cinema, I would say the role of all actors is to be a vehicle in which to convey a message on the screen to our society. It is in this context that I, as an African woman actor, contribute in bringing a message to our people. I want to make my contribution to the development of African cinema.

What has been your general impression of the image of African women in African cinema or in visual representation in general?

It has been very positive. Of course, it was very difficult at the beginning because at that time our societies did not understand. However, at the present there is beginning to be an acceptance. In the past, to see a woman in the cinema was a problem in Africa. Now it is changing, people have understood that it is art and they accept us.

*In Med Hondo's film, **Sarraounia**, you played the role of the great queen Sarraounia. The film was awarded the grand prize, the Etalon de Yennenga at FESPACO in 1987. Perhaps it is not a coincidence that Princess Yennenga, after whom the prize is named, was also a formidable woman. One may compare*

Sarraounia to the strength and courage of Yennenga. Could you talk about your experience as Sarraounia, and how you felt in this character?

You know, the history of this woman fascinated me. I don't know if you have heard about the Central African Mission led by the *Colonne Voulet-Chanoine*. These men did a lot of damage to Africans. Sarraounia, voluntarily celibate, decidedly celibate, had as her sole ambition to fight and liberate her people. She refused to bow to the *Colonne Voulet-Chanoine* when they arrived in Niger. She was a very brave woman. I admired the history of Sarraounia and I also loved playing the role in the film. I felt that I actually lived her character.

At the beginning, Med Hondo had chosen me for a minor part, the character of Amina in the film. However, after the selection at the first casting, I was his choice for the role of Sarraounia. I think this was because Med saw me in my family setting where he witnessed a brawl. I was fighting with a young man. I think this scene stayed with him. When he returned later, in the context of his film, he asked my nephew Djim Mamadou Kola, who is a Burkinabé filmmaker, "By the way, your aunt, the tall, dark-skinned one, I saw her fighting here one day, what has become of her?" "Ah" he stated, "she is around, she is married now." Med Hondo declared "Anyway, I want her to play in my film." My nephew replied "Well, okay, let's go see her husband." They went to see my husband and he had no objections. And that is how I passed the test. Although he had chosen me for the minor role, after having done a preliminary filming, he stated "No, she is the one to play Sarraounia." And I think that I was able to capture the personage that he had intended.

What could possibly follow this role as Sarraounia? What films have you acted in since?

I must say this character made me very popular in Burkina Faso, in Africa, as well as internationally. I must first take the opportunity to graciously thank Med Hondo, I owe him that. Because every time that he speaks publicly about the film, he speaks about me, his actor. The film has had an especially tremendous success because it was the greatest of African films in 1987. It was awarded the Etalon de Yennenga, the prize of Air Afrique, and the prize of OAU. It was awarded a total of five prizes. The film was a great success and my popularity came from this.

After *Sarraounia*, I played in *Mamy Wata* by Mustapha Diop. Though I don't speak in the film, I act with my eyes. I played the role of a woman in love. In Africa, you know, we have a certain pride that we hide behind our love. I was in love with a rebel, but I refused to declare my love to him. I followed him everywhere with the hope that he would declare his love to me, which continues right until the end of the film, when he still says nothing, and I leave disappointed.

After that, I played in the film *Les étrangers* by Djim Mamadou Kola. He was a prizewinner at FESPACO 1991, where he was awarded the prize of CDAO, the prize of OAU, and the special prize of the jury.

I also played in the film *Haramuya* by Drissa Touré [Burkina Faso 1995], which was also well received. I played in the film *Message pour Beijing*, a documentary for television by Martine Ilboudo Condé. Another film in which I played a role, was *SIDA dans la cité II* by A. Cissé of the Ivory Coast; it was also a film for television, which is being broadcast in Burkina Faso at the present time. Like the others, it was also well received. My role in these films also contributed to my popularity.

Perhaps you actually seek out certain films. For instance, **Sarraounia** *and* **Mamy Wata** *are legendary personages in African history, and you acted in both of these films. Do you see yourself as a certain kind of character in the roles you play, such as a very strong woman, or a woman with a great deal of confidence, strength and power? Are there certain roles that you feel more within your character as a woman?*

I would say yes. Let's take the film, *Sarraounia*, where I played the role of a woman who had a strong character, who was afraid of nothing. She tormented her neighbors and everybody around her. I was very satisfied in this role. I felt the presence of this force. On the other hand, in the film *Les étrangers*, I played the role of a submissive African woman.

It's true that the real talent of an actor is to be able to act in any role as if it were her true character....

Yes, the actor has to be able to do all. That is what I was saying at the beginning. We are attempting to convey a message. Thus, the actor must be versatile. When you are asked to play the role of a madwoman, you put yourself in the personage of a madwoman, you play that role. To play the role of a prostitute, you place yourself in the character of a prostitute. To play the role of a "grande dame," or a businesswoman in a company, you put yourself in the body of a businesswoman. That is an actor, in fact.

You were not an actor before playing in the film **Sarraounia**? *It was this film that got you started in the cinema. What did you do before acting in films?*

Yes, *Sarraounia* was my first film: I had never acted before, neither in the cinema nor in the theater. My profession outside of the cinema is secretary at the Centre Hospitalier National Yalgado Ouedraogo in Burkina Faso. I was trained as a secretary.

How do you manage the role as secretary and actor at the same time?

I would say it takes a certain talent. You know, our country, Burkina Faso, assists African filmmakers considerably. When we have a film production, I am given authorization or I arrange for vacation time during the shooting of the film.

Does an actor keep a bit of her role with her after the end of the film in her everyday life? Somewhere within you, was there, or is there still a part of Sarraounia or the other characters that you have played in other films?

No, I am simply Aï Keita-Yara. But, of course, in the streets when someone sees me and says, "Hey Sarraounia," sure, I say hello. I know they are my fans so I go to them to greet them.

Wanjiru Kinyanjui

Kenya

Several conversations took place by electronic mail during the month of February 1999 between Washington, DC and Kenya.

Wanjiru, you are among a visible group of women from Kenya who are emerging in the field of film, video, and television production. Could you begin by talking about your experiences with the image while growing up in Kenya?

I've always been fascinated by storytelling and the theater in which I used to take part in school. When I was young, my imagination seemed to function visually. For instance, I could make believe the creatures I was reading about were around me somewhere and what they looked like. An example is that when I read Erich Kästner's "Emil and the Detectives" in 2nd class, I transplanted the whole story into my everyday location, Nairobi. The characters were mainly little boys wearing tattered khaki shorts and shirts, all ganging up together in the streets. It is only when I studied Erich Kästner at university level that I realized that it was a German story, a German storyteller, and a German location!

My experiences of cinema and images are the Saturday nights in boarding high school where we were shown films like old James Bond, Mary Poppins, and other rather innocent films. Outside of school, we would sneak off from home to go into Indian films, which we understood without language: We were teenagers and curious about love and romance. At English language class outings, we would go to the British Council in Nairobi to see mainly BBC Shakespeare productions (in class, we read Hamlet and Macbeth mixed up at random with some African writers). I studied English, and later drama for a Master's degree and German Literature in Berlin. Significantly, and some say perversely, considering I am "third world," my thesis was entitled "Shakespeare's King Lear: Loss of

Identity and Discovery of Self." It had a lot to do with seeing: visual, inner-vision, seeming, being, and so on.

So this began your evolution in the cinema?

Well, my love for story telling rather than writing academic papers got the better of me, and before I finished my MA degree, I had decided to make the plunge into a world which is full of characters and their stories. I therefore applied and was accepted at the Deutsche Film und Fernsehakademie (DFFB), where I felt I had found "it"! At the film school, my basic problem was to get the Europeans to co-operate with "an ignorant black woman." We had to work very practically and help each other in each of our productions. But no one in my class would invite me to work on their projects, because they probably did not think I was capable! Well, beginners generally are not, and I therefore decided that I had to resort to another plan in order to gain practical experience there. I decided to do as much as I could on my own productions. So I ended up writing my own stories, doing my own camerawork, directing, and editing, rather than ask people who would not let me do theirs for them. Well, it worked quite well until I got to do the last projects, for which I got friends of mine.

The film school was definitely a great opportunity for me because we had no theoretical exams. Our papers were actual films and we could, therefore, experiment on each film we made after every seminar or workshop. Some cinemas in Berlin provided us with free tickets and it was possible for us to watch as many different films as we had time for. I could choose my own subjects, my own format, and the people I would work with. In a way, it was a freeing experience.

You stated that your basic problem was "to get the Europeans to co-operate with 'an ignorant black woman'." Could you elaborate on this?

At university, my colleagues were shocked by the fact that I could score the top marks at various subjects, including Latin and English. They did not expect this, and I guess they had no idea that I came from a very competitive school environment in Kenya and I had always done well in school! At the film school, the same attitude repeated itself: I was sort of "invisible" and not to be taken seriously. It meant being isolated from the working groups the students set up and which forced me to resort to plan B: ignore them too and go ahead and do what I set out to do. I guess that I am not an isolated case, because there is a general attitude that we are backward and we survive on donations from them. Well, African governments have not done much to correct this misconception of Africans, especially women. They are more concerned in getting donor aid and misappropriating them even. Of course, the reports on American/European TVs on Africa are usually negative: Hunger, epidemics, AIDS, street children, war, and corruption are what make news, not the people who lead normal lives in poor or posh or middle-class homes, whose children go to school or help their parents to survive. Not the efforts of ordinary citizens and their bravery in countering even catastrophes.

What are some of the productions that you did while in film school?

My school productions include: a short documentary on the daily life of a female African student in Berlin; the work of a traditional African musician teaching traditional music in Berlin and Germany, a visualized poem of my own; an essay on Africans in Berlin; and, finally, the full-length feature, *The Battle of the Sacred Tree*, which brought me back to my home village as a location! *The Battle of the Sacred Tree* was my rather ambitious graduation project, for which I had to raise more money than I actually could. But at last, a very low-budget film was completed and I was on my way out of the sheltered and spoiled life of a student!

In Germany, I had also written and directed two short dramas, thirty minutes each, for ZDF German Television. These were stories for a multicultural project which were made by a multi-cultural team about Berlin's mixture of "tribes": Turks, Germans, Africans, South-Americans, Poles, Czechs, and whoever else was a professional in the fields of writing and directing. Well, mine were dramas around African-German connections. One is witty, but the other one concerns a neo-nazi attack on an African man who has an eight-year-old daughter by his German wife. The little girl, through whose eyes we see, is suddenly thrown into an identity crisis: Am I not German? Where do I really belong?

Could you talk about the production of the film, **The Battle of the Sacred Tree**?

Shooting in Kenya was something of an adventure: the conditions are as different as day and night. I could get no one to volunteer to work for me. They all figured it is just like any other foreign-financed film with a lot of money to distribute. But the actual atmosphere was more friendly, more humorous, and less stressing than shooting in Germany. I would get really upset and some actor would tell me, "Don't worry, it's only a movie!"

Had you ever studied at any Kenyan film institution?

No, I have not studied at any Kenyan film institution, but I was a resource person at the Kenya Institute of Mass Communications at a three-week production seminar. During the first week, the participants developed two ideas into a five to ten minute script which they then shot and edited in two crews. One of the films was good, the other one a mess. It was my first experience at a Kenyan film institution which trains people on technical aspects of film. Most of the video/filmmakers in Kenya have gone through this institution.

Could you talk about some of your film projects since returning to Kenya?

Well, I have been based in Nairobi since 1995. In 1996/97, I made two short films for a German TV series "The Rights of Children". In Nairobi, I wrote and directed a film based on the right to attend school plus the right to know both parents. The leading character, Koi, cannot go to school because her mother is only a street hawker and is also single. Koi, inspired by "The Ghost of Children's Rights," tracks down her father and literally blackmails him into paying her school fees. So she kills two birds with one stone. The twelve-minute story is a comedy of sorts.

The second film was shot in Kigali and is based on traumatized children. Gatashya, a ten-year-old boy, lost his whole family in the genocide but survived somehow. He meets another orphan boy in the city who introduces him to his orphanage. The personnel at the orphanage try to help him to work out his trauma and get over it. These two films were shot on Beta and broadcast on ZDF in German-speaking countries. The series has won the "Erich Kästner" award in Germany.

Could you elaborate some on the genocide that you focus on in the film?

During the 1994 genocide in Rwanda, Tutsis were killed by the hundreds of thousands. Hutu sympathizers were also killed. The genocide did not spare neighbors or close relatives who had got mixed up in the ethnic division. Hundreds of children were orphaned. No one in Rwanda was spared, because many are still traumatized. The survivors all lost many of their kin and friends. A trauma psychologist who works with children told me stories about children watching their fathers and mothers getting chopped up. It is unimaginable! After doing some research, I decided to do the short film on this subject— which is actually too hard for children, but it happened to children! I found it difficult to make a film (it was for German TV) which is palatable to children who have not gone through this. But even then, it is still terrible.

You have many projects in process at varying stages. Could you talk about them?

In 1997, I wrote the screenplay, "Sweet Sixteen" for a full-length feature film which is now in the fund-raising stage for production. *Sweet Sixteen* dramatizes the fate of a sixteen-year-old girl who gets herself pregnant. In Kenya, it is the end of the road for many a teenage girl: at least 10,000 a year lose their places in school while some lose their homes. (It is not a depressing story! It is about dealing with an extreme situation and beginning to rise again).

In November 1997, I started shooting *African Children* which favors the girl-child and which is now in the editing stage. It is a documentary on African teenage girls. The film seeks to give a differentiated image of how others see Africa and its people. The general image that goes through the media is Africa's helplessness, poverty, chaos, war, catastrophes, etc. It is certainly far from being about "typical" African catastrophes, as it concentrates on the daily lives, beliefs, dreams, and expressions of these girls. Very few reports show normal girls going to school, eating, laughing, being cheeky like any other teenagers, leading a normal life. This film is educational in terms of informing people out there that Africans are just people despite the setbacks. And people are people. This film is about strong schoolgirls who lead very normal lives, according to themselves. It is told by themselves and not by a commentator. The girls give their own stories the way they will, they share their daily life with the audience. They are ambitious and strong and they are very hard working.

Since 1998, I have been writing a thirty-minute script for Zimmedia's "Mama Africa Series," a project by six African women directors; we attended a writer's workshop in January (1999) in Zimbabwe. My plans are to finish the doc. editing and concentrate on the script. In between, I've been to many different festivals with *The Battle of the Sacred Tree* including one of my dream festivals, Creteil/Paris in April 1998, where it had a "gala evening" which was fantastic.

What actually drives me is the need to give Africans images they can say are truly themselves and not what Hollywood gives them. I would like to hear, as I heard from many Kenyans after they saw *The Battle of the Sacred Tree*, "that is just the way us women in groups behave." We have to learn to enjoy our own stories, which portray our joys, follies, vices, and virtues and to go on to say, "We are alright! We can do it, we can be proud of our people." In short, it is a quest of identity. Many Africans think that the more foreign they look and behave, the more acceptance they will get. But they forget that there is strength in just accepting their own past, present, and future as their own, and therefore as the source of their own survival.

Could you elaborate on the International Women's Film Festival at Creteil (France). At the 1998 festival there was a focus on African women. What were your experiences?

The focus on African women at Creteil was a good thing because we don't realize how many women are busy shooting in Africa, and on how many formats, and on what variety of subjects! Certainly, Creteil revealed that women in Africa are certainly working on their own image and struggling to get things done, and getting them done! It gave us African women a chance to air our views, show what we are doing, show how diverse we are and in how many colors we come (four of us were white). And, my own film had the honor of "opening the focus on African women" and that felt great. I felt I was treated, to my own surprise, like a star! Well, I had no objection at all!

One of your short films focused on African-German relations. Could you talk about your experiences as a black person in Germany in light of the racial tensions that exist there? There is an active group of Afro-Germans, some of whom I met during their visit to Washington, DC here at Howard University. I have also read the book **Showing Our Colours**. *Have you had any experiences with this group?*

Yes, I knew and worked with some of the Afro-Germans in Berlin. I met the late May Opitz at an Audre Lorde poetry workshop. Audre Lorde encouraged the Afro-Germans to write the book *Showing Our Colours* and I remember it coming out. I was very saddened by the death of the talented, beautiful, and resourceful May Opitz.

The Afro-Germans, mostly raised by white mothers, have had a very depressing past. In fact, their past is distorted by the fact that many of their black fathers never seemed to care for their existence and their white mothers could hardly cope with their lot: society rejected them on account of their black children. One way or the other, few seemed happy to me. It dawned on me that I was very lucky to have had a healthy childhood in Kenya, one in which my identity and purpose seemed clear!

Once, the Afro-Germans invited me to show my film, *A Lover and Killer of Colour* and we traveled together to the venue, Duesseldorf. During a discussion about their parents in the van, I was thrown off-balance by the accusation by one of them: "Do your men have to scatter their sperms everywhere?" I was struck dumb, and I thought later that this should actually be discussed with our African men. In Kenya, we ladies complain about them too: many just dump us as soon as we admit we are pregnant! And sixty percent of Kenyan mothers are single! Over to you, African men!

Nathalie, another friend of mine from the group, has been collecting images of black people on advertisements and she talked about it in my film, *Black in the Western World*. She noted that they are negatively portrayed, too, although this is not obvious at first glance. Others in the film are Mahoma from Malawi, who was hurt during a racist attack; Felix from Namibia, who was also bashed up on some occasion; and Tsitsi Dangarembga from Zimbabwe, who was at that time busy trying to understand life as a black woman in Germany. This film has been shown at community centers in Germany where Germans would get very upset about Africans summarizing their points of view. They would be angry with me! Well, that is their own point of view. But I'm glad I don't do—or feel it is my duty to make—such films anymore. *A Lover and Killer of Colour* won me an interesting comment from a TV editor in 1989 at the Oberhausen Short Film Festival: "It is just like South Africa, uncompromising." And I replied: "Well, South Africa is not free yet!"

The Battle of the Sacred Tree, in its proposal stage, won me the critique: "This is not an African film! Anybody can see that the writer is completely westernized!" That one I could not respond to! It was too "civilized," too modern, too green and lush (location in Kenya), too un-village oriented, that I was declared non-African! Well, this is the film I enjoyed doing most: I was telling a story like any other, albeit on African culture. It is about a group of Christian women who want to be rid of the "primitive, savage and hateful past" by getting the old, sacred tree chopped down. They cannot mobilize people to do it, so they decide to do it themselves; but before they strike it on a moonlit night, they are attacked by God's own creatures, the biting safari ants which live and thrive under the tree. At Mill Valley, they called it "a hilarious comedy of errors" and, apparently, audiences enjoy it very much. It is my pleasure.

You studied and worked in film in Germany and now you are back in Kenya working as a filmmaker. Could you compare your overall experiences in film within a German context and in Kenya, within a Kenyan milieu?

In Germany, there are enough professionals to choose from if you are directing a film. Things are sometimes more organized (depending on the funding, the production conditions, etc.) But in Kenya, one has to rely on a small group of people, most of whom have had no professional training or exposure, especially as heads of their departments, like costume design, properties, film music, scriptwriting, directing, sound, etc. This is one of the areas people need further training in, so that when a film project comes up, you are confident with the crew and you don't end up worrying about details in every department yourself. There have been people who have worked on Hollywood films shot here, but they are employed as runners and third assistants. This means that we have a vicious circle: for chief positions, one might have to resort to a foreign crew! It makes the logistics more complicated and extra funding necessary! But all the same, it is much easier to work with Kenyans because they are friendly, open, humorous, and easy to get along with. Shooting in Kenya is full of pitfalls, but it is more pleasant in the long run.

In the German context, I had a problem of identification: I was asked by a co-student why I made all my films on black people. I asked, why shouldn't I? Of course, it is because I was a foreigner and we shared not only problems of non-acceptance, but a common heritage. And also, if I don't, who is going to do it? The only problem with this is that one ends up in a ghetto—people want to keep you in it. I was getting sucked up in a spiral of having to deal with racism in everything I do—radio programs on black people in Germany, lectures on racism in film, teaching children about Africa, writing poems on my surroundings, etc.

In Kenya, my mind is free to roam into whichever subject it fancies. Nobody asks me everyday, as a matter of course, where I come from and whether I intend to stay in Germany or go back to pest-ridden Africa. The everyday stress is gone. I don't even talk about racism anymore, but about our government, our views on it, etc. And I find people just that much more alive here.

Are you looking to start your own production company?

Though I do not have my own production company so far, I plan to as soon as I can get some capital together to start one. Also, I prefer to be on the artistic, rather than the organizing side! So for now, I am still consolidating my position before I make that jump.

What do you see as your role as a filmmaker?

As a filmmaker, I see my role as a cultural worker. Historical distortions have made Africans lose confidence in themselves. We tend to ignore our past and rush headlong into things American and Western European. A white person commands more respect for us than one of us black people. The whole problem lies in the brainwashing that took place during and after colonialism. In Kenya, for example, African music, religions, and cultural life were prohibited during colonial days. The Christian missionaries convinced us of "the evil which evidently was inherent in our past and present." The promise of going to paradise pertained only to those who abandoned their "primitive" gods and embraced Christianity. Today, everywhere we look, we see terrible symptoms of our injected inferiority complex. A white person gets away with anything in Kenya.

A person who has been to America is a "been-to," as Ama Ata Aidoo, the poetess from Ghana, terms them. In every film I do, I try to correct the negative image we have of ourselves by trying to portray Africans from the human side. Of course, human beings err and are never perfect, but there are also positive sides to us which never surface in films made by outsiders. These I try to include in my films. And if I portray a character as basically negative, it is because we also have such characters, which exist everywhere. It is a quest to question, to probe, to rediscover qualities using cinema as a tool.

Could you talk about African cinema?

African Cinema depends on the maker and his/her location. Francophone films tend to be more anthropological in their approach—Africa revisited like a museum. This is alright, as our past needs reconstructing. But sometimes I get impatient and wish I knew more about the present life and the present struggles. I don't exactly like museums because they show stagnant lives. I like films which connect more to us today or at least depict how things have changed and why. Anglophone films tend to be more development-oriented—again, this is restricting us to a world populated with suffering Africans. Where are the films which embrace the whole character of Africans? Where are the films which can make us laugh, which appeal to our emotions and which show us who we are? I feel the same as a filmmaker (I forget who it is) who said that the greatest appreciative comment for him would be "that one is behaving just like my neighbor next door." In short, African Cinema should also produce films which not only portray life as it is, but have characters whose world is accessible to us today. I mean, villages are nice romantic places, but there are cities in Africa too. There are the high and mighty who can be sub-

155

jects of satirical critique. There are career women and brilliant children. There are normal issues of life.

Could you talk about what is going on in Kenyan cinema? With women in Kenyan cinema?

There have been a few productions in the past few years. Anne Mungai made *Saikati* in 1993, then I made *The Battle of the Sacred Tree* in 1995, Albert Wandago made *Metamo* in 1996, now Anne has launched *Saikati 2*. Dommie O. Yambo is planning *Forbidden* and I am planning *Sweet Sixteen*. It is not very easy to get a film going here, it depends on one's connections. There is no supportive government policy to make our progress easier. There is one in Burkina Faso, which is a much poorer country than ours! Of the above, there are three women and one man. There are other women in the "industry" and they seem more tenacious than the men!

Would you say that a woman's sensibility exists? How would you describe/define it?

A woman's sensibility? Oh yes, definitely. We just have to go into the African literature of this century. African women have not written much, but most of their work has a positive approach. When describing corruption and government, they can be more humorous and more human: they don't read like a grinding thing which drags the reader down. An example is Faty Sow Fall's *The Beggars' Strike* which makes us laugh, but, of course, is a caustic critique of the political hypocrisy which is crippling the continent. Women, I think, are closer to the heart and are more sensitive to emotional lives. A man can be quite dry in the same subject.

What importance do you see in African women taking part in film criticism?

African women should take part in film criticism because they can correct images of themselves and even of their surroundings. Their point of view is important, seeing that they comprise at least half the population of the continent; and also, they can also tell us how they really see men, either as a suppressing group, as husbands, as fathers, as rulers, etc., and be able to pinpoint some discrepancies evident in the way they apparently "are" or how they "think".

Discourse on images of black women in the cinema is emerging as an important category in African film criticism. What are your views?

Black women are very strong people in general, from Africa to the Diaspora. They uphold the societies they live in. They are the ones who struggle against all odds to feed their children. If we look at how they have been portrayed, we notice that there is a big difference in, for example, white films where they are whores (*Mona Lisa*) or big, nice, caring, and subservient Nannies (Hollywood), or creatures in deep trouble (films commissioned by development NGOs), or mythical creatures in some African films. The reality of the strong African woman still needs more emphasis, especially in today's world—where she's fighting a battle of liberation from both traditional and "Victorian" laws which keep her down.

Strong images would give her more confidence to stop believing that she needs to be like this or like that, depending on societal beliefs and notions. I like her image when she is shown to be of an independent mind, when she is not a passive being who is too busy following false tracks laid down for her by others who are more interested in "keeping her in her place." One should give her the opportunity to define where her place is! And cinema, because it allows us to travel in a projected world of the possible, not necessarily the present reality, is a great opportunity!

Amssatou Maiga

Burkina Faso

Interview held at FESPACO 1997 in Ouagadougou, Burkina Faso, combined with several conversations via electronic mail during the summer of 1998. Translated from French.

Buud Yam is a sequel to the film **Wend Kuuni***. The story continues the experiences of the character Wend Kuuni and his sister Poghnéré, as young adults sixteen years later. Poghnéré portrays the same charm as a young adult as she exhibited as a young girl. Could you talk about your character Poghnéré in the film* **Buud Yam***?*

I play the role of Poghnéré in the film *Buud Yam*. In the film *Wend Kuuni* my character is the only daughter and child of my parents. One day I have a brother, and then we live together, we love each other. When I play the part in *Buud Yam*, I feel that it is a certain reality for me. I truly feel that I am living this character in the film.

I was touched by the friendship that your character shared with the young woman who was also the girlfriend of your brother, Wend Kuuni in the film. Did you actually feel a sense of kinship towards her?

In *Buud Yam*, she was a friend that I had since childhood. She was a friend of Poghnéré' in *Wend Kuuni* and the friendship continues in *Buud Yam*. We grew up and matured together, she is my best friend in the film. Because Poghnéré and her friend are so close, they were often called twins. If you look closely in the film, you find that their mothers are also very good friends. They were also childhood friends who grew up together, married, and supported each other, and they continue to be friends.

While Serge Yanogo played the same character in both **Wend Kuuni** *and* **Buud Yam,** *Rosine Yanogo played the role of Poghnéré in Wend Kuuni. How were you chosen for the role of Poghnéré for the film* **Buud Yam?**

It was a great pleasure for me to have acted in *Buud Yam.* I attended a casting where several young women were present. I passed the first casting and then there was a second one. During the third casting, I was told that I was chosen to play the role, and I was very happy.

Actors certainly contribute to the image of African women in the cinema. What has been your impression of the visual representation of African women in the cinema? Do you feel that as an actor you can contribute to the positive image of African women?

I don't know if I can say that I have really thought about it, the African woman in cinema. Well, people have not really seen the importance of the woman in African cinema. Perhaps when they see a woman acting in a film, they don't give much significance to the role of the African woman. Perhaps in seeing a film such as *Buud Yam,* or if other films are made with more roles for women, things will evolve. So, yes, I think that perhaps with the little experience that I have that I can contribute to the positive representation of images of women.

Gaston Kaboré was awarded the Etalon de Yennenga [the grand prize of FESPACO] for the film **Budd Yam.** *What was your reaction?*

Like everyone else in life, one is allowed to dream. During the festival, my dream was to win the greatest prize. In fact, that is what happened. I was very, very happy, for myself in particular, because it was the first time that I acted in a film—and, on top of that, in a feature film by one of the great filmmakers, Gaston Kaboré. I was also very happy for the entire team because everybody did such a beautiful job, a job that merited such a grand reward as the Etalon de Yennenga. I must say that I was very touched that day.

Of course, you were quite young when the film **Wend Kuuni** *was first made in 1981. Nevertheless, the film has become quite a legend in Burkina Faso and still continues to be shown even today. Do you remember when you first saw the film as a young girl?*

Yes, I remember very well having seen *Wend Kuuni* when I was a little girl. I don't even remember how many times I have seen the film.

Do you remember how you felt about the film then? What were your general reactions and, in particular, your impressions of little Poghnéré?

In general, I remember liking the film very much. When I saw it for the first time, the personality of the two young actors is what impressed me the most. They had two very important roles and they were able to embody the characters with such subtlety. They were quite admirable. I always enjoy seeing the film again and again, if for nothing but to admire little Poghnéré. I think she did so well in her role. While I don't know for sure, she certainly must have attended acting classes. Otherwise, how could one explain such a wonderful performance? Perhaps I may be exaggerating somewhat, but it was top-notch acting.

Having followed little Poghnéré yourself as a little girl, did you ever imagine that as a sequel, when Poghnéré grows into a young woman, that you could actually play the role?

Sincerely, I never imagined that I could be Poghnéré. But as one is wont to say, life is full of surprises, even the greatest of surprises. In reality, it was as if I was dreaming. As I said before, I was very, very excited about having been chosen for the role. When I was chosen for the first casting I thought certainly it must be a mistake. Then when I was called for the second casting I realized that this was really serious. I began to think about what I was going to do on the set, because, in fact, I had never acted in this capacity before. It's true that I had acted in a school play, but that was far from the reality of acting in a film. I felt an enormous responsibility when I learned that I was chosen to play the role of Poghnéré. Later I realized that nothing was impossible in life and that I would simply do my best, what the director expected of me. As I can tell, it turned out very well.

Perhaps the legendary Princess Yennenga gives you a double sense of pride. She was an important female figure in Burkinabé history and the grand prize of FESPACO bears her image. How did you learn about Yennenga? Were you taught about her legend at school?

Yes, at the primary school level we are taught about the history of Yennenga. Yennenga was a princess of the Mossi Kingdom and a great warrior who fought in defense of her kingdom. Hers is a history of an entire people.

How do you feel when you see your image on the big screen? What impression does it give you?

I don't know if other actors have the same reaction, but when I see my image on the screen I only see the negative aspects. I think, "Ah, I could have done better." In other words, I correct myself while viewing my image on the screen. However, in the final analysis, the audience can better judge the actor.

What are some future projects? Another film perhaps?

I don't know. This is my first film, so I don't know quite what I will do next.

What kind of work do you do when you are off-screen?

I pursued secretarial studies and I am now working as a medical secretary in a pharmacy. I enjoy my work very much.

Sarah Maldoror

Guadeloupe/Angola

Interview held at the 15th FESPACO in February 1997, Ouagadougou, Burkina Faso. Translated from French.

While you are from the African Diaspora, you hold an important place in African cinema. Several of your films have focused on themes of struggle in Africa, such as the internationally acclaimed film **Sambizanga**. *What is African cinema to you?*

First, for me, African cinema does not exist. African cinema will exist when it is seen first in Africa. When Africans go to see African films, it can be said that an African cinema exists. For the moment, we are making films for others. That is the drama of African cinema.

You came to cinema during the decade of African independence. Much of your political awareness, which is reflected in your work, was sharpened during that period. What was it like during that time—the spirit of that era, the interests of African filmmakers at that time?

I came to cinema during the years of African independence. Before independence there was not an African cinema, and even now that there are African films, what do you really call an African cinema? Before there is a cinema that can be called African, there must first be a national cinema. And for there to be a national cinema, there must be cinema houses, there must be a sufficient number of African films. African films must be seen by Africans. They must go see their own films with their faults or whatever. There must first be an African public!

You are Guadeloupean, a woman of the African Diaspora who has made films in Africa, about Africa, as well as films with a focus on Africans from the Diaspora. Where do you situate yourself within African cinema?

Of course, I have done many films in Africa. But I feel, in the first place, that there are no borders. Let's get that straight! Whether it is in Africa, in Guadeloupe, or the United States. What I am saying is that cinema is the only art where there are no borders. Of course, I feel much closer to Africa than I do to the United States.

But at the same time, I am affected by the United States and its tremendous will to crush the world. I feel that on this point you Americans hold your own very well. Your cinema is everywhere. You have imposed your cinema. There is not one person in the world who does not know a Western or an American film in general. You have imposed yourself, and we must protect ourselves from you. You have invaded the world with your Westerns. And you have all the right to do so, but what can we do? Today, can anyone do without American cinema? No. We even go to see *Malcolm X*. You Black Americans have a cinema, you go to watch your own films as well as others, which is not our case. That is where your strength lies.

*The themes that you treat in your films are in general what are called **engagé**. You have a commitment to the history of the liberation struggles of African peoples. Do you feel that this is your role as a filmmaker?*

What do you want me to do? What films do you want me to make otherwise? When I see all these short films that are being made at the moment, I don't know if you have seen them, where the black woman is portrayed only as a whore. It's disgusting because the black woman is not that. There are women who work, there are women who are honest, there are women who fight for their children. But now, one has the impression that the more often black women take off their bras, that they are shown nude...I say no! Of course, some of that does exist. There are women who act that way. But that is not all there is. And that is what disturbs me!

How, then, do you see your role as filmmaker?

My role as filmmaker is cultural. What interests me is culture, to research films about African history, because our history has been written by others and not by us. Therefore, if I don't take an interest in my own

164

history, then who is going to do it? I think it is up to us to defend our own history. It is up to us to make it known, with all our qualities and faults, our hopes and despair—it is our role to do it!

You say that you are disappointed in the portrayal of African women in contemporary African films. Would you say that the representation of women in earlier African films was more positive?

At the present time, there seems to be a descent into hell. In earlier films, you would have never seen an African woman, a black woman naked. But now, it is difficult to find a film in which a woman has a particular reason for undressing. She seems to undress for no apparent reason at all. I find that offensive. As a woman, I have had enough of these images. Other things must be shown. If the kinds of films that I do are what you call *engagé*...I think that without a political stand we will never get out of our present condition.

Although my purpose is not to bring up a drama of the past, I would like to talk about an event that happened several years ago and it appears that it has not yet been resolved. In 1991, FESPACO devoted a part of its platform to a workshop for African women in the cinema. Unfortunately, the tension between African and African diasporan women brought out quite a bit of emotion. You attended the conference. Could you talk about the events and how you felt about it?

We were told to leave because we were not considered African. We are in Africa, of course I am African. Certainly, my parents were Africans. Why am I Guadeloupean? Because my parents were sold into slavery. I am part of the group of Africans who were enslaved and deported. I am part of that deportation, but I am African, Antillian perhaps, but I could have also been born in America and be a Black American today. Therefore, when we were told to leave because we were not African, what could I have done otherwise?

Such a lack of culture! I don't know what else to say: I was stunned. There were women who came from the United States, they were told to leave. What difference is there between a Black American, an African, and me? We all come from the same land. I found it outrageous. That is why we will never get out of our condition, because we cannot accept ourselves. *Voilá!*

Yet you have done films in Africa, about African history. You are accorded the status of Angolan within the context of African cinema. How, then, can you be told that you are not African? What determines who is African?

165

Let me say this: yesterday I presented a film about Léon Damas. It is a film where Leopold Senghor and Aimé Césaire discuss the works of Damas, it was not in competition. Why it was not in competition, I have no idea. All the other films throughout the festival were shown three times, in cinema houses here in the center of town.

However, my film was screened in a faraway location, in an area that was extremely dangerous. There were three people in the cinema house. Three! Of course, I am grumbling, and no one can make me keep quiet. I was there to present my film to three people. However, every morning in the cinema houses where I went to see other documentaries, afterwards when someone asked, "Is the filmmaker present," the answer was nearly always "No." I am sent to the other end of the earth and I go, even to present to three people. I complain perhaps because I cannot accept this treatment, and because I am not accepted. I am not welcomed here at FESPACO.

Perhaps because you say what you think, because your films make very strong statements.

I don't know, but I will not be silenced. That is over. I am not of a generation that keeps quiet.

I see you as a pioneer in African cinema. You studied film in the ex-Soviet Union with Ousmane Sembene. You worked alongside the others who debuted some thirty years ago. What do you think about the evolution of African cinema?

To the contrary, it has gone backwards. I think that there has not been any criticism about the kinds of films that are being made. I am for anyone who wants to make a film to be able to do so. However, if we never say that a film is not good, then any and everybody will become a director, even if they have no talent. If they have nothing at all to offer they will make a film, and no one will say the film is bad. Because if they do, one will say, "It's because I am black you are saying this; therefore, you are racist."

I say no, I can make a film and I can fail. I failed because I made a bad film, I did not fail because I am black. Which means that now everybody is making films, yet there is no critique to judge if it succeeded or not. So what do we want? The more films we have that are average, mediocre, and minor, the more black culture will be stifled and crushed. And we are going to accept that? Well! Well!

You say that now anybody can be a filmmaker without there being a real film criticism that addresses the quality of the work. What do you think the criteria should be for making films? Should everyone go through film school? What specific training should one have?

Training is necessary. If you go to school, good for you, but if you do not, it does not matter. If you work as an assistant to, I don't know, Milos Forman or Spike Lee, you are learning your craft. That is actually the best school, learning is what is the most important. Whereas today, there is the attitude: I am going to make a film, no matter what, and here it is!

Do you feel that at the beginning of African cinema, for instance, during the time when you started, that there were some real differences in terms of approaches to filmmaking, compared to today?

I would say there were certain morals at that time. *Voilá!* We thought, perhaps mistakenly so, that we were respectful of a country that we did not know, of a history that was misunderstood. This history was to be respected; we believed in it. I think that is what is lacking now.

Do you think that filmmakers of today are more attracted to images and experiences, or things in general, that happen outside of their countries, and perhaps they are not as interested in their own history?

Of course. For instance, pornography is in fashion. They think: "This is what is being made in other films, therefore, let's put some pornography in our film."

Do you think that it comes from filmmakers wanting to attract the largest possible public?

Of course. It is very simple: I make a film about the great poets Léon Damas, Leopold Senghor, and Aimé Césaire, and no one comes to see it. I went to see a film early this morning where the African woman was portrayed as a prostitute and the cinema house was packed full. It is evident that the filmmaker who made this film has a public, and that I do not. That is also the reality. So who is right, he or I? The public or I? I think it's that simple.

There is much discussion about the problems of the distribution and exhibition of African films in general. What are your thoughts?

There is no actual distribution of African films because Africans do not go to see African films. They will go see an American, French, German, or English film. But they will not go see African films because they find them inferior. And, as I said before, as long as there is not an African public who will go to see African films, there will not be an African cinema.

There may be African films, but there is not an African cinema. There is a Japanese cinema because the Japanese go to see Japanese films. There is an American cinema because Americans go to see their own films. So as long as we do not go to see our own films we cannot say there is an African cinema. It's not true.

And the exhibition of films?

There is none. You saw the condition of the cinema houses!

Do you have an audience for your films? What has been the reception of your latest film?

It depends. If the film is shown outside of Africa I do well, generally. I have very good reviews. The film about Léon Damas received awards everywhere. However, I do not follow my films, or else I would spend all my time at festivals; either they will receive an award or not. Then I go to Africa, and not only is it not chosen to be in competition, but also, on top of that, my film is screened on the other side of the world. And of course, that is disappointing. It is an insult. Moreover, it is a total disregard for Damas, a show of contempt for Césaire, indifference toward Senghor. It is disrespect for literature in general. I have no choice but to accept this, but I will fight nonetheless.

In spite of your disappointment about the state of African cinema, what do you see as the future of African cinema?

We must do greater films now. We must get away from the "calabash films," the "village films," the little stories. Now we must take history and look at it as it is, with its convictions, with its ideas, for or against its principles. We must do these films with space and greatness, really!

And your future projects? Are you working on a film at the moment?

I am working on a film about Louis Delgrès, who was a colonel and a violinist. You know, today everyone can study music. If you have children who want to play the piano or the violin, they can do so. Of course, if you have money, they can study whatever kind of music they want. But can you imagine in 1789, during that time, what it meant to be a violinist? Well, it was pretty extraordinary.

Delgrès fought with the French army against the English. When Napoléon reestablished slavery, he did not accept it. He fought and he lost because the French and the English—who previously fought against the French—joined together in a collaborative attempt to defeat the black army. This same black army fought against the English alongside the French army. I am going to do a film about this man.

Have you begun filming?

I am looking for funding.

Ouméma Mamadali

Comoros

Interview held at the 15th FESPACO, February 1997, Ouagadougou, Burkina Faso. Translated from French.

*It was interesting how you used storytelling to bring together the issues of democracy, gender, and the economy in the Comoros Islands. Could you talk about your film, **Baco**, and the themes that you addressed in the film?*

Well, it is my first film. I have done short documentaries in Comoros about the problems in the agricultural sector, and about peasants. However, in terms of fiction films, this is my first professional fiction film. I co-directed *Baco* with a man named Kabire Fidaali.

The story takes place in Comoros and is, in fact, a satire on democracy in the Third World, but the story is presented in the form of a tale. A child recalls what happened in his family. It is a story about his father, who has several wives. Ninety-nine percent of Comorians are Muslims. Baco, which means the elder, the wise man, or the grandfather, is the principal character. He is married to ten women, has fifty children and a hundred or so grandchildren. He is a peasant who lives a relatively comfortable lifestyle because he owns several plantations.

I will note that Comoros is the premier producer in the world of fragrant flowers, and in particular *ilang-ilang*. *Ilang* is a flower that goes through a distillation process and its oil serves as a base for all the great perfumes. Baco has several plantations where he cultivates *ilang*.

He begins to notice that his wives, children, and grandchildren do not agree with him anymore. Because the price of *ilang* has fallen considerably, they no longer want to plant it. There is a protest in the family, and Baco decides to call democratic-style elections to choose a chief of the clan, who is the person who will manage the domain.

Could you talk about cinema in Comoros? Are there other Comorian films?

Cinema in Comoros starts with this film. There has never been a Comorian film. Before two years ago, there was not even television. Moreover, there is not yet a national television in Comoros. The film was co-produced by Cinéjou Productions, a small French company, and MTC (Musamudu Télé Culture), a small community television company, which was created thanks to the initiative of a few Comorians. So this is truly the first Comorian film.

Therefore, this is a first and an important Comorian contribution to African cinema....

Yes, yes, definitely so.

What are your thoughts about African cinema? What does it represent for you?

African cinema, in my view, is a cinema on its own.... At the present time I have the impression that everybody, even the European audiences, are drowned out by U.S. culture. I even think that this is a pretty critical state because soon we will no longer have our own culture. There is a mass of information that comes from the United States, and everyone is becoming attracted to the same things. While I would differentiate African cinema from this, at the same time, it has difficulty finding a place in the world of cinema.

You stated that it has only been two years since television exists in Comoros. Does that also mean that there are no cinema houses?

Yes there are, but we cannot really talk about cinema because the theaters are closed in Comoros. There are several neighboring regions that came together to buy a videocassette player and monitor, and every night people gather and watch television together. I would say that it is a community television. People come together in families and they all watch it together.

Generally, the programs are broadcast from the TV5 channel, CFI, and there are many Indian films. The Comorians, as all other Africans, are very fond of these films. Otherwise, cinema does not exist, or no longer exists. Cinema houses have since closed because of the lack of means to maintain the theaters. There are a few projectors that no longer work and Comoros has been completely abandoned by everyone. If you look at other African countries that receive a lot of funding from France, Canada, and different other francophone countries, you will see that Comoros has been completely abandoned.

So *Baco* is the first film. Of course, it will take some time to make people aware that there is a cinema that is coming alive in Comoros. That is why I thank you for giving me the opportunity to speak about it.

What are your thoughts on the emergence of African women in African cinema?

Up to the present time, we see a good many filmmakers who are men; it is true that there are not many women in the cinema. Now women are making films in greater numbers, documentary and fiction. We are seeing a sensibility in these films that is different from men. It is true that the subjects of the films made by women are more touching, when it concerns the woman directly.

In Africa, the woman has a role that is very different from the Western woman. It is true that there are many problems that concern women. The subject of a film made by women is treated in a way that is particular to women, with a woman's sensibility. I feel that each person who creates something has a sensibility that is superior to someone else's. However, the fact that it comes from a woman means that there is a different perspective than that of a man, *vis-à-vis* the problems of women. I made the film with Kabire Fidaali, who is a man, and to have worked with a man allowed the subject to be treated from two different angles; it brings a richness as well.

You stated that you see a certain sensibility particular to women. How would you characterize this sensibility?

A woman's sensibility, well, I don't know exactly how to describe it. Perhaps it would be to actually see films made by women, and then sense this perspective. One may perhaps feel that it is more touching when a woman talks about her grandmother, her mother, the conditions of women, of her family; it is another vision. Because it is a real-life experience, you understand.

Would you say that this sensibility is specific to African women?

I think it is universal: you can find this perspective in a film made by a woman in France or other countries. I can sense this sensibility in a subject treated by a woman, but that is a personal observation. I think a woman has a different way of looking. It is complementary. I also find that male filmmakers have done exceptional work in their treatment of the condition of the African woman, of the Muslim woman, and these films are very touching.

There is another thing, when we are involved in it; it is sometimes difficult to separate ourselves from the subject. I think that is the danger of being a woman and dealing with the problems of women. As in any research, when we are directly concerned we must know how to keep a certain distance in order to show something. It is up to the individual woman to know how to do this.

You speak about a certain complementary vision that a woman brings. You worked with Kabire Fidaali, who is a man. Could you describe this feminine/masculine complementarity that was present in making the film together?

It was a very special collaboration. Kabire is Malagasy and lives in Madagascar, but spends every vacation in Comoros; I was born in Comoros. Also there is a difference in age, Kabire is much older than me; he is fifty and I am thirty. However, at two different periods we were taught the same thing. We grew up in a similar environment. Although we have a different perspective as a woman and a man, we have a similar sensibility that allows us to create something together. I think there is a richness that comes from working with a man and a possibility to be able to discover a common sensibility and way of seeing things. Even though there is a twenty-year difference in age between us, for me it has been a very rich experience.

Would you say that he has discovered and appreciates your sensibility as a woman?

Yes indeed. First of all, it is very difficult for two people to make something together, it takes a great effort. As I just stated, we have something in common. We have a vision that is complementary, as a woman and man. For example, the personality of the women in the film evolved from our combined effort. We wrote the dialogue together. I had my ideas but he added to them. And that is what is very rich. I think the roles of the women, as well as the men, would have been different if I had work with a woman.

While you and Kabire directed the film together, you both had specific tasks. What was the division of work between you and Kabire?

174

The film was made thanks to the work of Kabire. He trained the technicians while he was in Comoros. It was truly his personal and private initiative, with the help of no one. With a small television subsidiary, Kabire trained the entire crew. Now, thanks to him, Comoros has a technical crew capable of making films. I do not have the technical capabilities, Kabire was the technical partner and I did the producing and writing. Kabire did the camera; he trained a sound person on location. I did the directing and *mise en scene.*

So Kabire Fidaali developed the complete training program from start to finish?

Yes, it was Kabire who developed the program entirely. In fact, he taught here in Ouagadougou at INAFEC (Institut Africain d'Education Cinématographique). He taught cinematography at the film school at the University of Ouagadougou.

How did you begin your collaboration with Kabire?

He came to this project as a professional; for me it was an adventure. I had not done film studies at all. I plunged into it while looking for work. I had studied Asian languages, then received a Master's in communications, and afterwards I was looking for work. When I did not find work, I began writing. My father manages this small community television in Comoros. He was working on a project for a short film while I was visiting him, and he suggested, since I had nothing to do, that I should write a story. Then, everything evolved from that. I had known Kabire for a long time, since he is a friend of my father. I showed him what I had written and he was very enthusiastic about it. Then we started working on it and here is the result.

How has your film been distributed and exhibited so far?

For the moment, *Baco* has been viewed only by Comorians, because I have not yet been able to show it elsewhere. However, I think that it is mainly a problem of finding important contacts. I am a newcomer to this profession. In the world of cinema, people know each other; for the moment I don't know anyone. FESPACO is my first festival; I hope that I can show my film elsewhere. It is a télé-film, it is not cinema, but on the level of television broadcasting, I hope that it will interest someone.

What was the reception of this film in Comoros?

It was quite particular: the women liked the film very much, and the men felt frustrated. It is true that it was the women and not the men who said all the important things. Towards the end of the story, the people realize that it is a woman who is winning the elections and not a man. A man stands up and says, "These elections must be recalled, it's a disgrace," although it is one of Baco's daughters who is winning in the elections.

In Comoros, it is interesting because it is a Muslim society, but it is based on a matriarchal system. When the woman marries, her father must build a house for his daughter and it is the husband who goes to live with his wife. That is surprising in comparison to other Muslim countries, where this is not found. In Comoros, the woman has a great deal of power. Through her spouse or son, she decides everything, and she is the one behind every decision. In the cultural arena, it is the woman who comes out often and who organizes the events. I think that may be the case in many parts of Africa. But in any case, in Comoros, the women are much more dynamic and hardworking than the men.

This is you first film. Is this the beginning of a career in the cinema?

I don't know if it will lead to a career. I hope so. Because, you know, once one gets a taste of it, it's contagious. There is a desire to continue and do more. I have finished a second script and this time it will be a feature film, again set in Comoros. Because I want to make my country known. Now that the script is finished, I am looking for funding to shoot it, again in collaboration with Kabire. Once we find that we work well together, we want to continue.

Salem Mekuria

Ethiopia

Interview held at the 15th FESPACO, February 1997, Ouagadougou, Burkina Faso.

I saw your film **Deluge** *at the Ethiopian Mini-Film Festival in Washington, DC in 1996. I found it very intense and engaging. It is also being screened here at FESPACO. Could you talk a bit about your film?*

The film is titled *Deluge* in English, it is called *Ye Wonz Maibel* in Amharic. It is a sixty-minute documentary, a personal story talking about an historical event. I finished it a year ago, but then I re-cut it so that it could be transferred to film so that it would be shown in festivals. It is on 16mm film and that is how it is being screened here.

You narrate the film and you talk about your own personal process and how you felt while making the film. You also talk about going to Ethiopia to do the research and the shooting. Could you talk about your experiences while making the film?

In the film, the story that comes through is a personal journey. The time line of the story is from the end of the Haile Selassie era to the end of the military dictatorship, which happened between 1974 and 1991. But the making of the film itself has its own time line.

I started working on it in 1991, right after the fall of the military dictatorship, at which time I went home deliberately to make a film about that period. Basically, I started researching and filming at the same time because I didn't know exactly when the military dictatorship was going to end and how or what I was going to do about it, although that thought was in my head for most of the time since my brother disappeared.

When I went home in 1991, I took my camera with me and started talking to people. I really didn't know exactly what I was looking for or what I was going to end up doing. And so for three years, basically, I went back. Twice I went with a crew and started talking to everybody I could find who was willing to talk about that experience. Then I would come back and start to edit it. My initial thought was to make this big official history: this happened, this happened to so and so. But it became so unwieldy; every time I would come back and put together a rough-cut of some sort, I couldn't stand it myself, let alone other people who were not as close to the story as I was.

Eventually, after a lot of cuts, after a lot of thinking, then I realized that I was not really looking for the official story, I was looking for that personal story, what happened to my brother. And what happened to my best friend. So with the help of my daughter, who could see a lot clearer than I could at the time, because I was too overwhelmed with the magnitude of this story, I realized that that was what I wanted to do.

Eventually the final product came through as both a journey for me, in terms of trying to discover what happened—although I don't discover exactly what happened—but also as a personal journey as to how I understood this story, what my part was in it, what my brother's part was in it, and how that fit into the big official story. That really was what eventually came out.

Did the impetus for the way you tell the story come out of your being, I don't know if I could say, in self-exile, or as an Ethiopian diasporan?

Part of the difficulty in telling the big story was that I was not there when it happened. So, as a distant observer, I had a lot of discomfort in saying this happened and this happened. It was just too distant for me. Part of it also had to do with my feeling, "Who am I to tell this official story when I was not even there?" So yes, part of it was being away from it, although I didn't call myself or consider myself an exile, because it wasn't something I wanted to identify with. I always dreamed about going back the next year and the next year. So exile would mean, sort of saying, "I am here" and I still don't admit to that, I guess that's my difficulty. But yes, it had a lot to do with the fact that I wasn't there. It wasn't a story that I had the authority to tell.

I finally got closer and closer to that thing that really concerned me, that was the impetus in the first place for me to want to do something about it, which was the disappearance of my brother. Then I discovered the relationship between my brother and my best friend, in terms of the movement and the revolution, and what happened to the two of them who ended up on opposite sides, basically, and eventually they both died, fighting on opposite sides. That, to me, made it my story. I was capable of telling that story.

Fortunately, my brother was a great letter writer. He wrote me everything he thought, everything that he saw happening, so that dialogue was already there, with my brother. During our letter writing I asked my brother questions and he gave me some of the answers I did not have because I was not there. That enabled me to have a certain perspective and I got rid of the problem of the exile telling that story.

I also incorporated my daughter, who was born in the United States, and grew up in the United States, and really had no direct connection to that story. Through her need to know about my brother, I was able to bring her into it, too. So it became a family history.

There is an English and an Amharic version of the film. How has the reception been of both versions?

Many Ethiopians who have seen both versions tell me that they have a different relationship with the Amharic version. The emotional relationship has a lot more depth in the Amharic version than in the English version. The English version is closer to sort of an official history. The Amharic version is more personal, they say, because it incorporates that connection to the language, the culture. There are some phrases I could not translate into English correctly, to elicit that emotional attachment. In Amharic it was there, there was no need to struggle to make sense: "What is she saying?"

I also eliminate the tension between the subtitle and what the people are saying. There is always that. Even when I am watching the English version I tend to struggle between not seeing the subtitle and just hearing the people; that was eliminated. So they had a lot more direct connection with what was said. They said they were much closer to the Amharic version. I am myself much closer to the Amharic version.

How about the non-Amharic speakers who had to rely on the English version?

Well, actually, nobody from the groups who do not understand Amharic, who are Ethiopians, has come to tell me the difference. Because when it was screened in Addis Ababa it was the Amharic version that was screened. And there were a lot of people who came from different groups, but they basically did understand Amharic.

But the emotional experience I am pretty sure is different for people who are not totally Amharic speakers from the beginning or people who learned Amharic in school and who are now Amharic speakers. I am sure it is different.

I suppose I was thinking about people like myself.

Oh, non-Ethiopians. Well, for them English is the only way that they can get into the story. It's been phenomenal, the response. I really didn't expect that it would touch in the way that people have told me they have been touched. I really didn't understand how universal this story could be, being told from a very personal point of view and I guess that is the answer.

It was a human experience it was a story of loss—you lose a brother, you lose a best friend. Your best friend and your brother fight against each other, they die eventually, and nothing was gained by it. Those kinds of stories are very universal. I didn't think about that when I was finally figuring out that that was what I wanted to do.

As an African woman filmmaker, would you say that you take on a certain role because of your gender? What role do you want to play as a woman filmmaker— or perhaps I should ask, do you see yourself playing a certain role as a woman?

When I'm working, I don't think necessarily that I would operate as a woman filmmaker. It's when I am in front of an audience that I know I'm being looked at as a representative of some rare sort, especially as an African woman or as a black woman in the United States, and I feel somewhat responsible, to be responsible. Because I think we have a lot of work to do, I feel that if I don't do well maybe others won't get the same chance that I have. I'm privileged in many ways, that I have been able to do what I want to do, and so I feel like I should be so responsible sometimes, to make sure that I don't destroy...that I don't burn bridges for other women coming after me. It's not an easy thing to be, and maybe because I am always the responsible sort, I don't know, sometimes I feel that there is a burden that I have to carry. But at other times I feel really terribly privileged to be doing something that I love doing.

At other times I feel like I have to focus on stories about women because there aren't that many films being made about stories about women, by women especially. It's a mixed bag. There is real happiness that I am doing this, and there's a certain kind of tension of whether or not I can chose to do anything I want to do. Do I always have to focus in areas where I feel there is a lack? Do I have to fill a vacuum? Those thoughts go in my head at times.

But I love doing stories about women. Even when it has nothing to do with women particularly. For example, in *Deluge* I gravitate towards including women, more women than men, getting stories from the women because I feel that their perspective is neglected. So I feel that is my role as a woman filmmaker. I also feel that I can do it better, because I feel that women open up more to me than they do to men, or they open up in different ways than with men. There is a certain comfort, there's a certain kind of shared experience, they don't have to explain to me. So I feel I have a better handle sometimes in getting some of the stories from women. I feel that is also a part of my role as a woman filmmaker.

How about as an Ethiopian woman filmmaker? Are there other Ethiopian women filmmakers?

No, but I think there are some coming up. And I am really looking forward to sharing my experience with them. In exile, in the large Diaspora, as far as I know, as a practicing filmmaker—and there are three or four films that I've made—I'm the only Ethiopian. But there are other women in Ethiopia who are employed in the government. Especially as an independent, there is only me.

But there are women in school now, there are women coming up. There are women who have just graduated who are struggling to make their first film. There is hope. One of the discomforts actually of being an Ethiopian, or African, or Black woman, is that you are sort of looked at as a rare bird. I am not the sort of person who likes the spotlight and when they push you in there I sometimes resent that. I am not rare, I just had the opportunity that I was able to grab and others were not. I was just in the right place when there were doors opened. That's part of the discomfort.

In 1991, there was a workshop for African women in cinema here at FESPACO, where women throughout the continent met for the first time. Were you involved in the meeting?

No; my first time at FESPACO was in 1993.

Have you been involved in the association that has been formed as a result of that? I know that there is an Eastern Africa regional branch as well.

181

No, it's very difficult. The distance, the lack of resources. We don't have the infrastructure, we don't have time. I'm teaching and making films and raising a child by myself. Also we don't know each other really, unless we meet at places like this. Some work in their homes, some work everywhere around the world. I have no way of being involved.

I am now really trying very hard, not only with women, but with other Ethiopian filmmakers, to set up some kind of structure so that we can communicate and share ideas, and perhaps even resources that we can share with each other, so that we can enable each other to work, and know about each other's work. I know that the first time that Ethiopian filmmakers saw my work was when I went back to Ethiopia last August. Before that I had made three films, they had never seen anything that I had done. It's really hard. In short, I don't know what's going on with the organization, if there is one.

Zanele Mthembu

South Africa

Interviews held at FESPACO, February 1997 and in Washington, DC, June 1997.

You have a background in television and are now adding to your experience in the media by studying film. Could you first talk about how you became involved in the media?

I started in television in 1992 and I worked as a production assistant, with the aim of becoming a director. I started out with a small company that had a very good reputation in South Africa and has done a lot of documentaries, educational programs, dramas, and so on. I was there for about four months when the producer decided she wanted me to direct my own program. I did a short five-minute program for prime time. The show was something similar to "Good Morning America" in the United States. It was actually called "Good Morning South Africa." The program that I did focused on how violence affects children in South Africa.

The producer realized that I had a lot of potential, so from that time on I started directing my own documentaries on educational programs. I covered issues on health, housing, and voter election programs for the elections. We did profiles on all the main people who were running for election at the time. I worked on a lot of topics for the South African Broadcasting Corporation, mainly on burning issues in South Africa, educational programs in particular.

Did you come to television through a training program or did you study at the university?

I have an Honor's degree in communication and I majored in broadcasting in South Africa, which is equivalent to a four-year degree in the United

States. My main focus was education and the media, particularly television and education. The education system in our country is structured in such a way that a lot of hands-on experience is not available at school because of the lack of facilities, equipment, and that kind of thing. I only got hands-on experience when I started working for Penguin Films in South Africa. It was the first time, in fact, that I understood the whole process of pre-production, production, and post-production. I really began to appreciate what goes on during those phases because we had never really gone into that at school. I was actually thrown into it when I did the children's program.

Could you talk about some of the programs that you worked on?

Everything that I did was for the national television, the South African Broadcasting Corporation. The programs that I made were for the different channels that we had within the South African Broadcasting Corporation. Most of the programs were in English, subtitled in the different ethnic languages, while others would be only in English targeted for the main English-language channels. Some were made for either morning or evening prime time.

What were the African languages used?

Zulu and Sesotho. One channel was for mainly Zulu-speaking people and the other channel was for Sesotho-speaking people. The decision was made that certain programs would be subtitled in Sesotho, and some programs in Zulu. Most of interviews that we did with the people were in their own languages.

Why were the programs mostly in English with subtitles? Even though these programs were subtitled in Zulu and Sesotho, didn't it mean that people who were not literate in those languages and did not understand English would not have access?

It was the executive producers who made the decisions on the languages used. And at that time I was not part of the decision-making structure. As I became more involved in these decisions, I had a lot more input on what should be done and I could talk about the expectations of the people. Being a black South African and having grown up with other people making decisions about the kind of programming we saw, I now had a lot to say about it. However, the ultimate decisions were still out of my hands, really, because the people much higher up were the ones who made the decisions about the language used. The reason that was generally given was that more people understood English, since we have actually nine ethnic languages in South Africa. Zulus make up about sixty or seventy percent, then Sothos, and then the others.

It was unfortunate that I never had the kind of influence that was necessary to change the thinking. I had no access to the people who had the money and the people who were making the decisions. I had no access to those decision-making structures. But my belief is, and what I have seen indicates that the programs that really have an impact are those programs that are made in the people's languages.

The other problem in South Africa is that we still do not have regional television. Everything is centrally controlled. All the broadcasting is done nationally. There is no regional broadcasting like in the United States (where, for instance, you have a local Fox television station in Washington, DC dealing with issues in the Washington, DC area). With national broadcasting it is easier to control what goes out to people.

Could you talk about your evolution from television to film studies and why you want to add film to your media experiences?

One of the main reasons that I wanted to move into film as well was when I realized that a whole lot of documentaries are actually made on film. I had never realized that when working in television—because we aired most of the films from Beta SP—that there are a lot of connections between film and video. These films are shot on celluloid, transferred to video, and broadcast on television. I want to learn the process of making film and the connection between the two media. I want to know the chain from film to television and how that works. Coming to the United States was the only way that I saw that I could get that information and experience. At the Discovery Channel, where I work, everything is shot on 16mm, and some on Super 16. Wildlife films are shot on 35mm for television broadcast and brought down to Beta SP. I am learning about the various steps that take place before a film is aired, such as quality control, and so on.

You are currently a film student, why did you choose the United States, and why Howard University?

It so happened that I got a scholarship at the Discovery Channel. In order to be close to the headquarters, which is in Bethesda, Maryland, the most logical step for me was to go to the nearest film school, which is at Howard University. And the fact that it is a historically black school, well, I thought that would be fine.

Could you describe some of your experiences as a student, and some of your interests?

At Howard University there is a lot of hands-on experience, one has to do it oneself, which gives one a better idea of what goes into being a director of photography, how to do the sound, how to edit. It gives a holistic idea of what goes on in filmmaking, which is a good thing for me, because when one goes back to edit, one realizes the mistakes, the missed shots. This builds directorial skills. In the editing room is where it all happens.

What are some of your objectives when you return to South Africa after your studies in the United States?

I think the biggest influence I can have is as a producer because it is in that capacity that one can really make decisions about what goes out. Producers make editorial decisions, they are the people who put everything together. That is where I want to be, but at the same time I would also want to direct and edit what I do, to have the control of the material and the means of putting that material together.

I am picking up a lot since I have been with the Discovery Channel. I have contacts with producers, people who can make programs. And having been back home and looking at how things are done has really made me realize that I need to be able to be in the structures where decisions are being made, and if you have the kind of education that I am getting here, you get that respect.

In addition, I won't have to rely on an editor to edit things the way that I see them and the way that I believe that my people will see them. I think that a lot of black South Africans like myself will see images in the same way that I do because we have the same kind of background, we grew up under the same conditions, and I know the kinds of things that made us very angry and still make us very angry with the kind of programming that goes out. So I will be able to control the content.

Could you give some examples of the content that made you angry?

There is one incident that stands out. During the elections we put together voter education programs and I participated in making those programs become a reality. Most of the writers who wrote for these pro-grams were white writers, not black writers.

They had jokes that they believed that black people would understand and consider funny. There was one joke that really made me very angry about an Austrian hat. I didn't know what an Austrian hat was, I don't know much about Austria. If you are going to make an Austrian hat joke in a language outside of that context, you are making a joke about some-thing that people don't even have an idea about. I asked, "What is an Austrian hat and who are you talking to, who is your audience?" The response was "No, it is really funny." I then replied, "Yes, it is funny to you because you know what an Austrian hat is. I don't know what an Austria hat looks like."

Could you tell me what an Austrian hat is?

It is a very small hat, I don't know how to describe it. It is very small with a very long feather and it is part of Austrian traditional dress. That was a joke that was going to be incorporated into this whole thing and people were supposed to find it funny. They went ahead, of course, and used the joke. That really made me realize that we needed to be in deci-sion-making structures where we could change such views, where we could make decisions that are good for our people. We cannot rely on other people to make decisions that are good for us. Something as simple as a joke that people do not understand in a program really indicated to me that white people in South Africa do not know about us, and have no intention of knowing about us. And these are things that we are expected to consume as viewers.

What has been your experience with images of Africa, growing up, and more recently?

Growing up I had a lot of influences from American movies. However, there is one South African film that I remember, I think it came out in the 1970s, I must have been about five years old or something like that. Though it was very sketchy because I was so young, I remember it was about twins and there was a witch doctor who lived on a mountain. One of the twins went up to the mountain to do something and then she fell to her death. I don't remember the story but it had a lot to do with people's beliefs and practices. I would really like to see that film now that I am grown and to really understand what it was all about.

There were films like *The Gods Must be Crazy*. It was funny but it demeaned the Bushmen as a people, and I am glad that it came out when I was much older and I could appreciate what was happening in the film, unlike before. There were other films that were made some while ago that I remember. In all the films that I have seen, Africans were what are considered here in the United States as coons. They make people laugh running around doing this, doing that, you know like this one guy who passed away some years ago Ndaba Mhlongo. He was a coon, he made people laugh, he was a funny looking man, always making people laugh. That is one thing that I remember.

I read a book that described the images of black Americans in film, and when I saw some of the images, I actually saw the similarities between what happened in the United States and what was happening in South Africa. There are some films that I would like to go back to view to be able to understand what was going on and to compare the portrayal of black South Africans in those films with black Americans in the United States.

Could you talk about cinema in South Africa, and how you see your role as a filmmaker within the context of this cinema?

I don't know much about cinema in South Africa because we are bombarded with American images. There were even special cinema houses for European films. The only time that I really began to know or even to see films from other countries was when I went to a cinema not far from where I worked in the suburbs, where French, Italian, and Japanese films were shown. That was the only way of knowing about anything other than American films. Of course, this brings up the issue of distribution, exhibition, and ownership.

There has not been that much work by South African directors or producers, and when there has been, it has been mostly work by white directors and white producers. As people in exile come back into the country with skills in directing, cinematography, and other areas, I see this as a beginning. I see this stage as very important because we can really come together and show what we as black producers and film directors can do.

How were you introduced to African cinema?

Before coming to Howard University I did not know much about African cinema because we did not get many films from Africa at home. So being at Howard University has exposed me to African cinema. As I stated before, the kind of education we got in South Africa was structured in such a way that I knew more about European cinema than African cinema. At Howard University I have access to literature about African cinema and I am able to have discussions with colleagues and professors.

The first time I heard of Ousmane Sembene was when I talked to a colleague. I then read a book about the works of Ousmane Sembene by Françoise Pfaff, but I had never realized how important this man is. At FESPACO a colleague of mine said to me, "Look there is Ousmane" and I thought, "Ousmane," but it did not register, and I said "Ousmane who?" and she said, "Ousmane Sembene, the filmmaker" and I said, "Oh, him, oh I heard about him." Then I kept hearing people talk about him. It was then that I really realized the importance of this man: he is considered the father of African Cinema. All of these things about African cinema I learned when I came to Howard University. It is ironic that I had to go to the United States to learn about cinema in Africa.

The African films that I have seen tend to differ from region to region. West African films, the few that I have seen, tend to be more experimental, whereas Southern African films, such as those I've seen from Zimbabwe, seem to be more didactic. I have been impressed with what people have done with little things that one wouldn't think could make a visual story. It is amazing how a little story could be made into a beautiful film. An example would be someone's desire for a car, this one obsession in owning a car could build into a whole story. It is amazing how little things can make a beautiful story.

How would you compare your training in the United States to that in South Africa?

Since I have been at the film school at Howard University I feel that as black people there are still a lot of things that we need to do in terms of improving what is our own. This also means being able to be in control of what we have with the intention of making it better for people who are going to come later. I found Howard to be much better than what we have at home in terms of access to equipment and facilities.

In terms of hands-on experience, the black universities in South Africa do not have the equipment and there is not the access to internships where you can get that hands-on experience. Here in Washington, DC there is so much, even at the undergraduate level. There are possibilities where one may go out and work for different companies and get the benefit of the hands-on experience that is needed.

The curriculum at Howard University has been really an eye-opener for me, having taken courses like "Blacks in Film" and "African Cinema." We learn about what is happening in our own films, how we are portrayed by white producers and white directors, as well as how we portray ourselves. My interest in being a producer makes me think about how I would portray other black people. I have become more sensitive to and aware of some of the things that are still burning issues in terms of images of black people in the media. In that way, Howard opens your eyes to these things.

In South Africa there was no way that I could learn more about Africa. There was a lot taught about Germany, England, Europe in general, and America. In terms of Africa, if I had not come from the family I came from I would not have known much about Zimbabwe. My father was a journalist, so we had access to encyclopedias when we were very young. Of course the encyclopedias were skewed in their perspective, but at least we got to know about Africa as a continent, what it looks like, where Nigeria is in relation to the Ivory Coast, that kind of thing. We were able to know about the politics of the continent itself, of different countries, what was happening in Malawi, for instance. My father got an opportunity to travel to all these places so he would bring us a lot of information and pictures and we would get a better understanding of Africa.

I find that when interacting with American students, in spite of the sophistication of American media—everybody has access to television and films, and many to the Internet—there is still not that much being reported about Africa in terms of the continent itself, the people who live in the continent. The only time that one hears about Africa or sees about Africa is when there is something terrible happening in African countries.

That makes me appreciate being at Howard University, especially in the film school. As a film student, one learns more about Africa than what is being portrayed. Students interact with African professors, with people who have traveled and who know what Africa is about and what is happening in the film industry there. One gets to meet some of the people who have gone out and have even worked in those areas. Having looked at what other universities had to offer I didn't get the impression that I would be exposed to the theoretical aspects of film that I have been able to get at Howard, in terms of the focus on black issues in film and television.

As a woman filmmaker from South Africa, what role do you envision that you will take on in African cinema?

I think there is a big role that African women so far have played in terms of what goes out in film, and I think a big role that I can play as an African woman is in the area of documentary filmmaking. Just knowing there are so many women—and I know there are a lot more who I haven't met or who were not at FESPACO—when we get together and talk about these issues I hope that we will be motivated to go even further. I am glad that there are more African women like myself who are involved in film and who can tell their stories—not women stories only, but African stories in general, from a woman's perspective.

You stated that you have now been exposed to African filmmakers in general. What have been your impressions of the works by African women filmmakers, and do you think that you can use them as models for your own work?

At FESPACO I did see films by African women, but I have not really had a chance to go back and review those films. What I would like to do is find out more about the experiences of many of these women. I am starting from Southern Africa, with women like Tsitsi Dangarembga, because those are people who are very close to me, and we have so many similarities in terms of the problems that we are facing in Southern Africa. I am looking at her background, where she has been, the issues that she has had to deal with, and that kind of thing.

But in general, I have not been able to do as much research on African women filmmakers, to be able to learn about their strengths and weaknesses, the kinds of issues that they have had to deal with, what they are trying to do right now, where they are going. I would like to be involved in getting together to form some kind of unit as African women filmmakers to improve our conditions in this profession.

As you stated, there is an emerging presence of African women in the cinema. What place do you see African women holding in the future?

Being a black African woman has its own problems, aside from getting into the film industry. The film industry in Africa is dominated by men as much as Hollywood filmmaking is dominated by men. I am quite an ambitious woman and for me it is not only the process of making films, it is maximizing my audience, because it does not help to make films and try to convey certain messages to an audience if you do not have the kind of viewers that you want.

I know the biggest obstacle that I have is being black, being African, and, most of all, being a woman. Fortunately, there have been those who have gone ahead of me. What is important is to learn from their experiences, their mistakes, their strengths. I will take from those strengths and learn from the mistakes and make it work for me.

The world of filmmaking is evolving everyday. I am very positive and optimistic about the future and I believe that I will be able to achieve what I really want to do in filmmaking. It has not only to do with the portrayal of women in film. I am not concerned about the specifics. I am cognizant of all those things. It is also important to address the negative portrayal of black people. I am not only concerned about women, I am concerned about children, the way they are portrayed in film; about men, how they are portrayed in film. So you take all of these and make them work. As I said, I am fortunate because there are people who have gone before of me and have done this work. I am using them as a guide to get to where I want to go.

In a multi-racial, post-apartheid South Africa, how does one make the balance with the different races? While indigenous Africans are the majority, people of European descent continue to have an enormous amount of control. What do you see as a multi-racial South Africa in terms of programming, in terms of filmmaking in South Africa?

It depends on your audience. In South Africa it is predominantly black. And even though it is predominantly black there are still a lot of ethnic groups within South Africa, so we need filmmakers and television producers who will make programs that are targeted at different groups.

On the other hand, though we all have different needs, there are programs and films that are going to be accepted by everyone, films that people watch and enjoy as a unit. For instance, people in the urban areas would enjoy the same kinds of things; however, there are distinct differences in the rural areas. There are also films that I believe can be cross-racial. We need to be able to sort out the needs of people and find out the kinds of things that interest each group, the issues that they would like to see addressed when we go to regional broadcasting.

Thembi Mtshali

South Africa

Interview held in November 1998, Washington, DC.

Thembi, you have a long list of accomplishments: you are a celebrated artist in various fields of creative expression as actor, television personality, playwright, vocalist, and choreographer. Could you give a bit of your background?

I was born in a little village called Sabhoza in Zululand and I grew up with my grandmother. My grandmother took care of me because my parents were working in the city, in Durban. My mother was a domestic worker and my father worked as a sales clerk. They only had one room which could accommodate them so that when they were getting ready to have the second baby they had to take me to my grandparents, so I grew up there. I grew up in the rural area where we would go get water from the river and carry it back on our heads. We would go to the fields to plow. I used to look after my grandfather's kettle. There were no boys in the family to do those chores, so I had to do it. I grew up as a tomboy, fighting with the boys in the fields. My schooling started there. I moved to the city when I was fifteen. That is when I moved to live with my parents. It was also because of my schooling. In the rural area, classes only went to a certain grade, after which there were no other schools, so I had to move to continue my education.

You grew up in South Africa, where your artistic talents were nurtured. Your grandmother's storytelling had a great influence on you. What stories do you remember and how did you experience them as a child?

Well, my grandmother was a very good storyteller. It was a tradition that has continued. Every grandparent could tell stories. Those years I regarded as pre-school for me. It was very informative and very educational. The stories taught us how to take care of ourselves; we learned a lot from those stories. I value them very much, even now. When I look back, I regard myself as having been very lucky to have had that kind of background.

Having had storytelling as a basis in your early education, do you find that you later transferred many of the elements to your work in theater?

I had this background and knew a lot about my traditions. Whereas many of my fellow actors had grown up in the cities and the only life they knew came from growing up in the urban areas. I had a great deal of knowledge about our traditions and the stories of my people. It helped me to be creative in the arts. It also influenced the way I tell stories through music.

Your theatrical debut began when you played in **U Mabatha***. It was actually in the theater where your artistic journey took form. Would you say that is where your career started?*

Yes, that is where it started, although being in the arts for me was not a planned thing because when I was at school...you know, your parents try to protect you and for me as a girl, in those days, you either become a nurse, or a teacher. Your parents then feel that you will have a secure job. Being an artist implied that you wanted to be a "street girl," that you were running out of control. No parent wanted her child to be an artist. It was not regarded as a profession. For me, becoming an actress—I never know whether to say actor or actress....

What is the difference for you between actor and actress?

Well, an actor is an actor, whether you are a female or a male, so I take myself as an actor. A doctor is a doctor; you do not say "doctress." Or they never thought women would become doctors [laughter].

It happened that I dropped out of school because I got pregnant. I then had to look for a job because my parents told me straight out, "Now you have decided to become a woman you have to take care of yourself." Having a baby is not child's play, so I had to go look for a job. Having to leave school, I had to find menial jobs like being a maid. But music had always been my love: at school I used to sing in the choir, at church I would sing in the choir. We would form little groups at school, so I really loved singing. Becoming an actor was something else; it had not yet entered my mind.

So you had not made a connection between these two art forms?

No, not then...when I was working as nanny, I used to sing for the kids that I looked after. The family that I worked for grew very fond of me and they always told me, "You don't belong here, you are an artist!" But at that time, I was only concerned about having that job so that I could earn money and buy things for my child. It so happened that there were auditions advertised for the play *U Mabatha,* which was a Zulu adaptation of *Macbeth* in Uzulu. *Macbeth* was portrayed as a Zulu king. In fact, it was this family that encouraged me to go to the audition. The auditions were done at the University of Natal. I wondered at the time, were they trying to get rid of me [laughter]. As it turned out I auditioned and then I got the part. Fortunately, the rehearsals were in the evening; so, it did not interfere with my job. I could go to work during the day and rehearse in the evening.

At the same time, I had a problem in the evening because my father did not allow any of his children to come home later than a certain time in the evening. I spent most of my time sleeping outside at the toilet, which was outside of the house, because my father said straight to me, "If you come home and the lights are off, do not bother knocking at the door, because it means that we are sleeping." I spent most of the time sleeping at the toilet until someone would wake up and open the door so that I could come into the house. But I was really determined to make something out of myself, to be somebody, better than just being a nanny. At that time when I was doing the play, I began to see a little light, of me becoming a professional performer.

We performed the play at Natal University. Of course, in those days, we still performed for segregated audiences. There would be days for black audiences and days for white audiences. Unfortunately, at that time my parents did not make it to see the show. The play got invited to go to London and my father said to me, "Oh, so you are going overseas, you will never come back." I told him, "Yes I am going to come back." I know he was trying to make it difficult for me, but at the same time, I knew he was being protective of me. It was not because he hated me. We went to London, and when we came back, he was the first person to say to everybody, "My daughter has been overseas." He invited me to come to his job so that he could introduce me to his co-workers. After that, I join another play, which was called *Meropa*, which means "the drums of Africa" in Sesotho. My first work in the theater was mostly musicals.

So you performed and sang in the musicals?

Yes. The play that really took me on the road around the world was the musical play *Ipi Tombi*. It played around the world. It was then that I could really call myself an artist. Also, because I played the leading role, I really became a celebrated artist.

What was your role in that play?

I was the bride getting married every day. Sometimes, I say, maybe that is why I am still not married [laughter]. I got married for four years every day. To different men, because they would change the actors for the character.

Could you talk about your experience as an actor in cinema and television? Was it a natural evolution from the theater to these media? Was it a natural process?

It was a natural process. After *Ipi Tombi*, I concentrated a lot on singing. I worked with Hugh Masekela and Miriam Makeba. I performed as a backing singer in their concerts. During those days, I was living in New York, in the late seventies and early eighties. It was when I moved back to South Africa that I started to work in television. When I first left South Africa, there was not yet television. The first time I saw a television was when we went to London. I remember being glued to the television set. I did not want to go to sleep, I tried to stay awake as long as I could, and I did not want to miss anything.

Are you saying that there was no television set where you lived or that there was none at all?

In the whole country, there was no television. Television started in South Africa in 1976. It was only in the eighties that black people were even featured on television. When it started it was only one channel, which only presented white people. Slowly it increased and then we started seeing black faces. There was another channel for black people in the eighties. When I came back in 1985, I started on television by doing music shows. I began to present a music program for television called "Inselelo."

Then I joined the Market Theater. It was the Market Theater that really launched me as an actor. All the work that I had previously done in theater were musicals. I had never done straight drama and acting, you know "real acting." Musicals are different from straight drama. In musicals you sing and dance and everything is dramatized through singing. We workshopped the script, "Have You Seen Zandile" with a friend of mine, Gcina Mhlope. We presented it at the Market Theatre. I remember the director at the Market Theatre saying; "Well, I don't know if Thembi is an actor or a singer." In that play, I had four different parts. The play was based on the life story of Gcina, how she grew up. We almost had the same background. Her grandmother raised her as well. We could share many stories. I played her grandmother, I played her mother, I played her friend, I played the friend of her grandmother and in all those roles, I simply looked back at my grandmother. In doing so, I became my own grandmother. I transformed into my grandmother. I did everything my grandmother did. I was telling her stories in the play. The play did very well. It was taken to the Edinburgh Festival. We got a "Fringe First" award. We toured around Europe. In fact, that play took me to another step in my career. People started respecting me as an actor. I started getting roles as an actor. That is when I auditioned for the film, *Mapantsula*. We were in the middle of rehearsing the play *Have You Seen Zandile*.

*In **Mapantsula**, you play the protagonist Pat, that was ten years ago in 1988, and it was your first film. What do you remember most about your role in the film?*

Well, I remember when I was invited to audition for Mapantsula. I did not even believe...I did not even think that I was going to get the part. They wanted women around the age of twenty-three to twenty-five and, at that time, I was almost thirty-seven years old. However, my agent encouraged me to go. Well, I got the part...

The film was made during the apartheid era. Could you talk about some of your own experiences during the film production?

That was the first political movie made in South Africa, in the late eighties, during the state of emergency in our country. A lot was happening around us. I remember that the casting was very closed. During the interview, they wanted to understand what your political views were and, of course, they really had to be careful. Everything was underground. It was done clandestinely. Finally, we started filming. Most of the shots were done in Soweto, in this woman's house. Most of the whites who were working with the film were liberals. The whole thing was done right under the nose of the system, without them knowing it. Before they knew it, the film was outside the country. It was introduced at the Cannes Festival.

What was its impact on you as an artist? How did you experience your role in the film?

I was not aware of the impact of it at the time. To me, I just thought, well it is one of those films that will end up being screened in little places, at political rallies. I did not really think that it was going to be big. I was very, very proud at the end. I remember being invited to a women's conference called "Malibongwe" in Amsterdam, which was organized by the ANC women, and it was at the same time as the release of *Mapantsula*. It was a huge thing. I thought, "Oh my, I am in Hollywood or something!"

*With the film **Mapantsula**, it was the first time that you had seen your image on the big screen. What was it like?*

I do not know how to describe it. It was amazing. We were all invited to this big cinema for the preview and I thought, "Oh my, that is me!"

Compare the impression you got from your experience of seeing your image on television....

Well, when watching television, you are at home, it is very relaxed, whereas in the cinema, there are all these strangers, and they are looking at your image. It was a very different feeling.

How did people respond to you in general? You spoke some about your experiences at the women's conference?

The film was difficult for a lot of people who were in exile at the time. It was very touching. Seeing that it was done at home, seeing the surroundings, people commented, "Oh my, this is near my house." In fact, many people cried, but they were also excited by the fact that people in South Africa were using any means to expose the brutality of the South African government.

So you were often in audiences of South Africans in exile?

Yes, it was only screened outside of South Africa. It was only released in South Africa after 1990.

What did you think about your character Pat? I know this was a while ago, but do you remember her and how she was portrayed?

Pat was this girl who had just moved to the city looking for a job, and the first job that she could get was as a domestic worker. I do not know how she got caught up with that guy Panic, who is a gangster.

The fascination of this lifestyle perhaps?

Maybe the protection, because she was new in the city. If you are seen with "the" guy, you feel that you are protected. Although I view Panic more so as a survivor. People do anything just to survive. If you do not have a job, you have to find another way of survival. Pat did not look at herself just as a domestic worker. This was the beginning. She wanted to step forward and do other things—for instance, when she gets involved with the union guy, who introduces her to secretarial work. She had other ambitions for herself.

You said that you had been a nanny. How did you, as the actor in the film, connect with Pat's experiences?

In fact, I did not act in that movie. I just became myself; I just did what I did when I was a nanny. It was funny, because the woman who played the role of my madam is a very nice person. We worked together at the Market Theater. She found it very difficult to be harsh. They tried to push her saying, "You have to be harsh to be in this role." After the take she would come and say, "You know, I did not mean to do that." I would say to her, "Please, come on, we are acting here!" She would take it so personally. She would wonder if she was being too pushy. They would tell her, "In fact, you must be more pushy."

What is the Market Theater? Could you describe its purpose and objectives and give details of the people involved in it and the works that came out of it?

Market Theater Company was formed by Barney Simon, who was the Artistic Director and, Mannie Manim, who was the Managing Director, together with a small group of highly talented young actors. They converted the 1913 Indian Fruit Market into an arts complex, and committed themselves to a theater that would not only entertain, but present to their audiences a reflection of the world in which they lived.

And, of course, Market Theater gave birth to a lot of workshopped productions, many which were dubbed as protest theater. Market Theater gave a lot of artists like myself pride, respect, and a home for creativity. It was primarily dedicated to the development of indigenous work that reflects our aspirations and lives. And even today, it is committed to our community in a time of need, for healing, understanding, sharing, and reconciliation.

You also write songs, plays, and stories. Would you say there is a connection from your childhood, where you actually want to write the stories that you heard or experienced?

Well, in fact, the person who really nurtured my capabilities as an actor and writer, who really encouraged me, was Barney Simon. He passed away about five years ago. He really was my teacher, as far as theater was concerned. He could see through you. He could see what you could produce as an actor. I remember one time he called me and said, "You know Thembi, I have an idea for a play, I think you and I can write this play." I said to him, "Barney, I am not a writer, I am an actor." He said, "No, you are a writer, you have a story to tell." With him we would talk and he would ask, "Where did you grow up," and other questions.

During the time, whatever we would talk about would become a script. I remember another play we did. When I wrote the song, "My Sister Breast-fed My Baby," we were doing a play called "Women of Africa." Barney said to me, "What kind of woman would you want to portray?" I said that I would love to portray a domestic worker because I feel that domestic workers in this country and all over the world have contributed so much in the society.

In South Africa, there is hardly any white household that does not have a domestic worker. All the kids grow up being taken care of by our mothers, by our sisters, by our aunties, and they all grow up being nurtured by that love. When they grow up, they become different people. I told him about when I looked after these children and I had already had my own child by that time. Yet I had to leave my child and had to go look after these kids. He asked me who was taking care of my child. I told him that my sister was taking care of my child. That is where we got the title,

"My Sister Breast-fed My Baby." Because my sister breast-fed my baby, while I was looking after other people's kids. We wrote that song.

I remember one time I was singing this song in the play and there was one white guy sitting in front. He started crying. He went out of the theater. After the show, he came backstage and cried again and said, "You know the reason why I am crying is because I just came from enrolling for military duty. I am working in the townships and everything that you said in that song, I have just been through it. A black woman also raised me, so everything that you said in that song just tears me apart. I can see this woman that raised me, and now I have been drafted so that I can shoot the kids in the township." It was a very powerful message.

So "My Sister Breast-fed My Baby" was a song and a play?

It was a musical theater piece. In "Women of Africa," we did storytelling and music about situations in South Africa. We were different women, and each woman had her own story. My story was based on domestic workers, as I just described. Other women had different themes.

You have been quite visible on the television screens of South Africa; you have been both TV host and actor. You are particularly well known for your role in the television series "It's Good, It's Nice." Could you talk about the series and your role in it?

The woman who was producing this series called me up. We were already friends; we had worked together on children's programs. She was both a producer and director. We became very close. She was white, she trusted me, I began to trust her. She was not the type of person that imposed things on you. She would present certain things and I would tell her that I could not do this. I could not do a children's program that does not say anything to our black kids; we have our own stories. If we are going to have a program for our children, because I am doing this program for black kids, I cannot tell them about Cinderella and others. We have our own stories that are never told on television. Our kids are always watching Bugs Bunny and so on. She would listen to me and further explore what I said.

When she first wanted to do this comedy, she had a different thing altogether in her mind. Yet it turned out to be something else when we started talking about it. She had somebody to write the script, he is a very celebrated writer. She told me that he had agreed to write this comedy for us and asked if I could perhaps assist her with the casting. I said to her, "The first thing, this person is white, he does not understand anything about black humor." Many times, for me, with white comedy, out of ten laughs maybe I would find one laugh. Their humor is different from ours. I said that if we are going to focus this comedy on black people, we have to have someone who understands our humor. She then said, "Well, we don't have anybody who could write." I told her that the actors that we were going to cast in the play could work with us to work-shop a script. We all know how to laugh. We have so many stories to tell that can make us laugh. We have so many stories in the townships that are funny that we could create into a comedy.

So, then we started in this way. Afterwards we did the casting so that we could get together and workshop the script, step by step. It worked. From the time it came out on television, it was a hit.

What role did you play in the series?

I played the part of an actor who had just come to Johannesburg to find fortune and fame.

You also hosted musical shows for television, are you interested perhaps in producing your own show?

I would love to, which is why I think that my chances being at DCTV (Public Access Television of Washington, DC) will allow me to grow step by step.

What do you think about the concept of community television?

I think that it is a great concept because in South Africa we do not have these kinds of facilities. I am really excited about it. I would never have thought that I could see myself operating a camera and shooting something. And I have already produced something. I really see so many possibilities coming from this experience of learning the concept of community television production and its inner workings. I see myself growing in this and being able to produce my own shows, my own children's programs. I love working with children. I would love to produce plays for children, educational programs.

*Your credits also include the **Lion King** soundtrack. What was your role?*

The opening soundtrack for *Lion King* was done in South Africa. I was one of the singers who was invited. You know the part that goes; *nans ingonyama bakithi* sung by Lebo M. We also did quite a lot of other songs for the film. That is why *The Lion King* on Broadway now has about ten South Africans in it.

As a vocalist, you have performed with renowned musicians such as Dizzy Gillespie, Miriam Makeba, Hugh Masekela, Abdullah Ibrahim, and Ladysmith Black Mambazo. Miriam Makeba especially influenced you. Could you talk about your experiences?

Well, growing up in South Africa, a lot of our music was cut off from us. The music that we could get from the radio was music from America. We grew up not really appreciating our own music. And of course, we could never hear Miriam Makeba because her music was never played on our radios. Although there were many other groups coming up and their music was played, there was never an appreciation of our own art. I think that it was a matter of being brainwashed that prevented us from appreciating our own music, our own talent. When I started going overseas, I met Miriam. I had always loved her music. Those records that could be smuggled in, I always loved listening to her. When I saw her perform for the first time, she just electrified me so much, the powerful messages that she had. She really made me love and appreciate our music. Instead of thinking that I could become a Diana Ross, I thought, "I could become Thembi." Working with Miriam and Dizzy Gillespie, two pioneers on each side of the ocean, has been a real highlight of my career.

You are living in the United States, at the moment. Could you talk about your experiences?

I just did a workshop at the University of North Carolina. What was so interesting was that you think, "This is a class of Masters students, where should I start?" This is African American Theater, African Studies, you expect people to have a certain level of knowledge about Africa, and South Africa. But in fact, you really have to start from scratch. Many people think of Africa as one country. You have to draw the whole map of Africa, so that they can realize that Africa is a big continent with different countries. Growing up in South Africa, I never knew anything about African Americans, only those that we saw in the movies. Before coming, I thought that America was paved with gold and glamour. I never thought that you could find slums in America as well. Whenever I go home people say,

"Oh, in America, you have a lot of money." They do not think that when you are here you do not even have a car, you walk in the streets, you get on the buses. They do not think of this. It is a way of communication, of getting to know about each other's situation.

What are some of your future projects, ideas, or plans?

Like I said before, when I go back home I hope that I can be in a position to have my own production house and produce my own work and share the knowledge that I have acquired all these years.

Catherine Wangui Muigai

Kenya

Interview held during the 15th FESPACO, February 1997, Ouagadougou, Burkina Faso.

Catherine, could you talk about yourself and how you came to be a producer?

I am a video and film producer in Kenya. I have always been interested in films dealing with women's and children's issues. As I am a woman, I feel that I am more conversant with those topics. I read the different scripts that come to me and if they interest me, and they are along those lines, I choose them.

There are not many films from Kenya and it has only been recently that a cinema tradition has emerged. Could you discuss filmmaking in Kenya and women's presence in this field?

There are not many women filmmakers, but there are a few of them, one of the women that I work with, who has produced a feature film, is Anne Mungai. The film *Saikati* won several awards during FESPACO 1993, and I feel that she is an authority in that field, and I am very happy to be working with her. We are working on her next feature, which will be called *Saikati II*. I am looking forward to it. In fact, we have already started. We have shot the first few scenes and we are continuing to look for the funding to continue. We have gotten a lot of goodwill, as well as equipment and lighting for free.

We are working with other production companies in Kenya. We have come together and are working as a team. We have the Kenya Film Producers Association and most of the association members have agreed to help us initially without having to ask for money up front. Of course, funding is important in our completing the project, and the lack of it has become a real problem. This is why you don't find women producers, because it is a very hard job going around raising money to make films.

We are determined and so far we have gotten a lot of goodwill from individuals, from different organizations, like the UNDP (the United Nations Development Program)—they have agreed to do the posters for us. We have some aerial shots and the AMREV has agreed to give its airplanes. So, what we need to do is to get enough money, though we have a little, to pay the actors and others, as well as the out-of-pocket expenses. It is a struggle but we are determined.

As you stated, there are not a lot of filmmakers in general nor women filmmakers or film producers in Kenya. Would you say that you are one of the few woman film producers? What role do you play in this field?

Yes, well, as I told you it is not an easy task. We have problems getting money. Another trend that you are finding is that, because filmmaking is very expensive, there are many people who are only working in video. However, we feel that film is a very effective way of reaching out to people. It is a very, very powerful way to reach the public and we do feel that it is important as well.

If women are trained in filmmaking and are able to do films about themselves, as well as the nation, and the country in general, it is an efficient way to portray the woman positively. I think we as women are in a position to fill that need and to be able to express it much better than perhaps men would. Although I must say, I am impressed with some of the men who have been interested in portraying the woman positively.

Do you think that there is a certain perspective that is particular to women in terms of film directing or cinema in general?

I think so. I think that a woman knows the needs of other women. They feel those needs. As women, we are exposed to the variety of experiences and problems that women go through. We are able to feel it, be it within our homes, or with the children. These experiences may be as victims of discrimination, or of not feeling completely free to do what one would like to do. So I think these issues undertaken by women in filmmaking may be presented much more practically and effectively.

You stated that you generally tend to gravitate towards scripts that focus on issues that relate to women. Could you talk about the scripts that you receive?

206

Right now, women-focused issues are what I am really interested in doing, because I feel that this is the area that is really lacking. Of course, it does not mean that these will be the only issues that I will address.

Could you talk about some of the specific themes of the scripts? I find that in the area of women and development, issues such as health, women's rights, and education have been important themes in films that attempt to raise the consciousness of women, as well as the general population regarding the issues that concern women.

Yes, Anne Mungai's last film *Saikati* is an example of how the focus on education is brought into the film to raise the importance of the education of girls. *Saikati*, the protagonist, had plans to graduate and become a flying doctor, after which she could go out to help in the community. The education for girls is one of the many issues that we are trying to raise, and films can play a role to encourage it. If girls are educated, they will be able to uplift their families. Women are very important in society: if you uplift a woman you are actually uplifting the whole family. You are also empowering the woman.

She is able to get a good job, she is able to handle higher positions within society and become influential in the country and become a good leader. We need women leaders; we need them in every field. I think we can do a good job and we have the capacity to succeed in whatever area we pursue. It is about time we encouraged our women to go out and do the things that have been stereotyped as men's jobs. I am sure that we can do them quite well.

You said earlier that you were encouraged by the portrayal of women in some films made by men. Based on the films that you have seen, and on your knowledge of African cinema, what is your general attitude about images of women in African cinema?

The image of African women has not been very positive. The woman has always been portrayed as a weakling or as a sex symbol or someone who just sits around the house, is dumb, and does not know what she is doing. We should try to get away from that, because the woman is able to do what the man can do. I feel that this is a challenge and this is something that we as women in filmmaking must do, and providing positive images of women is what I want to be involved in.

There was a merger between your film company and some others. Could you talk about the merger of the film production companies, how you came together, the goals and objectives of the company, and also some of the needs and interests that you address?

In Kenya, film production is not a very big industry as such. So you have people with their own little companies and everyone is trying to do everything themselves. This does not always work out very well. You are the producer, the director, the scriptwriter; you are running around, you are doing everything yourself. We have all gone through those problems and we have seen that we do need a force, a united and strong foundation, to get these things going.

We started by talking to a few people as well as with the KFPA, the Kenya Film Producers Association. In that association, we identified different people that we could work with. Anne Mungai used to own a company known as Joyana. My company was called Amp-Sonic Ltd., and there was another company, Gone Fishing Productions, owned by Clive Haines. So we all joined forces so that we could work together as one. The name of the new company is Sambaza Productions. This is the only way to go, really, because we need to work together. And because of the lack of finances and other things, you know, when you are a group you can agree on certain ways to make things happen as opposed to struggling by yourself. So we have been working quite well.

In 1991 a PanAfrican organization of African women in the image industry was formed. Were you involved in this organization at the time when it was established?

My partner, Anne Mungai, is involved in it. This is my first time to come to FESPACO.

There have been regional associations that have been established as well. In Kenya, have you been involved in the East Africa regional association of this pan-African organization?

Yes, I have been assisting.

Could you talk a bit about some of what has been going on in the association?

Well, it is not that active as such. But we hope to get it going. Anne has been very busy and we are recruiting a lot of people. I can't say much about it for the moment.

What do you see as the importance of women in the cinema in general? The necessity of having women in your position as producer, as well as having women directors, scriptwriters, and in all areas of the industry?

The woman's position in society, I believe, is a position that is very, very important. If a woman is well represented, and is involved in what is happening in the film industry, I think that this would be a very good thing, and it is something that will add to the film industry. Because, as I said, if you uplift a woman, you uplift a nation—and the world, really. So I think that it is important that women get involved in this area.

Fanta Régina Nacro

Burkina Faso

Interview and press conference held at FESPACO, February 1997, Ouagadougou, Burkina Faso. Translated from French.

Fanta, you have the distinction of being the first woman of Burkina Faso to do a fiction film. Could you talk about how you became interested in filmmaking?

It was quite by chance. When I was younger, I liked cinema quite a bit. I had a neighbor who knew about a film school in Burkina, and since I was very interested in films, I asked her for more information and she told me about INAFEC (Institut Africain d'Education Cinématographique). I studied at the film school for three years. As I continued my courses, I realized that I was interested in directing. However, the curriculum required that the students first learn scriptwriting and editing, and then work with an assistant director before learning to direct. Thus, I did a bit of everything before doing my first short film.

Your first short film, **Un certain matin**, *received several prizes, the Tanit d'Or for short film at Carthage in 1992, the Licorne d'Or at Amiens also in 1992, the First Prize Air Afrique in Milan in 1993, and Special Mention in Montreal, also in 1993. Could you talk a bit about this film?*

It was a glimpse into the life of a peasant in Burkina. He wakes up one morning and, like any other morning, he goes to the field. However, on this morning, before going to the field, he has three bad omens; he bumps his left foot, he kills a newborn black chick, and he hears the chirping of a bird that sings off-key. He then asks himself, "What is going to happen to me today?"

While he is working in the field, he hears a young girl crying for help. He looks around and notices a man with an axe who is about to kill the young girl. He thinks, "There is not a moment to lose," he then picks up his rifle and shoots him. The madman falls to the ground, he is covered with blood. We then hear someone say "Cut!" In fact, it was a production shoot and these two people were the actors in the film. Since he had never seen a production shoot and the crew was hidden on a hill, he could not imagine that these were actors. He actually thought that the girl was in danger. So, the film is about this story.

Your next film, **Puk Nini,** *is among the short films in competition here at FESPACO. Could you talk about the film and why you chose this theme?*

Puk Nini means "Open your eyes, be vigilant." It is a Mossi expression. What it is saying, in fact, is that when a problem comes, do not stand idle with arms crossed, do not be pessimistic. Stand up and move, go forward and find a solution to one's problem. The idea occurred to me because I have many male friends who were colleagues at INAFEC and are married and still quite young. Yet, they have already had two or three extra-marital relationships.

I wanted to know why, after one year of marriage, that they found it necessary to have a mistress and a relationship outside of the marriage. Often they have relationships with women who come from Togo or Ghana. What I came to understand is that my colleagues find that these women treat them in a manner that they are unaccustomed to when they are at home with their Burkinabé wives. It is from this idea that I decided to make this film.

As it turns out, the woman who you chose to be the seductress, was neither Togolese nor Ghanaian, but in fact, she was Senegalese. Why did you decide to choose a Senegalese woman?

Why a Senegalese woman? Well, I had the choice among Togolese, Malian, and Senegalese women. I chose a Senegalese woman because I saw a film that gave me some ingredients for my story. The film is called *Djali Djali,* by Senegalese filmmaker William Mbye. In the film the ingredients of seduction are described, such as, how to use incenses, how to perfume oneself, how to wear the *djali djali* around the waist. Those were the elements that helped me in the evolution of my script, and so I chose a Senegalese woman.

You stated that your married colleagues have mistresses outside of their marriages, yet Astou, the Senegalese seductress, appeared to be a prostitute. Why was she portrayed as a prostitute and not a mistress?

In fact, she is a mistress, not a prostitute. A prostitute walks the streets while a mistress does not; she is in her house. Perhaps she will go out to have a drink, and it is in these situations that she will meet lovers who are looking around, but she is not going to walk the streets to look for clients.

However, the second time that Salif, the male protagonist, went out with still another woman, she also appeared to be a prostitute. It seems as if the couple was coming out of a room in a brothel, which confirmed my initial impression that Astou was a prostitute. Based on how she was introduced in the story, I got the impression that she was looking for someone for the moment. She did not appear to be looking for a relationship, nor did she appear to be looking for someone in particular.

Again a distinction has to be made between a prostitute and a mistress. In the end, it really is the same thing. A prostitute goes out with someone who is not her husband; a mistress does the same thing. The distinction is the approach that is used to obtain the client. For instance, when Salif goes out with the white woman in the bar, she is not a prostitute but rather an adventure that he has with a white woman. Perhaps the white woman is married, but we don't know in the film. However, because the man is married he cannot bring her to his house. So the only thing that he can do is take her to a hotel or a *maison de passe* [a place where a couple goes to engage in discreet intimate activities], in fact.

What has been the reception to this film? I know it has been seen here in Ouagadougou, has it been shown in Senegal? What are the Senegalese reactions to this film and the responses in general?

In general, it has had a good reception. At FESPACO, after the three screenings, the audience had a positive reaction. They understood that it was a comedy and they allowed themselves to experience it within this context. They were amused, and they laughed. Of course, it provoked much discussion among them.

There were generally three kinds of reactions. The Burkinabé men felt that they were mistreated, that I have a bad impression of them, and that I portrayed them all as women chasers. The Burkinabé women were also disappointed because they thought that I presented them as primitive, as women who do not know how to seduce. Then there were the Senegalese women who felt that I portrayed them as prostitutes, that I mistreated them as well. Those are the three different negative reactions.

There were positive reactions. Some Senegalese women felt that it was a song in praise of the Senegalese woman. There were Burkinabé women who welcomed it, because it permitted them to think further, and perhaps to reflect upon the crisis that exists among couples. Because no matter what we say about African life today, there is a crisis among couples that is alarming. It is necessary, at least for me, to think about the relationship between women and men.

Do you think that you portray a certain sensibility in you work that comes from being a woman filmmaker?

I would say that there is a human sensibility. Ever since I saw a film called *Femme d'Alger,* which was made by a man, with what one may even call a woman's sensibility, I've come to realize that there is really no woman's or man's sensibility, but there is simply a human sensibility.

If another woman were to make *Puk Nini,* the scenario of the film would not be filmed in the manner in which I did it. If I were to give it to a man, it would be again a different way of filming it. So, each person films in relationship to her or his sensibility, as well as past, daily life, and dreams of the future.

You were trained in a film school in Africa; you have worked with African filmmakers Idrissa Ouédraogo, Dikongue-Pipa, and Kitia Touré. You have had experience as editor and scriptwriter. Could you talk about African cinema as you see it?

To talk about African cinema is a bit complicated because it is a cinema that is going through a tremendous crisis. A crisis of scripts and stories, a crisis of distribution, a crisis of production. In spite of all these crises, I try to find funds to make short films. Because I feel that short films are the best training ground in the evolution to feature films. Nevertheless, it is true that it is very difficult, though, at the same time, things are possible.

African cinema, or more accurately African cinemas—because there are many African cinemas—is going through a turbulent period. With the restructuring of the FEPACI [Pan-African Federation of Filmmakers]—because our foundation, which has been in existence for twenty-five years, is going through a crisis—we need to consider new ideas in order to redirect this cinema. Perhaps this restructuring will help us come out of this ghetto. The problem with African cinema is that it has been a cinema that has looked to the outside for its audience, in the hope that it would make a profit in order to do other projects. We quickly forget about our own public.

At the moment there is a brainstorming group based in Bamako whose objective is to come up with ways to make our films profitable on the continent. We have a significant population—however, only ten percent of the African population sees our films. Even if they pay a small amount for entry fee into the cinema house, if ninety percent of the African population goes to see our films, perhaps we could succeed in resolving the problems around production. At this moment we are going through a complete overhaul: we are reflecting, we are pulling our efforts together to give a new orientation to this cinema which will become even greater.

Ouagadougou, Burkina Faso, is often called the capital of African cinema. Besides the crisis, do you think that here in Ouaga, and in Burkina in general, there is more of an awareness of African cinema than elsewhere?

Yes, we speak a great deal about African cinema and Burkina, indeed, as the capital of African cinema. We are numerous in terms of filmmakers and we have had the chance to benefit from a tax that is charged on foreign films. Although it is not as effective as before, this money allows at least the possibility to pay for equipment and to pay technicians. We have a conscious policy *vis-à-vis* African cinema, which is very important in Burkina, and it facilitates the production of our work. When there is already material and technical assistance, and the support of Burkina, this offers a credible dossier when we present a film project and budget to outside financiers. The politics and the actual endeavors of Burkina regarding the cinema are significant.

In 1986, while studying film at INAFEC, you and the other students had the opportunity to collaborate on a film project with African American film students and film professor Abiyi Ford from Howard University, who came here from the United States. Could you talk about this experience?

What can I say? I had very important relationships and professional connections with black Americans or—what did you call them?

African Americans....

...with African Americans, as they are now called. They were very positive relationships. I also later met Zeinabu Davis and other filmmakers.

The experience with Abiyi Ford from Howard University twelve years ago on a collective film by students was our first cinematographic experience. It was very important for me and allowed me to define my role in this profession.

Could you envision making a film about African Americans or a film that makes a connection between Africans and African Americans?

I really have not thought a lot about this subject. I had thought there was a possibility for us to work in collaboration with African Americans from the United States, but I realized that American money does not leave the American continent. What would perhaps be possible to do is a co-production or a part of the shooting that takes place in Africa and the post-production in the United States or a part of the shooting that takes place in the United States. However, the United States is so far away from our continent and the transportation is very expensive, this collaboration would be somewhat difficult.

On the other hand, to do a film about black Americans? I don't have an idea yet, but why not? I would have to spend some time in the United States and live with African Americans in order to come up with a script idea. However, if one could succeed in doing a film that would permit the two African communities to come together, that would be a good idea.

We now see more and more Africans and Caribbean people who are living in Europe, or at least who spend a great deal of time between Africa and Europe, like yourself, as well as the United States. What do you think about doing a film that speaks about black people and their experiences in Europe?

To be quite honest, no, not yet. My *imaginary* in terms of cinema is based in Burkina. When I look for an idea for a film, I base it on Burkina, the capital, or my village. My reference has not yet gone beyond the limits of my borders. On the other hand, perhaps that will happen when I am ready to go beyond those limits. I did do a film on video recently for the black community living in Paris. It was a film for the Soninké, called *L'Ecole au coeur de la vie*. It was a film to teach families how to better help in the education of their children.

As a Burkinabé woman, what do you think about the grand prize of FESPACO, the Etalon de Yennenga? Yennenga was a legendary woman of the Mossi Empire.

216

The fact that Yennenga was a legendary woman who made a great contribution is very important, and every Burkinabé woman and every African woman should be proud. To show her as an emblem, to give distinction to a film in her name, is important. However, I have at a certain given moment, questioned what it really means to have the prize Etalon de Yennenga. What can it give, for better or worse, to a film or the director. I don't know, especially when I see the films that have been awarded the Etalon de Yennenga during FESPACO, later to only remain in a drawer, when the prize should have meant a successful commercial release. So what does this prize really mean? This is a question that I am posing at the moment. I have not yet found a response.

What is your next film about?

It is a short film called *Le truc de Konaté*. It is a comedy about the constraints of condoms in the rural areas. You know we are a very traditional society and everything that is foreign poses a problem and it is a comedy based on this.

Do you have any future projects that you are working on as well?

I am writing a script for another project that is a film adaptation of the novel by Mariama Ba, *Une si longue lettre* (So Long a Letter). It will be my first feature film. It is a project for an African production by Bassek ba Kobhio, who bought the rights. I have done a first draft of the scenario. Now I must work with an actual scriptwriter to put in place the structure and the organization of the narrative.

*Mariama Ba's **So Long a Letter** is a very beautiful and poetic story and, of course, her work has been well received in the literary world. Do you think it is an important practice to take African literature and adapt it to film? Why did you choose **So Long a Letter?***

I like *Une si longue lettre* very much. It is a novel that I had an opportunity to study at school. In rereading it for the adaptation, I realized that it was a wonderful story on the condition of women. It is still contemporary although it was written perhaps twenty years ago. It continues to be a reality because the problems of women have not actually evolved, the problems around education have not evolved, the political problems have not evolved. I actually feel closer to the women in this book than some of the women of today. I think that the themes raised in the book are important.

217

The only problem was that since I did not have the technique for adaptation to film, the process from novel to screenplay was a bit long. In addition, the problem with adapting this particular story is that since it is a very well-known book, each person who has read it has an image already in her or his mind. To be able to visualize it in a manner that allows everyone who has read the book to get into the film narrative will be very difficult. I hope that I will be able to find a consensus, so that each film viewer can find what she or he envisioned when reading this novel.

Press conference after the press screening of *Puk Nini* at FESPACO 1997; questions by various members of the panel and audience.

*What inspired you to do the film **Puk Nini?***

It came from a dear friend of mine who works for the television station, where he presents issues and situations relating to society. I also wanted to reflect upon love relationships between women and men to try to understand a bit more about the cultural aspects of our society.

Africa is rather vast, and cultures are very diverse; therefore, one must be clever enough to draw from various sources in order to create her or his own cultural perspective.

I saw the film and I liked it for its humor and its light-heartedness, and at the same time for the serious treatment of the subject. Also some scenes were risqué. Were those scenes difficult for you to choose?

It was not difficult because for me it would not have been a film without those scenes. It is a film about love relationships and I didn't want to be hypocritical to the audience and myself. People can interpret it as they want, but for me it was essential.

...What lesson should women learn from this film?

The objective was not to recommend that Burkinabé women do as Senegalese women do. The importance for me was to show that one must think about how we can each day nourish the flame in an intimate relationship between a woman and a man.

Judging from the end of the film it seems hopeless, it seems that men will not stop having affairs.

I don't think that men's behavior is rectifiable. But they were not the only ones that I criticized. I think that everyone in this film had her or his turn to be scrutinized, whether it was the Burkinabé woman, the Senegalese woman, each in one way or another had her responsibility to assume. I did not mean to accuse the woman or the man, but to simply show that there is a combination of things and that mistakes must be shared between the woman and the man.

At the end of the film the scene of the two women did not enter into a cliché, but rather you showed the complicity between them, and perhaps that is the solution. However, at the end we see that the man goes out with a European woman....

There are two reasons: we have always had fantasies of those things coming from the outside...

Perhaps the foreigners have fantasies as well!

Indeed, foreigners have fantasies about Burkinabé women, as they may have fantasies towards others. Frenchmen may have fantasies about Swedish women. So having fantasies is a rather universal concept. I did not want to end the film when the two women [the wife and former mistress] became friends, which could have been interpreted as, "If you discover that you have a rival, meet her and become friends with her and everything will eventually straighten itself out." I did not want to give this impression. No one is perfect; each person must find the solution that works for her or him.

There are women who think that the film is a first step towards the making of a pornographic film in Africa...

Not at all. First, one must understand the difference between a pornographic film and an erotic film. I think that my film is, simply speaking, sensual.

Has your film been aired on Burkinabé television, and have you discussed your film with the Burkinabé public?

No, the film has not been broadcast on television. However, excerpts have been shown to give an idea of what the film is about, which brought about the debates that have been written in the newspapers. There have been several positive as well as negative reactions. Among the negative

219

reactions, it was felt that the film is somewhat pornographic. Also, some Burkinabé and Senegalese women have felt insulted.

People are hypocritical, at the same time they participate in these activities and then express negative reactions when they are revealed....

I am for these reactions, which is why I made the film, in order to have a debate. It is through these debates that we may resolve problems and I am delighted that the debate brings in controversy. There have been lively discussions between men and women about this film. Some of these discussions pose the question about the responsibility of each person in a relationship.

Did you have problems with the actors, especially during the risqué scenes?

Not at all. I explained that to play in a film is not to reenact daily life, but rather we interpret a character. I think that our actors had a certain maturity, which allowed them to forget their own feelings about the subject and to embody the character and show her or his experiences, and that is a plus for African cinema. I am a bit sad, however, because the woman who played the role of the Senegalese had a few problems with her companion. However, things have since been worked out: I think that he eventually understood that in reality she is not a prostitute, she is a very intelligent and ambitious woman.

At the end, I realize that there was no solution. Because when the woman approached her rival, she stated, "I have a technique and I will teach you," but yet the wife stated, "No"!

That was important. Perhaps it was what we might call a modern reaction. I wanted the Burkinabé woman to respond in this way. I wanted her to think about the steps toward a solution rather than to be pessimistic.

Ngozi Onwurah

Nigeria

Interview held at the African Literature Association Conference, East Lansing, Michigan, April 1997.

In another conversation, we talked about your identity as an African woman filmmaker based in London. You stated that you wanted to describe some of the ways that you find that portrayal problematic, especially when it is imposed externally.

As a black woman filmmaker, I get invited to a lot of different things and sometimes they want me to wear different hats. Sometimes I am a woman filmmaker and that's the priority at that particular event. Where it gets particularly muddy is when it has to do with being an African filmmaker. Because the way that black America has appropriated the word *African American*, the context in which people refer to Africa gets very muddy.

As a filmmaker who works out of London, the problems that I have making films are completely different from a woman who, say, lives in Nigeria, who lives and works in Zambia, or Zaire, or Tanzania. The problems that she has as a filmmaker are completely different from the problems that I have as a filmmaker, or the people who we make the films for are different. So, in terms of who I am on a professional level, it gets very complicated.

It is less complicated on a personal level. On a personal level, I know who I am; I know where I am from. But in terms of talking about it, you cannot lump together a woman who lives in London, who gets funding from the BBC to make films, with someone who is living in Nigeria, where literally the budgets, the facilities, everything, would be completely different in terms of how she has to work. So it gets complicated and sometimes I don't think there is enough differential made between black people or people of African descent working outside of Africa and people of African descent working in Africa. It is two different experiences.

In terms of how you bring your identity into your work, would you say that your work often centers around being of mixed race within the context of being British as well as Nigerian?

The fact that I have a white mother and a black father is essential to my identity. Obviously, it gives me a unique perspective politically. Politically I am black; emotionally I'm black. But once you say that "unequivocally, I'm black," there are specifics that come out of the fact that I have a white mother and a black father and that I lived half my childhood in Africa and half my childhood in an all-white neighborhood in Newcastle in England, that give me a specific viewpoint on everything I see.

On another level, there are issues around a kind of polarization, especially in America, but also in England, though nowhere near to the extent as in America: The two races are incredibly polarized in America, there's black and there's white and they seem to very rarely mix. They seem to very rarely live in the same neighborhoods, and that's not the case in England.

If I had to choose...if someone says to me, choose...if there was a war between black people and white people and someone says choose who you are going to shoot, obviously I'd go over to the black side, but I don't particularly want my mother to be my enemy and I think that informs a lot of what I do. Basically, the woman, the person who has loved me most in my life—who has loved me more than Malcolm X, who has loved me more than Mandela, has loved me more than any person on the face of this earth—is my mother; second my grandmother. These are two white women. These are the people who have formed me. And yet I am completely removed from them culturally and politically, there is a whole world between us. This is a strange place to be. It informs everything you do basically.

*In the context of African cinema, how do you situate yourself as a filmmaker in terms of being African, in terms of being black British? You talk about different hats, I had not before necessarily associated you as an African woman filmmaker, I am familiar with you more as a black British filmmaker. A lot of your work appears to address your experiences as a black British, as a mixed-race woman, where, as the director of **Monday's Girls**, you are viewed as an African woman filmmaker.*

It's more complicated than that.

Could you talk about these complicated identities?

It is incredibly complicated. All I can say is that my whole life has been a training ground to live this life. Basically, since I came out of my mother's womb it's been a chameleon situation for me. It's much more complicated than saying I have a lot of hats I wear. I have a lot of hats I have to wear but I wear them all simultaneously.

You say a lot of my work before *Monday's Girls* was about my black British identity, but I wouldn't agree. My work has always been specifically about being three or four things simultaneously. It's about being black British, it's about being bi-racial, it's about being African and it's about being all those things, because that is what I am.

Up until the age of twelve I lived completely in Nigeria, Ibo was my first language. I was the doctor's daughter on the compound, I knew nothing else. I was light-skinned compared to everybody else, but it was not really an issue. I may be considered slightly prettier, maybe I would have a higher bride-price. The fact that I was lighter-skinned in Nigeria was not a big issue. And where it was a big issue, it was a positive issue.

There was a bit of a backlash against my mother because we were Biafrans, and England had supported Nigeria during the Biafran Civil War, so she got a bit of a stink. But, basically, Nigerians, Biafrans, Ibos, Africans, in general, are too friendly, they take people for what they are. My mother never encountered the level of racism a black person would encounter in Britain.

So when I arrived in England at twelve, I arrived completely as an African child. I arrived in November in Newcastle, but it was an African child arriving in Newcastle. Newcastle, for those of you who don't know, it is a completely white city. I was the first black person at my school and everywhere. Everywhere we went we were the first black people the city knew and they laughed at us, they could not understand a word we said. I did really silly things; I used to carry my schoolbooks on my head, because that is what I used to do back home. I used to carry my brother on my shoulder; I used to take my shoes off when it was hot. So I made all these cultural faux pas if you like, and I lost my accent. My mother says I lost my Nigerian accent within eight months of arriving in England. It caused me too much grief.

So I assumed this neo-white identity, where I was trying to blend in as much as I possibly could with all the other children so they wouldn't make my life hell, and then I couldn't handle it. I actually left Newcastle when I was about fifteen or sixteen with my mother's blessing because it was such a nightmarish place to be. I came to London and became black British. So I have these three identities that are concurrent with each other and yet the only natural one, the only one that was natural and not forced on me in any way was the one I had in Nigeria up until the age of twelve.

Coffee Coloured Children is about an African child with a white mother growing up in Newcastle. *Still I Rise* follows the journey from Africa all the way to America and to Britain, of black women and how they are perceived. For me as a filmmaker, I have two eyes always, constantly; I am both on the outside looking in and the insider reporting out. And I think that is something slightly different in my work from other black women filmmakers, whether they are African filmmakers, or black British filmmakers. Quite often I have an insider's eye and an outsider's eye on the same situation and that goes through all my work. So that when I made the film in Nigeria, it was both as a Nigerian and woman. Because I knew how to treat the chiefs, I knew the traditions, I knew the order and hierarchies, I knew the procedures. But on the other side, I was not a Nigerian living in Nigeria.

*There appears to be a dichotomy, or separation in relationship to **Monday's Girls** and your other works, which are not viewed as African films. It is true that **Monday's Girls** is not your work as an independent filmmaker, at least that is the impression I get. What is this separation of **Monday's Girls** from your other works?*

And like *Monday's Girls*, there was *The Desired Number*, another documentary that was done in Nigeria. If I were to talk aesthetically, artistically, and structurally, I would say that *Monday's Girls* is my most European work. In terms of the formal way that it was filmed. Because what I inherited coming from Africa and living in Africa until I was twelve, the thing that was the most important to me, was storytelling. I was told a lot of stories. My whole approach to storytelling comes from what I grew up on in Africa.

In Africa, stories are neither realism nor non-realism, there is no line between what is real and what is non-real. So the spirit's world, or whatever, co-exists side-by-side with the real world. And they are not one thing or another. And what I think about European filmmaking, even African-American filmmaking, is that it is very much lodged in realism.

Storytelling is realism, so that if you are walking down the street, you are real, you are three-dimensional and what is going on in your brain is something that you cannot see. If you look at all of my other work apart from *Monday's Girls* there is a certain amount of mixing of reality, what's called reality, and what's called non-reality.

In *The Body Beautiful*, the mother is having the love scene with the younger man. That didn't really in actual fact happen; that happens in her head, but you bring it to life and the daughter is watching it. In *Wellcome to the Terrordome*, the Africans go underneath the water because they are trying to walk back to Africa and we see what their life is like underneath the water. These are all things that are absolutely comprehensible to Africans. If you look at a lot of African literature, it deals with the spiritual world side by side with the real world.

Monday's Girls is completely literal, it is completely observational filmmaking, and therefore completely the most European of my work. I think it has a lot to do with the eyes of the people and the stereotypes that they have in their head. That means that if you see a picture of an African woman in Africa wearing certain types of clothes, that's real African filmmaking; and then if you see a film, like *The Body Beautiful* or whatever, that's European filmmaking and that's so ridiculous.

*You stated during the film screening discussion of **Monday's Girls** that as a woman filmmaker, **Monday's Girls**, which was commissioned and produced by the BBC, would not have been what you would choose as a film. You also stated that it was "another case of naked African women dancing around, painting their bodies." So are you saying this is a European vision of African women?*

The problem with a situation like this is that you end up also denigrating Africa. I think it is brilliant that there are these ceremonies, there is nothing wrong with African women dancing naked. European women have far too many hang-ups about what should and shouldn't be covered.

What I am saying is that the European is willing to finance films that show Africans in that context because, in their eyes, that is the only part of Africans that they see. That is the area in which they are most easily able to absorb the information. The "Discovery Channel" kind of programs or the "National Geographic" kind of programs, these are how they expect to see, or are interested in seeing Africans. Whether they are liberals and they are looking at it as the noble savage kind of thing ("These simple people know things that we don't know, without complicated lives") or whether they straight up expect to see African women naked; so when they see them naked, it completely meshes in their mind that this is how it should be.

But for me there are all kinds of other things that if I had the choice to make, if I had the amount of money given to me to make something else rather than *Monday's Girls*, there are at least ten or fifteen other subjects that I would have chosen way before I got to making a film like *Monday's Girls*.

Such as? Would they be situated in Africa?

Yes, that is literally too big a question because there are so many. And also I am a professional filmmaker, so I am quite used to the notion that there are certain programs that the programmers want and that they don't. So even if they had given me a brief that says we want a film about African women or Nigerian women going from adolescence into woman-hood, it would still not be a brief that I would choose as first choice. But since we were going to be disciplined and professional about this, this was the brief of the program.

What was interesting to me was the way those girls/women were dealing with the fattening rooms, the generational gaps in terms of what the elder women wanted from them, what they wanted to do, how they interacted with me as an African American/African British woman coming over to them. Naomi Campbell popped up in their everyday conversations, and it was quite a visual juxtaposition to see these girls in their completely traditional African dress, sitting talking about how Naomi Campbell puts on her makeup. It was a scene you could have shot in Brixton or you could have shot in Brooklyn. These black women were sitting around basically "dissing" the way this girl puts her makeup on [Ngozi sucks her teeth to mimic the girls].

In the context of the fattening rooms in *Monday's Girls*, there could have been a lot of parallels made. Even in terms of how a lot of them were reacting with the camera. A lot of them knew what to do in front of the camera. When you turned the camera on, they were one thing; when you turned the camera off, they were something else—which is exactly the same thing it would be in Europe.

There were all these things about how they thought people were viewing them when they were being watched in Britain, outside of Nigeria, because a lot of them were aware. A lot of times these girls played African for the camera because a lot of times they knew what people were expecting from them. There were a lot of interesting dynamics in that. But the brief wasn't that. The brief was that they wanted to see some girls go into a room and come out fat.

You have stated that what critics and intellectuals can do for African cinema is to watch a range of things coming out of Africa. You also said that oftentimes the West dictates what films are made in Africa. So you feel that African filmmakers are particularly sensitive to the attitudes in the West in terms of the work they do?

That question has two answers. The fact of the matter is that American cinema has conquered the entire world so that even this myth that people have—that if you go to the cinema in Africa you'll see African films—is preposterous. If you go to the cinema in Africa you will see: firstly, American films; secondly Hong Kong/Kung Fu films; thirdly Indian films; finally, and occasionally, African films. So the bigger question is where the money comes from.

Indigenous filmmakers that live on the continent and produce films and television programs do so primarily for their national broadcasters. Nigerian filmmakers working in Nigeria work for Nigerian television and the money and resources are so limited. There are very few Beta cameras. A lot of people still work on U-matics for broadcast. There is so little money.

The indigenous audiences, what they want primarily from their broadcasters are news programs to find out what is going on in Nigeria, what's going on in the Democratic Republic of the Congo, and local soaps. That's what they want from their broadcasters, which is different from the imports, because they get "The Cosby Show" imported, they get Eddie Murphy films. What they want specifically from their broadcasters that they can't get from American imports or British imports are the news programs and the local soaps. So these two sections gobble up the tiny budget that is available for indigenous filmmakers to make indigenous programming.

Above and beyond that, if you want to make anything else other than that, you need to get money from somewhere else. If you are from a French-speaking country you'll get it from the French authorities or the French TV or French funding or the EEC. And if you are from English-speaking countries, you have to scrape around to get the money. But then what you're doing is applying around somewhere else for money. These people are not charities. They don't give you the money to go off and make films or programs just for that audience back home. There is a crossover audience. You have to then make the films to be watched outside of Africa. If you are from Burkina Faso, the biggest audience that you will get for you film will be in France. You might somewhere along the line make videos and there'll be copies made and people in Burkina Faso will see it. But by far the people that will pay to see it, the people who will decide to give the money for you to make another film because you've made a profitable film, or you didn't make a film that made a loss, will be the French. You are answerable to the French and the people who go to see it in France. The hope is that a lot of black French people or black people living in France will go see it, so you will have to compromise less.

When I make a film that you go to see, rather than my old white headmistress to go see, I am making less of a compromise. There is still a compromise involved for me to make it for you, because Americans, especially, are notorious for never setting foot in a theater with subtitles, and that includes black Americans as well as white Americans. Black Americans will not go see subtitled films.

So you are already dealing with a situation where a filmmaker might be forced...say I come from Nigeria; in Nigeria a lot of people speak English, but the language of emotion is Ibo. Where I come from, when they are really happy, when they are really mad, the formal language is English, but the language they speak among themselves is Ibo, but I might be forced by an American financier to make them speak in English. And what you have is a very stilted performance.

Even now, when I swear really badly—and I'm nearly thirty, and I left Nigeria when I was twelve—but when I am really angry and I swear, I swear in Ibo, its the language of emotion still for me. So you have these emotional films, these people are speaking English, and it's wrong, it's completely wrong. You have made a fundamental change to the story. So when we are making films we are still answerable to European audiences.

So, then, when it is said that this is an authentic African movie, they are not actually seeing an authentic African movie. An authentic African movie has not yet been made. When you think about black cinema in America, it has been only recently that you could see authentic black films being made. Because Spike Lee and all these people still have to get their money from Hollywood and they are Hollywood-dictated. So it's pretty obvious that African filmmaking is still even more removed from the source than that, so you have to actually answer to others.

Therefore, liberals and people that run institutions like this must open their eyes and think, just because in *Monday's Girls* these girls are wearing traditional clothes this isn't the only concept of Africa. People must begin to say, "If I see African films, I am willing to watch something that might be challenging me as to what I thought my definition of Africa was." So that would be the only way that we would get money to make films that tell you more about us. You guys must know so much about our initiation ceremonies. You guys probably know more about our initiation ceremonies than the people in the next village know about the village next door, because they are the ones that get made.

228

Would you say that you bring a woman's sensibility to your work as a woman filmmaker?

A long time ago, I made the decision to disconnect myself from the female film circuit because what was happening was I was always getting invited as a woman filmmaker. When I first came on the scene—when I first came out, if you like, on the filmmaking scene—the first group of people that literally tried to swallow me up was the female filmmaking circuit. Because it was a predominantly white circuit. And the notion of this very young (I was only about twenty-two) black woman coming out, they kind of literally jumped on me.

The situation that I found myself in at these festivals, was confronting a sea of white women's faces. And somehow I was supposed to have the same experiences as these women, and I didn't. If I were standing in a room full of black guys and not one single black woman, I would have still had more in common with everybody in that room than with a sea of white women. And what they expected me to say was so phenomenal. They "dissed" their men in a way that I can't possibly "dis" black men. For them, it is very easy to say men do this, this, and this. For me, it is absolutely impossible to say in the same way.

So for a long time I went around denying the fact that I was a woman filmmaker simply because I did not want to be associated with this. Just on so many fundamental levels, the campaign against abortion and for contraceptives. As black women, we don't have any problems with getting abortions. They will whip your baby out of you faster than you can cough. In Nigeria, there are millions of women, Catholic women, liberal women all setting up clinics. This is not our problem.

Now I can relax, and yes, ultimately I have a female sensibility, whatever that is. It's like Haile, you know Haile Gerima, he said your grandmother used to tell a story and your grandfather used to tell a story. It would be the same story but yet it would be told completely differently. If you notice, I have made twenty-two films and twenty of them must be about women. I definitely do have a female sensibility, but how you define what a female sensibility is, and where a black female sensibility differs from a white female sensibility, and where an African woman sensibility differs from a black woman sensibility, they are all very complicated.

I can say that stories are really important to me, but then if you look at Charles Burnett, stories are really important to him. I like filming violence, where a lot of people would say it isn't a woman's sensibility to film violence. But I have always thought that the big thing about film is to show people a lot of what happened to us in history. Everyone acknowledges that the Holocaust was a really bad crime, partly because everyone was white, and partly because they have images to see how horrific it was. There were none of those images from slavery because, if there were, they would be every bit as bad as the images from the Holocaust, but there are no images. What I have always thought is as a filmmaker my job is to show some of these images of what really happened and for me that means being violent sometimes. Whereas, if you've got someone like Julie Dash, she has a very poetic sensibility. So I think that it is so impossible to categorize.

You and I know why we are women and why we are not men. But how do you explain it to someone? It's not about having a period, it's not about—but it's absolutely impossible to explain what makes me a woman and why I like being a woman. I don't like having periods; I don't particularly want to push a baby out of my womb for twenty-four hours. I think the big difference between Africans and Europeans is that I am quite prepared to accept that there are some things that I don't understand, I will never understand, and that I am not meant to understand. You guys, and the guys in Europe you want to logically explain everything. There is no logic, I am female, I have a female sensibility, I make female films, and when I die God will explain to me what the difference was [laughter].

Franceline Oubda

Burkina Faso

Interview held at the 15th Edition of FESPACO in February-March 1997, Ouagadougou, Burkina Faso. Translated from French.

You have certainly been visible on the media landscape in Burkina Faso. How did you enter the world of cinema?

I am a director at the National Television of Burkina Faso. I see film and television as a vocation. I entered in the field of television in 1985, through a recruitment campaign for journalists to enhance national television programming. Once there, I observed that there was no programming for women. Thus, I decided to create a program called "Women and Development", which actually focused on the participation of women in the development process. After creating these programs, I went into directing.

For me, directing is not making films as such, but it is a means of expressing myself in relationship to women. Whether it is a panel discussion, or field reporting, or a more elaborate treatment such as a documentary film, I do it all. It is in this context that I evolved in this profession, and the reason that I became a filmmaker, especially in documentary filmmaking.

Would you say that your role as filmmaker is to focus on the experiences and conditions of women? Do you expect to work solely on topics that relate to women?

I think that women are in a better position to deal with the question of women, because they have lived these experiences. If I broach the problem of polygamy, even if I am not myself in a polygamous marriage, perhaps I have a sister, a mother, or aunt who lives this situation. Indirectly,

I have already seen how this woman experiences this life; I am a privileged witness who treats this subject. That is why I think a woman is in a better position to deal with the question of women, because she takes on the role of educator in society.

If you were to go into a household and see a woman and a man, you will find that it is the woman who is the backbone of the household. Even if you speak about a man, the care that surrounds and supports him is provided by the woman, she is the foundation. She prepares the children's meals, she dresses them, she nurses them, as well as her husband. I think that the woman is in a better position to talk about women, because she lives it both directly and indirectly.

One of your films was screened as part of the TV/Video Competition during FESPACO and then we saw another film during the colloquium in commemoration of the International Day of the Woman, held yesterday, March 8 and today. Could you talk about your films and their themes?

As I stated earlier, since 1985 I have done films that touched on many subjects. I have made at least fifteen documentaries with a focus on women. I will cite a few of the films that were awarded prizes nationally as well as internationally. At the 1993 FESPACO, I received the first prize for the Television/Video Competition with the film called *Accès de la femme à la terre*. At the 1995 FESPACO, I received the second prize for the Television/Video Competition for the film *Sadjo, la sahelienne*. Also at the 1995 FESPACO, I received another prize, "Développement humain durable" presented by the UNDP [United Nations Development Program] for the film *Femme de brousse, survivre à tout prix*. The film focuses on women's fight against desertification. Of course, there are the two films that you just saw, *La destinée* and *Elle pour refaire le monde*. The latter film was presented at the Beijing conference in 1996. I was designated by the Burkina government to make the film to present the point of view of Burkinabé women at Beijing. I made other films such as *Les cracheurs de farine*, which focuses on milling operations.

The film *Femmes de Yatanga* is about women in the rural sectors. In the region where the film takes place there is an association called "L'Association Six 'S'" which means, *savoir se servir de la saison seche en savane au Sahel* (to know how to make use of the dry season in the savanna of the Sahel). Despite the rapidly approaching desert, women have developed initiatives to fight against desertification and to survive it. The film *Femmes de Yatanga* focuses on their activities. For example, we see them using a new method of rearing sheep. They learn to fatten the sheep in a more intensified manner than the traditional practices in Burkina, which use a more extensive feeding system. They also use an anti-erosion method to fight against land erosion. We also see how they employ a technique for germination when there is not sufficient rain. In the documentary, I was able to show the women using these techniques.

In 1993, I was also awarded a prize "Sud-Nord" at the Rencontres Médias Nord Sud in Geneva. In that same year, I also won the prize "Images de femmes" and the prize "Regard sur les télévisions africaines" both at Vues d'Afrique in Montreal, for the film *Accès de femme à la terre.* In 1994, I received a First Mention for the film *Sadjo, la sahelienne,* also at Vues d'Afrique. In 1993, I won a prize from the FAO (Food and Agriculture Organization) for the series "Femme et développement." I have been awarded a total of eight prizes for the work that I have done.

During the question-and-answer session after the film screening there was a debate about the freedom of choice on the subject matter of your documentaries and to what extent you are free to treat the themes of your films. What role do the funding agencies have in the choice of the subject of the films that they finance?

In fact, when we make a film that has been commissioned, we must work within certain restrictions. We are obliged to respect the specifications of the agency. However, we often have the possibility of treating the subject as freely as we want. We have just developed a script and have submitted it to outside institutions, as well as those within Burkina, to produce it.

Our television station does not always have the financial means to produce our programs, so we have to become producers as well as directors and are forced to seek outside funding. Of course, in those cases, we do have limitations. For example, there may be an institution that is interested in a topic on AIDS, but its objectives for treating it are to focus on economic development while the area of social development is not the point of interest. We are, therefore, required to address the issue as it relates to the needs of the commercial market. For instance, the topics relating to AIDS are very much a public focus especially in the area of awareness-building and, thus, we are required to gear our program to these interests in order to obtain funding. Sometimes it is difficult to say loudly and forcefully what we want to say.

Who is your audience? The Burkinabés in general? Are you able to distribute your films to neighboring countries or outside of Africa?

We produce for the National Television of Burkina, and our audience is within a fifty-kilometer (thirty-mile) broadcast range around Ouagadougou. However, now, eight provinces out of forty-five are served by the CRT (Centres regionaux de télévision). At the present we are attempting to install antennas in those provinces in order to receive Ouagadougou—which is the main station—on live broadcast.

What we have also done is organize small screenings where we can discuss and debate about the subject matter presented in the films that interest certain NGOs and women's associations. This also allows us to have a certain contact with the public, to really talk about particular topics. But these screenings do not always render large results: as you notice, in the theater there was not a large audience.

Is there a system in place where films can be screened in the village areas and people can discuss afterwards?

There is a possibility, if there is a demand. Yesterday, I was asked to present my two films to a group about thirty kilometers from here. It is an association of village women who wanted to organize an activity for March 8, on the International Day of the Woman. They wanted to have a film screening and debate. Even today, when leaving the auditorium, there were Burkinabé members of human rights groups who asked if I could show my film *Elle pour refaire le monde* in Doridori, which is almost two hundred kilometers from Ouagadougou. Though it is very far, for this kind of screening, even if it is only done periodically, we are able now and then to go to certain villages. However, it is still limited.

We also have been able to present films by using video projections as well as through video-clubs. Now, in the villages, people show videos and ask for an entrance fee of twenty-five or fifty CFA. When this structure exists in the village, we schedule a date and we go to those areas, screen our films, and discuss the films with the people to see if they identify with what we are presenting.

What has been the general response to your films?

I make films about women, their accomplishments, their perspectives, and their experiences. It is a way for me to present examples of women who can be used as role models, as well as give a new perspective on certain preconceived ideas that people have. Let's take the example of the film *Sadjo, la sahelienne.* In Northern Burkina, there are Peuhl women who are very beautiful, and who like to make themselves up. Here in the Burkina capital, there is the general impression that they do not like to work. But, in fact, they do work. Because they like beautiful things and they like to beautify themselves, they have an incredible talent as craftswomen. Northern Burkina has rich land for cattle breeding. When a sheep or ox is killed, the hide is removed and the women work with the skin. They make shoes and other items, it is really quite something to see. When a film such as this is shown to people who have preconceived notions of the Peuhl, their attitudes are changed.

In your film La destinée, you raised an important problem about the impact of foreign images that inundate the television and movie screens in Africa. Could you elaborate on this? As you showed, these films do not reflect the reality of the African youth, and yet, the influence on them is significant. Could you also expound on the phenomenon of these outside images on popular culture in Africa?

We are realizing that we do not have the power to control the influx of these outside images. We are bombarded with these images and perhaps what is necessary is a policy within African countries to find a way to examine these images and their influences. It is a very complicated situation. People buy satellite dishes and connect to whatever network they want. It is very difficult. We also sense that Africans do not like their own images. They actually prefer foreign images. This comes from the fact that we are not used to seeing our own images. And I think it is up to us as directors to fight in this regard and assist our public in developing an appreciation for our cinema.

It is a cinema that speaks of our reality, of our development, and we must reach this objective. It seems that even the people in the North do not like our films. They have another vision of us. They have always portrayed Africans as spectacular and sensational, or naked and hunger-stricken, with swollen-belly children. We do have value and worth and it is up to us Africans to value our culture, what we have. As a result, others will also appreciate our culture and our images. This is the only way that our cinema will evolve. If we are only content with images that are thrown at us, I think African cinema will never thrive.

Do you notice a certain alienation among the young generation from their own culture that comes from wanting to be like the people and images that they see on the screens? You have already stated that Africans do not identify with their own images; what does this mean for the future of African culture?

235

I think that, in fact, there is a certain alienation because the impact of the image is very powerful to the extent that it can change attitudes. When our young people see these images, they attempt to identify with certain actors and characters and, as you see, the cinema here is Kung Fu, and the Japanese cinema is still something else. Our youth like foreign images because they want to express themselves in different ways than they find in their own culture. As I portrayed in the film, when the French television series "Hélène et les garçons" comes on the television, all of the young people run to see it. If you notice, AIDS in our country is very developed. The young people who watch these shows do not realize that these are characters on the screens that are making love in a spontaneous way, but, in reality, people are taking precautions. This has to be stressed to them, and I tried to show this. These images create fantasies in our young people, who in turn want to imitate them. It is true that the lesson in the use of contraceptives appears a bit didactic. However, I tried to demonstrate that while these acts are shown on the screen, that in reality young people must know that there are places where they can go to find information about the real facts about these practices.

In the film we see a certain fantasy that the village girl has vis-à-vis *the city. She sees all the images that are representative of a city sophistication. She finds the hairstyle, clothing, and manners of the city girl beautiful, chic, more interesting....*

In the film, my purpose was not to present a village/city relationship. Of course, when going from the village to the city we see the contrast in housing and furnishing, but I was not really interested in focusing on this aspect. But yes, it does exist. The girls from the village admire the girls from the city because it is another "look" [stated in English]. For instance, in another film that was screened, we saw a village girl take the wig of a woman while musing "I look like a city girl." Their main objective is to become like them. They think that the girls in the city have a better situation and they want to have the same lifestyle. On the other hand, when a girl from the city comes to the village, she is often disappointed to see the way that the girls and women dress.

Would you say that village girls experience a certain alienation as they strive to identify with city culture?

Yes and no, it is a way of imitating. It is a change of mentality that comes from the images that we receive. There is a strong westernization in the villages, because the people of the city are viewed as the models. I wouldn't say that it is necessarily alienation, but rather a way of identifying with what is considered better.

You work in video and television; could you talk about the technology in terms of the advantages and disadvantages in comparison to working in film?

With film and video production, it is a question of the physical medium. It is not because one works in video that the theme is not treated in the same manner. A feature fiction film can be made in video and perhaps it will cost less. And I think that it is better for me to work in video, since we are already troubled by the lack of financial means. Thus, in this case we have less anguish. Video is much less expensive, it is practical, and we are able to show much more of our work to the public.

On the other hand, 16mm or 35mm is not accessible to everybody. One has to have many contacts to have the funding to make films in these formats. To gain the confidence of financiers is very difficult. You see filmmakers that since the beginning of their career have never been able to complete their films, whereas, during this same time, those of us who use video are doing a maximum amount of films.

I would assure you that if I had the means, I would do six video-documentaries in a year, whereas, if I worked in 35mm, I would take five to ten years without having done one film. I think we should turn towards the means that are more accessible.

What do you feel is your contribution to African cinema? You have already talked about your work in the area of women and development, and I have seen several of the films in this series. You were also one of the co-organizers of the colloquium in commemoration of the International Day of the Woman, where a few African women in cinema presented their work.

I think that I have been able to contribute to African cinema by doing a few films that have been seen and awarded prizes, that have toured around the world, and that have raised questions about problems that exist. I am sure that there is a great deal more to do because the contribution of one person, even if it is important, is not enough; since there are a great many problems that remain, and there is still a lot to do.

I have contributed a great deal to the emancipation of women because all the films that I have done have focused on women, especially in my country. I have been in this field for the last eleven years. Whether they are documentaries, television debates, or reports on particular situations, I think that I have contributed much to the emancipation of women. I would like to continue in this direction so that women may become more aware of their situation in order to better participate in the development of our country.

As a Burkinabé woman, what are your impressions of Princess Yennenga?

She is a hero.

As the symbol of the grand prize of FESPACO, does she represent a symbol for the future of African women in the cinema?

You have seen that in a conscious or unconscious way, the image of Princess Yennenga is the grand prize of FESPACO, which is very significant. It demonstrates the importance of women in society. And I think to have this prize is a crowning achievement. And we women must fight so that women will achieve this.

If we succeed in obtaining the Etalon de Yennenga, the efforts of women will be crowned and we will have reached a certain objective. Princess Yennenga was the proof of courage and bravery, the proof of endurance, and she was a woman who did a great deal in Burkina history. I think to fight for a woman to obtain the Yennenga is truly a step forward, and it will be for the greater welfare and improved standard of women in general.

Aminata Ouedraogo

Burkina Faso

Interview held at the 15th FESPACO, February 1997, Ouagadougou, Burkina Faso. Translated from French.

Aminata, you are a visible presence in African cinema, especially as organizer and general coordinator of the Union Panafricaine des Femmes de l'Image, UPAFI (Pan-African Union of Women in the Image Industry). Could you start by talking about your background in cinema?

I entered the cinema when I began my studies at INAFEC (Institut Africain d'Education Cinématographique). It was a film school at the Université de Ouagadougou here in Burkina, where some two hundred students throughout the continent were trained between 1976 and 1987. The core curriculum at INAFEC was multifaceted. Therefore, we touched on many areas, such as radio, television, print journalism, and film. After completing the core curriculum, there was the choice between two divisions, one for those who specialized in cinema; and the other for those who specialized in communication.

After this training, I went to Paris to continue at IMAC (L'Institut du Multimedia et Architecture de la Communication). During my professional career, I have done four films—one fiction film and three documentary films. The first film was about the new world order of information. The second focused on the SIAO (Salon international d'artisans d'Ouagadougou). The third examined the use of stimulants by students preparing for examinations. And the last touched on alcoholism. Two of the films were shot on 16mm and two on Beta.

Within the discourse on women and the cinema, there is much discussion about a woman's gaze or a woman's perspective. Do you feel that there is a certain sensibility that women bring to their films?

If you mean sensibility in the popular sense of the word, I would say yes, there is a certain woman's sensibility. Evidently, sensibility depends on the personality of each individual. The fact that we are women means that we have a sensibility that is different from men. And then, it depends on the subject. Let us take a car accident as an example. When looking at the accident, each person is struck by an aspect that touches her or him. Generally, a woman would be more sensitive to blood. And if she were to speak about this accident, she would put more emphasis on the presence of blood. If she were sensitive to other things, perhaps, these would draw her attention, because there are many factors involved. If she were a mother and if it were a young person hurt, her maternal instinct would be roused, which would perhaps be different from the vision of a man.

I think this sensibility spans all spheres. For example, a woman and a man enter a store. The woman would automatically go towards the dishes and chinaware, or foodstuffs or beauty products or children's clothing, if she has children. Instinctively, the man will go towards hardware or household maintenance, because there is a general attitude that men are much more handy in the area of home repairs, where *a priori* women are less likely, unless she is professionally disposed to it. This aspect is also included in the notion of gender sensibility.

However, when it comes to cinematic creativity, I do not think there are subjects that have especially a female orientation. I think women may treat any subject. There is no male or female subject matter. The subjects are the same and we treat them according to the message that we want to get across, for the reasons that drive us to do the film. Whether we are women or men, we may deal with any subject, but it is true that the process would be different.

Even if we were to take into account the nature, character, or the treatment of a subject, the process would be different according to the person. Take for instance a written essay. When you give a topic to a class of twenty-five students, you will receive twenty-five different ways of treating the same topic. It is informed by the person's temperament and individuality.

However, I do not feel that there is a subject that is designated only for women. Moreover, I think that it is also up to us women to rectify this impression. To use the term "feminist film" or "woman's cinema" does not mean that there is a cinema exclusively for women. When there is a minority, it is always this minority which has to speak out, to protest or make a call for action. It is simply due to the fact that in the field of cinema there are not many women. People have always thought that cinema was a male profession. Thus, attitudes had to change, there had to be a great deal of evolution, and women had to be encouraged to go into film.

The woman, in essence, is the one who calms the situation; she is viewed as the reasonable person. And I am not saying this to be in opposition to men. If she invests in the area of film to address the many afflictions that plague us today, such as war, famine, illness, she will be heard. As women tend to speak little compared to men, therefore, when she does speak she draws more attention and her words have more power, because they are rare.

"Women's films" or "images of women" as a concept must be interpreted in a positive way, and not in a sense that will ghettoize or pigeonhole women because they have made a certain film.

I do not know if you are familiar with the filmmaker Kitia Touré. He made a film and, though a man made it, it made a significant proclamation to women. It spoke of the role of the woman in the home, the household, as educator of the children, and he also addressed women's negligence in certain areas. Though it is a film open to criticism, it is a positive film. One must look at it and discuss it. Yes, the film was an expression of his sensibilities, and though there are questions that may be posed about it, there is still something valuable that can come from it.

When one speaks of "women's films," it is principally to let people know that in the area of cinematic creativity, there are women, women make films—not *women's* films, but films made *by women* and this must be encouraged. It is equally important that women enter in this domain.

In the area of film criticism, there is much discussion about the visual representation of women. What are your impressions of the image of women in African cinema?

I think that people focus too much on the image of the woman. I do not think that initially filmmakers really made their films thinking, "I must have a 'feminine' presence." Human beings are composed of man and woman. The woman is everywhere, so you cannot make a film without her. There are two images, a positive image and a negative image.

Let us take the film *La noire de...* as an example, the position of maid in our culture, at least in Burkina Faso, is held by girls. In Europe—though I am not in a position to talk about it in a detailed way—generally women are the maids. It is for that reason that [in French] they are called *femmes de ménage,* because one thinks that housework is women's work. Nowadays we see men doing housework. One can also do a film where a man does the housework, and then ask men how they view the image of men.

However, in general, I think that we have certain images because men are the ones who have made films. They are behind the camera, and women are in front of the camera. I do not think this was a preconceived idea, it was not consciously done.

We do see African films where the woman's body is objectified. There is no apparent reason for the nudity or the specific attention that her body is given....

It is true there have been male filmmakers who have used the woman as a object of pleasure, and that is due also to the influence of Western films that they see. It is in the West that we see the woman nude, the woman kissing a man, the woman making love with a man on the screen. Individuals can be influenced and filmmakers are also influenced, because we see these films on television, on the screens, and these are films that are commercialized to make money. Films that are now being made have been influenced by these images in order to be sold.

In Africa, sexuality is not banalized as it is in the West. There is modesty and a sense of respect. This distinction must be understood. Westerners think that it is because we are "primitive" and "uncivilized"—and of course I ask, "civilized in relationship to what?"—or not liberated or evolved that we don't view sex in a banal, common way. Nevertheless, it is a question of understanding. In their societies it is acceptable, and they do it. In our societies, we do not. In addition, I totally disagree with the notion that we must imitate them. I do not see how that helps us. When we think it is useful or good for our population, we will do it. We do not take all from the West; we take what is good and leave what is not. I do not see at this stage of our evolution, of our civilization, that these images are actually good for us.

Some will say that it is because it is not allowed or because we do not make these kinds of films that people want to see sex. We *can* show sexuality, but it is *how* it is shown. There is a way of portraying it. To go even further, I will note that in Europe today, unwanted pregnancies are not known as they are in Africa. The practice of abandoning infants is not known in Europe as it is in Africa. The young Western woman who becomes pregnant, wants to become pregnant. She has decided what she wants, she knows her body, she knows what sexuality is, and she goes into sexual relationships aware of the consequences. She lives her life freely.

How many parents here in Africa talk about sexuality with their children? We must first start to speak about sexuality correctly with our children, without resorting to vulgarity. We can speak with them about any subject because we are their parents. We are the ones who have a direct interest and are the only ones who can tell the truth and speak objectively to our children. No one else can do it for us. Parents must prepare their children for this and not let them learn about life from the exterior, through films and television shows. Though I am mainly talking about girls, I include boys as well—because respect for the girl cannot happen if the boy does not know that he is supposed to respect her. There is a lot of work that has to be done and ground that must be covered.

What part do women play as filmmakers?

We who create, who are behind the camera, who want to get a message across, whether we are women or men, if we want to use women, it is not sex that should be the dominant feature. Nothing in particular adds to a film or enhances it by using sex; on the contrary, it often does a disservice to the film. If you were to ask people what kinds of films they would like for the youth, they would readily say educational films. The violent or *risqué* films are not as popular, though people do watch them privately. It has to be discussed because each person has a point of view on the subject.

I am a filmmaker, but I do not know if a film with a black woman or white woman used as an object of pleasure would be a subject that I would want to focus on one day. Perhaps if I were to do so it would be done in a manner much more respectable, more subtle, without—if I can express myself in this way—lowering myself, as I have seen done in other films, and I don't agree with this portrayal in these films.

You have raised some interesting points in the context of images of women. I do not often hear or read film criticism by African women or critiques of images or films by African women. African women as film critics are not very visible, at least not to me in the United States. Does a visible film criticism by African women exist here on the continent? If so, how does it manifest itself? If not, do you see it emerging?

Of course, it will come. Do you know why you do not see African women in the area of film criticism? Because in the film arena in general women are not well represented. And as long as this is the case, there will not be women visible in the various spheres within the field of cinema. When women enter in larger numbers in these different areas, you will then see women film critics doing objective criticism and analysis of films. It is not because you have not seen any that there are none. If you were to attend the debates that take place after the film screenings during FESPACO, you would see that when women take the microphone to talk they do critique the films that they have seen, they give their opinions about the films that they have just seen. Perhaps there are no written essays, but there is a critique.

To return to what I said earlier about African films and even Western films where women are used as objects of pleasure, this is not the image that we want of women. When making a film there is often more emphasis on women than men, and I do feel that it is done unconsciously, because what actually attracts people's attention is the woman. A man may pass by nude and it will not be as shocking as if it were a woman. People will turn to look because it is a woman.

Women are symbols and represent something for a society, no matter what society. Women inspire respect and consideration. If a woman lowers herself to a certain level, it is shocking to a society. It is also a rejection of that society. I think it is in this way that the image of women should be interpreted. Fundamentally, the image of woman is positive. We must not render it negative, whether we are women or men; I am speaking of the society in general. We must insist on this.

In 1991 at the 12th FESPACO, an African Women in the Cinema Workshop was part of the official FESPACO platform. As the organizer of this workshop, could you talk about the organization and the needs and interests that made it a reality?

We organized this workshop because we realized that, ever since Burkina Faso established this festival, there was a female presence in front of the camera, but the female presence behind the camera was minimal. However, we are seeing the emergence of women behind the camera, and there are increasingly more films made by women. There have not been very many women trained in this area in Africa, and the first women to have made films are not actually on the continent. Compared to African men, African women make films far less frequently.

A workshop was organized to make women's place known and understood by the international and local public. The objective of the workshop was first to pay homage to the African woman for all the work she has done in front of and behind the camera and to make this work known to everybody. It was not a workshop organized to fight against men. It was an event organized with FEPACI (Pan-African Federation of Filmmakers) and FESPACO, in agreement with all the concerned officials of the country. This permitted us to bring together some fifty women, with different perspectives and from different countries. It allowed us to see that, in fact, there are many women who work in this industry, who have various funding needs and diverse problems, and thus it was important to find out what solutions were needed, as well as to exchange ideas. Perhaps you have noticed that the presence of women at FESPACO is more visible.

What has happened since this event?

During the past six years...as you know, like any other new organization there are difficulties. Unfortunately, we in Burkina Faso are the only ones who are doing something for African cinema and culture, and the government supports us. These concerns must be supported by all African states and must lead to concrete action. For instance, during the 1991 FESPACO, funding was available to invite the women because outside partners have become more aware of the presence of women and their importance. They understand that this presence also benefits the entire society. However, the funding did not come from any initiatives by African states. It has to be the concern of our own countries. They must have an interest in initiatives such as the workshop. They must have an interest in the place that women will occupy in the cinema, so that this structure that has been established may grow and be strong enough to stand on its own.

There are still many realities that cannot be overlooked. There is the problem of the financing, production, and distribution of films, which are the same problems that male filmmakers have. However, certain considerations must be taken into account, due to the role of woman as it is defined in her social context. She is a woman, she is a wife, she is a mother, and she is a daughter—therefore, she has responsibilities towards her parents—thus, she has responsibilities that are not the same as male filmmakers.

Today, in order to get a film financed there must be a lot of networking. It is a world where one must have many contacts, or one must be known. It is a kind of a closed group. No one will approach you. No, you must knock on all doors. You must run after people in order to make yourself known. It is easier for a man to do this than for a woman, for logical reasons. For example, because a woman has a baby, it is more difficult for her to travel. To travel she must have money, for herself and for the child. She must care for the child if she takes the child with her. That is one restriction. Either she has children and afterwards she works,

245

or she works and then has children. If she has young children, she cannot be as efficient. A man has a baby, it is not he who takes care of the child, it is the woman. Whether he is married or single, it does not play a role in his being able to go out and meet people to find funding. In Africa, women are not sufficiently organized to do so.

There are no economic structures in Africa that invest in the cinema. Prospective financiers are not convinced that it is an industry that can bring in money, but this must happen. Africans must understand that they can invest in the cinema and can make money from it. And when this happens, our cinema will not be as reliant or dependent upon others as we are today. In the same way, the "Union panafricaine des femmes de l'image" would not be as hesitant as they are today because of lack of funds. We must start relying on ourselves. We must start working with our partners and stop depending on them. We have a saying that goes: "While one washes your back, you must wash your own face." If somebody helps you, you have to do your part. This attitude must be followed in Africa.

During the 1991 workshop, African women expressed the need to meet among themselves in order to get to know each other before opening the forum to others. At the same time, women of the African Diaspora considered themselves African and felt that they were part of this group of African women. This difference of opinion, in terms of who was considered African and who was not, caused a tension and ultimately a terrible misunderstanding. I would like to revisit this event in an attempt to have an open discussion between African and African diasporan women.

I would like this event to be de-dramatized, because I see the event as being a misunderstanding. Women of the Diaspora and African women do not live the same reality. Our problems are similar but are not posed in the same way. The meeting in 1991 was the first time that we ever came together. Because it was the first time, there was a foundation that we wanted to establish, and we needed to talk among ourselves. We needed to get along together and to instruct each other. We did not know the problems that existed in Southern Africa, in Central Africa, in East Africa, in West Africa, in North Africa. First, we had to create a platform in order to discuss, to understand each other, and to reach a common agreement on something.

This workshop was planned during FESPACO. FESPACO is an international event, it is open to everyone, and many people attend. The fact that this was the first time that "Women of the Image" met also meant that there was a great deal of interest and a lot of people wanted to participate. Of course, that was not a bad thing. Nevertheless, I think that if you want to participate in something, if you are interested in something, you say it and you show it; we have to try to understand each other. We were a large group, and so there was this misunderstanding.

We asked the women of the African Diaspora to let us first talk among ourselves before meeting them. Since we did not speak the same language, in terms of experiences, and since we did not speak about the same things, we could not understand each other.

Today, if I were to speak about poverty or the situation of women in Burkina Faso, I would emphasize the problem of schooling, the problem of health, of housing, of food and nutrition, and so on. If I had to have this debate with an American, we would find that these are problems that are not her problems. Her problems are on another level. In order to be able to speak to others, I must first know for myself what my problems are, what I want myself, and then I can talk and exchange ideas. However, if I speak about food and nutrition because I do not have enough to eat, and she speaks to me about hairstyles, etc., evidently, I would say that is not my problem, at the moment. I am not worried about my hair; my first concern is survival.

This is to say that there was a misunderstanding, and I also feel that there was a dramatization of the situation. I went out and attempted to talk to the women, but they did not want to understand. One cannot force someone to discuss if that person does not want to. They consider themselves Africans, they feel they are at home in Africa, they are entitled to these feelings. I can understand how they feel. However, I think they relied too much on this aspect when, in fact, it had nothing to do with the situation in question.

I think that if we really want to work together, we can go beyond these misunderstandings. I am prepared to discuss this problem with anyone interested. I am prepared to give whatever information, whatever clarification possible regarding this incident and, in my opinion, it should not be the end of the world. Things happen. We have a saying that goes: "In the mouth the tongue and teeth mix together, but sometimes the teeth bite the tongue." Thus, in life, we may come together, but a misunderstanding may happen. However, there must be a dialogue to resolve this misunderstanding.

I think that it is a problem that does not have to persist. I do not see why we cannot undertake something together if we see the need to do so. On the contrary, I think we should get over this in order to understand that, after all, there was a problem in the planning of the workshop, they came with another perspective, there was a misunderstanding, but at the end we had the same objective. We want to achieve the same things and we can work together.

I do not think the problem was that big and, what is more, everything has an ending. We did not have the same understanding on one particular point. We can collaborate and come together on other things. We made a decision on this point because we had to organize at that particular time. Today, if we were to go to a festival in the United States and we wanted to participate in something, either we are accepted or we are refused. We cannot impose ourselves. In the case of the workshop, it was not a rejection; it was a moment when we asked them to let African women meet among themselves. They could have tried to understand our reality, to see how we could all do something together. It was a pity, but it is over.

What do you see as the future of the organization of African women in the cinema?

The project that we are working on at the moment, and that was one of the objectives at the time, is to compile an index of women in the cinema. This document will include a list of women filmmakers and their needs, a list of the names of partners, a list of organizations that are interested in promoting women and their works, a filmography of works by women, a list of organizations that are interested in the promotion of women, and a list of the various festivals.

Since the first meeting, at each subsequent FESPACO we have met to talk about the association, and to support the women. It is a slow process, it is true, and there is even the impression that we are not doing much; but in reality the association does work, and we see an increasing number of women just about in every sphere of the cinema.

We are working towards the promotion of women in cinema. If you read the revue *Ecrans d'Afrique/African Screen*, you will notice that each time that a woman has done something, we talk about her, we promote her work. However, the work that we do is not yet visible today. The Italian organization, Centro Orientamento Educativo (COE), based in Milan, also plans to do something regarding African women. In 1996, in Harare, we had a women's workshop and the women of Zimbabwe have formed an association. Every time the opportunity comes, we must seize it. Though it is not only up to women to do this work, men too must do it because the work that we do benefits everybody, men as well as women.

And you, in terms of the work that you are doing, you are in some way a mouthpiece. Others will know that this association exists and that there are women filmmakers, editors, scriptwriters, and other women in the cinema. Consequently, more people will know about African women in the cinema and about the films made by women.

Françoise Pfaff

Guadeloupe/France

Interview held in Washington, DC, November 1997.

You are Professor in the Department of Modern Languages and Literatures at Howard University. How did you become interested in African film history and scholarship, and what do you see as the importance of scholarship in African cinema?

Well, I came to cinema first in France. I studied in Paris and took a course by the well-known film critic, Michel Ciment. He is one of the people who created the journal *Positif.* He gave very interesting classes on American cinema, not only the history of American cinema and the films that were landmarks in that cinema, but also how a film reflected a society, how it could criticize or celebrate the values of that society. But there was always a link established between the filmmaker and, of course, the milieu in which the work was being made.

I started to appreciate film from a more critical point of view. It was no longer pure entertainment for me; it was something that was meaningful, something that conveyed particular images, symbols, and metaphors. This is what led me to consider cinema more seriously and also to be interested in American society. Perhaps this is what led me to come to the United States. This is how my interest in film began.

After I came to the U.S., I ended up teaching at Howard University in Washington, DC, and became interested in seeing the correlation between literature and film. I taught novels by African writers, and a lot of African American students had that very mythical and idealized image of Africa, but no concept of its reality. I used films at first to illustrate African reality, so that students could see the context of the books they read.

Then in 1976, I believe, Howard University invited Ousmane Sembene to lecture and we saw his film *Black Girl*. I remember it quite vividly.

That was the first time that you had seen the film?

Yes, and I met Sembene. I was teaching French and was interested in meeting him because he was from a francophone country, and I had read his novels. However, I had never seen his films. I became more and more interested in his work and used his films in my courses. As you know, most of his films are adaptations of his novels, so I could teach his novel in class, and we could see the film and discuss the differences between the written work and the film. It was also at that time that I met the Ethiopian filmmaker Haile Gerima.

Then my friend Abiyi Ford, professor of film at Howard, invited me to give a lecture on the cultural components of Sembene's film *Emitai*. I explained the context for the film—the Second World War, the concept of colonialism and the French presence in Senegal—how Senegalese men fought in the French army and how villagers' produce was taken from them and given to the French. Afterwards, this information enticed me to do more and more research.

I had touched history. I began to see more films. I would do research dealing with African religions, then look at various ethnic groups and their particular socio-cultural facets, and one thing led to the other. It was no longer only film per se that interested me. It was also the culture expressed in the film, and I have continued this research to now. It is a never-ending process if you want to be thorough and up-to-date in what you provide to your students.

Starting with literature, I went to film, and my interest in film has branched out to many other spheres. For example, in order to write an article on film as an anthropological tool,[1] I had to understand anthropology. You have to study other fields in order to grasp the reality that is expressed in film and the meaning and significance of film as a medium and also as a tool for social change. You have to learn everything you can about the society on which the film was made.

So that is how I came to African film, a little bit because I was interested in film research, and then, when I came to the States and started teaching francophone, Caribbean, and African literature, film also became a pedagogical tool for me. Since I was teaching French, I focused on francophone cinema, and this led me to specialize in West African francophone cinema. I don't know a lot about anglophone African cinema.

Was there a cinema component in your dissertation research?

Yes, there was also a focus on cinema, how the tools of literary criticism can be used in cinema. I had done some work on the images of blacks in American films.

So it was at the Sorbonne that you began...

Actually it was at Paris VII. I started at the Sorbonne, but then after 1968, I followed some of the teachers who seemed to be more progressive to Paris VII. It was interesting how it all worked. You are right, I started with American cinema, then, because of my identity as a black woman, I became interested in the plight and destiny of African Americans and how they were portrayed in film.

Do you think that is what piqued your interest to ultimately teach in the United States at a historically black university?

Yes. When I first came to the States, I taught for a year as a teaching assistant at Bates College. Of course my primary purpose for coming here was to know the United States but also to focus on the African American community, maybe to find myself in that community. I do think there is a relationship between, as you said, my interest in the African American community, my study of that community on film, and then my branching out to the "motherland."

I have seen your presentation on stereotypical images of Africa in film. Having studied both, do you see similarities in the treatment of African Americans and Africans in Western cinema?

Definitely, because as Abiyi Ford says, "cinema is not benign." It is a vehicle for a particular ideology. And since bankers who loan money to make films, investors in films, and people who head the film industry in the United States are usually part of the dominant social stratum, most of the ideas reflected in their films are ideas of this social sector. When you have a dominant group with a policy of racial segregation based on black racial inferiority, of course films are not going to celebrate the heroism of African Americans!

Until the 1960s, you had this image of African Americans as animals and rapists—you remember Griffith's *The Birth of a Nation*—or else they were inept, stupid people, as in Stepin Fetchit's films. You had all those animal-like stereotypes of African Americans, but in the 1960s, although gaining a cinematographic "humanness," they were also viewed as victims in films such as those with Sidney Poitier.

The image of Africans in Western cinema is about the same. Some motion pictures show Africans as savage natives, with painted faces and spears poised to kill the poor explorers who venture into their territory. This manner of presentation shows not the explorers who disrupt the peace of the community, but the natives who are evil because they hamper the explorers' journeys! You also have the image of violent, stupid Africans as part of the background for the daring white treasure hunter, usually male. This representation of Africans in Western media corresponded, of course, to the system of colonialism.

On the one hand, you had slavery and segregation that fostered certain derogatory images of African Americans in Western films, and, on the other hand, you had colonization that permitted no positive portrayals or heroism among the colonized. The same types of stereotypes were developed. In an article on stereotypes of African Americans in American literature, Sterling Brown found similar stereotypes. Films that convey the dominant ideology condone the systems accepted by that ideology. What is propagated by the dominant group is sustained, so you find a correspondence between them. Art forms convey ideology. That is why you have correlations between the images of blacks—Africans and African Americans—in Western films. It is definitely part of a system of expression and maybe part of a system of control, because you proffer those images to whites but also to blacks, which says to the latter: "Stay in your place, you are subhuman." Film is a very tricky way to control people. It's a great medium, but it can also be misused, abused, and used as a controlling element in a society.

You have contributed a great deal to African cinema scholarship in the United States. You have written several books including the first book published in the U.S. devoted to an African filmmaker. You have organized conferences as well as other activities in the area of cinema. Could you talk about these contributions?

The other day I was teaching a class for my colleague Mbye Cham, professor of African Studies at Howard, and his students had my book on Ousmane Sembene. It was published in 1984, and I was very happy to see that thirteen years later it is still being used. I felt I had not wasted my time in writing the books on African cinema because they are still considered relevant today.

My first book, *The Cinema of Ousmane Sembene*[2] has been termed "an explication of text" by the Malian film scholar Manthia Diawara. This may be accurate, because I felt at the time that Sembene's film texts had to be explained and placed in their proper socio-cultural perspectives. They are not easily understood by people who don't know anything about Africa. The book has been used as a reference for many subsequent books, so I think that, in all modesty, it may have made some kind of impact.

My second book, *Twenty-five Black African Filmmakers*,[3] is a compilation of biographies and bibliographies of works by twenty-five black African filmmakers. It too is widely referenced and is owned by a number of university libraries. Writing those books and being one of the first scholars to publish books and articles on African film in the United States might have contributed to making African film a serious topic in this country.

At the beginning, when I proposed my first course on African cinema, people in my own department laughed. They said: "She is just going to show films! She doesn't want to teach! It's going to be a relaxed class. African film...who has ever heard of it?" I believe that my scholarship, with its serious approach to film, has contributed to creating a field that is now explored by others. So I think that is what I have modestly contributed. I have also written some notes for African film festivals.

Another contribution that I consider rather important was my work as curator of the African component at the 1988 DC FilmFest, the annual Washington, DC, film festival. I think that by organizing panels, inviting people from France and Africa, critics as well as filmmakers, I contributed to the seriousness of the topic.

You are a professor at Howard University, which perhaps can be seen as a hub of African cinema scholarship: I'm thinking about Mbye Cham, Abiyi Ford, yourself, and Haile Gerima, all of whom are at Howard. What is it like for you to teach at a historically black university, and what is its potential in the area of African cinema scholarship?

Yes, I think we have key people at Howard University, and we also have a unique group of students, largely constituted of African Americans. I am teaching an African film class this semester, and out of twenty-five students there are eight Africans. This fosters an exchange between African Americans and Africans in ways that perhaps would not happen otherwise.

The context of viewing and criticizing African films brings those two groups together, I feel, because they share their experiences. The African students are sometimes from Senegal, sometimes from Cameroon and elsewhere, and I show films from those countries. The Africans can add to the discussion from their personal knowledge of their own society. So I think it brings, beyond the film, another dimension of communication between the students, based on the criticism and viewing of African cinema.

I tell the students, "I am going to show you Africa, maybe not as you dreamed about Africa, but Africa as seen by African filmmakers with a certain amount of realism, and you might not be very pleased." Because members of the African Diaspora can have the idea of Africa being a mother and a paradise. We have a dream about Africa, but when we go there, we are disappointed because it doesn't match our expectations.

I tell them, "I want to prepare you for your first trip to Africa by showing you a realistic approach to African society." And then a student will say, "Well, why can't we keep our dreams; after all, aren't we entitled to dreams?" I respond, "If you want to keep your dreams, fine, but the purpose here is to show that Africans are people like everybody else. They have aspirations, they have disappointments, they have evil and good people in society just like any other society. And one should not mythicize 'Mother Africa' but rather see it realistically."

What are some of the films that you show to give them this reality?

For instance, Sembene's *Xala*. It was interesting to see how African Americans and Africans would discuss the issue of polygamy and of corruption. The film is also very comical, so we discuss its farcical aspects. I also show how it was used with political intent to ridicule the corrupt bourgeois and celebrate the solidarity and power of the powerless, the beggars in the film—that is a film that had an impact. And, of course, the final scene of the film, the spitting, is usually not acceptable to African Americans. They say, "Oh, what is that? It's disgusting!" And, of course, you have to explain that in the Senegalese context, it may mean something different.

There are also some cultural aspects of African societies—the practice of excision in *Finzan* by the Malian director Cheick Oumar Sissoko, for example—that have a great impact on African American women. They have heard about it, but to listen to a woman shouting at the end of the film while she is being excised, I think this is something they will never forget. They inevitably ask, "How can you do that in your country?" and the African students explain it and mention movements that are fighting this particular tradition. People are beginning to understand that excision entails dangers and certain kinds of problems. It is being eradicated, and Howard students are overwhelmingly against the practice. The film creates a climate of dialogue, and I think it is very enriching for African Americans to see a visual presentation of what they might have heard about before.

Then, in terms of the oral tradition, in *Finzan* you have the Koteba theater[+]. A lot of my students do not know that there is a popular African theater in the same way you had the Commedia dell'arte in Europe that influenced Molière and others. In Africa you have the Koteba theater influencing Sissoko in making *Finzan* so as to be able to relate to popular audiences.

The whole issue of what African film is, how you have to get rid of your conceptions of film as entertainment, of film as Hollywood, of film as the *Towering Inferno*, special effects, big budgets; you know, to get into African film is an effort for African American students.

At first they say, "Oh, my God! It is so slow! There is no action!" Later, as they get into it, they appreciate it. So it allows them to penetrate other cultures and maybe to reject the almighty sense of mono-culture which is widespread in the United States and sees American culture as world culture.

I think it is important for them, as minority people within a society, to see the cultural differences that exist in Africa, because many of them have the idea that Africa is all the same. Until you stipulate the differences between Senegal and Cameroon, they have never really thought about it. They thought Africa was Africa, which is again a misconception conveyed in the U.S. as a dominant ideology.

Hopefully, by the end of the class they will have a better idea and a sounder judgment in terms of Africa. And they will have a better relationship with their colleagues who are Africans. We have this myth at Howard University that everything goes the best way possible between African American and African students, but this is not always the case. I think that this type of course might create a better understanding.

You have also focused on images of women in African cinema, particularly in the works of Ousmane Sembene. Could you describe your research in this area?

Well the image of African women, Senegalese women in Sembene's work, for instance, has been rather significant from the beginning of his career. I believe he thinks that, as a Marxist, he is going to challenge the structures of society that divide it into the oppressors and the oppressed, the haves and the have-nots.

Therefore, gender division in a society and oppression of the female group is going to be rejected by Sembene, and I think that he sees the African woman as a symbol of liberation. He believes that as long as she is not liberated, society is not going to be free, and this has been an element from the beginning of his career. He has also used women as metaphors, as symbols. For example, in *Ceddo* all the men are killed or dismissed and unable to carry on the leadership of the group, so the princess takes over. In *Emitai*, when the men are away fighting the war or hiding in order to avoid being enrolled in the French army, it is the women who collectively protect the village.

In Sembene's novels women play a very significant part—for instance, the prostitute in *God's Bits of Wood*. I think that Sembene has decided to give roles to women in his films—and to give roles to women in society—that are different from the subservient, stereotypical ones often assigned to African women.

Recently, Med Hondo chose to make his film *Sarraounia* about a female warrior who participated in the resistance against colonialism, which is again a way to celebrate "Mother Africa." Perhaps this African woman is too mythicized in *Sarraounia*; she is larger than life and has lost a lot of her femininity, and maybe some people would have a problem with that. But just the very fact of deciding to make a film about a woman we wouldn't know of otherwise is something very positive.

I think that a number of filmmakers, such as Cheick Oumar Sissoko, have studied the status and role of African women and have used film so that people gain consciousness of their oppression and hopefully will fight for their liberation.

If you were to compare films made at the start of African cinema with contemporary films, how would you contrast their representation of women?

From the very beginning, African filmmakers have given certain strength to their portrayals of African women. Now the way this is done may have changed because times have changed. Maybe feminism was more militant in the 1970s and is less so in the 1980s and 1990s. Except for *Sarraounia* and Souleymane Cissé's *Waati*, I don't know if there have been other recent films entirely devoted to an African woman. Sissoko's recent *Guimba* is certainly not. I did not go to the last FESPACO, but it seems that there are few significant women in Gaston Kaboré's *Buud Yam*, which won the grand prize. Maybe they are seen in a less militant fashion than they were, let's say, in the 60s and 70s, for example in *Ceddo* in 1976, and *Emitai* in 1972.

Perhaps the themes or the subjects themselves that filmmakers focus on are more urban, rather than historical, mythical, or legendary.

But even a mythical film like *Guimba* doesn't have a real strong female portrayal, and neither does *Buud Yam*. I haven't seen the film but I read about it, and I don't think it has strong female portrayals. Maybe there is a mild regression in this.

*In **Buud Yam** there is more of a focus on the protagonist, Wend Kuuni, than on his sister Poghnéré, whereas in Kaboré's **Wend Kuuni**, we really feel Poghnéré's presence in the film.*

And she expresses feminist views; she asks why girls can't go in the field like little boys and keep sheep. She has a dream that she is a little boy and can do what Wend Kuuni is doing. And in *Wend Kuuni* itself, you have the woman who rejects her impotent husband, and he later hangs himself. So here you have women who are very assertive, which may not exactly reflect the reality of the time of pre-colonial Africa. Some critics did not see how women could have been that assertive in a patriarchal system. They say that the socio-historical context of the 1970s and 80s influenced Kaboré to give those women a voice rather than to represent reality faithfully. But it doesn't really matter, the results are the same: they are portrayals of assertive women. *Finzan* is a more recent example. In Djibril Diop Mambety's *Hyena* and Jean-Pierre Bekolo's *Quartier Mozart*, the women are also assertive. Perhaps women's assertiveness in more recent films is portrayed in a different way, a more individualized way, whereas before they had collective impact and historical significance.

You were born in France of Guadeloupean and Alsatian origins, you live in the United States, and your research focus is on African cinema. How do you bring these together in your research and teaching?

I think it is not by chance that I teach African cinema. It is to help students but also to help me, myself, in that eternal search for identity which I may never find. It is the search for my father maybe, whom I look to see in Africa. A psychiatrist might give this sort of interpretation.

Also there is the need that we all feel, as members of the African Diaspora, to have roots, a sense of origin. Maybe it is true that in studying African cinema, I am looking at Africa as a cradle that has been stolen from my history because my father's ancestors were transported as slaves to the New World.

Subconsciously, my coming to the United States may have been a way to be part of a black community, which was not available to me in France twenty-five years ago. Perhaps now I would not leave for the States because the community in France is much stronger. There are black standards of beauty, there are publications, so it is much different. But I felt a bit lost in the 1960s and early 70s in France. I was a black person born in France; my parents separated and I stayed with my mother who, of course, gave me all Western culture and Alsatian background. But I knew I was different from my Alsatian cousins, and that is probably what led me first to the States to study African Americans in film, then Africans in films, then literature from the U.S., Caribbean, and Africa that dealt with black subjects. I think it is all interrelated.

African cinema studies in France has a long tradition. Would you compare African film scholarship in France and the United States? How would you situate yourself in both?

In France, my focus on African Americans in cinema was a pioneering step because no one had done that before. I think my name is vaguely known in France, but it is probably better known in the United States, in terms of scholarship in the field of African cinema. I think I have written more in English on African cinema than I have in French. I participated in a few colloquia in France. You have to make a choice. The French historian and critic of African film, Pierre Haffner, for instance, is better known in the francophone world than I am, in terms of his research.

Film scholarship in France was more significant in the beginning than in the United States, because film is seen there as something very serious. With people like Jean Vigo and a few others, the French really studied film as text very early on, even in the 1920s. They had theorists of cinema, André Bazin, for example. So it is no wonder that film scholarship on Africa started earlier in France and had more profound implications, because the view the French have of film is more serious in general than Americans'. Most Americans see films as entertainment. Of course, you have scholars in film studies in the United States.

In addition, France has its whole history in Africa, the colonial past, which America does not have. Some people are interested in African cinema because of that link to the French colonial past. In America you have African American critics like Clyde Taylor and Claire Andrade-Watkins, who, because they are African Americans, felt a need to explore African cinema. But the concept of cinema is different in the two countries, therefore, the approach to it is different, as is the approach to African cinema.

And there is a great deal of funding that comes from France for the production of francophone African films.

Yes, there is a French connection, and of course, the French Ministry of Cooperation subsidized the first African films. Then those films participated in French festivals and received awards; people wrote about them, and all of that started a budding scholarship.

I would like to discuss your 1991 essay, "Eroticism and Subsaharan African Films."[5] Would you talk about the issues you explored as related to the female body in African films? A great deal of the focus in Western feminist film criticism is on female objectification in Western films. Would you say this is an important issue to raise in African film criticism?

Less so. A lot of Western feminist critics have focused on dismemberment of the female body in film and exploitation of the visual representation of the female body. Because of the culture in a number of film-producing African countries—for instance, Senegal—you have the influence of Islam, which advocates covering the body. This has had an impact on the representation of women in Senegalese films.

Also, people like Ousmane Sembene always said they wanted to be different. These filmmakers did not want to show sex for sex's sake or violence for violence's sake. They wanted to do educational, not sensational, cinema. So that very concept, I think, has limited the exploitative representation of the female body. However, Sembene gives you a glimpse of Diouana's body in *Black Girl.* He gives you more than a glimpse at the princess's body as she goes into the water in *Ceddo*, and then of course you have Désiré Ecaré's *Faces of Women*, which was scandalous at the time precisely because it showed that eight-minute scene in the water where the bodies were naked. The characters were copulating in the water. People were shocked because the culture in a number of West African countries precludes the representation of naked bodies. In ritual dancing you may have a partially nude body, but I don't believe that this is as readily accepted in film because of the nature of African cinema and also the influence of Islamic culture.

It is not by chance that in a country like the Ivory Coast you have films that are a bit *risqué*, such as those by Henri Duparc. It is likewise not by chance that you have to go south to the Ivory Coast and get away from Islam to find more daring types of films like *Faces of Women*. The film *Le sixième doigt* by Henri Duparc was not even erotic, just gross. But, in the film by Idrissa Ouedraogo, *Le cri du coeur*, a black man and black woman make love in a very explicit manner on a couch.

However, the body is usually not uncovered, or if it is, only briefly. In many cases love scenes are not shown directly, which leads spectators to imagine them. For example, in *Touki Bouki*, there is the water hitting the rocks, the moaning, a woman on the ground not visible in the frame, the orgasmic grasping of the cross. All these things are a metaphoric way to suggest sexuality rather than directly represent it. In *Saaraba*, you see an eye, then a trembling lip, then a hand. You also have a suggestive allusion in *Toubab bi* in the interracial sex scene.

By the way, it is interesting to note that there are few interracial relationships in African films. I think this is because a lot of African filmmakers no longer show conflictive situations between blacks and whites. They focus on the situation within their own communities.

To summarize, I would say that African filmmakers do not exploit the female body the way their Western counterparts do, because of cultural components such as Islam, and also due to the very nature of African cinema. In 1975, the *Charte d'Alger* proclaimed that films should be educational and not erotic.

But you do find eroticism. For instance, the other day I was showing *Toubab bi* to my class and there is a scene just before the young man leaves Senegal to go to France to study film. In a very brief scene with his wife, she lifts her *pagne* and you can see her beads. Eroticism is evoked, not by showing the body of the woman, but the beads, accessories used in intimate moments, which suggest sexuality. So again, it is done in a subtle manner, and you have to know the culture to sense it.

My students ask, "What's the big deal with those beads?," and I explain the magic of perfume, of incense. I remember a Senegalese man explaining to me the power of those beads: you hear them when you desire a woman, then when you have intercourse with the woman you hear them, you smell them. So that when a man leaves, the woman may give him some beads so that he will remember her and not be unfaithful. Again, you have to know the culture to see how eroticism and sensuality are contained in film. It is not necessarily obvious to the non-Senegalese.

You have also focused your research on francophone literature. Your book on conversations with Guadeloupean writer Maryse Condé was published in French and English...[6]

My work on Maryse Condé was directly connected to my origins. I also met her at Howard University, so you see how the "hub" has had an impact on my life: first Sembene, then Condé. She and I later met several times in Paris. Finally, we decided to do a series of interviews and turn them into a book.

When I wrote a proposal to get a grant to do that study, I insisted on going to interview Maryse Condé in Guadeloupe, in her cultural context. This also reflected my personal interest in going to Guadeloupe, which was the native land of my father. So that again is linked to who I am and my trying to understand my origins, the culture from which Maryse Condé comes and my father came, the culture that triggers the kind of monumental literary work that she is writing. There is a link.

Because of my self-imposed mission as a teacher, for *Entretiens avec Maryse Condé*, I tried to figure out all the questions that could be asked by a curious mind to an author while that author is alive. A lot of people ask questions about authors who are dead. Since Maryse Condé is alive and well, I thought I had a golden opportunity to pose my own questions and the ones students and other scholars might have. The book is linked, I think, to both my origins and my profession.

I translated the book into English so that all my students could read it. The translation was a challenge because I had to render certain images and metaphors that are particular to the francophone Caribbean. She used words that were typically Guadeloupean in the description of her childhood. Doing the book on Maryse Condé was a chance for me to go back to Guadeloupe and then to popularize her work in the United States.

She has also done film criticism, so that is another connection between you.

Yes, there is that connection as well.

*The focus of your most recent work is Med Hondo's 1987 film **Sarraounia**, about a great queen of Niger, which he adapted from the book by Abdoulaye Mamani. Why did you choose this topic?*

A publisher in Great Britain invited me to write the book as part of a series on important, but neglected, films.[7] I accepted because I have always been interested in the film and am appalled by the limited circulation it has had.

Sarraounia is a film whose technique and language are very appealing and should be understood by a wide audience, so I am surprised and disappointed at how few people have seen it. *Sarraounia* is a great historical film, a great historical epic, the only film of that genre that celebrates an African queen, one who resisted French colonialism. I would think that Sembene would want to do his projected film, *Samory*, in the same vein, but there you have a male hero.

Sarraounia appealed to me because the heroic protagonist is a woman, because it is a well-made film, and because the filmmaker is Med Hondo, for whom I have great respect.[8] I did research at the Library of Congress in Washington and the Bibliothèque Nationale in Paris and studied the historical events that were translated in the film, in order to comment on them in explaining the film.

I was amazed to discover how faithful Med Hondo had been to the historical record. Sometimes he even underplayed reality, not expressing all the violence and cruelty that actually happened. He was very sedate in certain ways, probably because he believed that too much violence would divert the attention of the viewer. The study of all the history behind the film excited me in analyzing *Sarraounia*.

At some point I went even deeper than I needed to, because I wanted to see how French colonialism had been. I knew it was rather atrocious, but I did not believe it had been so extreme and so calculated. So I got all involved in French and African history at the end of the nineteenth century, which I would not necessarily have done without the study of *Sarraounia*.

Here again is an African film making you research sociology, anthropology, religion, and history. Film criticism is a really wonderful way to expand your horizons, if you want to be knowledgeable about what you write. Readers count on your accuracy, so you have to be precise and well-informed.

There are a lot of different places that you touch as a person of African descent from Europe focusing on Africa while living in the United States. How does this positionality work for you in terms of studying Africa from the perspective of a member of the Diaspora?

I think you are both inside and outside. Of Guadeloupean descent, but living in Paris, I was brought up in a French, white environment, and within that environment I always felt black, or different. With regard to African film, in one sense I am the outsider, with that French culture, that Cartesian way of analyzing the world.

On the other hand, I am the insider, a member of the African Diaspora who has a personal interest in studying Africa. So I am both involved and detached, and I hope the result is a good balance.

How is this different from an African perspective?

Africans may have a tremendous advantage because they know the cultures and do not have to research as much as I do. They know the language, know the proverbs, know the cultural connotations. Africans have this advantage as African film critics; but at the same time, the emotional involvement of, say, a Senegalese critic in the Senegalese environment might blur objectivity.

And that is what is expected, objectivity?

I think any scholar looks for a certain degree of objectivity. And I think a Senegalese critic might not insist on certain points that may be derogatory or too negative in the description of his or her own society, whereas someone from the outside would not have those preoccupations. I think it is a great advantage to be within, but, at the same time, this can create an emotional attachment to what you analyze and can lead you to emphasize certain positive points and neglect others that are critical of your society.

How about in terms of gender? Do you find that you have a particular vision or gaze as a woman who does film criticism?

Yes, I think that I have a gaze and a certain way of looking at some topics that are feminine. I am sure that my way of looking at Sissoko's *Finzan* or other films on African women is different from the gaze of a male critic. My sensitivity is different, my experience is different—therefore, my judgment is going to be different.

African cinema is still very much a man's world and counts few women directors, and the same is true in the area of film criticism. This obviously affects the content, style, and analysis of African films. Let us hope that, very soon, many more women will participate in the making, critiquing, and history of African cinema.

Notes

1. See "Africa from Within: The Films of Gaston Kaboré and Idrissa Ouedraogo as Anthropological Sources," *Society for Visual Anthropology* 6,1 (Spring 1990).
2. See *The Cinema of Ousmane Sembene, A Pioneer of African Cinema,* (Westport: Greenwood Press, 1984).
3. See *Twenty-five Black African Filmmakers: A Critical Study, with Filmography and Bio-Bibliography* (Westport: Greenwood Press, 1988).

4. Manthia Diawara describes the Koteba theater as played out in "Finzan"; see *African Cinema: Politics and Culture*, (Indianapolis: Indiana University Press, 1992), p. 145.

5. See "Eroticism in Sub-Saharan African Films." Reprinted in *Erotique Noire/ Black Erotica*, eds. Miriam DeCosta-Willis, et al. (New York: Doubleday, 1992).

6. See *Conversations with Maryse Condé*. (Lincoln: University of Nebraska Press, 1996); *Entretiens avec Maryse Condé* (Paris: Karthala, 1993).

7. *Sarraounia by Med Hondo* (Wiltshire, England: Flick Books, 1999).

8. See interview with Med Hondo, "Sarraounia: An Epic of Resistance." *With Open Eyes, Women and African Cinema* (Matatu 19), ed. Kenneth Harrow, 1997.

Monique Phoba

Democratic Republic of the Congo

Interview conducted at Vues d'Afrique, April 1997, Montreal, Quebec. Translated from French.

Your most recent film is being presented here at Vues d'Afrique and it was also shown at the 15th edition of FESPACO in February. Could you tell me a bit about yourself and your latest film?

I direct documentary films, for the most part. I have worked in video up until the present, and I have done four documentaries. The last film, *Deux petits tours et puis s'en vont*, I co-directed with Beninian director Emmanuel Kolawole of the Benin Television. I have been living in Benin for the past two years.

Before relocating to Benin, you were based in Belgium for some time. Could you talk about your background and your experiences in Belgium?

From a very early age, I was interested in literature. I wrote poetry when I was very young. I also had a passion for history. I would always plunge into my father's newspapers and other literature, so that when I was ready to go to university I had already written two collections of poems. Everybody always said to me, "You will be a writer." I realized, however, that it was something that caused me to be too enclosed in an ivory tower. I was detached from reality. I wanted to escape from this tendency, since I was a bit of a recluse. I decided that I did not want to stay in this world of literature that distanced me from reality and people. I felt that I must try to find something else. And that is how I found myself in the field of communication. First I worked mainly in radio, where I stayed for five years. I also worked in theater and did all sorts of activities where I was required to interact with people.

While studying Economic and Commercial Sciences at Université Libre de Bruxelles, there was a radio station called "Radio Campus" where the students could express themselves. For five years, I was responsible for a one-hour program. It was actually quite a job. Every week I had to come up with issues and topics for the program. There were subjects of political, social, and cultural interests. Thus, I was able to develop the skills required to treat these subjects.

So it was through your experiences in radio that you evolved into cinema?

Yes, it was in working in radio that I acquired an interest in African cinema. At the time I met a compatriot—who is also present at Vues d'Afrique and was also at FESPACO—Ngangura Mweze, who directed *La vie est belle* in the early 1980s. It was through him that I got involved in culture and cinema. It was quite an experience for me to work with a Zairian and compatriot who made a feature film, which was also very successful. Gradually, I covered more and more issues relating to cinema in my radio shows.

I then went to FESPACO in 1987 and again in 1989. I was very attracted to the cinema, but since my studies were more in the area of marketing, I thought that I would pursue film production. On the other hand, since I had a skill in writing and I still had literary tendencies, I thought that I would go into scriptwriting. I didn't think that I could go into directing, having not studied it. Moreover, I had no time to study another area, since I had already spent five years in school. Therefore, I focused on the areas of scriptwriting and producing.

Then I had the possibility to attend a three-month workshop for documentary filmmaking. One could not pretend to be a documentary filmmaker after this training course. After all, it only lasted three months. Perhaps I can compare it to a method where one is thrown in water to learn to swim. Rather than take a year to learn, the person is thrown into the water and, depending on the ability to manage in the water, the person is either repelled by swimming or becomes a great swimmer. It was something to this effect.

We were taught for about a month how to manipulate the features of the camera; during the second month, we shot a film; and during the last month, we edited it. I remember how terrified I was. My film was a complete failure, but there were other colleagues who came out okay, who made a successful film—and that was the principle of this kind of training. They were at the same level as I was. They had never used a camera before, and the process of filmmaking also intimidated them; yet, they succeeded in doing wonderful films. Having blundered in my first attempt, I had to prove myself.

268

During that period there were national conferences for democracy. This was the beginning of 1990. There was a national conference in Zaïre and I wanted to attend. So I bought a camera on credit (I did not have money to buy it outright). As it turned out, the conference did not take place at that time, it was postponed for several months. Since I did not have much money, I felt that I had to film something, so I did a report about the press. There was a new *presse d'opinion* in Zaïre, which meant that there were new newspapers that appeared each day. I chose the five most important newspapers that played an important role in Zairian politics at the moment.

I had a small Hi-8 camera. I operated both the camera and the audio. Though the images were not very good, because I had so little experience, when I returned, people felt that the material was something that they had never seen about Zaïre before. So the success that the film did have came from the fact that I had spent a good deal of time in the field of communication, where I did a lot of interviewing and so on.

I met a leftist group with whom I quickly connected. The group members had other audiovisual perspectives on the African reality and the Southern Hemisphere in general. They had editing facilities and allowed me to edit. That is how I did my first film [*Revue en vrac*], which was awarded a prize here at Vues d'Afrique in 1992. This is how I evolved into filmmaking.

Do you find that there are similarities between preparing a story, report, or documentary for radio and preparing documentaries for video/film? In what ways did radio work prepare you for video/filmmaking?

I treat my themes in a specific way. I'll give you an example of what I did on radio. The war between Senegal and Mauritania is a situate that dates far back. During a period when the conflict resurfaced, I went to see Senegalese who lived in Belgium and France. I queried them about the history of the black and Arab Mauritanians who lived in Senegal and asked them why the problems had come to this. I did historical research in addition to the interviews. I also found music from Senegal and Mauritania. I searched to find the sounds that evoked the desert and sea, since it was a problem about the border and the Senegal River. I created my radio programs like a short film, a film with only sound.

I think that is why I moved toward cinema. Because it takes a lot of time and energy to do this kind of program, and radio programming generally does not allow this kind of time. It must be done quickly. Though I did not have the time, my projects became increasingly ambitious. I remember once I did a fifteen-minute segment for which I collected songs and music. Actors read letters during the program. This fifteen-minute segment required an entire night of editing.

My friends said to me "What are you doing? You are crazy. First of all you are doing it for free, you are not being paid! We are only students!" There was not really the means to do much. In order to really do more, you must spend money to rent equipment, to pay actors, and so on. What pushed me to leave radio was that it became a field too small for what I wanted to express. Going from radio to film was a logical step.

You were in Belgium, now you live in Africa, in Benin at the moment. Do you find that there is a great difference between working in Belgium and Benin? Going from Europe to Africa in general?

Yes. First of all, I must say that I have always more or less lived in Europe, aside from short intervals when I was in Zaïre, but not for a very long time. I spent time in Asia; however, I mainly lived in Europe. I think that I have always felt my identity as a Black woman among white people. This experience shaped a very particular personality.

I demand positive images of my origins, of Africa. I am very militant on this level because I have lived in an environment where oftentimes a black person is not valued. A black person is viewed only as someone to be helped, lucky to get this help, and then must say thank you for it. A black person is viewed as someone who never feels at home, who has nothing to demand and only something to be thankful for. This is a heavy burden. You are always on the defensive. This meant that I was very aggressive, very sullen, and very uneasy among those with whom I collaborated. Although things went well and the films turned out well, there was a very acute tension.

Coming to Africa, there have been other tensions, and different ones. Nonetheless, I am coming from Europe and I bring other kinds of behavior and other ways of relating, that's clear. And, of course, I also have problems. I would say that the main problem that weighed on me the most when I was in Europe, and that I no longer have, is that I did not feel that I was at home there. Of course, I am Zairian and I am not completely at home in Benin. However, I am in Africa, and the absence of this tension means that I am appreciating life and in some ways I am less militant in the sense that I don't always have to defend myself. What has always been important to me is to try to collect the positive things—because often we look for models from the outside—stock up on them, not lose a drop of these good things, and then broadcast them. I am in the field of communication and my role is to broadcast these things.

270

Benin is a country that is a kind of laboratory or experiment for us. It is an example of what will perhaps take place in Zaïre in five years or in Rwanda in ten years. We seem to always have to find experts from the West; we must become experts of our own reality. I cannot call myself an expert. I would say that I present the materials for the experts, those who are thinking about our future. Moreover, the image is important, it is emotional; it speaks to the guts. It provides the possibility to speak to many different audiences. I am not for an elite public. I don't think that I am a genius who can only address herself to other geniuses. I would like everyone to have access to my ideas so that they may be discussed and shared by many Africans.

You have worked on issues regarding the problems between Mauritania and Senegal; most recently, you have focused on events that have taken place in Benin. There is a certain pan-Africanism in your approach. Is this a role that you feel that you want to take on?

Yes, there was a part of me earlier on which was very pan-African. But also I pose the question, "Well, why not explore what is also happening in Latin America? Why not go see what is going on among black Americans?" Europe is always our point of departure. It is this certain Eurocentrism that annoys me. Besides, I am from Africa; in Africa I am from Zaïre; in Zaïre I am from a certain region. There are all sorts of identities that accumulate and it is important to try not to contradict oneself. There are many conflicts that are ethnicity-based.

There are people in Benin who say to me, "You are Zairian, what are you doing here?" That, I suppose, I should expect; in a way, I am immune by having passed through Europe. So this European experience has proven to be useful. My husband is European and has been very important in my process. He is someone with whom I discuss, with whom I work, and we think on the same level. That is very important for me. I am not anti-European. Nevertheless, I am only saying that we must learn to avoid the trap that tempts us. We are in a very competitive world, and those who say that they are helping you are not telling the truth: everyone has an interest. De Gaulle was clear: "France does not have friends, only interests." This frankness was one thing to his credit. We often forget these words, which are still very fundamental in Afro-European relations.

You have experience in literature, radio, and film, which are all in the area of communication. As a woman, in the media, what do you see as your role?

I would say that the woman can very easily accept being the carrier of a message, carrier of the message of hope, the message of change, the message of evolution. The woman can be a medium of transmission. We must not generalize too much, of course, but what I sense is that we have a personality, an identity that allows us this role. The "feminine" identity is in some ways the preservation of the nuclear family. Our aspirations are closely linked to the security of the community, of which we are psychologically, materially, and emotionally responsible. This means that during this period of evolution, the woman must commit herself, she must be there, because she must be the role model.

Could you talk about some future projects? We are seeing the eventual decline of Mobuto Sese Seko. Do you envision returning to Zaïre to freely cover the events of the country?

I have never felt separated from Zaïre, I think it shows in all that I have done. Even in doing a film about the return of "brainpower" in Benin—which was the subject of my second film, *Rentrer?*—there was always the question of how to manage the enormous Diaspora of Zairians outside of the country, which is similar to what came about in Benin. The problem in Zaïre is posed at the same time as it is in Benin. I film in Benin so that it serves for my country as well. Now that there will be elections at home, evidently, I feel the same way as I did regarding the elections in Benin. I have never spoken about any other country than Zaïre, but perhaps in another way.

Now I have film projects that I would like to do, that I am waiting to do, that I hope to do in a better climate. When I go to Zaïre there is something that makes me feel that I am being called by my land. It is something that speaks from the inside. It is almost overwhelming. It is astounding even. I am on the Zairian soil and there are so many things that speak to me—in the people, in the language, in the manner in which it is spoken.

When I first came to Benin I was not at ease, because although it was an African country, it was not Zaïre. This unsettled me. I expected to somehow find my country in the language, in the manner in which things were said, through gestures or an intonation. Well, it did not happen because Benin, was after all another country, it was not Zaïre. I was looking for these things, but they were not there. At the beginning, I was bothered by it to the extent that I wanted to take the next plane and leave for Zaïre. However, after two years, things have smoothed out; now I am very happy in Benin.

Something has touched my identity that I must resolve with my country and I will never be happy until I have the possibility of doing something there, even if I was to leave later. I am a traveling spirit; I have never been in one country for very long. I would never say that I will settle in Zaïre and never leave. Nevertheless, I certainly need to re-appropriate my country—for me, for my children, it is necessary.

Gloria Rolando

Cuba

Gloria Rolando visited Washington, DC in November 1996, during a tour in the United States. Her films were screened at Howard University and a question-and-answer session followed, from which excerpts are included. The interview was transcribed from a televised interview, which is part of *Reels of Colour*, a talk show series aired locally in Washington, DC, produced and hosted by the author.

Gloria, could you talk about your experiences as a filmmaker in Cuba, how you got started in filmmaking?

I started working at the Institute of Cuban Film in Havana in 1976 when I finished my studies in art history. I belonged to a group of students at the university with whom I started working in movies. We did not have school at that time, although we now have an international school and a national school. The people who were part of the Institute of Cuban Film at the time already had the practical experience of making movies, so we learned by doing films. We did the research, assisted the director during the production, during the shooting, and especially during the editing. This is how I started.

I mainly worked on documentary films, so I worked with the majority of Cuban filmmakers involved in documentaries. The documentary for us was and is an important genre to learn. Seeing the film evolve, from the moment of the idea until the end, was for me and for many others an important experience.

I notice that your films **Oggun** *and* **My Footsteps** *were shot on video. Do you mostly work in video?*

We used to work in 35mm but now we have acquired experience in video. Some of us filmmakers also belong to the National Video Movement, and now there is a possibility to continue doing documentaries. In my case this is how I made *Oggun: Forever Present* and also *My Footsteps in Baragua*, both in video.

Is this choice largely because of the lower cost and the ease, comparatively speaking, in making films in video rather than 16mm or 35mm?

To do documentaries in 35mm is expensive, while video is cheaper and it gives one the possibility and the access to do more things. The cost of video production is not so expensive and it enables one to move faster in terms of the production of the film.

In looking at these two films, I see themes of memory, of African mythology and storytelling within the context of African diasporan cultures in the Americas. Are those the themes that you most want to get across?

I follow the practice that I started at the Institute of Cuban Film, because there I worked on all kinds of topics, such as sports, politics, and art. The objective was to continue the cultural tradition, using the documentary. It is true that when I decided to do my own directing, the collective memory, the presence of the people that surrounded me in the neighborhood, in the culture that I know, the Caribbean culture—because Cuba is part of the Caribbean—is something that I was attracted to and wanted to reflect.

The history sometimes shows only one group of people, but it is a common history of many others. It is this kind of thing that we talk about, the Diaspora and the kind of African roots that we have in Cuba. In so many of the Caribbean cultures, like here, you need to talk with the elders because they can tell you the history and its connection with Africa. This cultural, economic, and social history also grew in this part of the continent.

Your background in art, how do you connect that to your work in film?

When you study at the university, you receive a general background in culture, which is mostly European culture. At that time, I did not learn too much about African culture or the culture of the Diaspora. Therefore, I learned it from a combination of things. During my years while working at the Institute of Cuban Film, I discovered that I was more connected to the culture in my country. I also attended conferences and lectures at the Casa de las Americas, a prestigious institution in Cuba, which opened doors to Latin American and Cuban culture. There I met many important writers and painters from Latin American countries and Caribbean countries. I became more open to understanding something that we call our identity. It is something that is part of your education and the environment that surrounds you. Moreover, to talk about our identity is a combination of the past, present, and also the future, and the history of the people that surround you. It is not something that I need to invent or that I am only seeing for the first time.

I was struck by the elements of interviewing, the fictionalization of the story of the Orishas, and the actual ceremony of the worship. Describe your experiences in making the film **Oggun**.

Well, *Oggun: Forever Present* was my first film as director. When I decided to make *Oggun*, I worked with Lazaro Ros, who is the most important Yoruba singer that we have in Cuba. The film is dedicated to him. Many people from Yorubaland in Nigeria arrived in Cuba during the slavery era, and it is amazing that this culture right to the present is so strong, with such a strong spirituality. It is part of the Cuban population, for both the people that practice this tradition and even those who do not practice it. We have many blacks involved in this tradition and some whites also.

It is a culture that is alive, it is in the street. You don't need to go to the archives to get the information. It is information that you can get with your neighbors, with relatives, with friends that invite you to the religious parties. You discover this kind of philosophy in the street, this kind of dialogue with nature. I made *Oggun* with these kinds of resources. I did the research in the street while Lazaro told me the history. Of course, he has a beautiful voice, but for me it was not only important that he perform in the movie. It was important that we have a long interview where he could explain his experience and his spirituality, that at the same time is a spirituality that lives inside of him, yet belongs to many other people.

Could you discuss how Oggun as the legend, and as one of the Orishas of the Yoruba religion, ties into the spiritual practices in Cuba?

Within the Yoruba tradition there is the worship of the Orishas, who represent the powers of nature and also some very human feelings. For

277

example, Oggun is the god of metal. Oshun is the owner of love, the owner of the river and of the sweetest element in nature, which is honey. Shango is the owner of thunder and the drums. He also represents masculinity. Yemanja is the owner of the sea, and life starts in the sea. So all these Orishas help in understanding the cosmology that comes from Africa, because sometimes it is thought that only the drums came from Africa. So they explain the world according to a cultural practice that took place in Africa.

In spite of the discrimination and exploitation that has taken place since slavery time, it is something that is still alive. Of course, we have lost a lot, but, through our films, recordings, and books, we are able to keep this collective memory. This worship is very rich in Cuba.

The name of the film is *Oggun* because Lazaro is initiated in this deity; he is the son of Oggun. He tells the history of the *Patakin* in Cuba, which means legend or mythology. In the film, he recounts the legend of Oggun, and around Oggun he narrates the history of many other Orishas.

In the film, you relate the relationship between Oggun and Oshun. Oshun was able to capture the love of Oggun. Is this part of the legend, that he stayed within his own world and he was not able to share his love and finally Oshun seduced him with honey?

Each Orisha has many ways that it manifests itself. The history that I told in fiction in this film is a relationship between love and war, and love conquers and attracts. Oggun tastes the honey that Oshun puts to his lips and he is conquered by the love. There are many versions and histories about this. My purpose was to show the universal values that are in all cultures, which can be presented in fiction form. Part of the narration was made by Lazaro, and I continued the history in the dramatization of this legend. I used both languages in the film, fiction and documentary.

*Your storytelling continues in your second film, **My Footsteps in Baragua**. When you say "my footsteps," are you talking about your actual footsteps in the process?*

The title is from a Trinidadian poem, "My Footsteps in the Homeland." We took the title *My Footsteps in Baragua* because I was trying to narrate the history as if I narrated it myself. So, I take the point of view of a woman who used to live in this neighborhood in the east part of Cuba called Baragua in the province of Ciego de Avila. Through her voice, I narrate to try to let people know about this neighborhood.

Could you talk about some of the people in the film and how you met them?

One of the people I interviewed was one of the last Barbadian women in the community, Mrs. Jones. When I met these people I said, "We need to do something about this history." She and many others arrived in Cuba—not only in Baragua but in other parts as well—at the beginning of the century with the hopes of having a decent life and with the idea of going back home. Some of them sent money back home because they needed to take care of the families that were in the rest of the islands. Most of them stayed in Cuba, they had families, and are now part of Cuba and their descendants as well.

It is a history of an immigration that ended many years ago, but we still feel the roots in the present. People are surprised when they come to Cuba and find that there are some black people that speak English and have English names. They often ask, "What are their roots?" *My Footsteps* is a tribute to all those people who arrived in Cuba and brought their culture. So, when we talk about the Diaspora and the oral tradition, this personal history is also part of this collective memory. Migration within the Caribbean Islands, where people search for a home and work, is still alive.

Are there autobiographical aspects of the film? Do you have ancestors in the English-speaking Caribbean?

I don't know, maybe. I live in a Caribbean island and everything is connected and is part of my life. So, even if I don't have these roots exactly, I feel a special commitment to tell something about this history. Even before I made *My Footsteps*, I had already found this history in the 1980s when I worked on the film *Haiti in the Memory*. During the process of researching and shooting this 18-minute documentary, I found black people who spoke English and I asked them where they came from. They told me that they came from Jamaica, Barbados, Antigua, and Montserrat. I knew that in Cuba there were some black people who had English names, so I tried to write something about this history, and I thought that *My Footsteps* could show more of this history.

To what extent are the people from the English-speaking Caribbean integrated into the Cuban experience and culture?

They are part of Cuba as well. In the film they talk about when they arrived in Cuba in 1914, 1915, 1920. They arrived as immigrants and, of course, they were integrated into the cheap labor force and worked in the sugar factory. At that time, they were very isolated because of discrimination. As time passed, the people who stayed in Cuba became part of the country. They respect their customs, but they are totally integrated into the Cuban society, they are not separated. While they are descendants of another culture, they have the same rights, go to the same schools, and have the same opportunities.

Do the Cuban-born descendants of these immigrants speak English?

Some of them do, it all depends on whether their relatives spoke the language. It is a personal relationship that they have at home. Some of the people try to speak English and to learn English—not like me, because my English is not very good. But, they learn English at school. Though some of them do not speak English very well, they understand because they have the elders, their grandfathers and grandmothers, who are still alive. So they are obliged to speak it.

There was a discussion in the film of the immigration from English-speaking regions of the Caribbean to Panama, and then these same people migrated from Panama to Cuba. Could you talk about that?

I knew about this movement from reading about it. However, I realized the importance of this part of the history when I visited Jamaica, and especially Barbados. I found books and pictures which showed that the movement in the Caribbean countries since the last century was to Panama. After the emancipation of the slaves, although they were free, they had to continue in the plantation system because they did not have work. The big movement and opportunity, which we call the "Panama Fever," came during the construction of the railroad and then afterwards the Panama Canal. Many people went there, and at the same time there was a separation. There was a disintegration of many families because it was mainly the men of the family who went to Panama for work. Many of them died during the building of the Canal. In 1914, when the construction was over, they had to decide whether to go back home where they did not have many possibilities, or to go to Cuba, where, at the time, there were opportunities in the sugar industry. So they decided to go to Cuba.

Gloria Rolando answered questions from various members of the audience after the screening of *Oggun* at Howard University.

Let me tell you a bit about my history. I belong to the Institute of Cuban Films, where I have been working since 1976, after finishing my studies in art history. I did not study movies because at that time we did not have a school. My generation and the older generation of Cuban filmmakers learned movies by doing movies. The people who teach in the international school are the same Cuban filmmakers who have been working in the industry for many years; they became filmmakers and afterwards they became professors. This generation will be more qualified than my generation; there will be more women involved in the technical areas in the future. Now in the Cuban cinema industry we don't have many women working in the technical areas such as, camera and audio. We write and direct but we don't have access to the technology. I think that for the younger people there will be better conditions. In general, it is difficult for everybody because of the economic conditions that we have now.

In 1977, I wrote my first script, which was about the traditions that came to Cuba through Haiti after the Haitian Revolution. I studied music many years ago, so I knew a little bit about the language of music. While studying at the Institute of Cuban Film, I put image with sound. So it was a big risk, but I think that this first project that I worked on opened a new world to me and I fell in love with this work. I know that it is not easy, I know that it is not cheap, I know that it requires much personal dedication and effort, but I love my work. It is not only to be able to make your own films, it is a responsibility that we have to conserve the culture and pass something on to the younger generation.

When talking about the economy and technology in Cuba now, it is very expensive to shoot on celluloid. Are you finding that more and more people are beginning to go towards video because it is a lot more accessible and the technology seems to be changing towards video for post-production, which is a lot cheaper than it is for film?

Your question is very interesting, because it is one of the areas that we are trying to develop. In Cuba the National Video Movement has developed, which means that if you have access to a camera that you can share with a group of people, you can form your own crew and no company is needed. Some of us Cuban filmmakers are now involved in video. *Oggun* was shot in video, in Betacam, and edited in the same system.

At the beginning, I worked mainly in the production of documentaries. We produced around fifteen documentaries every year, so we had plenty of work at that time. I had been working in this way since 1976, and suddenly the production went down. What could we do? Some of us were trying to do something in order not to lose the tradition. Though Cuban fiction film is important, I think that the tradition of documentaries is much more important, because it is really our genre. Many topics that we worked on in documentary form became fiction film, but sometimes it was not possible. We were also aware of the fact that through documentaries we could preserve our culture and spiritual values. I think that it is an authentic way, especially, to focus on black culture in Cuba, Cuban culture in general, but especially black culture, whose foundation is in the oral tradition.

When I realized this, I started working more in video. I made *Oggun* with a new company called Video America. I planned to do something in 35mm but it was very expensive, and a battle I could not start. For that reason I decided to create the video group, Images of the Caribbean, which came out of the National Video Movement in Cuba. I am now in the process of getting more technology to develop this group. *My Footsteps in Baragua* was shot in Hi-8, we had the same production crew as *Oggun*, and we edited it in 3/4.

I know that it is not easy when you have been working in a professional way and suddenly you need to change the technology and the conditions of production, but what could we do? Stop? Cuban culture is very rich and the reality is so strong—the elders, and the heritage that comes from Africa, the problems of the black people, how could we wait? For me—and I think that other filmmakers feel this way—we want to continue. Yes, if it is not possible to work in 35mm now, we will do it in video. I made *Oggun* in 1991 and it was only last year that I could shoot again. The worries that I had between 1991 and last year were too much—many dreams, so how could I sleep!

I especially liked the dramatic aspects of the film. When you interviewed Lazaro Ros, were you planning all along to dramatize his story? What was your approach when you first set out to make this documentary?

When I first decided to make the film about Lazaro, I interviewed him many times. At that time, he was still working at the Folklorico Nacional de Cuba. I had already had the script for three years, but nothing happened. When I found that the people of Video America were interested in doing the film project, I interviewed him again. In one of the interviews, he told me about the mythology about Oggun and Oshun according to the *Patakin* legend. I loved it very much and I decided to start the film in this way.

Some people asked me why I started in this way. Well, because I wanted to put the people immediately inside of this world, this magical world, this world that comes from Africa. I wanted to put them inside of the mythology, the spirituality, inside of the forest. Lazaro told me about this history, but I consulted with many other believers about Oshun and Oggun. It is not something that you need to consult in the archives. It is something that your neighbors within two or three blocks have, especially those who live in black neighborhoods like old Havana. I didn't need to go to the library; I talked with many others in the streets. I think it is very important to be open to the reality of our people.

I asked them if I could show Oshun without clothes and they said, "Yes, why not? Oshun is beautiful, Oshun is honey, don't you know love?" I decided to show the beautiful body of Oshun, because what we women do in Cuba when we want to capture men is give them honey. But it is part of the mythology and the reality that people live.

I decided to dramatize this when Lazaro told me that these *Patakins* have a meaning in the religion; in the practice they use honey, stone, the water that comes from the river and the sea, and the elements within the culture. When I decided to dramatize this, what counted was the relationship between people and nature, the plants and the animals. Everything is part of the cosmology because the African people consider human beings and nature as one, nothing is separate. This philosophy I tried to show through this dramatization. This is something that I had to open with immediately. I could not wait for it later in the film; I wanted to show it at the first moment, I wanted to signify it by starting this way. Of course, I had to combine it with some moments of Lazaro's own life. He talked about his concept of religion.

The second thing was where to interview Lazaro, because if I had done so in the studio I would have broken the fantasy. There is a relationship between the place that I interviewed him and the mythology, so it must be near the *ceiba*. In Cuba, nobody cuts the *ceiba*. The *ceiba* is a sacred tree like the baobab in Africa. All the ancestors, all the sacred ceremonies take place at the *ceiba* and also by the palm trees, because we dialogue with nature. I had Lazaro sit at the *ceiba*, which is in the same area where Oggun lives. That was the connection, and it was also a way to interpret the world that Lazaro was talking about. I did not want to separate him, shoot him in the studio and then show the mythology in another place. So everything must be integrated.

Could you talk more about the forms of worship that you documented in the film, Yoruba forms of worship, and the other forms of worship that exist in society, such as Christianity? What are the attitudes of the State towards religions in general and particularly the forms of worship that you have filmed?

Cuba is very rich in African tradition: people from Yorubaland in Nigeria, from Angola, arrived in Cuba. We have a tradition that comes from old Dahomey, and I am very worried, because those who are left are very old people and we have very little documentation about them. We have many influences. In Cuba, we also have a Haitian presence. To talk about a Cuban culture in terms of Africa is really very complex because in all these groups there are cultural manifestations of religion. They have their own drums, but something that all the drums have in common is that they were brought by people who were subjected to slavery. There are many influences from Africa, but the elders died before transmitting the secrets. The Yoruba tradition that exists in Cuba is only part of the worship, and for many years, the elders did not like to have films made about this tradition. They were very careful and feared revealing Yoruba secrets, but now they are more open.

But we must also be careful. Do we want to make a spectacle of the sacrifices, as many Europeans do when they come to Cuba? Or do we want to show the spirituality? I need to ask myself many times, "What would I like to show? Is it an ethnographic movie, or is it a film to recreate the atmosphere of the spirituality that the people have inside?" I have had the experience of seeing many people arrive in Cuba: they shoot, they talk with the elders, they promise many things. Really, they do not respect the culture, and they do not show the real face of it. The tourists talk to the black people who play the drums. But what happens? They never talk to people like Lazaro. I decided to give a voice to these people. We have a diversity of manifestations. I am not interested in describing the worship. The worship is a religion: if you want to know, you must be involved. We need to protect the religion and not exploit the religion; they are two different things. I think that people in Brazil and many of the Caribbean and Latin American countries play a lot with this culture, they use this culture, and we have some of these same manifestations and I am scared of that. The only way that I can fight and do something different is with films like *Oggun*.

I also want to develop something about Shango, because Shango is the owner of the drums. All these drums come from Africa, and if we have this diversity of religions, it is because the Orisha who was king in Oya brought this through the Middle Passage, through the history. It is this kind of thing that I want to reveal.

284

When I visit the black churches here in the black community in the United States, I am surprised how African they are, even if they are Baptists or Episcopal. They play the drums with the body, the hands, with the voice, and it is beautiful, it is Africa. We ask, "Where is Africa in the Diaspora?" The colonialists say, "You speak English, Spanish, you speak French, you are Protestants, you practice Voodoo, you are different." No, we have more things that are in common than are different, and this is the analysis that I would like to show in a film about Shango. I hope that he will help me do it.

It is true that you cannot expect that prejudices will no longer exist. Even with the revolution in Cuba, some people have prejudices; some ignore the real value and use it only for tourism. It is a long process, and I think that we people who work in the media have the responsibility to give another kind of answer and to educate.

Discrimination within this culture is something that has happened since the time of slavery. Cuba was colonized by the Spanish, and Africans were obliged to accept Catholicism. However, some Africans were permitted to organize under what is called the *cabildo*. They had to accept the Catholic name in the front. For example, you pray for Santa Barbara, but in the back you pray for Shango and have the drums. You have San Francisco but in the back, you have Orunla. There is the Lady of Mercy but it is Obatala who is clothed in white. In my neighborhood, which is in Old Havana, there is a celebration on 24 September, which is the day of the Virgin of Mercy that in the Yoruba tradition is the birthday of Obatala. The church is full, because they love the church, but also because it is Obatala. And Obatala is the owner of the head and for that reason people cover their heads in white, and everything is in the head. When people are being initiated you can no longer touch their heads, only the elders can.

Because of this kind of tradition, it is something that you cannot stop because it is part of the Cuban culture. We have deep, deep roots and it is impossible to take them up. The first ones to preserve this culture were the Maroons who keep to themselves, but they also keep the traditions. There are some whites that are involved, because they discovered how powerful our religion and culture are.

Could you talk about what was involved in filming the party?

The camera operator and I tried to figure out how to hide the microphones because this was something very important. Normally this kind of party takes place indoors, but if the party had been indoors we would have had to use lights, and the weather in Cuba is a little bit hotter than here, and secondly, it would have created a distance with the people. We used two Betacam cameras. We invited people with whom Lazaro wanted to share this party. We decided to have it outdoors in an old building in Old Havana in a complex where people would not feel distant. The sound operator had many microphones around the Obatala drums. He was with the Nagra recorder in one place in the back and controlled the camera and the microphone that was always with Lazaro. And in this way, we separated Lazaro's voice from the drums, which were very powerful, and the choir, but it was not easy.

I brought the crew to different parties to study. I advised them that we need to respect the order, we couldn't repeat any dance or song, we couldn't stop. It was only one time that we had the chance to catch everything and also to follow closely because you do not know what is going to happen during this kind of party, if the people would become possessed.

Could you talk about the icons and symbols that were used—water, light, wind and fire, and steel? When you were dealing with steel at one time, you stepped outside of the narrower environment and went to a larger steel factory with more powerful technology. This caught my attention; it was a bit out of the norm. Were you aware of that, was that what you wanted to do?

When I was doing the research, Lazaro told me that Oggun exists in the present, which is how I got the name of the film *Oggun: Forever Present*. So it doesn't mean that he exists only in the past, he is in the present also. I decided to shoot in an old place in Havana where metal is melted. The place was so dangerous and I was so scared. One camera operator was with the big melting machine and I was downstairs where it was less dangerous. I told the camera operator, "No, you can go alone and shoot." It was hard, but I decided to do it because I wanted to recreate the atmosphere of the metal, its beauty. I tried to show not only the expression of love, but also the transcendental aspects of his work. I decided to shoot the place where Oggun worked in one color, in the color of the metal.

What is important when doing this kind of work is to convey to the people what you want, and they will be involved with you in the same atmosphere. During the shooting of *Oggun*, when we were filming the honey, something magical happened. When we were shooting, a ray of sun appeared, and suddenly Raoul, one of the camera operators, said, "Look what is happening now, close to the honey!" It was Raoul who discovered this ray of sun. I said, "Do something, we need to shoot immediately!" He said, "Wait." When you see this, you will see that there was a reason that he wanted to wait, and it is very important. It was not a special effect. It was because he was involved with the spirit of what we were trying to show that he caught this magical moment. The meaning of the honey was revealed through this effect. We could have done this with a special effect, but this was natural.

When you are shooting, you have to be open. You may have written something else but the reality is so rich that you cannot be so closed and think, "No I didn't write this in the script." No, shoot and then you see what happens. There were small elements, such as the dog sleeping. We didn't know the purpose of the dog, but afterwards when I was editing, suddenly it worked because it helped to make the transition. The dog was awake while Oggun was working. Then she was tired and went to sleep; yet Oggun continued working.

We shot the rest of the animals in the zoo, not in the forest, because we didn't have time. We didn't have permission to go inside the cage, so we shot the two parakeets kissing each other from the outside. Our presence caused a big disturbance inside the cage. And apparently the couple became angry and decided to go into the small house, we immediately got the camera, we only had seconds to shoot, we didn't know how long it would last, so we had to be open.

To make films it is very important to have a budget and the technology, but also to have experience and a good heart, as well as to be able to convey to the people that work with you the importance of catching everything that happens. During the shooting of *My Footsteps*, it rained for two weeks. Raoul finally said, "Let's go shoot the rain, because it is raining everyday." I used some moments of the rain to help me capture the sense of time passing, and the sense of nostalgia. You never know, even if you write everything, something else will happen, and you have to shoot, you have to catch these ideas.

In the dancing there are times when the dancers became possessed. Should we not see it? Does the culture allow that to be seen? Does the culture not allow that to be seen? If the culture does allow that to be seen, what restricts the filmmaker from showing it? Respect for the culture?—which does not make sense in this context—or the filmmaker's interpretation of how that might appear for a different consuming audience that may not understand what they are seeing, and therefore would like to keep that away? There is this dilemma of how do we censor ourselves in showing our culture because we may think that in the West they may not understand it.

In my case, it is a question of respect and I know that they don't want the possession to be shown. We can show some things, but not the moment of the total possession when they talk. At this moment I didn't shoot. Even in the last dance for Oggun at the end of the film, the man went to the shrine and took the machete. He was there in the shrine, the image...we need to respect what happened to this man.

The drums are not only drums, they are deities. The drums are part of the initiation. They receive a sacrifice; the drums are fed also. It is through the drums that the Orishas are called. When the people are initiated, and the Obatala drums are played very well, sometimes people go into possession, even if the drums are not fed. It happened during the shooting. The strong energy spread during this moment and provoked possession. The woman that was dancing for Oya, she was out, completely out. So I showed parts of the possession with discretion, I did not shoot everything, I cut off the camera. I cut it off because I thought it was not necessary. I showed the film to the believers many times, and I also wanted Lazaro to feel comfortable with the film, to be happy with the film. Show the reality, the mythology, but also respect the people that he invited to participate in the party. I know that there are many others who want to show these kinds of elements, but we need to show respect.

[The following was an important point regarding the sensitivity around shooting possession that Gloria Rolando made at the African Literature Association (ALA) Conference at Michigan State University in April 1997]:

In Cuba it is not only the possession but the internal worship and sacrifice and many other things they don't like to show. They permit you as an artist to make art around the religion, but not describe the worship, they don't permit this. Maybe in some houses, maybe some people do it, but it was not my intention. In the case of the possession it happened the same way, they considered this as part of the secret of the religion. And if we want them to accept what we are trying to do as artists, we need to respect them.

What can the Diaspora in the United States offer you in terms of support of your work?

When I came here for the first time, I often heard the word Diaspora, the African Diaspora. What does the African Diaspora mean to you? What is the history of the African Diaspora? We need to recognize the history of what happened to the black people of this continent after they were brought here in slavery. If you talk about the African Diaspora, you need to study what happens in the Caribbean countries because it is part of our history. While this history happens in rural areas, I don't think it is unfamiliar to people who live in cities. In the United States there are many people who have Caribbean roots and I think that Africa isn't only the past, it is also the present. It is present in these ways, in this century, with these people who are still alive. It is present in the people who worked in Panama trying to get a better life; the people who migrate from Jamaica right now to this country to work. I saw a documentary called *H2 Worker* before I came here; it is about Jamaicans who got visas to come here to cut cane in Florida.

In Africa, you may find some cities, but the majority of the people live in the rural areas. It is a history that concerns all of us. I need to clarify this because I live in a city, but I know that it is part of my roots. Even if I don't have English-speaking Caribbean roots, I have Cuban roots. I want you to understand my culture and the culture of the black people in my country. We need to consider it a phenomenon of migration because it is something that belongs not only in the past, it also is in the present. We also need to come together because I think it is not only my personal work, we need to work together to defend our culture, our point of view. So I am trying to get technology to bring to Cuba not only for my own work, it is a collaboration between filmmakers, between people involved in culture, a culture that we need to defend.

Naky Sy Savane

Ivory Coast

Interview held at FESPACO 1997, Ouagadougou, Burkina Faso, February 1997. Translated from French.

You acted in the award-winning film, **Au nom du Christ**, *which won the Etalon de Yennenga in 1993, as well as many other films. So, you are quite visible on the screen. Could you talk a bit about yourself, where you are from, your background and career in acting?*

I am an actress and I am Ivorian. I am here at FESPACO because FESPACO is a bit like Hollywood for us Africans. Therefore, it is very important for an African actor to attend and participate in the festival.

In **Ecrans d'Afrique** *No. 7 [first quarter 1994], there is a photo of you on the cover page. In the revue, Alessandra Speciale focuses on African actresses in an article entitled "A Threefold Trial: African, Female and Actress." She profiles your experiences as an actress, and those of Felicité Wouassi. Could you give your reflections on some of the issues that were discussed in the article?*

It is true that in Africa it is very difficult for a woman to assert herself. Furthermore, if she chooses to be an artist or actor it becomes even more complicated. For me, it is three times more problematic because I come from a family that is very religious. I am the granddaughter of an imam, which does not simplify matters. For instance, where I am from, at fifteen years old an adolescent girl should already be married. Here I come along and try to jostle things, to do what I want to do. It has not been easy.

You have acted in both the theater and the cinema. What have been some of the roles that you have played, and your experiences in both of these media?

Yes, I come from the theater, I have already played in at least fifteen plays. These have included some of the great French plays by writers such as Molière, Racine—I acted in his play *Britannicus,* Jean Genet, Bertolt Brecht, and I recently played the role Antigone in the play by Jean Anouilh.

I also acted in some great African plays by playwrights such as Birago Diop. I have already played the role of Nefertiti in *Ramses II* in the theater. To summarize, I had many wonderful roles in the theater. In the cinema I played in *Le guerriseur* by Sidiki Bakaba, in *Le bal poussière* by Henri Duparc, *Le sixiéme doigt* also by Henri Duparc, *Afrique mon Afrique* by Idrissa Ouedraogo, and *Au nom du christ* by Roger Gnoan Mbala. I have acted in films made for television in my own country, the Ivory Coast.

Though actors are not given the recognition that you think they should have, people do know you and come out to see you on the screens and tune in to watch you on television. What message do you want to send your audience? As an actor, do you feel that you are contributing to African cinema?

Certainly! I learned very young that as an African woman I had to defend myself, no one would fight for me. We had to fight, each of us in her own way. At an early age, I handled things on my own. I decided to fight in the best way I could so that the African woman may have the place that she deserves.

I feel that the African woman plays a pivotal role in society. She works a great deal and manages the family. Because there are men who do not have work, the women go to the fields to work, or if they are not cultivating the fields, they are at the marketplace the whole day selling in order to bring money home. The woman cannot be overlooked. She makes a tremendous contribution to the development of her country.

In another context, you have stated that African audiences often do not distinguish between reality and fiction and that may cause problems when you act in roles that may be in conflict with traditional images of women in African societies. Though you have experienced some problems as an actor, in this respect you appear to be a committed artist. At the moment, there is a great deal of discussion about the image of African women. Perhaps as an African actor you in many ways, are that image, or become that image. Do you think in general that the role of the African woman and the images of African women in African cinema are positive? What are your thoughts about the visual representation of the African woman in the media in general?

Now the African woman is beginning to have a positive role in the cinema. It has started to happen. Because in the past she was always seen as a secondary character, the great roles were played by men. We have learned that we must work hard and work a great deal. We are chosen because we have talent. We have also learned that we must push harder to have roles created for us, scripts that are written with women in mind. We must even go as far as to suggest roles for ourselves. At the present we do not hesitate to tell a director to create a certain role or that we want to be a certain kind of character. At least I do not hesitate to do so.

The last film in which I acted *La jumelle* [The Twin] was by the young director Diabi Lanciné, who really values the African woman and supports the struggles of African women, such as the fight against forced marriage and excision, and the fight for the African woman to have the right to choose her own future. All these issues were touched upon in his film.

Believe me it was a great pleasure for me to play such a role because there are certain things that we cannot say in Africa. For instance, the fight against excision, we cannot talk about it, we must each fight in our own way, and as best we can. For many years, I have been fighting against this practice for my daughter, because she risks being excised. We submitted to it, we did not know. We did not know where to go. Moreover, I think there is one obligation that I have which is to protect my child and prevent her from being subjected to the practice of excision.

The cinema has the possibility of conveying messages, especially in the context of images and storytelling. What role as an actress can you play to struggle against excision?

I am already in the struggle against it. The fact is that I fight each year for my daughter because it is a continuous battle. You are vulnerable to this practice right up until marriage. However, most people are not ready to listen to this opposition, it is still part of our tradition. I think the best solution is that each woman in her own work, in her own society, fight to protect her daughter.

Cilia Sawadogo

Burkina Faso

Interview held at Vues d'Afrique 1997, Montreal, Quebec, April 1997.
Translated from French.

Could you talk about yourself, your background, and about how you became interested in animation cinema? It's fascinating, because we don't see animation films in African cinema.

I was born in East Germany. I lived there for eight years, after which I lived in Burkina Faso for nine years, and then I came to Canada. After having studied in various places, I received a diploma in communication with a minor in animation cinema, and that is how I came to cinema.

At first, I wanted to work in television, but afterwards I found that it was much more interesting to work in animation because I draw quite a bit. I genuinely like drawing and I think that it is a way to express oneself and to be able to express universal ideas. There are many of my films that don't have dialogue and this allows me to touch a larger audience, such as with the last film that I made *Le joueur de cora* (The Cora Player).

Could you expound on the themes of your films and how your films have been received?

I made my first film in 1992, which was called *La femme mariée à trois hommes* (A Woman Married to Three Men), based on a tale from the Zaïre. It was my first work, which took me a long time to do. It was very well received and I was awarded prizes for this film. Afterwards, I did two shorter animation films. One was based on a poem. The film was an illustrated poem called *Naissance* (Birth). The other film was called *l'Arrêt d'autobus* (The Bus Stop). The theme of this film was about racism and interracial relationships in Montreal. It was especially addressed to children, and presented in a light-hearted manner. It was a two-minute film, so there was not the possibility to go too deeply. It was just to give an idea, to give a glance.

The next film, *Joueur de cora*, which I have just completed, is being screened at Vues d'Afrique. It was also screened at FESPACO a few months ago and was awarded a prize. It is a seven-minute film, which is part of the collection "Droits au coeur." The "Droits au coeur" [Rights from the Heart] collection was initiated by the "l'Office national du film du Canada. Within this cadre, two parts—which include seven films in each part—have already been produced, all of which deal with the subject of children's rights as decreed by the United Nations. Since the films in Parts One and Two of the collection had only presented a Canadian perspective on the rights of children, or a Canadian interpretation of these rights, it was thought that it would be interesting to do a third part in co-production with countries from other parts of the world. A search began for co-producers and foreign directors, which in the end, included two Czech directors, two directors from India, one Cuban director, who is also a woman, and me as a Burkinabé filmmaker. Thus, we have the point of view of Indians, Czechs, and Cubans, and their perspectives on the rights of children and how they portray it. The film *Joueur de cora* is part of this collection.

You are Burkinabé, and you lived for some time in Burkina Faso. You are German; you were born in Germany. Now you live in Montreal, where you have been for some time. How do you live this multiple identity? I don't know, perhaps I can call you a "poly-cultural" person?

"Poly-cultural," yes. I think it brings something particularly interesting. I think it reflects the way that I make films. My films are never about a specific culture. They are films that always touch on a universal theme. I consider myself a citizen of the earth before anything else. I am an Earthwoman.

The fact is that I come from not only different cultures but also two races—I am half-white and half-black—I truly experience this in every sense of the term. When I was in Germany, I was told "You are black," but when I was in Africa I was told "You are white," I was put in the category "white" and viewed as such. When I arrived in Canada, I was again told "You are black." Thus, I lived in all my environments within a context of never being entirely part of a particular race. What was good for me in this experience was that I acquired a tolerance and a sense of a universality of many things. I also learned the acceptance of difference and the diversity of cultures.

Personally, I can say that I am a person who is multi-cultural in every sense of the word. Which means that I feel very European sometimes, often very African, and very Quebecois. I have lived in Quebec for seventeen years and have adopted much of the Quebecois culture, also. I feel very much at ease in all these cultures, and I feel at home. What I hope is that it will never happen that one day I am told, "Excuse me, but you do not belong after all." Though I do feel that I belong, I feel something more as well. I live this "something more" and I attempt to make the connections between different things. For me, there is no real difference; we are all similar with differences that are particular to the personality or culture of each person. However, these are not differences that should be used to form the judgment that one is better than the other.

You have been here in Montreal, Quebec, in North America, for a long time, which is neither Europe nor Africa; do you also feel part of an African Diaspora?

No, I identify very much as Quebecois. Though I will say that it often depends on where I am and with whom who I am. For instance, when I am at Vues d'Afrique, and when I participate in the events at Vues d'Afrique, I become truly African, I feel African. When I am at FESPACO, I am African. However, if one analyzes closely the way that I make my films, they are very Quebecois and they respond to Quebecois expectations and needs. I feel very Quebecois in my daily life.

Drawing from your triple identity, what do you feel is your role as filmmaker and perhaps more particularly as a woman in the cinema?

I think I can respond by using the example of the film I made called *L'arret d'autobus*, which was inspired by something that I actually experienced. For a period of time, I worked in the outskirts of Montreal in the suburbs where there were not many immigrants and people of different races, and people were very suspicious. However, at the same time, they were nice and I did not really have any problems.

However, at one point I was confronted with a woman with whom I was to work and who was straight out racist; to the point that she was ready to quit her job because she did not want to work with me because I was black. When I first arrived, though she had never seen nor met me before, she bluntly said, "I do not want to work with this woman." I quickly realized that I must not show a negative reaction. I must not get angry; although it is very frustrating and infuriating. On the contrary, I must go towards this person, because what has made her racist is ignorance. It was not a racism that had been generated by a hatred that is

297

often times found in violent hate groups. It was based simply on igno-rance. She was a woman who had never known black people, her only references was what she had seen in the media—which was a very false image—and she was afraid. Once she got to know me, as well as my family, she even came to me to say, "Really, I had no idea!"

At that moment I realized that it was important for us, who are per-haps the bridge between two races, to make an effort, because we are of mixed races, of mixed cultures, we understand the culture of the other. Often people are afraid because they do not know the other culture, and then they make mistakes and have negative reactions. It is up to us to make the bridge and go towards people who are afraid, because there is a great deal of fear in racism. We take up this role, those of us who are mixed-race.

So, do you feel that the role that you want to take on as a filmmaker is to bridge the gap, to mediate between cultures and races?

I think that what I like to be able to do as a filmmaker is to have the freedom to choose my themes. I do not feel obligated to only focus on themes about racism, or themes about Africa, or themes about black people. I think it is important to be free to work according to our creative needs and to go towards the things that interest us. I am black; I live in an environment where I am in the minority. Of course, these are the themes that interest me, and surely they will reappear more often in my films than other things. I see myself, with difficulty, trying to make a film about China, even if it is interesting. I would have to go to live there in order to know more about it.

Your films are often without dialogue, which makes them more accessible to a variety of audiences, since there is not the problem of understanding another lan-guage and reading subtitles. Has this facilitated the distribution of your films in other countries?

They have been seen in other countries such as the United States, France, Belgium, Germany, and in many places in Africa, TV5 has bought them, and of course in Quebec.

Earlier you said that you attempt to bring a certain universality to your work. Do you feel that you have achieved this? What have been the responses in other countries?

Yes, I think there are themes that interest everyone, tenderness, love, tolerance, poetry. I think the only difference is in the way that each person transmits the message, but I think that there is a universal message.

What are some of the specifics in making an animation film? What are the technique and process that are used?

Animation requires a different approach to filmmaking. Initially we draw everything. It is not like conventional filmmaking where you tell an actor to cross the street, then the actor crosses and you shoot the action. In animation if I want my character to cross the street, I draw the action in twenty-four images per second to show him or her crossing the street.

It is a great deal of work, which means that the cost of filming is very expensive. It demands a lot of time and work and there are many people who work on it, and they must be paid. It is an artistic concept that is particularly thorough because one must envision the scene down to the smallest detail and create the costumes and the decor. Drawing the decor is not like composing images and then photographing them, or setting up a decor and then filming it. It must be entirely envisioned and designed. It is a different approach. An animation film is envisaged. The film is actually drawn.

As you stated, animation film is an expensive medium. I remember reading that it can cost more than US$7,000 per minute. How are you able to find funding? Does this limit you to only doing very short works?

SODEC (Société de développement des entreprises culturelles), a funding agency in Quebec and ONF, (Office national du film), financed my first film. My second film was self-financed, it was very short. A friend financed a part of it and I financed the other. The third was also financed by SODEC, and the fourth was financed in co-production with the Office national du film, and Ciné-com Production, the company of Burkinabé filmmaker Gaston Kaboré. Thus, it was a co-production between Canada and Burkina Faso.

Animation films are often viewed as films for children. Are children your targeted audience? Is your objective to make films for everybody, adults as well as children?

Yes, we are often the victims of a certain stereotype when doing animation films. Especially when they are presented in festivals where there are no animation films at all. Moreover, people often don't really know what animation is. Yet, many animation films are made for the general public or even for adults only. Oftentimes children don't really understand what is going on or they are not comfortable with what they are seeing. I think in the West there is not a large market for animation films for adults. However, we find in Asia that adults watch animation films just as much as they do other films. Personally, I like doing films for children. It does not bother me at all. I enjoy it very much and I find that I have much more freedom. Because for children we can do things very "fly" as we call it here in Montreal, with much fantasy and fun, where the filmmaker can really let herself go. One is not obliged to be too down-to-earth, and I like that, actually.

Masepeke Sekhukhuni

South Africa

Interview conducted by Mbye Cham for the African Women in the Cinema Project in October 1998, at the Southern African Film Festival (SAFF) in Harare, Zimbabwe.

Masepeke, you are the director of the Newtown Film and Television School in Johannesburg, South Africa. Could you begin by talking a bit about your background, where you received your training and how you became interested in film and the general television and audiovisual media?

I was born in Soweto. When I was growing up, education was a very important aspect of everyone's life, the whole culture. In order to improve your life, in order for you to be a better person, you had to get education. By that, it meant having those kinds of formal secure jobs. If you are bright and doing well at school, you have to be a doctor, you have to be a scientist and all those kinds of things. When I was at school, during the Soweto uprisings in 1976, I was just about to finish my primary education. Due to that, our education was totally disrupted for two years. Some of us did not even finish our primary education properly. A couple of churches initiated a project where young people could go and finish their schooling but it was mainly for the secondary level. Some of us just squeezed ourselves into the secondary level and started learning things. We learned that way. I did that through a couple of churches.

Politically things were tense, our parents trying to cope with us. Through ANC connections, some of us were able to go abroad. I worked in England for about a year and a half in community centers working with young people, with young people who were truant, who did not finish school. I was trying to find myself, asking what it was I wanted to do. I knew that I did not want to be a doctor. I wanted something in media. Before I left home, I had taken some classes in drama, in theater. Even when I was working in the community center, we used to do drama classes. Something was hooking me to media. I wanted to study communications.

I went to Middlesex Polytechnic, which is now called Middlesex University of Communications. It opened a whole area for me; television, radio, film and everything. Starting off, I was more interested in print media. Because you are so used to expressing yourself on pen and paper, everything had to be in writing. So I started out that way. I also loved photography, I was self-taught. I learned how to develop photographs myself. I started freelancing with *Drum* magazine in Johannesburg. A friend of mine was working for them and said, "get some of these stories in *Drum*." I started doing that. My main area was music so I developed show biz stuff. Then there was a whole political thing of consciousness-type music about apartheid. There were specific musicians that one targeted in order to get the anti-apartheid message across, like Third World. There was Missing Roots in England and all those who were sympathetic to anti-apartheid. One was doing a lot of stuff around them, photojournalism, and all that.

Through the experience of photography, I realized that there was something more effective. It was frustrating trying to capture the musicians' movements on stage through still photography. I thought that there was a better way to capture these movements. I happened to hook up with a woman filmmaker in England who was a journalist before and who was also from South Africa. She was studying film. I talked with her and she said, "Yes, try film, let's take my Hi-8 camera and go do something." I thought, "Yes, filmmaking is the answer." I did my graduate program at Goldsmith College in London. They had a full-time film program, I was very happy with that. Ever since then, I have never looked back and I still believe that the best way of capturing anything is through film. It can be the smallest movement. There is nowhere that you can get closer to anything without using film and video. That is where I came from.

Could you talk about the school that your direct, how it came about and what are some of the various aspects of the school, and what you envision?

The school's history started in the late eighties when a group of mainly white, anti-apartheid filmmakers had a vision of equipping young aspiring filmmakers with video-making tools. What was happening in the country then politically was that most of those filmmakers or videomakers were documenting a whole lot of political activism that was going on in the country and sending it out to the world. There were areas that they could not penetrate; that only black people could actually get into. As people who lived within those communities, they were the ones mostly affected. The whole idea was also for black people to document what was going on in their own community. So, it started loosely like that and then became an informal project where they had weekly classes with the Alexandra Arts Center.

As the organization was growing, it started to have subcommittees, one of which was an education subcommittee. They drew a proposal, which was sent to Channel Four Television in the UK, proposing to actually set up a project, sort of a full-time program for training.

Fortunately, Channel Four liked the idea and gave seed funding for the project. In 1991 the project started off as the Community Video School (CVS) with twelve students from all over South Africa. The first students completed the program after two years, in 1993.

That is when I joined the school on a full-time basis. I got involved with the school very informally, just talking to people who were involved. After that, I got pulled in because I knew as someone who got her film and video training elsewhere, in England, it was important for me to impart it. More importantly for me, because these were black people who were being trained, it was more important for us to be involved to determine what kind of vision should be put through for the training.

In 1993, there were a lot of changes that we proposed in terms of moving the project, and not only being seen as a project but having a more long-term vision of a school. We pulled away from the original organizers of the school and set up an education trust. We moved from the location where the project was based; it was getting too small for the kinds of activities that we wanted to get involved in. We moved to an area called Newtown Cultural Precinct where a lot of artists were based. We called ourselves Newtown Film and Television School. We set up a new vision of the school with a full-time program, internships, linking with other international film schools and having more qualified black practitioners to teach at the school.

The curriculum itself was under scrutiny in terms of the steps that had to be taken to insure that students who come out of the school are not just technically competent but are people who understand the whole implication of cinema and video in terms of identity. In terms of them being a new generation that is going to come out of South Africa and start shaping a whole new way of seeing cinema, a whole new way of interpreting visual media itself; it was very important that in the curriculum we include those aspects of African Cinema, Black Cinema. So that students could actually have a broader base that is more relevant to them.

It is a two-year full-time program with a third-year internship. When people finish two years of the school, we place them with various companies. We normally ask for a minimum of six months. They are there for six months up to a year based on their performance in the industry, then they graduate.

So the areas that they are involved with are basically film and video...

Well, what has been happening is that when we started, even though the curriculum was film based, it was hard to work on film because of the expense. One, being the post-Mandela release and pre-new democracy, it was very hard—where you still find that in that era the political system itself was still within the control of the actual apartheid forces themselves. The school as it was, was something that made a big statement. Here we were training black people. For the first time, black people actually are being given those skills, of making films instead of being in front of the camera as actors.

It shook the white industry, so there was always that kind of antagonism towards the school from the industry before the new democracy, except for a few independents and progressive people. I remember when the first group of students was placed, you would find in various companies people even called them communists, because they came from the school. Visibly, Newtown was giving people power to actually have freedom of expression to write their own ideas, to know how it is done, to demystify the whole thing. Some of the big multi-nationals like Kodak—Kodak was not in South Africa then because of the sanctions—so Kodak did not have an office then at all, there were no ties. The film lab then, was very much state-owned in Pretoria. I remember one of our students when making his graduation film in 1994, decided to shoot it on film; we got some stock from Agfa. He went to the lab but the labs were not prepared to give any discount at all, they were not going to do it for us. Fortunately, the students had come to the Southern African Film Festival in 1993 and were introduced to a lab, CFL, in Harare. It occurred to him, "Why don't I go to Harare." So students got on one of these minibuses, traveled all the way, seventeen hours to come to CFL. For some reason, he had some misunderstanding with the owner of the lab then about the kind of arrangements that they would make for him. He thought it was free, but they gave him a sixty- percent discount. Later when I met the manager, he told me that he was so moved. This young man misunderstood the kind of discount he actually agreed with him, and there he is at his doorstep with his film under his arm and he has traveled all the way, he was very determined. He said he had to help him out.

Over the period of time that the school has been operating have you been trying to raise the number of women given the fact that in African cinema and the audio-visual industry in general, women are not that prominent in all positions?

That is one of the key policies, I think, of the school. The school itself has always been run by women. One of the key policies is to actively try to encourage women and promote women to come in. We have our selection criteria and at the top of that list is affirmative action for women. Every year we go out to make publicity about applications. Even within some of the women's magazines, though we may not agree with, we put an ad there. We do radio interviews, television interviews. We go to community groups that deal with women. To be honest, it has been a battle to get that kind of idea number of women. Because, although the young women come, when we start interviewing them, we find out that even when we have selected them for an interview, they do not want to do film. They don't want to. We run workshops before the selection, we do screenings, we start discussing how they are themselves perceived, certain ways that women have been represented in the movies. Then we go further than that in terms of behind the scenes: "here we are, this is what we do," and all those kinds of things. For some, it makes sense, and for some they just say, "No."

The first intake that the community school had, there were five women out of twelve. Of those five, about two dropped out before the end of the course, because they found out that it was not what they wanted to do after a year or so. The other three qualified and started working, two of which kept working up until two years ago. One of them said she has left the industry, it was just too much for her. She works for an insurance company; she just wanted a steady income. From that group, there is only one who is an editor now. She has worked for Transkei Television, SABC, and others. She is quite strong. The following year the intake was fourteen students and half the class was women. Out of that, the women who have made an impact, I think there have been about four of them. Four of them are still in the industry and are very strong. One of them was here at the Festival [SAFF]; she is never out of work. Wherever she goes people just want her, she chooses. When jobs come she says, "Which one should I work with?" Another one is a production manager. They both are making an impact.

We have had an interesting situation, in my current second year group, we are sixteen and eight are women. Three are South Africans and the others come from the region. We have two women from Zambia, and also one from Botswana and one from Zimbabwe. They are quite a strong unit, out of the group of women only one has actually dropped out.

We still have a bigger challenge of making sure that we find somehow a right approach of getting the women in. It is a bigger issue of the society. Because now even though a lot of women, and young women especially, are interested in television, they want to see themselves there, on the screens. That is what it is all about, they want to be presented. We have had people that we tried to teach and have talked to. They say, "No, I don't want that, I want to be a presenter, I want to be seen on televi-sion."

Among the ones that you have trained, what specific areas are they trained in, camera, editing, sound, producing, or is it a combination of all of those?

Basically, all the students are trained in everything at the school. The first year they have to learn everything: how to develop an idea, writing, etc. Every student is required to learn all the areas. So in their second year they are strong. It actually shows who is strong in what, who is capable of doing what. When they finish that first year, before they come back for the second year they have an internship for three months. They are placed within various companies bearing in mind what they are strong in. If someone has shown strength in directing then he or she will be a director's intern somewhere, or in editing, and so forth. But what I have observed now is that a lot of our women students seem to have the capa-bilities for producing and editing and writing, they are very strong in those areas for some reason, I don't know why. Writing, editing and producing, we got the women there.

I notice that one of the students that you have in your current class, I think in the second-year class, actually played the lead role in the Zimbabwean film **Flame**. *Are these the kinds of students that you are getting now, people who have already been exposed to some aspect of the industry, and as a result of that they want to go further?*

Of the type of students who come to the school there is a whole mixture. Some people had no clue. We take them in for affirmative action, there are very few who have had exposure. From what I have actually experi-enced, those who have exposure we usually have a problem with them because they think they know. For some reason, it takes them a long time to actually learn, because they have this blocking mechanism. Personally, I like the ones who don't know, because they are humble, they are open. The minute that they actually get in tune with what is going on, they go far ahead of those who actually had some kind of exposure, it is very interesting.

Especially the women students that we take in. We realize that we have a very small number of women applicants. Last year we had about three hundred applications and out of those, you would not believe how many women applied, only about twelve. So we make sure we interview all of them. When going through the applications it already indicates that they had no film experience at all. So we make sure that that is not going to be the criteria for the interview, for us to talk about the industry or whatever. We want to find out more about the person, what is it that they want to bring in to the course. What is it they want to bring in to the film industry. Have you got a story to tell? Tell us about your story. What really attracted you to film? Sometimes people cannot really express themselves properly to say, "I have this thing within." But you can just see it, that this person has got something. But due to the lack of exposure, they cannot express it. We have had good experiences with those kind of people. You take them in, and quietly the first few months they find their way, you find they are more practical people. As I said earlier, the ones who turn out to be far ahead later are not the ones who have already been there and are under the impression that they know what it is all about.

You said that the school has always been run by women. What is the composition of you staff? How many people do you have actually running the school and what percentage of that is women?

We are not really a big school. There are four full-time positions, and one part-timer, the bookkeeper. Of these four, it has always been women. The director, the program coordinator, the education programmer who does the library and extra-curricular activities for the students (like festivals, visiting filmmakers, seminars), our administrator and the receptionist, it has always been all women. We had one man before who was among the women, he was there to do fundraising and things like that, but there has always been women who have been doing it.

We do not have a full-time teaching staff who is there every day. All our instructors are on contractual basis; they are all industry practitioners. They come in for their special area per semester. Most of the time we have a pool of people who insure the continuity for the students. These people commit themselves; even when there are productions, they do it around the students' programs. Each instructor has three hours per week. Whether their class is directing, editing, etc., they come three hours per week. When students are on production, depending on who supervises them, they will be there with them for two weeks. The way we contract people, we look at their area of specialization. If for instance, we are looking for a directing teacher, we want to know if this person is a director of television, documentaries, drama, or performance. We want to make sure that the students get the most out of it. Not everyone who is a filmmaker is good in everything.

How is the school funded? Is it through student tuition, government funds or other agencies?

Funding has always been a kind of continuous handicap for the school. What was envisaged was that Channel Four would put up the seed funding with the hope that by the time that contract runs out there would be a new government. There has always been that kind of idea, that "it is our government which is going to help us." That has really, I think, hurt the school in terms of its long-term sustenance. I think currently we are suffering from funding strategies that were based on international donors. Since the new government has been in place we get a quarter of the budget from the Department of Art and Culture, but then with that there is no commitment for the long term.

What is happening now in South Africa, is that next year we are going to set up a Film and Video Foundation. It will be sort of a body that is going to look into the film industry, in the areas of training, production, co-production, and marketing South African products.

So yes, funding has always been sort of our handicap. The students pay minimum fees, but it does not even make up a quarter of the expenses that have to go into their training. We adopted the fees just as a matter of principle for people to actually take responsibility, not to expect that it is just going to be a handout for them. Even though it is minimal, they have a problem paying those fees. Our fees are now 7,000 rands. It costs us 40,000 rands per year per student. For them to get that 7,000 is a big deal. Their parents are earning how much? 2,000, or 1,000? So now, we have a new strategy where we are going to the corporate world and industry to have them set up a scholarship fund. That seems to be working at the moment. A number of people have committed themselves for the scholarship fund, the Video Lab was the first one. Now we have Times

Media Ltd. (TML), and others, as well as various individuals. We also monitor that because we feel that students should not automatically qualify. Because we never know whether they are going to drop out, so first they have to put up a deposit like 2,000 rands and after a semester, it is easy for us to sort out where they are. A lot of times we prefer to go for the second year because by then we know the students. We know their strengths, we know they are committed people.

Because the thing is, if we were to raise the fees to realistic figures that other film schools in South Africa are actually charging, like 20,000 or 22,000. What it does automatically is exclude black people and then it contradicts the mission of the school, which is to open access to black people in the most important areas of filmmaking, the creative decision-making. If we don't do it, no one else is going to be committed in South Africa. That is the truth, no one else would be committed to make sure that black people get in and that they are well qualified and well trained.

How do you see the situation of women in African cinema in general and in South African cinema in particular, how would you assess that? In terms of their participation at all levels?

I think that a lot of times the perception of separating women in cinema for me, personally, is problematic. Because I think that all the problems that women go through, men need to be part of those discussions. Men need to be made aware of their attitude and their approach. As fellow filmmakers, African filmmakers, I think they also have to question themselves, a lot has to be confronted by our fellow African filmmakers to actually make sure that they support the women. They take it upon themselves as a matter of principle, that, "I want to see more African women participate in the cinema."

I always say that women are the best storytellers in Africa. That is where I start, and in trying to encourage young women I say to them, "It does not matter whether you call those stories gossip or chit chat or whatever." Women have them; they have those stories. Then you move further than storytelling. Women are producers, they control the budget at home, they direct. When they come they have those natural skills, they have those skills already and our men should recognize that. They should know it, and help us in this battle to insure that there are more women. When women are here, they are given that opportunity to use those skills that they have.

This whole thing of mystifying the difficulties of making films, I think that it is all male games, it is about power, basically. Men just like to be in a position of power all the time, to mystify everything. They have to sort of confront themselves to say, "We know how women are, I know my mother, I know my sister, I know the kinds of skills that they have, and so I have to make sure the opportunities are there for women."

What are some of the prospects that you see for women and South African women in particular? Do you have any women filmmakers now coming up? I know you have some of them because they are coming through you, actually, at the Newtown Film School. With the situation in place right now, how would you assess it generally speaking?

I don't want to be very pessimistic or dismissive. I think we have started somewhere. We have started somewhere: at Newtown we are training young women. Outside of Newtown there are very few individuals that I know that are out there trying to make a mark, trying to negotiate for their space. I think what we need is a strong network, this is what I am always saying to the sisters. I say, "Look, we should have a strong network to know who is actually good in what area and make sure that those particular persons impart their skills, that they go further, with the involvement of men, as well." To some extent, we still have a lot of work to do. You also look in television; a few women have also been given powerful positions. The head of Channel 2 at SABC is a woman, at the head of the radio there is a woman, on the board there are women. I think we are making headway somewhere. Because we have started, all we have to do is to make sure that we will intensify and actually recognize that we are there.

I think the other problem is that we don't really recognize and feel confident that we are there. We need to be even very vocal about it, to say, yes we have made headway, we have started. Now strategically, what is it we need to do to insure that other people are further developed and other people are coming in? I think that men have to be more involved in terms of insuring that women are moving forward. I don't want to get into the whole rhetoric and emotional issues, like, "as women we are marginalized." I just want to see us practically, identifying where we are, how do we get there, and making sure that we are working together with men to insure that there are more women in the industry.

You talked about networking, how would you see that working in terms of relations between South African women filmmakers in particular with other women filmmakers on the continent as well as in the African Diaspora? Do you see any potential in those linkages, in that kind of networking?

The potential is there, but what has been the obstacle is the lack of information. As you know, South Africa has been isolated for so many years. The few women who are in the industry hardly know other African women who are in the film industry. Through some of us, and through the school in terms of our network, we are seeing the awareness coming out. I think we still are at a very early stage where I think people are searching, inquiring, "How do we start to network, now we have heard there are other women, how do we get in touch with them?" I get those kinds of questions from people all the time, who ask, "How do we get in touch, how do we insure that we can talk to other women about their experiences?"

In the region itself institutions like SAFF, the Market, which have initiated those kinds of venues for people, are opening up the borders for people to start talking. FESPACO itself is a very important institution, I think that we have a long way to go to actually insure that a lot of women especially from South Africa participate more in the continent. On the other hand, you get this feeling that FESPACO is a big body and it is just too overwhelming for people. For some reason, it needs to be demystified for a lot of people who don't know what it is. In terms of its profile before the festival actually happens there is a lot of work that has to be done within my country. To say this is FESPACO, this is what we stand for; there are definitely some mystifying things about it.

There is a lot of discussion about gender issues particularly about the notion of a female sensibility. Do you feel that there is a female sensibility that comes out in a woman's film? In the process of training your students, especially by the fact that the school is run mostly by women, does this issue come out, especially with the young women that you are training?

For me it is very difficult. Even with the experience of working with the young women in the school, people have different personalities, to sort of generalize and see it that way is very dangerous. You see young men who are very, very sensitive. You look at the films that they have made, and if you want to generalize you may say, that film was made by a woman, and it turns out that it was a man. What I would personally recognize is that for me there are definitely different ways that men and women see things. There is definitely a difference in the way that we see things, the way that we solve problems. There is some sort of idea around this issue where you find maybe somewhere, somehow women have not adequately expressed their womanhood in their films, due to the whole production process of the filmmaking itself. Perhaps, due to the inhibitions that they actually come with or carry with them, actually being touched with this

311

medium. Knowing what the camera is saying. Knowing when you edit. How do you freely express yourself as a woman in that medium? As opposed to those principles which have basically been set by men, the principles of making movies. I would like to see it on a higher level than that as well; the principles of filmmaking itself have been basically defined by men.

Now maybe things have changed. I know some of the things that have always been kind of scary to women is equipment. They see these big cameras, these big machines. They are big, they are heavy, you need a certain strength to carry these things, if you push your finger through there, this will happen. All of those things, I think they have been very intimidating—"How am I going to carry this thing?" I think women have all the energy, the power. They put buckets on their heads and all those things. The invention of the equipment was made through the male's eye and the male perception. When we want to get into that issue, I would like to look at those things as well.

What are some of your own film projects?

Since I have been at the school, it has been very hard for me to work in the film industry. The last time I did a documentary was in 1995, which was a piece I did on African music for SABC. Now I am working with Joyce Makwenda in Zimbabwe, we are doing a series on the role of women in politics in the Southern African region. We are not just looking at hardcore politicians, but we are looking at all those other areas where women have been active to make sure that the politics of the region are happening. My personal favorite story is of the She-bin queens in the township. When the whole resettlement happened they refused to go to be housemaids. They refused to be nannies. They carried the whole economic independence. This is why, as in the case of South Africa, they were permanently raided by police. Because the whites did not under-stand why this one did not want to be their nanny. What we have today is that She-bins are the tourist attraction, people come to see them. At least they are given a bit more respect.

Is this going to be a documentary series?

Yes, it will be a documentary series. I am also working on another project, which is at the very elementary stages. I am working with Godwin Mawuru, as well, on the story of Nehanda. I was attracted to it also, while we were growing up. During the struggle we used to hear about this woman, Nehanda. When we switched on Radio Freedom, the combat theme was, "Forward Nehanda", but we did not know what it was at the time. I am doing research on this woman who was so strong, and through her spiritual medium gave guidance to all the guerilla forces in the region. She actually single-handedly stood up to the colonialists. She was the first one to actually be executed, they beheaded her. At the point when she was there with another man and they were both ordered to be baptized to be forgiven; she refused. The man gave in to be baptized and she refused.

Wabei Siyolwe

Zambia

Interviews held during two occasions in 1997: FESPACO, February 1997, Ouagadougou, Burkina Faso, and in Washington, DC, October 1997.

You have a particularly multi-faceted training in film and theater. Could you talk about your background and how you became involved in cinema?

I went to drama school in England for four years at the Guildhall School of Drama. So I was trained in acting for film, but also the technical side as well; it was a multi-disciplinary school. It was very practical so we did our own short films. We wrote them as well as acted in them. It gave us a very broad spectrum of all the things you can do with film and theater.

Theater is really my first love and I have done theater and music since I was very small. We used to live in Russia, so I did a lot of piano and music at the conservatory there. So doing film was a natural progression. I am used to all types of visual and performing arts but at the moment, I am doing a lot more film than I have before. Actually, my first professional work was in film. Even though I had majored in drama in school, the work that I did upon completion was mostly in film, big feature films such as *Cry Freedom*, which I worked on when I was eighteen years old, *Nuns on the Run*, and *The Crossing*. So I had been exposed to it as an actor, but I was always much more interested in the production aspect of it, behind the camera as opposed to in front of the camera. So, since 1986, I have been interested in film and decided that I was going to pursue that.

In another discussion, you told me that you prefer to be viewed as simply a Southern African. Could you talk a bit of your experiences growing up in Southern Africa?

I was born in Zambia. And if you know a bit about colonial history before 1884, my particular part of Southern Africa was called the kingdom of Barotseland. The people in this particular part of Southern Africa originally migrated from South Africa, so culturally speaking, our languages were spoken by the same people, Sesotho-speaking people. So that when I meet people from South Africa we have the same culture, the same cultural practices, the same language, only the dialect is different. It's the difference between Americans from southern United States and Americans from northern United States, it's the same language but it is different in sound.

My family is the royal family in that area and is still recognized as the royal family. So we still have very strong ties with South Africa. All my grandparents were educated in South Africa, Fort Hare where Nelson Mandela went, and Lovedale and places like that. I have always had strong connections with South Africa.

I was born in Zambia; my father is Namibian by origin, if you take in the divisions. He became part of a liberation party called UNIP in the 1960s. If you know the history of nationalism in Southern Africa, he was one of the first Africans to go abroad in the 1960s. He moved to New York and started the first mission for Zambia at the UN. That was the first place where I grew up, in New York City.

Zambia was the head of the front line states for the liberation movements in Zimbabwe, Mozambique, Angola, South Africa. So all of the liberation parties were attached to the Zambian embassy in a certain way. My father was responsible for all of the students and all of the health issues for all of these countries, because they had no representation since they were not considered legal at that time. They were considered terrorist groups as opposed to legitimate liberation organizations.

This brought me very close to Southern Africa in that sense. I grew up with all the liberation leaders in my own house. That is why when people ask me where I am from I say very strongly that I am Southern African. There is not one place that I consider home more than anywhere else because all these places are very much a part of me. And I actually don't recognize any of those borders myself, but if someone asks me where I am from, I say yes, I am a Zambian. I have a Zambian passport, but I also have British, American, and a bunch of other things.

Has your political background while growing up influenced you in wanting to do film? How do you want to see these experiences in your film stories?

I think life is political, every part of life is political, especially as a woman, I think it is very political. Everything that I was surrounded by was extremely political. I define the way that I look at the world as so. Those things that happen in history are very true for me. For example, I have cousins in Angola and I have to get a visa to go see my cousins. I have cousins in Namibia it is the same thing. So that kind of life that I have has influenced how I have seen the world, obviously. I think that I see myself as a very global person because I have lived in other parts of Africa.

I think that film has always been a mark culturally, in terms of people seeing visually who they are. And so for me having this sort of fragmented kind of history and life, I always thought that film was a very important thing for me. Because it is very necessary for people to see who they are. And the history of Southern Africa has always been told by someone else. I have recently been doing a lot of graduate study of my own history and its mostly been written by other people. But fortunately, one of the things about colonization is that there were a large number of people from my part of Southern Africa that were highly educated. And so there are very good books written by Silozi-speaking people.

It is all tied together, I don't see any difference between the written word and the visual word, really, but the visual media is the dominant media in the world right now. People don't pick up books, people turn on things, whether it is the Internet or the television. That is the thing that people connect with more than anything. In that case, that is what I want to be involved in, because I have a duty in terms of my own family to tell the right story. I have to tell our history from our perspective. That is the connection between why I think it is important, why I do it, and because it is the ultimate media.

What do you want to contribute to African Cinema, or more particularly Southern African Cinema?

I can talk about Southern African films because that is what I am familiar with. Some of the oldest movies in Southern Africa are films like *Come Back Africa*, which came out in the fifties. And most films were from South Africa in particular, dramatic films, the narrative films. They were made by whites who had their own agendas, some positive, some negative. These were mostly social context stuff, social issues that had to do with apartheid, and it was very informative. And I am glad those films were made. I am glad there was a record of who we were then.

I am not familiar with Angola or Mozambique, because South Africa was the only place that had a film history. Zimbabwe is very recent, and

317

Botswana it is pretty much non-existent except for films that have to do with social issues such as breast-feeding, or AIDS or those kinds of things. But as far as the narrative, South Africa is the only place where there was that kind of filmmaking. And those films have depicted Africans to be a certain way. Most definitely in a derogatory way, as savages, as non-human, as apartheid claimed they were. So that really is the history. There was a period in the sixties and seventies when white filmmakers in South Africa were making social-issue films that were quite good, but also from that perspective.

You have to be in Southern Africa to know that it is such a serious distinction between the life of a white person and the life of a black person, the life of a colored person and the life of an Indian person. They are very different in the ways they see the world, and they have very different positions in life. So these positions and views color the images that they paint of those worlds. And because all of the groups were completely separate and not allowed to mix in any way, it created a very surreal kind of fragmented idea of who people are.

Historically people in Southern Africa are dealing with such enormous things right now because history was written in one way, which was completely a lie. People are losing their jobs in South Africa and Namibia, because they wrote history in one way. I mean literally losing their jobs. So it is creating insecurity for people, all people. In terms of who am I, I feel that I am not completely attached to one kind of Southern Africa. So I think that I can fill in that gap and be objective in telling the story of certain groups and their history.

What kinds of stories, are you interested in telling? Are you interested in fiction, documentaries, docu-dramas?

Every job that one does fulfills a certain need in oneself. So I don't specifically see myself as only doing feature films, only doing docu-dramas, only doing documentaries. I like it all. I like to tell stories, stories that I think people should know, because I think certain stories help people understand who they are. And that is ultimately what I want to do, talk about identity, the issue of identity.

Earlier you stated that as a woman especially you think that life is very political. As an African woman in cinema, do you see specific sensibilities that may come out because you are an African woman?

Yes, I think so. But I think it would be the same if I were an African man. But, no I am being a bit trite. Yes, there are those specific things, because in that climate of colonization it did—like in America—create rifts between the sexes. There is the oppressor and there is the man and the woman, and the man ultimately oppresses the woman.

From my own perspective, I come from a matrilineal society so there was always a respect for women. Women always governed. In fact, a woman was always the queen of the two capitals. We had two capitals in Barotseland. So from that perspective women have always had a lot of dignity, but over the years during the nationalist years in Southern Africa, men seized the power. So historically, I think I am in a good position, because in my society women have had a lot of respect.

But there are these same social problems that are around the whole world, women being battered, and so on. My position is that yes, I have a lot of things to say that I think a man couldn't say. There are a lot of things I can see that I think Southern African male filmmakers can't see. And that is from being a woman. And I think you understand that yourself, there is a certain sensitivity that we have and there is a certain sensitivity that men have.

You have now ventured into another area of cinema. Could you talk about your studies in film at American University in Washington, DC and why you are studying film production?

I am doing graduate studies in producing. And it is the first producing program in the country, I have been told. I really want to learn to be a good producer. I've done a lot of directing, I've done acting. I am doing a 16mm film that I will begin soon. Over the last two years, I have been concentrating on film production, distribution, financing, and development for multi-media and for film and video. We will do managing and enterprise. Mostly it has focused on the business side, and that is what I went there for.

Creatively I am very comfortable; I know what to do with film. But I wanted to get skills in terms of finding the means to be able to produce good work and not necessarily always begging at development agencies. I have done a lot of stuff with Norwegian agencies, French agencies. When I was in Namibia I did a lot of stuff with international development agencies and I really didn't want to go that route anymore I really wanted to try and go the private route in terms of private financing with a specialty in Asia.

Now I am basically peddling. I came to FESPACO specifically to meet some people I know and with whom I worked on *Cry Freedom* about ten years ago. Over the years we have been researching and working on certain themes and concepts in the hope of making a feature film. So we met here and I will be going to South Africa in November 1997 for the film and video market there. I am starting to look for financing deals in South Africa. You are writing at the same time that you are meeting people, at the same time that you are traveling and building up the knowledge and the information that you need to do it. It is being done spontaneously it is not straight. The only thing that is straight is that I am in school and that's good, and it is challenging.

You mentioned that you will be doing a film soon. Could you talk about the specifics of the film that you are now preparing to shoot?

It's going to be a full-length feature film, it's about the life of a nineteen-year-old girl who goes back to Southern Africa to take part in the democratic elections, in search of her family and her identity. There was a big massacre in Angola in the 1970s called the Kasinga Massacre where a lot of young Namibians were orphaned. Many of them were taken to Germany, to the U.S. and to Cuba. And come independence they were all basically told, you are Namibian, you are eighteen, you have to come back to your country and vote. They tracked them all down. And it resulted in the biggest airlift in African history.

The story is about a girl coming back home to look for her parents. In the massacre, many children lost their parents. They did not know if their parents survived. It is quite a well-known history in Namibia, so that is what the story is about. So it's a political thriller essentially.

Do you find that films and filmmaking in Southern Africa tend to focus on themes of liberation and struggle? Perhaps you are not at the point where you make entertainment fiction and the "I love you" types?

Right, well we haven't done any of those "I love you's" yet. I think first we have to know who we are. And so to know who you are you have to go back a bit and figure out what happened, "How did I come to be the person that I am?" But I think within that we are going to mature.

The film that I make, the main story line, the main thread of the story, is going to be the politics. But essentially its going to be a story of a young girl coming of age. That is really what it's going to be about. And in that, she is going to fall in love, and all of those very human things.

But I think as I mentioned before, we can't escape from our history in Southern Africa, it is so intense. I couldn't think of writing a story like *Trainspotting*, or something like that. But I think those things will happen in time. Right now people are writing and telling stories based on who they are, because it is so fresh. It was only thirty years ago that other countries in Southern Africa first started to become independent, that's my lifetime, which is no time. People are going to free up a little on those heavy political things, but right now, I think it is very necessary.

Are there legends and stories in the oral tradition that you see that you may want to adapt into film?

Yes, in this film that I hope to make, one of the other threads is the oral history, the passing on of knowledge from grandparent to granddaughter, the initiation ceremony which I never had—and I am going to have one eventually—but it is very important for us, these rituals and ceremonies. I definitely want to have that as a very strong aspect of the story. I do not want it to be a narrative in the Western sense. I am struggling still to really find my own way of telling that story in the context of our own oral history.

Are there other Southern African women that you are connecting with, or other African women in general?

Well, right now I think we are very fragmented. Because some of us are or have studied abroad such as the director of *Everyone's Child*, Tsitsi Dangarembga, so people are just beginning to come back. So I cannot say in real detail who is in Southern Africa. Because we are basically just finding out who we are. But I definitely think within the film market in Capetown in November 1997 this specific one will be where I will see a lot more people. This will be the first time that I am going to go. In Namibia, there was one other woman who was a producer at that time, called Bridget Pickering and that is about it. In Namibia there are very few.

It's just beginning. The whole film industry in Southern Africa is still in its infancy, even though it has still been sort of going on for I think about ten years. But really in the last three years, it has taken off, especially with the elections in South Africa and the independence of Namibia in 1990.

Flame, a film in competition at this FESPACO, was directed by Ingrid Sinclair a white woman from Zimbabwe. With the multi-racial context in a lot of the Southern African states, will we find more black and white Southern Africans coming together, where race is not as much the issue in defining what is African?

The question sounds as if you are asking are we going to be able to work together.

I was asking in terms of identity, how will race be played out in defining who is African and how do you see this being presented in film?

We have to look at it in two ways. One way is that one group had all the means, all the access, all the legal rights to make films and show images of themselves and images of others. And on the other hand, you had a group that had no rights, no legal standing, no resources, no training. Apartheid was total, it was not just color, it was health. It was every aspect of the way you lived.

The latter group is the group that I am in. So for me personally, I don't believe that a white person can define who I am. Absolutely not, because they were separated from us in physical terms. It was not like in the United States when beginning in the sixties people could live right next door to each other. There was not that in Southern Africa. So for me I think that it is absolutely necessary for black people to make the films about themselves. Absolutely! I think it is perfectly fine if someone white wants to make a film or someone Indian wants to make a film about black people, but my question is "Why?" Why not get a black person to make that film about that, because they live that, and they know that? But I congratulate, and I have full support for anybody who is going to make films in Southern Africa because I think they need to be made.

For me, it was very gratifying coming to FESPACO because I can see where people are mentally, their treatment of the issues. It is totally educational for me to see people's films in general, whether they are Southern African or not. Because I think, film ultimately is an individual's vision of the world. And so if Ingrid Sinclair...if that is her idea of what the war in Zimbabwe was all about she has every right to that. Constitutionally, she has every right to say those things. But for me personally, because I will only be critical about my own, I feel that definitely I should be the one to write the history of Barotseland. For one, I've got the education, I've got the historical background, and I think I can find the means to do it. I have no problem with white people making films, but ultimately the person's film that I will appreciate and that I think will be in-depth enough, will be that person who has lived that experience, and who has black skin. Because we have two totally different experiences and you know it as well in America.

Speaking of the United States, what has it been like for you living in the United States? Could you talk about your relationships with African diasporans, and the links and connections that your have and want to make?

I think that African people right now are at a brilliant point, at the same time we are at the worst point. In Europe—you see what is happening in France—people are being deported, all these kinds of things that dig at peoples egos. But because we are at the worst point in terms of being excluded in really serious ways, I think people of African descent globally, are really recognizing their commonalties just because of the color of their skin, and also what we share in common culturally.

I have traveled enough to see that there are really some distinct issues and things that we do share in common so I think this is actually a good point for us. There are people who would never have come to FESPACO maybe, had it been another time. For instance, had it been in the eighties when things were more cushy for people. But now because life is more difficult, black people are coming more together. And I feel as much at home in South Carolina as I feel in Ouagadougou. To me there really is no difference anymore; the world is very similar. In a lot of places, people are dealing with the same issues. People are oppressed in the same ways, in terms of education and in other ways.

I am glad that I am very connected with Howard University, and Washington DC because that is a hub in terms of independent black filmmakers, non-Hollywood filmmakers who want to make films that touch on issues that are dear to their heart. So I am really excited and I am glad that I am in that location.

Do you see making a film with a Diasporan component?

Oh yes, this film that I am making is going to have that, because the protagonist is coming from the U.S. Essentially this character is American, she talks, walks, acts, thinks, American, but she is told that she is Namibian and has to go back. How does this person who is a so-called American, identify herself when back in Africa? That is what I really want to see played strongly in the film? Because that is what I am interested in, the cross-Diaspora situation.

You are the Artistic Director of your company Global Posse, could you talk about the activities and objectives of the company?

Global Posse began as a creative outlet for me and my partner Rodney Hopson when we were both at the University of Namibia in 1992. He was doing research in the Division of Social and Economic Research and I was a lecturer in the Department of Drama.

When I first went back to Southern Africa, I worked in Namibia, because my grandfather was born there, and as I said before, I have very long ties with Namibia. We found that in the development process of Namibia there was more focus on physical and material opportunity, rather than social and human development and change. So I thought that the arts would be an interesting way of addressing those social issues that were in place as a result of apartheid. I went out and looked for Namibian talent that never had access to any space where they were able to show their creativity, and we basically put on a show for the first time. That show, which was called "Afrika Festival Party" was a huge success, it was a historic event in the country, actually.

Because of it a lot of young writers, poets, musicians, and artists in general, approached me to direct, edit, and produce their shows. I started doing it and before we knew it, we had established a production company, because there was so much activity happening. We registered the company, wrote proposals to development agencies, and got funding to stage, produce, write and direct all sorts of productions for film, video, and commercials.

Could you talk about the actual name "Global Posse"?

I have always had a sort of global perspective of things, looking at that bigger picture. Posse is a term that's got a lot of meanings, actually. But the meaning that I am familiar with was that of a pack of people that are fighting against a force, a negative force to that group. I thought of Global Posse in terms of a group of people who have got global concerns, that are fighting against being marginalized in any kind of way; and in our particular way it was through media.

Because it is global, I suppose you can take it and use it wherever you are. How do you use it in the United States?

How we operate is that the company is registered in Namibia, where we still have very strong connections. We still consult with people there on many levels on different projects. I still write proposals and plan to continue to do productions there. I was back there a couple of years ago doing a radio series. I am always going to be connected to Southern Africa, that is never going to change.

We also became incorporated in the state of Virginia and basically run it in the way that we run it in Namibia, which is finding funding and finding young people who have a desire to learn about production. We put on productions or co-produce video productions, and get involved in a variety of things. So we are doing exactly the same things, just in another country, and it is a similar kind of situation, because most of the people that we work with are black youth, which is the focus of the company.

Do you actually do training in video, film and theater work?

We train them to do different things. For example in a proposal for a documentary film, I'll say that I want to use young people from a certain area, and I would like to be able to film the process of putting on a production with these young people, from the casting, to the performances and even beyond that. It takes on many forms, that is the thing about Global Posse; we take it wherever it goes.

When you taught drama in Namibia, did you connect acting for the theater with acting for cinema? Did you also combine your Global Posse activities with your drama teaching?

I taught both acting for theater and cinema. Global Posse was separate from the University of Namibia's drama department but sometimes we would work together. Sometimes we would co-produce. For example, if I wanted to bring visiting artists from different parts of the world and I wanted to have them perform at the theater or work at the University of Namibia, then we would do it together, and we would have an equal share in the responsibility. It is a very fluid company. The mission is to use the visual and performing arts as a vehicle for social change in manifestations of film, literature, dance, music, drama, multi-media, it is quite wide. And that is what I am going back to school for, to narrow it down a little, if I need to.

You also taught at the University of Virginia, could you talk about that experience?

I was an adjunct professor in the drama department. My main responsibility was putting on productions. I put on a South African play called "Joys of War." For a year, I was basically preparing to produce and direct that, but I was also teaching the basic theater techniques. I gave workshops for a number of weeks on stagecraft, voice and speech, and movement.

Do you see the trajectory from theater to film to be a fluid, interchangeable process? How do you bring them together?

Well the disciplines meet in so many ways but they are very different. The production approach is pretty much the same, you have pre-production where you are doing your research, you're doing your casting, you're doing your writing, (since I usually write my own plays that I produce), and then you've got production and then you've got the post-production where you are putting the pieces together. At times, it crosses over, but it is a very different medium. The time line is much longer for doing documentary.

Film is not so accessible in terms of being able to just pick up and do it because you need so many physical things to do it with. Whereas with theater, I used to do theater in the bush with my students. We would go on tours around the country and perform to villages, without any sets or props, just the actors and the audience.

In terms of the two media which one would you say, really, in terms of access, availability of equipment, and financial means, is more within the reality of African people? If I could talk about this in the context of an equal exchange between the art and the audience.

Most definitely theater, in fact, personally, the more that I have gotten into film the more I have felt that it is kind of pointless, making films right now in Africa. For several reasons, one, our culture is oral, that is what we are about. Whereas with visuals, we absolutely have no access to them.

The technology is changing so fast because there is so much competition in terms of who is going to rule the technology, it is very expensive because it is changing so fast. Once you have mastered one format, another format is in place, is on the way. Right now, high definition television, HDT technology is coming in and so the video equipment that you are using right now, well the shelf life is going to be very short. So now as filmmakers, we are having to think about the format that we are going to work in. Even with projects that I have started, I am thinking now that I'm not going to shoot in a certain format any more because it is going to be obsolete in a couple of years.

So to answer your question as far as Africa, for me the most satisfying thing, I think, is working with theater, because you have your response right there. You are much more in touch with your audience, as opposed to film, which is so elitist right now. Even getting to see a film is a problem if you are in Africa; the ticket price, the location. In Namibia, there was only one movie theater and maybe two drive-in theaters, now there are one or two more since 1996. Black people do not got to the movies in Namibia, they can't afford it, and they cannot get there, there is no transportation.

But I love film, I love working with it, I love that long struggle to get that piece of tape out and I love the fact that you can hold on to those memories. But logistically, it doesn't make any sense. And the more I do it, the more I feel that way. That is why I try to tie in any production project that I do with real life performance, with real contact with real audiences. Because they take away a lot more. I think the times that I have worked with people in theater, I find that it is much more organic, I keep more in touch with the people that I work with in the theater than with people I work with in film.

Film is a very fast industry and there is a high turnover. Even movies that are made ten years ago, people don't really watch them today. It is all about what is out at the moment, about first week box office receipts, and the rest is history.

What are some of your future plans, thoughts, dreams for Global Posse?

We would like to make the company more viable, so that it could be self-sustaining. Oftentimes, young production companies collapse after a few years because there is not a clear business plan. Because ours started so spontaneously, I was afraid that that was going to happen. So I decided that I had to definitely go back to school to learn about running a business, so right now I am working on a business plan for the next five years.

Pittsburgh will be our base in the United States after 1998. *Insh'Allah,* God willing, we will also be having something in Cape Town because I am part of a consortium that is bidding for the first free-to-air television station in South Africa. I am really trying to get into broadcasting, because that is much more where Global Posse is going. Broadcasting is much more accessible to Africans. As satellite continues to expand it will also be much more of a threat to Africa, even those free-to-air television stations are not going to have that much say because it will be cheaper to satellite something that is coming from Murdoch down to Africa. It will be much easier for news corps to send us news feed than for us to produce our own stuff.

Global Posse also has several feature films in development. We are now in the process of starting a limited liability company called Global Posse Television, which is going to be a group of people that will run it. We would like to be based in the U.S. and in Southern Africa. We would like to produce info-mercials, community service programs, documentaries, animation, a variety of things that can be on television.

In another discussion, you expressed your interest in getting in the mix of cyber-technology, where do you see Global Posse in this context?

For me I would want to make this new technology more accessible to Africans in Africa. I have been working on a proposal for a multi-media information kiosk that would be in a public space. For instance in Windhoek, there is a public square; it could be there. It would be a solid feature, like an ATM machine and it would be for the public. The feature in the kiosks would change every three months. It would always be about some kind of social issue.

The proposal that I put through was for an interactive kiosk for teens. One month it would be about sex, teenage pregnancy, and so on. It would have a video feature, the computer would ask questions, and the public would answer them. It would also collect data. It would allow people to touch it, to see what is this information age that people are talking about.

How will you continue to include theater?

I work with a lot of writers in Africa, in Southern Africa in particular, and I still love to direct theater plays. I would like to do as many African plays in the United States as possible and involve film in some way in terms of documenting the performances, as well as interviewing the directors, or presenting the concept of what they are doing.

My hope is that Global Posse becomes much more cross-cultural in terms of black culture, more multi-lingual. We have worked with lusophone and francophone projects before. I would like Global Posse to be in a position to provide programming from London to Brazil, to be doing things that black people all over the world can identify with, even if it has got subtitles, even if it is in another language.

Najwa Tlili

Tunisia

Interview held at Vues d'Afrique, April 1997, Montreal, Quebec. Translated from French.

How do you express yourself as a filmmaker from the North African Diaspora, as an Arab woman and a woman of the African continent?

I cannot say that I am a filmmaker or artist, I can only say that I try to make films. How do I situate myself? First of all, I am an Arab woman living in Montreal. Recently, I was speaking to a friend regarding Africa. I told her, "Well, we don't ask ourselves the question 'What are we?'" In my case, it is within the context of immigration that I position myself. The question that drives me the most is, "What kind of cinema will I do?"

Yes, I am African, I am from the African continent, it is a part of who I am. At the same time it is more than a continent that I feel, it is this sense of a psychological and emotional proximity that I have with a person. I do not feel out of touch with a fellow African from Niger, Mali or Burkina, nor do I feel that I have a completely different dialogue than she does. I feel a closeness to African women, not only among filmmakers, but with all women, and of course, women from Egypt, and the Maghreb in general. In fact, I am all of these women at once. I think that the actual identity of my cinema is my identity, at the same time one and multiple, and sometimes fragmented.

Could you talk about your identity as it informs your films?

My first film, *Heritage*, was a Tunisio-Canadian production, yet for me it was a Tunisian film. It was a voyage deep in my memory, a memory of the footprints that I left in Tunisia. I traveled in these tracks.

My second film is a documentary called *Rupture*. It is a 52-minute documentary produced here in Canada. It is a film that addresses the problem of conjugal violence lived by Arab women in Canada. While doing this film about conjugal violence, I discovered the complexities of this inquiry, a complexity that is linked to the context of immigration.

I focused on women who lived in Montreal and who at the same time were connected to the welcoming country and its culture. It is a film that is Canadian in terms of the country that produces it, I am shooting it here, and I will complete it here. However, somewhere, there is something that I want to go touch, which is essential. Beyond this complexity of violence, I find myself doing a film about the Arab woman, the condition of the Arab woman, which is not different from the condition of the Arab woman living in Tunisia or any other Arab country.

So this film reflects your multiple identities as well?

It is very difficult to situate myself in relation to this film, to say what identity I should give it. I would say that it is the identity of the moment. I find myself invested in this film, inhabited by this film, and finally it is allowing me to have a certain reconciliation with myself. At certain times I think, "It has been seven years since I have lived in Montreal." I lived for a long time in Tunisia, then France, and then I went back to work in Tunisia, and I re-immersed myself in the Tunisian culture. While in France I thought, "I am an Arab woman living in Paris." Now this film is a kind of quest, in order to understand: "Who is this Arab woman? What is she like?"

I am doing a documentary whose style facilitates this quest through the kind of research that is required. You know, this documentary evolves everyday. I encounter women who I think I have gotten to know, and then afterwards I discover that there is not only one world of Arab women, but there are many worlds of Arab women.

So for you, filmmaking is in some ways a quest?

Well, I would say that one does films to grow, and yes, I am growing through my films. I have been concerned with the question, "What kind of films am I going to do?" In some ways, this decision to let myself grow with my films has been reconciling.

At a given moment I thought that I would not be able to do a film about Quebec, the Quebecois people. I wanted to let this country come to me gradually. At one time there was a fear, of being completely dried out, of not being productive, of no longer being able to make films. How-

330

ever, it is not true, because we are all constantly surrounded by questions. Of course, I cannot do a film as a Quebecois of 100% pure wool, would do it. At the same time, I do have my own perspective, a perspective of this multiple woman regarding this country as well. A perspective of the people, of their reality. My fear is that it is an exterior gaze. It is a fear that we can overcome only at the moment when we are doing a film. We are afraid to have an exterior gaze, and at a certain moment, we accept that we are from the outside and we will have an outside gaze up until the time that we actually go towards the inside. It is perhaps then that we can speak of universality, and then we must take on the task. However, I do not think that these are things that will be fulfilled overnight, the next day when we awaken. It does not happen that quickly.

So you film from the inside and outside?

Well, I am attempting to resolve this question, which goes in the direction of my film. Because when I talk about the condition of the Arab woman in my film, I realize that there is a reality that surfaces in which the Arab women who are here are trying to overcome their situations individually. They do not do so within a community. There is no movement to propel this process; there is no revolution. In the Arab world, it is the same thing; women only come out individually, in Africa as well.

I decided that I would start with me. Through my films, if I find myself...I cannot pretend that we can actually overcome our situation by doing a film, whether it is a collective film, an Arab film, or a Canadian film. These expectations frighten me. It is for this reason that I attempt to do films, it is certainly an inside look from the outside, a look at a certain reality. It is a quest. That is the privilege of doing cinema. Of course, in making films we realize many things, we make mistakes and correct them.

I give the crew with whom I work the opportunity to evolve with me from day to day during the shooting, to have another perception of things. If one, two, or three of them can be touched by those moments of contact with others, that would be remarkable. Of course, I do not pretend to change the world. I try to do the little things in which I believe, in a humble manner.

There is an impressive number of Tunisian women filmmakers. Could you speak some about this phenomenon?

It is true that more and more women in Tunisia are making films. It is extraordinary because we know that for men and women of the Southern Hemisphere it is very difficult to make films from the inside. I think that these women are very courageous. Why is there this movement of women filmmakers? I think that it follows other movements as well. There is theater, and there is literature, whereas cinema is relatively new for us on the African continent.

I think the first woman in Tunisia began to do films, now about twenty years ago, if I am not mistaken. As I just stated, there is this movement in cinema, I think, that follows other movements in Tunisia. These women who were able to break into cinema while living in France and elsewhere are working very hard, because to work in the world of cinema is not easy, especially when you do not know anyone, and when you come from the outside.

Fortunately, the number of women who are able to do films is increasing and it is very important to have many of them. Let us hope that there will be many quality films. It is a new look at society, and certainly a transformation. It is a phenomenon that perhaps cannot exactly be explained, and yet, it is essential. I hope it will bring a new vision that is female, that is particular to women, with all its beauty and sincerity. It is also another way of looking at things.

I think that it is time to stop saying that others are responsible for our problems, that others are speaking for us, or that it is the media that is distorting the image of women. There is a space that we have to fill ourselves. We are not in a period of mass militancy, but we are at a particular moment in time—I don't want to call it "feminist militancy," because it is often viewed as aggressive to say feminist today, it has become like a bad label—perhaps it is a modern form of feminism, to go forward, to simply express oneself, to say things the way they are lived and felt by women. This is in itself an act of life.

Do you feel there is a certain woman's sensibility that women filmmakers express in their work?

I think so. It is a truth that is very simple. There is a woman's sensibility and a man's sensibility. For a long time men have spoken in our place, even the most militant, progressive men who make films about the condition of Arab woman.

Nonetheless, it is a man's point of view, with all its sincerity to understand from the outside. However, this vision could never take the place of a woman's.

I speak of a woman's sensibility in the sense where...in the case of my film, I speak of violence. It is not only the woman who is beaten by her husband who understands what it is like. I always say that I suffer for all the others, for this chain of women behind me, that I have in my genes, which I feel are here inside me. One has it or one does not. A man can feel it and understand it; he does not live it. I live it. I live it through my mother, within my own self, through my daughter. This brings a certain treatment to the subject, the questioning is different, the vision is different. Even from one man to another, one filmmaker to another, and even from one woman to another. This vision that comes out of women's experiences is problematized in another way, for better or worse, but nonetheless, differently. Here, we are talking about a woman's sensibility.

You spoke earlier about positionality in terms of where you make your films and the identity that informs your filmmaking. Though you live currently in Montreal, do you envision doing a film in Tunisia?

As I stated earlier, I was afraid of only being able to do a film in Tunisia. Now I am doing a film here in Montreal. It is true that sometimes the scripts go through cycles, where one takes priority over the other. I could do a film in Tunisia, but the truth is that the reality of Tunisia, I am living from a distance today. I no longer touch the daily life of Tunisia; I am living it from a distance. If I were to use the same script that I wrote several years ago when I was there, and were to rework it today, it would be from my point of view in exile.

My country, I take within me, but there is also another reality. Yes, I could go live for several months there and perhaps some things will surface, it is somewhat complex. It is a "no man's land" [stated in English]. At the same time, we are everywhere and nowhere. Perhaps that is particular to the first-generation immigrants, my daughter, perhaps will not experience this fragmentation.

My culture is always there, I carry it with me and I struggle not to see it in a nostalgic or exotic way. No matter what we say, "No, no it is not exotic"; this discourse frightens me, because somewhere, nostalgically, we want to rediscover certain things that are dear to us. If I have the privilege to be able to examine culture in relationship to me, I would have to ask, "What is it?" Because the word culture is vague, and besides, what is *this* culture?

In the end, it is not whether to do a film here or there. Today we Arabs, women and men, have the responsibility to question this culture that sometimes becomes dogma. We think: "It is our identity, and therefore it cannot be touched." With this attitude, anything and everything is allowed. No, this culture, once so beautiful, needs to be questioned today, by us, so that we may live it fully and be able to be at home within it.

Today, when we look at the Arab culture with its calligraphy, architecture and music, we see vast influences—especially from the eighteenth and nineteenth centuries—of the Golden Age of the Arabo-Muslim civilization, when it was open to the entire world. Today we are closing ourselves within our culture. No, it is worth rethinking. We must look around us and ask questions. With the rise of integrationism, we Arab women are now living in a period where we must question the issues around religion. We are living in a very complex period, very rich, of course, but very complex.

The problem for me at the moment is not whether to do a film here or there. If I could, not financially speaking, nor on the production level, but if I could, emotionally—because the technical side can be applied anywhere, there are no borders—but emotionally, if I could do a film in Tunisia, yes, I would be delighted. If I could do it in France or elsewhere, I would be equally pleased, but there is a core that exists that will follow me wherever I go, my commitment. That is why I am in cinema.

Of course, I do films for the pleasure of it, but also to have at least the impression that we are not on this earth to be ineffective. I think that we each have a mission. Not a mission guided by a flag, but rather to take life, not as a banality, but as richness. This life is worth looking at from our point of view, with our own passion and emotion.

Prudence Uriri

Zimbabwe

Interview and after-screening question-and-answer session held at Vues d'Afrique, April 1997, Montreal, Quebec. Also included is a conversation that took place by electronic mail in September 1998.

Prudence, perhaps you can begin by giving some background of yourself. Could you also talk about how you came to film and television?

I did some information work during the Zimbabwe Liberation War. I was a freedom fighter then, but I was working under the Department of Information, so I got some hands-on training in news gathering and dissemination. Basically, I would say that was how I started getting involved in information work. Then I went into printing where I stayed until after independence, when I joined the Zimbabwean Broadcasting Corporation. At that time, I went through different levels of video and television production work until I got training in the United Kingdom as a film editor. Between then and now I have been to Germany and Denmark in and out of different courses in various aspects of film production. When I returned home, I continued working for the Zimbabwean Broadcasting Corporation. I left ZBC in 1991 to join Capricorn Video Unit where I am still working.

Information collecting, as you stated, was a task you performed when working at the Department of Information. Could you talk about your role in the Zimbabwean Liberation War and how it prepared you for the work you are doing now?

I did not see my role during the liberation struggle as separate from what everyone else was doing. Because at that time it was more about the distribution of work at different times to different people who could do a particular task at a specific time. There were lots of things that different people got trained in. Some went to the forefront to fight. Some transported ammunition to bases toward the borders, which I did for a very short period. However, my main job was to work in the Information Department and I always went back there. I think being involved in the liberation struggle opened up many ways for me to know what I wanted to do, what I stood for as an individual. I think that the role that I now play in my own society has been shaped out from the kind of background which emphasized that if you believe in something that you want to do, do it, and try hard to get it. I wanted to do work in information and that is what I am doing now.

How do you see your role as a woman filmmaker, in the context of information work?

I am interested in gathering information whether in print media or for radio. I think it is by chance that I did television work. Overall, I think information work is what interests me the most. In my country, we have a problem in that the infrastructure does not provide for everybody or cater to every nationality in terms of information dissemination. The current infrastructure can only adequately reach urban/semi-urban areas. I see my role as being very useful. It is important because I am contributing a lot by informing the general public through the use of video. I do a lot of development-related programs. I work with a lot of women's NGOs, not only Zimbabwean NGOs but with other international organizations as well. So I get a lot of support from being in this kind of situation and through networking with relevant people.

Do you feel that you have a sensibility as a woman that you bring into your work?

I really do think so, maybe that is also one of my motivations for going into information work, coming from a background where the woman's role was not recognized by society. Women have always been taken for granted and it is felt that what they do does not have to be acknowledged. I feel that it does have to be acknowledged and I have to play a part in making my own society realize that women contribute a lot to the development of the society. Not only now have women made contributions, but since time immemorial, they have always played a role.

Could you talk about your films, the themes that you focus on, and some of the experiences you have had during the film production?

The types of films that I make have specific objectives. One of the objectives is really to talk about the issues that are of main concern to many people. I like to talk about problems that people are facing, probably not to find a solution but to open a debate, to open a dialogue, for people to have information in order to be able to talk about certain things. It is only when they have access to this information that you can open windows for dialogue. So, I have been working on films about women's empowerment. I have worked on films on health; I have done some films on AIDS. I also worked on another film about cervical cancer which I am now translating into the two vernacular languages, Shona and Ndebele, so that the grassroots people who may need that kind of information may be able to understand the problems around this disease. Most of these programs are commissioned. Different organizations are involved in a variety of projects. They come to us at Capricorn to ask if we can make a video for them. We actually work quite well together. Sometimes, however, we do films that we initiate ourselves.

Was your film **The Whisper** *commissioned by development agencies or was it your idea?*

My most recent work, *The Whisper,* was my idea, but it was not so difficult to get funding for it after approaching several development agencies with whom we normally do development work.

How was the film produced and funded?

MS, a Danish NGO that supports several development projects in Africa gave all the funds needed to produce, package and make versions into two main local languages in Zimbabwe. SUCO, a Canadian NGO, gave money for the French version. MFDI, in the United States, is distributing the English version. We have done a lot of similar videos for development agencies for their own use in their work on different projects. So I got a very good response right from the very beginning.

I do get support for film projects that I initiate because people often are willing to support an idea if it is about something that they believe in. As a result, I have often been able to get some information and materials to work with in order to get the work going.

The Whisper *reminded me of the fiction film* **Neria** *by Godwin Mawuru, which was also set in Zimbabwe. In this film, there was a similar kind of situation where the protagonist was disinherited when her husband died. Is this a practice that frequently occurs and, thus, a common issue on which to focus?*

337

It is one of the many problems that Zimbabwean women face after a spouse dies. There may be some similarities on the theme but our approach to it differs. Nevertheless, this reflects that it's a problem and that people need to accept that it exists, that changes should be done, and that they have to comply with the realities of the dynamics of culture in a modern world.

The aim of *The Whisper* was to provoke a debate between the government, those making the policies, and the general public who are affected by these policies and should actually be the ones who benefit from them. So it seems like the public is left behind. When new laws such as these are introduced, the people themselves should participate in the process. But as it is, they don't contribute to the decision making to decide what is good for them. They are expected to accept whatever comes along. So the main objective for making this film was to initiate a more focused dialogue between the government and the general public; and also to involve the NGO's that are doing work towards bringing about this kind of participatory type of governance.

Another objective was to find out what kind of work is being done by women's organizations in educating people about these new laws and how they are affected by them. Most important, it is to see how representative their approach is towards educating women about their rights, and how to go about things should problems occur. In terms of the rights that authorities must deal with, in some cases the documentary reveals that, some of these authorities do not also understand what they are supposed to enforce. At the end of the day, you would conclude that education in this context should not only be directed to women but society at large.

Women's participation in the Zimbabwe Liberation War was particularly significant. Your combined first-hand experience as a freedom fighter in the liberation war and background in filmmaking makes you well placed to do a film about women in the war for independence. Have you considered making a fiction or documentary film that brings together your experiences and those of your comrades?

I've been thinking about doing something like that, but I find it very difficult to talk about my own story. My own story is one of the many things that happened there involving many people that were taking part in the struggle. So I am thinking more of looking at the situation in the camps for example. I would like to address the problems that people who were not there may never get to understand or even imagine.

If we want people to know about these experiences, it is high time that we talk about them. I don't want to put that kind of message to people in a heavy way that will make them feel sad. Rather, I want to make it light, like an entertainment thing, but at the same time looking at the real things that took place. We also had fun, it was tough but we had our fun there. We had adjusted ourselves to our own situation and through thick and thin, there were highlights. For example, one's first day as a trainee soldier, how individuals from different backgrounds behaved in this totally new and complicated environment. I wouldn't want to preempt my ideas now. But I am thinking about it. It has to be a series because there is so much to say.

Discussion with various members of the audience after the screening of _The Whisper._

You interviewed many women who talk about how they were affected by the disinheritance laws, were you able to talk to the families-in-law to get their side of the story?

No, the particular family who victimized their daughter-in-law, which I gave as an example in the film, was not keen on even seeing me. It was unfortunate that I could not talk to any members of the family because I happen to be a sister of the victim who lost property. She had just lost her husband and I helped her to go through the legal process to get a peace order. So they knew me pretty well and they knew that the film would be seen by all and thus, they did not want to talk to me.

So they viewed you as taking sides with the woman...

Yes.

Why **The Whisper** as the title of the film?

It is a sort of whispering documentary. I think that it comes from the idea that people are not yet very keen on talking about issues like that outside of their own little communities, or sometimes the discussion does not go beyond their households. They do talk about such things, but to do so openly is not so common. That is why I chose to call it _The Whisper_ because still it's like a vibration, I also knew that it is a hot issue and for some time it will remain so. I had to choose a persuasive, catchy title, something that would make one anxious to see it.

How long did it take you to make the film?

It was just six days of filming but more than two months of research. I tried to travel as widely as possible in the country to get different views from a variety of people. So most of the money and time was spent on research as well as traveling to those places to film.

Were people very responsive to your questions in terms of giving responses to what you wanted to know? Did you have any bad experiences?

I think the most difficult experience that I had was when I found an interesting story, but the person could not tell it because she was not used to speaking about her problems to people that she did not know. Another problem was the lack of money to really spend the time needed with people in order to really get to know each other, so that they could feel at ease in discussing their experiences. Still another problem was that while I could get people who would be willing to talk to me, they were reluctant to do so in front of the camera for fear that their financial situation would be compromised. Sometimes a woman's situation had to do with how her husband was treating her at home, and if she talked about it in front of the camera, she feared that it might be seen on national television. Of course, which would mean the end of their marriage.

Instead of waiting for a solution from men, or for men to change, perhaps women should struggle themselves against these laws, work should be devoted more toward making women more aware.

I think, in general, what is lacking is proper education. We are talking most particularly about the laws themselves, and the focus of this film is mainly about the impact of these new laws that have been introduced to women. I wanted to show that first and foremost, it is important that women understand these laws before they can be implemented. You find that traditionally there are certain rules that bind women. Women who were brought up two decades ago feel that there is a conflict between the laws that existed then and these new laws, which they feel are geared more to the younger generation. So what really needs to happen is to introduce these new policies at a pace that people can accept, understand, and feel that they are part of. At the present, they feel that these laws are being imposed on them. Some of the laws are actually very positive, however, people are not always aware of them.

From a conversation by electronic mail, September 1998.

Could you talk about some of your current projects?

In August 1998, I took some locally-produced films to rural areas as a pilot project. The objective was to make people aware that there are a lot of relevant films around which they should gather to see, to provide entertainment, and to discuss their views about the film we make with their participation. But the films usually end up as information suppliers. The films never get back to them and they usually do not know how we use the information they give us. In a way, it is giving them back what we as filmmakers take from them, allowing us to assess what issues they feel are important to be discussed through film.

The response was overwhelming and my only problem now is that I have created an expectation. Often they asked if in the future we would maintain a continuous schedule and keep them updated through visuals. I intend to use this experience to raise money for a relatively on-going mobile festival in the rural areas. I came back with some very specific film ideas from the discussions that I had with the viewers there.

Zara Mahamat Yacoub

Chad

Interview held at FESPACO, February 1997, Ouagadougou, Burkina Faso. Several written conversations took place during 1998 by electronic mail. Translated from French.

Zara, you have been a pioneer in Chadian television history, could you talk about your career in the visual media from the beginning to the present, and about your role in the evolution of television production in Chad?

After completing my studies at the Université de Chad I competed for a slot at the l'Institut national de la communication audiovisuelle in France. Upon my return to Chad, equipped with a diploma in communication with a specialization in television production I signed a contract to work as a senior ranking civil service employee. At the time, there was no television network in Chad. Therefore, I assumed a post in radio as producer and announcer. The moment that a television network was created, I was called to come on board. Not only was I the first woman, I was the only woman. I occupied successively, the role of programming manager and head manager of the National Television of Chad. In addition, I worked in South Africa as journalist/director at Channel Africa TV in Johannesburg.

*You have made three films, **Les enfants de la guerre** (Children of War), **Les enfants de la rue** (Children of the Street), and **Dilemme au féminin**. Could you talk about the films and your experiences while making them?*

Les enfants de la guerre, a fiction film, is a portrait of three children, a girl and two boys, all orphans of war. These children, who have lived through war, experience on a daily basis, the trauma and nightmare of war. The film is a TVT, Belgium Television and Sophilm production with the financial assistance of La Coopération Française, L'Agence de la Francophonie and the European Union.

Les enfants de la rue, a documentary, is a story about Oumar, the leader of a gang of "society's rejects." Oumar and his friends live in the streets and steal to feed themselves. They are exposed to all kinds of illnesses, as well as the many risks that are associated with being young children alone on the streets, among which is the danger of pedophilia. The film is a TVT and Centre Culturel Al-Moumna co-production.

The documentary film, *Dilemme au féminin*, talks about excision. The film is a fiction-documentary about a young girl who is a victim of this horrible practice. She takes us through the multiple contours of the excision operation. The viewer will witness an actual operation followed by the opinions of various leaders. Muslim and Christian representatives give their position regarding this practice. A doctor explains to us the consequences and after-effects of FGM [Female genital mutilation] basing his arguments on concrete cases that have been revealed to him during the course of his medical career. A TVT Production, this film has been awarded several prizes. The film has been shown in Europe and North America.

Your film **Dilemme au féminin** *received a lot of attention in 1995 and as you stated it was awarded several prizes; the "Prix du Club du Sahel" at FESPACO 1995, as well as the awards "Images de Femmes" and "Regard sur les télévisions africaines", both at Vues d'Afrique 1995, as well as an Honorable Mention. After its release, there was a great deal of controversy surrounding it in your country, Chad. Why did you choose this subject? What has been your role in African women's struggle against female genital mutilation?*

Born and raised in a society that practices female genital mutilation, I live the daily suffering of women and children who are victims of this practice. This is what motivated me to join the struggle against it. *Dilemme au féminin* is a film that speaks about excision. And as you may know excision is practiced practically everywhere in Africa. But in the past, excision was also performed in Europe and in other countries. The consequences of excision are terrible. Today voices have been raised across the world denouncing the phenomenon of excision. It is a reality; I have seen young girls die from excision. I have seen women who have remained infertile for their entire lives as a result of having been excised. I have seen women who have suffered in their souls because of excision.

Thus, I assert that it is more so a health problem. I am making a statement about the practice of excision and as I just told you, my role is to expose, to take note, to report to people when things are not right. And I attest that excision is not a good thing. Excision is causing so much damage, and so it must be stopped. Thus, the reason for my film, *Dilemme au féminin.*

Unfortunately, the release of this film in my country, Chad, presented many problems for me. However, I told myself that this was all part of my day-to-day job. When one espouses this profession, one must expect the worse. And yes, I suffered a great deal, and unfortunately, there are still repercussions. But still I did what I felt was my duty.

The film was viewed just about everywhere. The film was viewed in my country, Chad, and I was very touched and very pleased because after the tour of the film a little girl who once said to her father "Papa, papa I want to be excised," after having seen the film on television said, "Papa, papa if that is what excision is, I don't want to be excised." So I said, no matter what problems I encounter, what is essential is to convey a message. And the message is delivered. That is what was crucial for me. This is my role, it was my duty.

You are among several women in Africa who utilize the media to visualize the experience of girls and women subjected to the practice of excision. There is Soraya Mire of Somalia who made the film **Fire Eyes**, *and there is Anne-Laure Folly of Togo who made the film* **Femmes aux yeux ouverts**. *In addition, there are also Senegalese Awa Thiam who wrote the book* **La parole aux negresses**, *Somali Asma El Deer who wrote the book* **Woman, Why do you Weep?**, *and Egyptian writer and doctor Nawal el Saadawi, among other women of Africa. Could you speak about the importance of African women to join the struggle against excision and how women in the media, can be vehicles in this struggle?*

African women have a very important role to play in the struggle against female genital mutilation to the extent that this practice concerns, first and foremost, women. In Africa, there is a tendency to reject everything that comes from the outside that puts one's "culture" in question. This makes our role even more important. But this does not mean that we Africans must exclude our European and American sisters from this struggle. Because of immigration, female genital mutilation is practiced just about everywhere in the world. Thus, social awareness about it and the struggle against it must not be limited only to African countries.

There was a backlash after the release of the film. The Islamic Council of Chad showed a strong negative response. What were the consequences for you after the film was released and viewed by the Chadian public?

Well, the consequences, I can speak for the most part, about how it affected me directly. Imagine that you live in a society, your own society, that you live in a community that is your community. I am Muslim. I belong to a Muslim community; suddenly there is a rupture. Suddenly you are banished. Suddenly when you walk down the street everyone says, "There she is." Suddenly wherever you go, you expect that people will speak to you and they don't. If people say "Look, she has done a lot of things, she has done good things," that's alright. But when people say "She is a bad woman, she has dared to insult Islam, she has dared to do this or that," well, that hurts. And then all day long, you hear in each and every mosque people talking about you.

I don't think this experience will leave me right away. Many feelings still remain and I continue to suffer as a result. Today, however, I can leave my house, I can go to my job, I can go visit my friends. But I do not take the risk of going to certain places, the places that are often frequented by fundamentalists, for fear of being viewed as provoking the situation. I tell myself, "No, you must not incite these people," because even if I go without any particular motive, they will think that I am trying to instigate controversy.

You stated that no matter what the consequences were, that it is your role and duty to make films that send a message. Has this experience influenced your filmmaking or the subjects that you choose? What impact has it had on your work, your vision?

It is true that since the film and the aftermath of it, I have been much more guarded in my actions. I submit to a certain self-censorship. No one obliges me to do so, but I censor myself in one way or another as it relates to certain situations. It is true that it has put restrictions on the manner in which I view certain things. Especially when I did my last film.

Now, each time I want to film something, though I have already written it in the script, I think twice about how I present it. On location, I am much more cautious about what and how I am going to film. I say to myself, "Be careful you did a film where you had problems. This time you must look before you take your next step." The moral after-affects remain. If I were to tell you that I am no longer affected by my past experiences, I would not be telling the truth. For weeks on end I stayed secluded in my house, I could not leave. When I did go out, each minute I looked behind me to see who was at my side. Even now, though I no longer have problems, certain things remain with me.

*Since **Dilemme au féminin**, have you had difficulty finding a producer, a crew or actors for your subsequent projects?*

For my latest film, [*Les enfants de la guerre*], I brought in a crew from Belgium. The film was produced with the financial assistance of the Agence de la Francophonie, the Ministère de la Cooperation, and the European Economic Community. The film was also co-produced by a Belgium television company, the Chadian television, and a film production company based in Paris. Though the production crew was from Belgium, I also had Chadian compatriots who participated in the production of the film. While the principal technical crew—the sound technician and the camera operator—was mainly Belgian, the assistants and other production members were Chadians.

*In the context of the theme of the 1997 edition of FESPACO, "Cinema, Childhood, and Youth," there are many films that are being shown that treat the subject of children in diverse situations. Your film, **Les enfants de la rue**, focused on the theme of children, as well as your most recent film. Why did you choose this subject?*

My latest film is *Les enfants de la guerre*, or what I call "in the *oubliette*," because the surviving children are the forgotten ones. It is a film that speaks about the traumatism that haunts children who have lived through war. My film does not only reflect the reality of Chad; it also speaks about the children of today, whether they live in Rwanda, Burundi, or Liberia. It speaks of all the situations where there has been war.

What moved me to address this problem in my film is the need to record this phenomenon. Because today when there is a war in a particular part of the world, all eyes are riveted on the country where it takes place. The whole world precipitates to this location; the press, the humanitarian organizations. The world is focused on this country, on the children and women who die. As soon as the war is over, there is not a word spoken about this place and the aftermath of the war. No one even attempts to find out what happened to the survivors.

In a war, it's true there are the dead, but afterwards there are certainly those who escaped, who survived. But no one searches to know how

347

those who remain are continuing to live. In my film, I bring out the trauma suffered by the children who were left on their own, who are still there living with family members, in orphanages or in the streets.

They continue to be haunted by images of the war. However, there is no one who stays behind in an attempt to care in some way or another for these children. These children, whether we admit it or not, are sick. They are sick from all that they have lived through during and after the war. Thus, the reason for my film, *Les enfants de la guerre*.

You have made several films that focus on social and human conditions in Africa, especially as they relate to women and children. Do you feel that this is your role as a filmmaker, to bring out the conditions and events that take place in your country, in Africa, around the world?

I have always defined myself as a communicator rather than as a director or journalist or filmmaker. This I will say and I hold my position. I feel that I have a duty as a communicator in relationship to my society, *vis-à-vis* all that surrounds me. My role is to make known, to bring out what is not right. My role is to draw attention to certain problems. I see that I have a duty towards my people. I have a duty towards each and every person. My role is to inform people, to make them aware of the problems that need attention. This is my role as communicator.

There is a great deal of discussion about cinema and culture. There has also been a great deal of emphasis on women and development. What are your thoughts about the notion of cinema, culture and development, and how can cinema be used as a tool towards the objectives of women in development? Could you talk about this especially as it relates to your own films and the role you see yourself playing in development?

You know cinema is only a reflection of a society. When speaking of a society, one speaks of culture, absolutely! And one cannot really talk about cinema without speaking of culture. And we increasingly find that one cannot talk about culture without speaking of cinema. Though it is true that cinema is a recent tradition in Africa, the fact remains that it is imposing itself on the continent. Thus, when one speaks of culture, cinema has its place within it and vice versa. Whether it is an African film or a film from America, Russia, or elsewhere, a film always refers to some elements of culture.

*Do you feel that in the film **Dilemme au féminin**, where you expose the problems around the practice of excision, that you are connecting cinema and culture
with women in development? In other words, does the use of the medium of film
used to expose a practice that is harmful to women facilitate women's development
within society?*

Absolutely!

How do you see this happening?

Today, I would say that there is not a tool more effective than the audio-
visual medium, and especially films that raise women's consciousness, and
that assist women in general. When one says "women and development,"
when one says, "Henceforth, women must participate in development," I
feel that the direction to follow to sensitize women is through the media.
It is clear and very simple.

If one looks deeper into this assertion, we know that today in Africa
the majority of women are illiterate. With images, whatever the situation, these images speak for themselves. In the campaign for the promotion of women, I certainly feel that the audiovisual medium can assist
women to fully participate in the development process. Throughout the
world, we find that there is no development without the participation of
women. In any country in the world, you will see that there are more
women than men, 52 of 100 percent in a great many countries. As I
stated earlier, and to emphasize it again, television, video and film are
very efficient means to facilitate women's development in society.

*We know that distribution and exhibition of African films is a particularly com-
plex problem in Africa. What are some of your thoughts?*

You have evoked a very serious problem. Especially for African cinema.
We encounter enormous problems when making a film but the problem
that weighs considerably is that of distribution. For example, I can make
a film in Chad, but that does not mean that it will be seen throughout
Africa. Thus, the means of distribution remain a big obstacle. I don't
know how to resolve this situation, and of course, it will not be today or
tomorrow that we can do so.

However, I think that in time Africa will be more integrated, and it
will follow that our films will be integrated as well. I would say that
there has been an improvement in the last five years. For instance, though

we may not be able to see a Burkinabé film in Chad right away, eventually, in a year or two we are finally able to see it.

So, there has been a change, an evolution. I think that we will not only be able to see each other's films throughout Africa in the future, but they will be seen increasingly in the United States, in Europe and across the globe. African films are viewed in large festivals, in large cinema houses with larger and larger audiences. Now when one speaks of cinema, African cinema cannot be ignored, and that is a good thing.

Could you talk about the production company that you have created? What is it called, and what are some of the goals and objectives of the company?

The project for the creation of the production company dates back to 1994 but we have waited until 1998 to concretize it. The company is called SUD-CAP Productions. My co-partner officially manages it, since I continue to work for the Chadian government in an official capacity at the National Television of Chad. The objective of SUD-CAP Production is to produce and direct films, videos, TV magazines, advertisements, illustrated reporting for television, and radio reporting.

What are some of your future projects?

One project is a documentary entitled *Eradication des MGF's: un defi du 3ème millénaire* (The Eradication of FGM: A Challenge of the 3rd Millenium). This film will speak about women's struggle against this practice throughout the world. The film will be shot in Africa, Europe and North America. It will be directed by a Canadian woman, and co-produced with the Canadian company PAX Production and my company CAP-SUD Productions. We have already received financial assistance to solicit interest in the film project from Vues d'Afrique's Nord-Sud Production Fund. The film budget is estimated at around US$300,000. We are counting on the financial backing of the European Union, l'Agence de la Francophonie, the Cooperation Française, SODEC, Téléfilm Canada, among others.

I am also producing an international series entitled *Avoir 50 ans et un monde.* I am at the scriptwriting stage. Otherwise, I have several other scripts for fiction films that are waiting for funding. One film that I plan to complete in the very near future is the story of an eleven-year-old girl who works as a domestic. I also have begun research on a film about desertification, in particular the desertification of a village located north of Ndjamena.

Florentine Yaméogo

Burkina Faso

Interview held at the 15th FESPACO, February 1997, Ouagadougou, Burkina Faso. Translated from French.

I find the focus of your film, **Melodies de femmes**, *about women having their say through songs particularly fascinating. Could you talk about it?*

Melodies de femmes, which is 24-minutes long, is told from the perspective of a young girl from the city. She recounts the lives of the women of her village who express themselves through their songs. The songs are used as a means of expression in traditional society.

Could you describe your experiences while making the film and why you chose this subject?

I chose this subject because often when I went on vacation in the village, the women sang a great deal. They sang when they were grinding millet, on their way to the river to wash the clothes. Generally, they sang when they worked. When they sing they send a message and sometimes this message expresses their joy, pain, suffering or aspirations. I was struck by the singing and asked them why they sang. I was told because they did not have the right to speak, particularly in public. When they left their homes, they could not express themselves. It was forbidden for a woman to raise her voice. The only thing that was tolerated were songs, which allowed them to express whatever they wanted.

Often these were societies where there were polygamous marriages, and there were several co-wives. When there is resentment among co-wives they sing to show this. When they feel that their husband favors one wife over the other, they sing about this while working. The husband feels that he is being attacked but he cannot really hold it against them. And this goes for other situations that they live. Thus, singing is their only means of expressing themselves.

I have observed as time goes on, that the women sing less and less. Before, I noticed that they worked mainly at the mill where they crushed grain, which was prepared for batter made of millet or corn and then cooked for the main meal. Today, with the modernization of technology, there are automated mills that are being installed just about everywhere, even in the most remote villages. This means that the women now go to the mills only to drop off the grain, they line up their recipients in front of the mill and they return home. Of course, this also means that they no longer sing. They also go to the public faucets where there is running water or to the water pumps, rather than to the river. Often there is jostling and pushing, one woman declaring to the other that she arrived first. This means that not only do they no longer sing, but they also squabble among themselves.

In the past, the singing was a very elegant means to live their experience. When I realized that it was disappearing, I wanted to preserve this practice by doing this film. I also wanted to let the children, especially the city dwellers who do not know about this tradition, discover that another way of expressing oneself exists.

So, it was through the young girl who lived in the city that this story was recounted. I also noted that there was a parallel between the girl from the city and the girl from the village. The story, which was a message recounted using the oral tradition, was also told in epistolary form. While writing the letter, the young girl actually narrates the story of the film.

Yes, the young girl as city dweller has the chance to go to school and she can write her feelings about her experiences. That is something which did not exist in the traditional society. It was through the oral tradition rather than through the written word that things were transmitted. It also gave her the chance to express herself by writing about it. Through this adolescent girl, I reveal what existed and what is now disappearing.

Also, there was the juxtaposition between oral expression in Moré and written expression in French, the administrative and colonial language.

Yes, this parallel was made as well.

*Burkina Faso is the country that hosts FESPACO and is very committed to Afri-
can cinema. Does this have a direct influence on the Burkinabés in terms of their
appreciation of the cinema, especially African films?*

The Burkinabés are very much cinema lovers. One observes this through
their participation during several events that are organized during
FESPACO. Even outside of the festival, they go to see films often. Of
course, one knows that images relay messages and different aspects of a
culture are passed on from the perspective of the person who is behind
the camera, who writes the script, and so on. Therefore, because there
are more films that are produced outside than those nationally, this means
that people are beginning to forget their own culture. I think that it is
the role of the filmmakers in their respective countries, to attempt to
restore our culture that is about to disappear, by bringing it to the screen.

Melodies de femmes *was told through the perspective of a young girl, and as
you stated, you made the film with young people in mind. By the choice of themes
for your films, do you actually attempt to target young people?*

I made another film that also focuses on the youth. It speaks about the
extra-curricular activities that young people are involved in, and is ear-
marked for city dwellers. It is a portrait of a student, who in his spare
time, plays in a "Do-Do" troupe, which is a cultural group in the neighborhood. The film is used as an example to show that although one goes
to school, one may also have an interest in one's own culture.

The children involved in the Troupe Do-Do create masks made of
sponges to make different forms of animals. Then they play music, and
the animals dance. It is very beautiful to see. This film I also made for
children.

I do remember seeing these wonderful masks. What do they represent?

It is something that came to us from Niger through Islam. The people
adapted it to the culture of this country. Each year during Ramadan there
is even a national competition of the Troupe Do-Do. Each neighborhood
has its Do-Do troupe, and I did a portrait of a child of one of these troupes.

*The theme of FESPACO 1997 is "Cinema, Childhood, and Youth." The theme
was chosen in order to highlight the importance that cinema has on young people.
Do you feel that your role as filmmaker reflects this?*

I was very pleased with the choice of this year's theme, "Cinema, Childhood and Youth" because it was a theme in which I was already interested. Through this topic, I felt that we were given the opportunity to really think about the impact that images have on our children. I work for the television and we have very few national programs for children. We know that children like to imitate, and so everything that they see on television they try to imitate. We are realizing that if we make films that address their needs in particular, that treat themes and subjects that interest them, that, in fact, we will actually participate in their intellectual, cultural and physical development.

As it relates to themes on and for children, I had the chance to participate in a workshop organized in France in 1994, which focused on this theme. We were sixteen participants from different African countries, and there was a second session on the same theme where fifteen other African participants attended; all the participants were women. From this workshop, we ended up with some thirty different subjects since we each had to produce a particular topic.

Unfortunately, we were not able to find funding to complete the project. It would have been wonderful to see these thirty films at FESPACO, directed by women around the theme of children, for children. Personally, I have three or four projects for children that are completed. I am now looking for a producer who is interested.

You just mentioned that the participants at this workshop were all women. Would you say that children-focused films and programs tend to be made by women?

Yes, I would say there is a tendency. I have observed that when there is an opportunity to participate in a workshop that is organized to bring together several African countries—and I have myself participated in two workshops for children—the majority of the participants are women. Other women participants also notice in their countries—and I am again talking about national television—that this is an area that is designated for women, because men generally do not consider focusing on this area. Women tend to be much more interested. Perhaps it is also in part a maternal response. Women are generally the ones who educate the children, and perhaps it is for this reason that a great many more women than men are interested in the needs of children. Of course, this is a personal response.

What has been the response to your film? Has it been seen throughout Burkina?

Yes, it has been broadcast on television. It has been well received but I have not had direct feedback. However, I do get impressions from people who see me in the streets and say they have seen the film and appreciated it, and there may be a discussion about it. However, there is not an actual opinion survey in order to really know what the reactions are. There has to be many more films such as these to truly know.

What about the possibility of these films circulating in the schools or cultural centers for the young people to see and discuss?

No, unfortunately this does not exist. To have such a setup, equipment must be adapted for this kind of endeavor. We directors would really like to do something like that, whether it is for women or children. We make films hoping that they have a much larger impact because oftentimes it is limited to the larger cities that receive the broadcast. Thus, the people in the rural areas do not get to see these programs, yet it is there where we often work, where we go to get these images, and that is a pity.

I have noted from your discussion that there are certain interests which women directors have, as well as certain roles that they see themselves playing. Do you feel that there is a sensibility that one can say is particular to women in the context of cinema?

I think it does exist. I do not think that a topic given to a woman and a man would be treated in the same way. Of course, between two men or two women it would also be different. However, between genders I think the difference would even be more so. There is a certain intuition that women have, I think.

How would you concretize or describe this sensibility?

It is difficult to describe. I feel it, but I am not able to specify it. It is through our work that it perhaps manifests itself.

Have you had the opportunity to present your films elsewhere? In other African countries, in Europe or other places around the world?

For the films, there is an exchange network of programs that is done with the CIRTEF, a francophone organization. The Burkina television receives films that come from other francophone countries and we also send our films, there is this exchange. Therefore, people in francophone regions have been able to see my films through this system. Exchanges made directly between televisions are rare. There are also programs that are bought by European televisions, but this is rare because there are certain criteria that must be met. It must be a very good film on the level of image quality, and also according to their aesthetic interests. The content must also be of interest to those of the North, which, coming from our television, is rare.

What are your impressions of African cinema and what do you feel is your role within it?

When speaking of African cinema I think of it in terms of the content of the films that convey something cultural. There is always this notion of culture that turns up repeatedly. If we make films that truly reflect who we are, I think that it can be accepted everywhere, and we have the same level of technical experience as people anywhere else.

Why do we speak of American cinema? When we see American films we already have an image, we immediately think of action, often times violence, and so on. When we speak of Indian cinema, we immediately think of poetry, of love, of songs. That is the image that people have here of those films. Therefore, when speaking of African cinema we must be able to give it an identity. So that when one thinks of African cinema there is immediately an idea that it is this or that. Today I cannot tell you what it is because it is very diverse. Each country brings what is particular to its culture.

The Princess Yennenga symbolizes the grand prize of FESPACO. Do you know the history of the Princess Yennenga?

Princess Yennenga left an important mark on the Mossi Empire because she was the daughter of the King Gambaga. According to the story, the Mossi come from there, it is in the north of Ghana and the south of Burkina. The princess lived with her father and she was raised as a boy. She rode a horse and like the men, participated in war. She wanted to get married. And according to the story, she became pregnant. The court guardian returned to tell the king that the princess was expecting a child. She would have been chastised if she remained in the country so she left her family and sought refuge in the forest. There, she came across a house, and in it lived a hunter called Riale. The hunter befriended her and they fell in love, they stayed together and had a son. In memory of the horse that brought her to her lover, the couple decided to name the child

Ouedraogo, which means "male horse" in Moré. This woman symbolized defiance. We can see in this gesture a search for the new.

What do you see as the importance of this prize?

The Etalon de Yennenga has opened many doors for numerous African filmmakers. Although I came to cinema not very long ago, I did follow it when I was a student. And I observed that many of the important film-makers that we love and with whom we identify, began their career with the festival of Ouagadougou, some of them have received the prize of the Etalon de Yennenga. Thus, it has opened doors.

Perhaps African women in the cinema experience a certain pride in the fact that a woman symbolizes the grand prize. How do you feel about the fact that it is a woman who is the symbol of the grand prize?

Whatever one may say about the domination of women by men, the woman is the real winner in many ways, because she is glorified through this Etalon. I think we must work so that one day a woman may be awarded the Etalon de Yennenga, because if my memory serves me well, a woman has never won the prize of Etalon de Yennenga. Nevertheless, I think it will come because we see increasingly good films by women, including feature films.

Summary

"African women in the cinema" is not a monolith. Ngozi Onwurah even asserts that there needs to be more distinctions made between the disparate technologies, locations, and conditions in which African women work. There is, nonetheless, an exciting phenomenon that is emerging. Women from every region of Africa are using the diverse mediums of film, video, and television, in the various formats of 16 and 35mm, Beta, Hi-8, and ¾ video, to produce feature, short, documentary and animation films, which are shown in movie houses, on television, at film festivals, and ciné-clubs. While they come to cinema along different paths, for different reasons, and at different moments, they share a common goal: to bring images to the screen.

This compilation of conversations brings together a collective voice of women of Africa from the diverse areas of cinema. It reflects the multi-faceted lives of women throughout the continent and extends to the Diaspora to focus on women who connect to Africa in their film work and cinematic practices. The representation of women in this collection spans all regions of Africa—north, west, east, central, and south. Though not exhaustive in its inclusion of all women in this arena, it is representative of the concerns, problems, histories, and futures of women of Africa who share the media as a common interest.

The scope of the book covers a continuum of experiences: from the pioneer women to women film students who are making their debut in the film arena. Producers, film critics, and organizers are an integral part of the filmmaking process and their perspectives add an important dialogue to the conversation. Actresses, the visible subjects on the screen, voice their thoughts about African cinema and their role in the larger context of visual representation, culture, and society.

The interviews that make up this book show the wide spectrum of experiences that shape the cinema of African women, as each adds her brick, in the words of Valerie Kaboré. Some share their journey along the path to cinema, others reflect on personal feelings around identity and its influence on their work. Some focus on the themes of their work, which span the personal to the political. Their films probe intimate and personal issues around sexuality, women's responses to male infidelity, conjugal violence, and forced marriages. The films also examine societal laws and statutes that deny women's personal, legal, and human rights. They also probe broader political concerns of democracy and free elections, and the consequences of civil war and its devastating effect on women and children. Some women talk about their direct involvement in national liberation struggles and the importance of raising consciousness around AIDS and other health issues, as well as women's literacy and education. Still others contemplate their role as communicator and catalyst for change, stressing the need for women to organize among themselves and come together as a collective body to realize their objectives. As their diverse experiences converge under their common interest in cinema, the thread that weaves their voices together is their commitment to "visualizing herstories."

FILMOGRAPHY*
(Film, Video and Television)

Adagala, Esther (Kenya)

Women in Health. Documentary, 1984.

Adamou, Aissatou (Niger)

Gossi. Video, 26 min., color, documentary, 1996.
Les Femmes pénitencières. Video, 20 min., documentary, 1995.
La Réhabilitation des femmes handicapées. Video, documentary 1994.
Les Femmes du troisième age. Video, 25 min., documentary, 1991.
Le Gavage des femmes à Gaudel. Video, 26 min., documentary, 1988.
Les Femmes de la vallée du fleuve Niger. Video, 26 min., 1988.
La Retraite active. Video, 20 min., documentary, 1987.
Les Femmes Sorkos. Video, 20 min., documentary, 1986.

Adjiké, Sanni (Togo)

L'Eau sacrée. Video, 25 min., documentary, 1993.
Le Savon de l'espoir. Video, 22 min., documentary, 1993.
Vivre du poisson. Video, 25 min., documentary, 1993.
L'Eau potable d'Anazive. Video, 13 min., documentary, 1992.

Aina, Shirikiana (USA)

Through the Door of No Return. 16mm, color, docu-drama, 1997.
Brick by Brick. 16mm, 37 min., color, documentary, 1982.

Albuquerque, Fatima (Mozambique)

No meu pais existe uma guerra. Documentary, 1989.
Entre a dor e esperanca. Documentary, 1987.

Le Son c'est la vie. 16mm, 14 min., documentary, 1987.
As Nossas Flores. Documentary, 1986.
O Abc da nova vida. Documentary, 1985.

Amari, Raja (Tunisia)

Avril. 35mm, color, 30 min., fiction.
Le Bouquet.

Ashong-Katai, Seth (Ghana)

Triple Echo. Video, 125 min., fiction, 1997.
For Better for Worse. Video, 120 min., fiction, 1995.
Child at 6.30. Video, 110 min., fiction, 1993.

Atangana, Rosalie Mbélé (Cameroon)

La Production d'Africa Jin. 1994.

Aymadji, Opportune (Chad)

Tatie pouvait vivre. Video, color, 14 min., 1995.

Baccar, Selma (Tunisia)

Habiba M'Sika ou la danse du fer. 35mm, 100 min., fiction, 1995.
De la toison au film d'or. 35mm, color, documentary, 1985.
Au pays de Tarayoun. 35mm, color, docu-drama, 1985.
Fatma 75. 35mm, color, docu-drama, 1976.

Badarou, Michèle (Benin)

Les Tresseuses de natte de Gbangnito. 1985.
Bénin le temps au féminin. 1985.

Bell-Gam, Ruby (Nigeria)

The Cult, (Co-directed with David Urur Iyam), 1985.
My Child, Their Child. 1984.

Ben Mabrouk, Néjia (Morocco)

A la recherche de Shaïma. 16mm, color, 1992.
Pour vous servir. 16mm, BW, 1976.

Benhachem, Khiti-Amina (Morocco)

Ileïkoum. (Monthly television series), 30 min., 1974–1991.
Sindbad. (Bi-monthly television series), 30 min., 1991.

Benjelloun, Dounia (Morocco)

Le Barrage d'Aoulouz. 16mm, documentary, 1993.
Kheir El Ardh. 16mm, documentary, 1989.
L'Architecture de terre. 35mm, color, documentary, 1987.

Benlyazid, Farida (Morocco)

Keid Ensa. 35mm, color, 90 min., fiction, 1998.
Sur la terrasse.
Aminata Traoré, une femme du Sahel. Video, 26 min., documentary, 1993.
Une porte sur le ciel. 35mm, color, fiction, 1988.
Identités de femme. 16mm, color, documentary, 1980.

Bhar, Mounira (Tunisia)

Trésor. 35mm, color, fiction, 1993.
Itinéraire. 35, color, documentary, 1993.

Boni-Claverie, Isabelle (Ivory Coast)

Le Génie d'Abou. Video, color, 9 min., fiction, 1997.

Bornaz, Kalthoum (Tunisia)

Keswa el Khayt Eddaya (Kwesi the Lost Thread). 35mm, color, 96 min., fiction, 1997.
Regard de mouette (The Glance of a Seagull). 35mm, color, fiction, 1991.
Trois personnages en quête d'un théâtre (Three Characters on a Quest for a Theater). 35mm, color, fiction, 1988.
Couleurs Fertiles (Fertile Colors). 35mm, color, fiction, 1984.

Un homme en or (A Golden Man).
Nuit de noces à Tunis (Wedding Night in Tunis).
Forêt d'El Medfoun (El Medfoun Forest).

Cherabi, Nadia (Algeria)

Fatima Amaria. (Co-directed with Malek Aggoun), 16mm, 22 min., documentary, 1994.

Chiluba, Annie Chimbuvu (Zambia)

The River Too Far. Video, color, 45 min., documentary, 1997.

Coulibaly, Fatoumata (Mali)

N'Golo dit Papi. Video, color, 46 min., color, 1997.

Dangarembga, Tsitsi (Zimbabwe)

Everyone's Child. 35mm, color, 90 min., fiction, 1995.

Diegu, Omah (Nigeria)

Note to My Son. 1994.
The Snake in My Bed. 1994.

Diop, Adrienne (Senegal)

Le Sida au Sénégal. Video, 52 min., documentary, 1992.
La Pêche artisanale au Sénégal: enjeux. Video, 13 min., documentary, 1991.
Le Riz dans la vallée du fleuve Sénégal. Video, 52 min., documentary, 1990.

Diop, Rokhaya (Senegal)

Le Groupement de femmes de Cascas au nord du Sénégal. Video, color, 4 min., documentary, 1994.
Les Réfugiés Mauritaniens au Sénégal. Video, color, 10 min., documentary, 1994.
L'Ecole primaire au Sénégal. Video, 6 min., documentary, 1993.
La Crise économique au Sénégal. Video, 7 min., documentary, 1993.
Portrait d'un jeune musicien. Video, 6 min., documentary, 1993.

Djebar, Assia (Algeria)

La Zerda ou les chants de l'oubli. 16mm, color, fiction, 1982.
La Nouba des Femmes du Mont-Chenoua. 16mm, color, 115, fiction, 1978.

Douamba, Benjamine (Burkina Faso)

Souley et ses copains. Video, color, 35 min., fiction, 1996.

El Fani, Nadia (Tunisia)

Tanitez-moi (Give me an award). 35mm, 26 min., documentary, 1993.
Du côté des femmes leaders. Video, 30 min., documentary, 1993.
Fifty fifty mon amour. 35mm, color/BW, fiction, 1992.
Pour le plaisir. 35mm, color, fiction, 1990.

Elisabeth, Marie-Claire (Seychelles)

Magazin Ekonomik: Pti Metye. Video, 39 min., documentary, 1989.

Fani-Kayode, Lola (Nigeria)

Drive and Stay Alive. 1993
Mind Bending. Series, 1990.
Iwa. 1988.
The Dilemma of Father Michael. 1988.
Mirror in the Sun. 1984.

Fares, Nadia (Tunisia)

Miel et Cendres. 35mm, color, 80 min., fiction, 1996.

Faye, Safi (Senegal)

Mossane. 35mm, color, 105 min., fiction, 1996.
Tesito. Video, color, 27 min., documentary, 1989.
Elsie Haas, femme peintre et cinéaste d'Haiti. Video, color, 8 min., documentary, 1985.
Racines noires. Video, color, 11 min., documentary, 1985.
Ambassades nourricières. 16mm, color, 52 min., documentary, 1984.

Selbé et tant d'autres. (In the series *As Women See It*), 16mm, color, 30 min., documentary, 1982.
Les Ames au soleil. 16mm, color, 27 min., documentary, 1981.
Man Sa Yay. 16mm, color, 60 min., documentary, 1980.
3 ans 5 mois. Video, color, 30 min., 1979–1983.
Goob na ñu. 16mm, color, 108 min., 1979.
Fad'jal. 16mm, color, 108 min., fiction, 1979.
Kaddu beykat. 16mm, BW, 95 min., fiction, 1975.
Revanche. 16mm, BW, 15 min., 1973.
La Passante. 16mm, color, 10 min., fiction, 1972.

Ferhati, Jilali (Morocco)

La Plage des enfants perdus. 1991.

Fobé Fombé, Margaret (Cameroon)

Ces gosses qui bossent. Video, 15 min., documentary, 1997.
L'Union fait la force. Video, 26 min., documentary, 1995.
Ma'a Nwambang (The Woman who Collects Palm Nuts). Video, color, 28 min., documentary, 1995.
Femmes et hommes en milieu rural camerounais: rôle, tâches et responsabilités. 1995.
Siri cow (Woman Butcher). 1994.
Les Femmes pompistes. 1990.
Portraits de femmes. Video, 37 min., documentary, 1980.

Folly, Anne-Laure (Togo)

Sarah Maldoror ou la nostalgie de l'utopie. 16mm, 26 min., documentary, 1998.
Les Oubliées. Video, 52 min., documentary, 1997.
Entre l'arbe et la pirogue/From the Tree to the Dugout. 52 min., documentary, 1996.
Les Amazones se sont reconverties. Video, 13 min., documentary, 1995.
Femmes aux yeux ouverts. Video, 52 min., documentary, 1994.
Femmes du Niger. Video, 26 min., documentary, 1993.
L'Or du Liptako. Video, 13 min., 1993.
Le Gardien des forces. Video, 52 min., documentary, 1992.

Forjaz, Moira (Mozambique/Zimbabwe)

Um dia numa aldeia communal. 1981.
Mineiro macambicano. 1981.

Foumane, Blandine (Cameroon)

La Leçon de français. (Tele-film), 1992.
Contes du Cameroun. Video, 42 min., 1991.
Passe partout Cameroun. Video, 8 min., 1991.
Miseria. Television series, 28 min., 1990.
Silence on joue. Television series, 30 min., 1989.

Gebre-Egziabher, Lucy (Ethiopia)

Weti's Poem. 16mm, experimental, 4 min., 1997.
Tchebelew. Video, 15 min., fiction, 1996.
Bag-Age. 16mm, color, 10 min., non-fiction, 1996.
Emancipation. 16mm, b/w, 7 min., non-fiction, 1995.

Genini, Izza (Morocco)

Pour le plaisir des yeux. Video, color, 50 min., documentary, 1997.
La route du cedrat, le fruit de la splendeur. 30 min., 1997.
Concerto pour 13 voix. 90 min., 1995.
Voix du Maroc. 1995.
Retrouver Ouled Moumen. 50 min., 1994.
Airs en terre berbère. 16mm, 2 x 26 min., documentary, 1992-93.
Moussem. 16mm, color, documentary, 1991.
Cantiques brodés. 16mm, color, documentary, 1990.
Gnaouas. 16mm, color, documentary, 1989.
Malhoun. 16mm, color, documentary, 1989.
Louange. 16mm, color, documentary, 1988.
Rhythmes de Marrakech. 16mm, color, documentary, 1988.
Marco corps et âme. Documentary series, 11 x 26 min., 1987-1992.

Guerra, Mila (Algeria)

Merci Monsieur Monnet. 35mm, color, fiction, 1992.

Hachemi, Baya (Algeria)

Le Citoyen face à la justice. Monthly television series, 52 min., 1983-1989.
Visages de femmes. Television series on women, 52 min., 1975-1977.

Hakizimana, Sham-Jeanne (Burundi)

Marie-Louise: Femme aux multiples facettes. Video, 25 min., documentary, 1998.

Hima, Mariama (Niger)

Hadiza et Kalia. 16mm, documentary, 1994.
Katako (Wooden board). 16mm, documentary, 1987.
Toukou (Barrel). 16mm, documentary, 1986.
Falaw (Aluminum). 16mm, documentary, 1985.
Baabu Banza (Nothing is thrown away). 16mm, documentary, 1984.

Ilboudo, Henriette (Burkina Faso)

Vénégré.

Ilboudo, Martine Condé (Guinea/Burkina Faso)

Bi Mussoya. Video, 26 min., documentary, 1998.
Messages de femmes, messages pour Beijing. Video, color, 52 min., documentary, 1995.
Féminin pluriel. Video, 26 min., 1994.
Un cri dans le Sahel. Documentary, 1994.
Jazz à Ouaga. Documentary, 1993.
Artisanat 1993. Video, 10 x 3 min., color, 1993.
Siao. Documentary, 1992.

Kaboré/Silga, Valérie (Burkina Faso)

Parlement des enfants du Burkina. Video, 15 min., documentary, 1998.
Citoyens du monde. (With Quentin Van de Velde, Belgium), video, 26 min. fiction, 1997.
Kado ou la bonne à tout faire. (In the series "Naître fille en Afrique"), video, 26 min., fiction, 1996.
Les Vrais faux jumeaux. (In the series "Naître fille en Afrique"), video, 26 min., fiction, 1996.

Voix unique...Pour Beijing. 1995.
Scolariser la fille, une priorité. 1995.
Regard sur l'ONEA. Video 30 min., documentary, 1992.
De l'eau pour Ouagadougou. 1992.

Kamani Konham, Augustine (Cameroon)

Tazibi. (Co-directed with Rosine Kenmoe Kenyou), video, 95 min., fiction, 1990.
Cadeau de Paix. Video 43 min., documentary, 1989.
Engrenage. Video, 43 min., documentary, 1988.
Portrait d'une femme rural. Video, 27 min., 1988.

Kamau, Wajuhi (Kenya)

Mine Boy. Video, color, 120 min., fiction, 1998.

Kamugwera, Jeanne d'Arc (Rwanda)

Les Métiers marginalisés pour les femmes. 1993.
La Femme rwandaise dans la démocratie pluraliste. 1993.
Les Orphelins du sida. 1992.

Kenmoe Kenyou, Rosine (Cameroon)

Grandes fêtes, petits prix. Video, 24 min., documentary, 1992.
Tazibi.(With Augustine Kamani Konkam*).* 1990.
Un jour à la campagne. Video, 22 min., documentary, 1989.

Kinyanjui, Wanjiru (Kenya)

*Rights of Children (*Two short films for German TV series). 1997.
The Battle of the Sacred Tree. 35mm, color, 80 min., fiction, 1995.
Black in the Western World. 22 min., documentary, 1992.
The Bird with a Broken Wing. 1991.
A Lover and Killer of Colour, 1989.
Clara has Two Countries

Konaté, Kadiatou (Mali)

Musowbemi (Dreams of Women). Video, color, 2 x 26 min., documentary, 1995.

Tieni Kisseman (L'Enfant Terrible). 16mm, color, 12 min., marionette animation. 1993.
Circulation routière. (Co-directed with Kabide Djedje), 1993.

Kourouma, Suzanne (Burkina Faso)

Branmuso (Mother-in-Law). 35mm, color, 1994.

Krim, Rachida (Algeria)

La Femme dévoilée. (Co-directed with Hamid Tassili), 35mm, color, 9 min., fiction, 1998.
Adieu galère.
Sous les pieds des femmes.
Pourquoi pas.
El Fatha.

Letlaka-Nkosi (ka), Palesa (South Africa)

Mamlambo. Color, 20 min., 1997.

Lhape, Kilaba Ngansem (Democratic Republic of the Congo)

Oeuvre Maman Mobutu. (Co-directed with Bokufa Bosomba).

Liking, Werewere (Ivory Coast/Cameroon)

Regard de fous. Video, color, 93 min., documentary, 1988. (Film adaptation of a theater piece *Dieu Chose*).

Makwenda, Joyce (Zimbabwe)

Zimbabwe's Township Music from the 30's to the 60's. Documentary, 1990.

Maldoror, Sarah (Guadeloupe-Angola)

Léon G. Damas. 16mm, BW, 26 min., documentary, 1995.
Vlady. Documentary, 1988.
Aimé Cèsaire, le masque des mots. Documentary, 1987.
Portrait de Madame Diop. 16mm, color, 10 min., documentary, 1986.
Le passager du Tassili. 16mm, color, 90 min., fiction, 1986.

Un sénégalais en Normandie. Documentary, 1983.
Robert Doisneau. 1983.
La Littérature tunisienne de la Bibliothèque Nationale. Documentary, 1983.
Le Racisme au quotidien. 1983.
L'Hôpital de Leningrad. 16mm, color, 51 min., documentary. 1982.
Un dessert pour Constance. 16mm, color, 51 min., fiction. 1980.
Un carnaval dans le Sahel. 16mm, color, 13 min., documentary, 1979.
Fogo, l'ile de feu. 16mm, color, 13 min., documentary, 1979.
Miro. 16mm, color, 5 min., documentary, 1979.
Un masque à Paris: Louis Aragon. 16mm, color, 13 min., documentary, 1978.
Paris, le cimetière du Père Lachaise. 16mm, color, 5 min., documentary, 1977.
Un homme, une terre, Aimé Césaire. 16mm, color 51 min., documentary, 1977.
La Basilique de Saint-Denis. 16mm, color, 5 min., 1976.
Sambizanga. 16/35mm, color, 102 min., documentary, 1972.
Et les chiens se taisaient. Color, 13 min., documentary, 1971.
La Commune, Louise Michel et nous. Color, 13 min., documentary, 1971.
Saint-Denis-sur-Avenir. Color, 13 min., documentary, 1971.
Carnaval en Guinée Bissau. documentary, 1971.
Des fusils pour Banta. 35mm, b/w, 105 min., fiction, 1971.
Monangambee. 35mm, b/w, 20 min., fiction, 1970.

Mamadali, Ouméma (Comoros)

Baco, (Co-directed with Kabiré Fidaali), video, color, 58 min., fiction, 1995.

Mango, Idi Rakia (Niger)

Les Chasses touristes. Video, 20 min., documentary, 1990.
Le Langui. Video, 24 min., documentary, 1989.
Femmes et exode. Video, 19 min., documentary, 1988.

Matton, Sarah Taouss (Algeria)

D'un désert, l'autre. Video, color, 52 min., 1996.
La Journée continue. 1994.
L'Age mûr. 1994.

Mbongue, Jerose Chantal (Cameroon)

Un parcours de produits vivriers. Video, 26 min., 1996.

Mekuria, Salem (Ethiopia)

Ye Wonz Maibel (Deluge). Video, 69 min., documentary, 1995.
Sidet: Forced Exile. Video, 59 min., documentary, 1991.
As I Remember It: A Portrait of Dorothy West. Video, 56 min., documentary, 1991.
Our Place in the Sun. Video, 30 min., documentary, 1988.

Melome, Marie-Constance (Benin)

Un groupement pas comme les autres. 1995.
Pudeur de femme. 1991.
Le Soja pour mieux vivre (Soya for Better Living).

Mengue-Bekale, Rose Elise (Gabon)

Santé en question. Television series, 1992.
Tison enchanteur. Television series for children. 1989-90.
Les Jeunes sont formidables. Video, 30 min., documentary, 1986.
Le Temps d'un regard. Television series. 1982-84.

Mensah, Vera (Ghana)

Broken Hearts. Video, 117 min., fiction, 1998.

Mire, Soraya (Somalia)

Fire Eyes. 16mm, 60 min., documentary, 1994.

M'mbugu-Schelling, Flora (Tanzania)

Shida and Matatizo. 16mm, color, fiction, 1993.
These Hands. 16mm, color, 45 min., non-fiction, 1992.
Kumekucha (From Sun Up). 16mm, color, 1987.

Moustache-Belle, Jacqueline (Seychelles)

Les hommes et les oiseaux sur l'Ile Cousin. Video, 37 min., documentary, 1988.

Mungai, Anne (Kenya)

Saikati, the Enkabaani. 35mm, color, 95 min., fiction, 1998.
Tough Choices. 52 min.
Usilie Mtoto Wa Africa (Don't Cry Child of Africa). 1994.
Root 1. 52 min., docu-drama, 1994.
Pongezi. 25 min., documentary, 1993.
Saikati. 16mm, color, 90 min., fiction, 1992.
Faith. 1991.
Productive Farmlands. 1990.
Wekesa at Crossroads. 1986.
Together We Build. 1982.
Tomorrow's Adult Citizens. 1981.
The Beggar's Husband. 1980.
Nkomani Clinic. 1980.

Nacro, Fanta Régina (Burkina Faso)

Le Truc de Konaté. 35mm, color, 32 min., fiction, 1998.
Puk Nini. 35mm, color, 30 min., fiction, 1995.
Un certain matin, 16mm, color, 13 min., fiction, 1991.
Visages d'hommes. 1986.

Nama, Benjamine (Burkina Faso)

Femmes et culture.
Les Droits et devoirs de la femme.
La Question de divorce.

Ndah, Martine (Ivory Coast)

Tresses à la douzaine.

N'Diaye, Maimouna (Guinea)

Warbassanga. Video, 30 min., documentary, 1998.

Ndongozi, Spès (Burundi)

L'Apport de la femme burundaise dans l'élevage. Video, documentary.
Portrait d'une chanteuse burundaise. Video, documentary.

Participation de la femme burundaise dans l'amélioration de l'habitat des pauvres. Video, documentary.

Ngeleba, Angebi (Democratic Republic of Congo)

Bakola Miziki. 16mm, 45 min., 1980.

Nyarku, Yvonne Kafui (Ghana)

Asanka Delight. Video, 30 min., non-fiction series, 1998.

Ogazuma, Debrah (Nigeria)

For Dela. Video, 41 min., fiction, 1991.
Magana Jari Ce. 52-part television series, 1989-90.

Okodo, Elizabeth (Kenya)

Immunization Spots. Educational video, 16 min., 1994.

Onobrauche, Evelyn (Nigeria)

Oghenetega. Video, 10 min., fiction (children's program), 1996.

Onwurah, Ngozi (Nigeria)

The Desired Number. Video, 28 min., color, documentary, 1995.
Wellcome to the Terrordome. Fiction, 1994.
White Men Are Cracking Up. (In the four-part film, *Siren Spirits*), 16mm, 20 min., color, fiction, 1994.
Monday's Girls. Video, 50 min., color, documentary, 1993.
And Still I Rise. 16mm, 30 min., color, non-fiction, 1993.
The Body Beautiful. 16mm, 23 min., color, fiction, 1991.
Coffee Coloured Children. 16mm, 15 min., Color/b/w, 1988.

Osoba, Funmi (Nigeria)

The Dormant Genius. 1990.

Otuka, Mary Wagaturi (Kenya)

Through Women's Eyes. Video, 26 min., documentary, 1996.

Oubda, Franceline (Burkina Faso)

Elles, pour refaire le monde. Video, color, 28 min., documentary, 1995.
Accès des femmes à la terre. 37 min., documentary, 1992.
Accès des femmes au credit. Video, 32 min., documentary, 1992.
Les cracheurs de farine.
Les 1000 filles.
La destinée.

Ouedraogo, Aminata (Burkina Faso)

Ak Patashi (Qui m'a poussé). Video, 16 min., documentary, 1992.
A qui le tour. 16mm, documentary, 1991.
L'Impasse. Video, fiction, 1988.

Patzanza, Miriam (Zimbabwe)

The Return. 1992.
Beyond Today. 1988.
Woman Cry. 1985.

Phoba, Monique (Democratic Republic of the Congo)

Un rêve d'independance. 16mm, 53 min., 1998.
Deux petits tours et puis s'en vont. (Co-directed with Emmanuel Kolawole), video, 47 min., 1997.
Une voix dans le silence. Video, 12 min., 1996.
Rentrer? Video, 52 min., 1993.
Revue en vrac.

Pickering, Bridget (Namibia)

Silba's Wedding. Video, Color, 24 min., 1996. (In the Series *Stories of Tenderness and Power*).

Proctor, Elaine (South Africa)

Manna pour Talisman. (Co-directed), 1997.
Friends. 35mm, color, 111 min., fiction, 1993.
On the Wire. 1992.
Palesa. 1990.
The Gift. Fiction, 1987.
Who Was it Who Cried? Fiction, 1987.
Sharpeville Spirit. 1986.
Re Tio Bono/We Will See. 1984.
Sun Will Rise (Co-directed), 1981.

Quashie, Veronica (Ghana)

Tears of Joy. Video, 114 min., fiction, 1996.
Twin Lovers. Video, 100 min., fiction, 1995.
The Action Plan. Video, 28 min., fiction, 1992.

Rolando, Gloria (Cuba)

Eyes of the Rainbow. Video, documentary, 1998.
My Footsteps in Baragua. Video, 53 min., documentary, 1996.
Oggun the Eternal Present. Video, 52 min., docu-fiction, 1994.

Roy, Danièle (Burkina Faso)

La Femme mariée à trois hommes. (With Cilia Sawadogo/Burkina Faso), 35mm, color, animation, 1993.

Saäl, Michka (Tunisia)

Eleonora. Super 16, color, documentary, 1994.
Tragedie. 16mm, color, fiction, 1993.
L'Arbre qui dort rêve à ses racines. 16mm, color, documentary, 1992.
Nulle part, la mer. 16mm, color, fiction, 1991.
Loin d'où. 16mm, color, fiction, 1989.

Saharoui, Djamila (Algeria)

Algérie, la vie quand même. Video, 50 min., non-fiction, 1998.
La moitié du ciel d'Allah. Video, 52 min., documentary, 1996.

Saïhi, Horria (Algeria)

Algérie en femme. Video, 26 min., documentary, 1996.

Salazar, Denise (Angola)

Marabu. 1984.

Sanogo, Kadida (Burkina Faso)

Un Siao des femmes. Video 26 min., color, 1992.
Le Joueur de kora. Super 8, 24 min., color, 1989.

Sawadogo, Cilia (Burkina Faso)

Le Joueur de cora. 35mm, color, 7 min., animation, 1997.
L'Arret d'autobus. 35mm, color, animation, 1995.
Naissance. 35mm, color, animation, 1995.
La Femme mariée à trois hommes. (With Danièle Roy/Burkina Faso), 35mm, color, animation, 1993.

Selly, Mariam Kane (Senegal)

Femmes rural. Video, 26 min., documentary, 1993.
Xessal. Video, 26 min., documentary, 1991.
Cars Rapides. Video, 15 min., documentary, 1990.

Shafik, Viola (Egypt)

Le Citronnier. Fiction, 1993.

Sinclair, Ingrid (Zimbabwe)

Tides of Gold. Documentary, 1998.
Flame. 35mm, 90 min., Fiction, 1996.
Sounds of the South. 1995.
Better Trees from Better Seeds. 1994.
Bird From Another World. Documentary, 1991.
The Sanctions Debate. 1990.
Wake Up. Documentary, 1989.
Mothers Don't Forget. Documentary, 1985.

Harriet Vyse. Documentary, 1983.
Kingsdown. Documentary, 1980.

Sita-Bella, Thérèse (Cameroon)

Tam-tam à Paris. 16mm, b/w, 30 min., documentary, 1963.

Skandrani, Fatma (Tunisia)

Derrière chaque porte...Tunis, la Médina: Habitat traditionnel en Afrique. Video, color, 26 min., documentary, 1996.
Les Rivages de la création. Video, 30 min., documentary, 1993.
Médina ma mémoire. 35mm, color, fiction, 1988.
Mille et une chandelles. 16mm, color, fiction, 1986.

Sona, Venessa Ebote (Cameroon)

Play Skul. 1994.

Sutherland, Efua (Ghana)

Araba: The Village Story. Documentary, 1967.

Sylla, Khady (Senegal)

Les Bijoux. Color, 23 min., fiction, 1996.

Tan, Florence (Cameroon)

Retirement - Life's End? Video, 26 min., documentary, 1996.

Thompson, Bridget (South Africa)

Heart and Stone. Video, 90 min., documentary, 1998.
Ernest Wancoba at Home. Video, 26 min., documentary, 1995.

Tlatli, Moufida (Tunisia)

Les Silences du palais. 35mm, color, fiction, 1993.
J.C.C. 1986. 16mm, color, documentary, 1987.

Tlili, Najwa (Tunisia)

Rupture. 52 min., documentary, 1998.
Héritage. 35mm, color, docu-drama, 1993.

Touré, Aissatou Laba (Senegal)

Profession Talibé. 1993.

Uriri, Prudence (Zimbabwe)

The Whisper. Video, color, 57 min., documentary, 1995.

Weiss, Ruth (South Africa)

South Africa Belongs to Us. 1980.

Wilson, Lindy (South Africa)

Sefela sa Tsela/A Travelling Song. Video, color, 54 min., documentary, 1993.
The Mont Fleur Scenarios. Documentary, 1992.
Robben Island Our University. Documentary, 1988.
Out of Despair-Ithuseng. Documentary, 1984.
Last Supper in Horsley Street. Documentary, 1983.
Crossroads. Documentary, 1983.

Yacoub, Zara Mahamat (Chad)

Les Enfants de la guerre. Video, 26 min., doc-fiction, 1996.
La Jeunesse et l'emploi. Documentary, 1996.
Les Enfants de la rue. Video, documentary, 1995.
Dilemme au féminin. Video, 24 min., documentary, 1994.

Yambo-Odotte, Dommie (Kenya)

The Baisikol. 26 min., fiction, 1997.
Women's Agenda. Video, 59 min., documentary, 1996.
Towards Autonomy. Program, 1993.
Offence Like Assault. Video, 12 min., non-fiction, 1993.
If Women Counted. Non-fiction, 1993.
The Chosen One. (Co-directed), documentary, 1991.

Yameogo, Florentine (Burkina Faso)

Seni, le petit joueur de cor. Video, 13 min., non-fiction, 1997.
Mélodies de femmes. Video, color, 24 min., documentary, 1994.
Sacrées Chenilles. 1994.
Le Jeudi de Gasoussou. 1994.
Femmes, sève nourricière.
De fil en aiguille.

Zamoun, Fatma Zohra

Leçon de choses. 1996.
Le Témoin. 1995.
Photos de voyages. 1995
Et les flocons de neige. 1993.

Zinaï-Koudil, Hafsa (Algeria)

Démon au féminin. 35mm, color, 1992.

Zoulaha, Abdou (Niger)

Journées portes ouvertes dans l'établissement scolaires. Video, 15 min., documentary, 1987.
Santé pour tous en l'an 2000? Video, 13 min., documentary, 1993.
Promotion de la femme: comment passer de l'intention à l'action? Video, 29 min., documentary, 1993.

Zowe, Léonie Yangba (Republic of Central Africa)

Paroles de sages. 1987.
Lengue. 1985.
Nzale. 1985.
Yangba-Bolo. 1985.

*This filmography does not claim to be exhaustive. It includes most of the fiction films, documentaries and tele-films that have appeared in film festivals. Other works listed are drawn from various sources that have documented filmmaker biographies, or from film-related literature. Perhaps the areas that are least represented are television programs and series, commissioned, institutional and educational films. With the exception of a work by one Egyptian filmmaker, Egypt is not represented.

BIBLIOGRAPHY OF RELEVANT SOURCES
IN ENGLISH AND FRENCH

BY OR ABOUT AFRICAN WOMEN OF
THE MOVING IMAGE

Abega, Mathieu Mbarga. "Speakerines de la télévision congolaise." Profile of three women announcers at the Congolese Television: Isabelle Thomage Anita, Beatrice Kenzo, Jeannette Mpoutou. *Amina*, no. 229, May 1989, p. 43.

African Training and Research Centre for Women/Voluntary Fund for the United Nations Decade for Women. *Women and the Mass Media in Africa: Case Studies of Sierra Leone, the Niger and Egypt.* Research Series, Addis Ababa, 1981.

_____. "Summary of Subgroup Discussions Conducted During the Study Visit of Women Journalists held at the United Nations Economic Commission for Africa at Addis Ababa, 24-30 September 1978." *Women and the Mass Media in Africa: Case Studies of Sierra Leone, the Niger and Egypt.* Research Series, Addis Ababa, 1981, pp. 31-38.

African Women Professionals of Cinema, Television, and Video. "Statement of African Women Professionals of Cinema, Television, and Video, Ouagadougou, Burkina Faso." In: *African Experiences of Cinema*, ed., Imruh Bakari and Mbye Cham (London: British Film Institute, 1996), pp. 35-36.

Ahyi, Véronique. Interview with Awa Sangare, Mali-Actress. *Amina*, no. 247, November 1990, p. 30.

ALA Bulletin. African Literature Association. Summer 1996, pp. 8-19. In Memoriam: Efua Sutherland 1924-1996.

Amarger, Michel. "Les images d'Afrique aux féminins pluriels." *Festival International de Films de Femmes Catalogue*, 1998, pp. 90-94.

_____. Interview with Safi Faye. Filmography and synopsis of her films. *Festival International de Films de Femmes Catalogue*, 1998, pp. 95-97.

_____. Interview with Alimata Saleméré, Burkina Faso-Director General for Culture and Communication, Agence de Cooperation Culturelle et Technique (ACCT). *Ecrans d'Afrique*, nos. 13-14, 3rd-4th quarter, 1995, p. 98.

_____. Profile of Farida Benlyazid, Morocco-Director. *Ecrans d'Afrique*, nos. 9-10, 3rd-4th quarter, 1994, p. 20.

_____. Profile of Moufida Tlatli, Tunisia-Director. *Ecrans d'Afrique*, nos. 9-10, 3rd-4th quarter, 1994, p. 23.

Amina, no. 318, October 1996, p. 30. "Les femmes aux avant-postes à la télévision togolaise (TVT)." Profile of two women at the Togolese Television: Rose Badadouwé Lémou, Announcer and Ayéva Amidatou, Camerawoman.

_____, no. 317, September 1996, p. 50. Interview with Maimouna Hélène Diarra, Mali-Actress.

_____, no. 317, September 1996, p. 49. Interview with Zara Mahamat Yacoub, Chad-Director.

_____, no. 316, August 1996, p. 44. Interview with Martine Condé Ilboudo, Burkina Faso/Guinea-Director.

_____, no. 316, August 1996, p. 45. Interview with Kadiatou Konaté, Mali-Director.

_____, no. 315, July 1996, p. 20. Profile of Mariam Kaba, Guinea-Actress.

_____, no. 304, August 1995, p. 10. Interview with Cilia Sawadogo, Burkina Faso-Director.

_____, no. 304, August 1995, p. 10. Interview with Florentine Yaméogo, Burkina Faso-Director.

_____, no. 303, July 1995, p. 20. Interview with Sanni Assouma Adjike, Togo-TV Director.

_____, no. 303, July 1995, pp. 18-19. Interview with Zara Mahamat Yacoub, Chad-Director.

_____, no. 291, July 1994, p. 12. Interview with Margaret Fombé, Cameroon-Director.

_____, no. 291, July 1994, p. 13. Interview with Mila Guerra, Algeria-Director.

_____, no. 291, July 1994, p. 14. Interview with Kadiatou Konaté, Mali-Director.

_____, no. 291, July 1994, p. 11. Interview with Franceline Oubda, Burkina Faso-TV Director.

_____, no. 291, July 1994, p. 10. Interview with Cilia Sawadogo, Burkina Faso-Director.

_____, no. 274, February 1993, p. 40. Profile of Rosine Yanogo, Burkina Faso-Actress.

_____, no. 253, May 1991, p. 10. Profile of Chantal Bagilishya, Rwanda-Producer.

_____, no. 253, May 1991, p. 27. Profile of Marie-Thérèse Gonçalves, Benin-TV Host.

_____, no. 253, May 1991, p. 20. Profile of Seipati Bulang Hopa, South Africa-Director/Distributor.

_____, no. 253, May 1991, p. 22. Profile of Clarisse Keita, Burkina Faso-Actress.

_____, no. 253, May 1991, p. 14. Profile of Anne Knuth, Zimbabwe-Director of Communication.

_____, no. 253, May 1991, p. 22. Profile of Flora M'mbugu-Schelling, Tanzania-Director.

_____, no. 253, May 1991, p. 16. Profile of Anne Mungai, Kenya-Director.

_____, no. 253, May 1991, p. 12. Profile of Aminata Ouedraogo, Burkina Faso-Director and Coordinator of the African Women in the Cinema Workshop FESPACO 1991.

_____, no. 231, July 1989, p. 45. Profile of Léocadie Baniekona, Congo-Camerawoman.

_____, no. 201, May 1987, pp. 30-31. Interview with Marie Antoinette Aoulou, Ivory Coast-TV Director.

_____, no. 191, July 1986, pp. 10-11. Interview with Félicité Wouassi, Cameroon-Actress.

_____, no. 152, December, 1984, p. 10. "Colloque à Dakar: Les journalistes d'Afrique francophone se sont réunis pour traiter d'un theme: femme, développement et communication."

_____, no. 134, August 1983, pp. 16-17. Interview with Rose Blé, Ivory Coast-TV Director.

Anani, Elma Lititia, "Women's Image in the Sierra Leone Mass Media." *Women and the Mass Media in Africa: Case Studies of Sierra Leone, the Niger and Egypt.* African Training and Research Centre for Women/Voluntary Fund for the United Nations Decade for Women. Research Series, Addis Ababa, 1981, pp. 3-10.

Andrade-Watkins, Claire. A Mirage in the Desert?: African Women Directors at FESPACO." In: *Cinemas of the Black Diaspora: Diversity, Dependence and Oppositionality*, ed., Michael T. Martin, (Detroit: Wayne State University, 1995), pp. 145-152.

Aristote, Diakouré Don. Interview with Georgette Paré, Burkina Faso-Actress-President of Casting-Sud. *Amina*, no. 335, March 1998, p. 26.

_____. Interview with Eveline Lompo, Burkina Faso-TV Announcer. *Amina*, no. 314, June 1996, p. 44.

_____. Interview with Joséphine Bertrand, Cameroon/Central Africa-Singer/Director. *Amina*, no. 308, December 1995, p. 72.

_____. Profile of Thérèse Tape Yobouet. *Amina*, no. 259, November 1991, p. 40.

_____. Profile of Habiba Dembele, Ivory Coast-TV Announcer. *Amina*, no. 251, March 1991.

Association des professionnelles africaines de la communication (APAC). *Femmes, développement, communication: quelles perspectives pour Nairobi 1985?* Proceedings from the seminar organized by BREDA, Dakar, Senegal, 1-10 October 1984.

Association des trois mondes. *Dictionnaire du cinéma africain.* (Paris: Editions Karthala, 1991).

Association of African Women for Research and Development/AAWORD, *Women and the Media in Africa.* Occasional Paper Series, no. 6, Dakar, 1992.

Atef, Ahmed. Excerpt from an interview with Asma al Bakri, Egypt-Director. *Ecrans d'Afrique*, no. 15, 1st quarter, 1996, p. 61.

Attia, Kahéna Réveill. "L'écran vaut le détour." In: *L'Afrique et le Centenaire du Cinéma/Africa and the Centenary of Cinema*, Pan-African Federation of Filmmakers. (Paris: Présence Africaine, 1995), pp. 345-347.

Aufderheide, Pat. "Interview with Sarah Maldoror." *Black Film Review*, 1989, pp. 8-9.

Ayari, Farida. "Images of Women." In: *African Experiences of Cinema*, ed., Imruh Bakari and Mbye Cham (London: British Film Institute, 1996), pp. 181-184.

_____. "Images de femmes." *CinémAction* (Special issue: Cinemas noirs d'Afrique), ed., Jacques Binet, Ferid Boughedir, and Victor Bachy, no. 26, 1983, pp. 136-139.

Ayissi-Essomba, André. "Les présentatrices de la télévision camerounaise." Profile of announcers at the Cameroonian television: Monique Maa, Sylvie Mguiamba, Michèle Ngoumou, Yolande Ambiana, Rosalie Ayinda, Pamela Messy, Lilian Nukuna. *Amina*, no. 221, September 1988, pp. 6-8.

_____. Profile of Marthe Ndomé, Cameroon-Actress. *Amina*, no. 194, October 1986, p. 15.

Bakari, Imruh and Mbye Cham, ed. *African Experiences of Cinema.* (London: British Film Institute, 1996).

Balogun, Françoise. "Visages de femmes dans le cinéma d'Afrique noire." *Présence Africaine* (Special Issue: Le monde en mutation depuis 1989/The Changing World Since 1989: Dossier II Femmes du monde/Femmes d'Afrique-African Women/Women of the World), no. 153, 1996, pp. 141-150.

_____. "Interview with Fanta Nacro." *Présence Africaine* (Special issue on Cinema and Liberty: Cinéma et Libertés: Contribution au thème du FESPACO '93) 1993, pp. 97-98.

_____. "Interview with Sarah Maldoror: Cinéma et engagement." *Présence Africaine* (Special issue on Cinema and Liberty: Cinéma et Libertés: Contribution au thème du FESPACO '93) 1993, pp. 121-125.

Bangre, Sambolgo. Profile of Abiba Diarra, Ivory Coast/Mali-Actress. *Ecrans d'Afrique*, no. 13-14, 3rd-4th quarter, 1995, p. 35.

_____. Profile of Monique Phoba, Democratic Republic of Congo-Director. *Ecrans d'Afrique*, nos. 9-10, 3rd-4th quarter, 1994, p. 32.

Barlet, Olivier. Interview with Safi Faye. *Africultures* (Special focus on African women: "Les africaines"), no. 2, 1997, pp. 8-11.

_____. Interview with Anne-Laure Folly. *Africultures* (Special focus on African women: "Les africaines"), no. 2, 1997, pp. 12-16.

_____. *Les cinémas d'Afrique noire: le regard en question.* (Paris: L'Harmattan, 1996). Includes analyses of works by Safi Faye, Anne-Laure Folly, Sarah Maldoror, Fanta Nacro.

Bassolé, Adama. Interview with Awa Sangare, Mali-Actress. *Amina*, no. 203, July 1987, p. 20.

Bettis, Lynn. Review of *Femmes d'images de l'Afrique francophone* by Najwa Tlili. *Ecrans d'Afrique*, nos. 9-10, 3rd-4th quarter, 1994.

Bitoumbou, Crépin. Profile of Philomène Minkouika, Congo-Camerawoman. *Amina*, no. 231, July 1989, p. 14.

Bobo, Jacqueline, ed. *Black Women Film & Video Artists.* (New York: Routledge, 1998).

Borgomano, Madeleine. "Visage de femmes: lecture intertexuelle de *Finzan,* film de Cheikh Oumar Sissoko et du roman de Kourouma, *Les soleils des indépendances.*" *With Open Eyes: Women and African Cinema*, ed., Kenneth W. Harrow. *Matatu* 19, 1997, pp. 111-124.

Boughedir, Ferid. *Le cinéma africain de A à Z*. (Brussels: Editions OCIC, 1987).

Breton, Emile. "Beautés noires: paroles d'actrices." *Africultures*, no. 9, 1998, pp. 14-16.

Carson, Diane, et al. *Multiple Voices in Feminist Film Criticism*. (Minneapolis: University of Minnesota Press, 1994).

Chalaye, Sylvie. Interview with Werewere Liking. *Africultures* (Special focus on African women: "Les africaines"), no. 2, 1997, pp. 5-7.

Cham, Mbye. "African Women and Cinema: A Conversation with Anne Mungai." *Research in African Literatures* (Special Issue: Women as Oral Artists), Fall 1994, pp. 93-104.

Chikhaoui, Tahar. "Stories of Women "Selma, Nejia, Moufida and the others." An interview with Moufida Tlatli and other Tunisian women filmmakers. *Ecrans d'Afrique*, no. 8, 2nd quarter, 1994, p. 11.

_____. Profile of Kalthoum Bornaz, Tunisia-Director. *Ecrans d'Afrique*, nos. 5-6, 3rd-4th quarter, 1993, p. 38.

Cinémathèque de la Coopération Catalogue, published by Audecam (Association Universitaire pour le Développement, l'Education et la Communication en Afrique et dans le Monde for the Ministère de la Coopération et du Développement). Catalogue published annually. Annotated list of the films in its collection.

Critical Arts. (African Cinema Issue), vol., 7, nos. 1-2, 1993.

Dagba, Edson. Interview with Marguerite Ahyi, Benin-Camerawoman. *Amina*, no. 248, December 1990, p. 52.

Deffontaines, Thérèse-Marie. Interview with Izza Genini, Morocco-Director. *Ecrans d'Afrique*, nos. 5-6, 3rd-4th quarter, 1993, p. 8.

DeLuca, Laura and Shadrack Kamenya, "Representation of Female Circumcision in *Finzan, A Dance for the Heroes*." *Research in African Literatures* (Special Issue: African Cinema), Fall 1995, pp. 83-86.

Demy, Catherine. Interview with Safi Faye, Senegal-Director. *Amina*, no. 315, July 1996, p. 21.

_____. Interview with Ingrid Sinclair, Zimbabwe-Director. *Amina*, no. 315, July 1996, p.20.

_____. Interview with Lieno Tsolo, South Africa-Actress. *Amina*, no. 303, July 1995, p. 12.

Diagne, Rokhaya Oumar and Souleymane Bachir Diagne: "Annette Mbaye d'Erneville: Une femme de communication/Annette Mbaye d'Erneville: A Lady with a Talent for Communication." *Présence Africaine* (Special Issue: Le monde en mutation depuis 1989/The Changing World Since 1989: Dossier II Femmes du monde/Femmes d'Afrique-African Women/Women of the World), no. 153, 1996, pp. 93-100.

Diallo, Assiatou Bah. Interview with Anne-Laure Folly, Togo-Director. *Amina*, no. 331, December 1997, p. 38.

_____. "Les femmes à la recherche d'un nouveau souffle." *Amina*, no. 253, May 1991, pp. 8-9. Summary of the events at the workshop on African women in the cinema, FESPACO 1991.

Diawara, Manthia. *African Cinema: Politics and Culture.* (Bloomington: University of Indiana Press, 1992).

Diop, Baba. "Ousmane Sembene, The Suburb of Women." Sembene talks about his film *Fat Kine. Ecrans d'Afrique*, no. 24, 2nd quarter, 1998, p. 91.

_____. Interview with Venus Seye, protagonist of *Fat Kine* by Ousmane Sembene. *Ecrans d'Afrique*, no. 24, 2nd quarter, 1998, p. 92.

Diop, Cheriff Amadou. "Recidak 96: When the Women of Cinema Take Action!" *Ecrans d'Afrique*, no. 16, 2nd quarter, 1996, p. 39.

Domingo, Macy and Klevor Abo. Interview with Akosua Busia, Ghana-Actress. *Ecrans d'Afrique*, no. 4, 2nd quarter, 1993, p. 6.

Ecaré, Désiré. "Quelques réflexions sur 'Cinéma et libertés' à propos de *Visages de femmes*." *Presence Africaine* (Special issue on Cinema and Liberty: Cinéma et Libertés: Contribution au thème du FESPACO '93) 1993, pp. 21-24.

Ecrans d'Afrique, nos. 21-22, 3rd-4th quarter, 1997, p. 45. At a Glance: Film review of *Pour le plaisir des yeux* by Izza Genini, Morocco.

_____, nos. 17-18, 3rd-4th quarter, 1996, p. 27. At a Glance: Film review of *Everyone's Child* by Tsitsi Dangarembga, Zimbabwe.

_____, nos. 17-18, 3rd-4th quarter, 1996, p. 17. At a Glance: Film review of *Honey and Ashes* by Nadia Fares, Tunisia.

_____, nos. 17-18, 3rd-4th quarter, 1996, p. 7. Flash: "Zimbabwe: An Association of Women Filmmakers."

_____, no. 16, 2nd quarter, 1996, p. 34. At a Glance: Film review of *Mossane* by Safi Faye, Senegal.

_____, no. 15, 1st quarter, 1996, p. 37. At a Glance: Film review of *Puk Nini* by Fanta Nacro, Burkina Faso.

_____, no. 15, 1st quarter, 1996, p. 7. Flash: "South Africa: Women in Cinema."

_____, nos. 13-14, 3rd-4th quarter, 1995, p. 49. At a Glance: Film review of *La Danse du feu* by Selma Baccar, Tunisia.

_____, nos. 13-14, 3rd-4th quarter, 1995, p. 7. Flash: "Chad: A Fatwa Against Zara Yacoub."

_____, no. 12, 2nd quarter, 1995, p. 34. At a Glance: Film review of *Ash-shaytan imra'/Le démon au féminin* by Hafsa Zinai Koudil, Algeria.

_____, no. 12, 2nd quarter, 1995, p. 59. At a Glance: Film review of *Puk Nini* by Fanta Nacro, Burkina Faso.

_____, no. 11, 1st quarter, 1995, p. 24. At a Glance: Film review of *The Battle of the Sacred Tree* by Wanjiru Kinyanjui, Kenya.

_____, no. 11, 1st quarter, 1995, p. 24. At a Glance: Film review of *Léon G. Damas* by Sarah Maldoror, Guadeloupe.

_____, no. 11, 1st quarter, 1995, p. 5. Flash: "National Bureau of the Pan African Union of Women in the Image Industry of Gabon."

_____, no. 11, 1st quarter, 1995, p. 5. Flash: "Pan-African Union of Women in the Image Industry."

_____, nos. 9-10, 3rd-4th quarter, 1994, p. 26. At a Glance: Film review of *Retrouver Oulad Moumen* by Izza Genini, Morocco.

_____, nos. 9-10, 3rd-4th quarter, 1994, p. 5. Flash: "Fifth Women's Regional Conference in preparation for the Beijing Conference."

_____, no. 3, 1st quarter, 1993, p. 5. Flash: "African Women in Film and Video - Kenya section."

_____, no. 3, 1st quarter, 1993, p. 45. Profile of Nadia El Fani, Tunisia-Director.

_____, no. 2, 3rd quarter, 1992, p. 29. At a Glance: Film review of *Saikati* by Anne Mungai, Kenya.

_____, no. 1, 2nd quarter, 1992, p. 35. Profile of Fanta Nacro, Burkina Faso-Director.

El Asmar, Marie-Jeanne. Inteview with Clarisse Keita, Burkina Faso-Actress. *Amina*, no. 250, February 1991, p. 8.

Ellerson, Beti. "Do They Remember Us." Interview with Shirikiana Aina, USA-Director. *Ecrans d'Afrique*, nos. 21-22, 3rd-4th quarter, 1997, p. 8.

_____. "The Female Body as Symbol of Change and Dichotomy: Conflicting Paradigms in the Representation of Women in African Film." *With Open Eyes, Women and African Cinema*, ed., Kenneth W. Harrow. *Matatu* 19, 1997, pp. 31-44.

_____, "The Female Body, Culture and Space: The Female Body in African Cinema." *Ecrans d'Afrique*, no. 11, 1st quarter, 1995, p. 28.

Emiliano. "La nudité dans le cinéma africain: Quand le nu chasse le beau." *Amina*, no. 253, May 1991, pp. 30-32. African women talk about nudity in African films: Hanny Brigitte Tchelley, Ivory Coast-Actress; Carmen Levry, Ivory Coast-Actress; Tassoum Lydie Doual, Chad-Sociologist; Mariam Yago, Burkina Faso-Actress.

Festival international de films de femmes/International Women's Film Festival Catalogue. The 1998 festival devoted a special section to women of Africa. A part of the festival catalogue is devoted to African women in the cinema.

Folly, Anne-Laure. "A propos du centenaire du cinéma: n'y aurait-il pas erreur de date?" In: *L'Afrique et le Centenaire du Cinéma/Africa and the Centenary of Cinema*, Pan-African Federation of Filmmakers. (Paris: Présence Africaine, 1995), pp. 343-344.

Fombé, Margaret. "Femme africaine, l'heure de défi." In: *L'Afrique et le Centenaire du Cinéma/Africa and the Centenary of Cinema*, Pan-African Federation of Filmmakers. (Paris: Présence Africaine, 1995), pp. 348-350.

_____. "New dawn of African cinema." In: *L'Afrique et le Centenaire du Cinéma/Africa and the Centenary of Cinema*, Pan-African Federation of Filmmakers. (Paris: Présence Africaine, 1995), pp. 395-397.

Foster, Gwendolyn Audrey. *Women Filmmakers of the African and Asian Diaspora: Decolonizing the Gaze, Locating Subjectivity*. (Carbondale: Southern Illinois University Press), 1997. Includes chapters on Ngozi Onwurah: "Ngozi Onwurah: A different concept and agenda," pp. 24-42. Devotes some attention to Safi Faye and Sarah Maldoror: "Other Voices."

Gabriel, Teshome. *Third Cinema in the Third World: The Aesthetics of Liberation*. (Ann Arbor: UMI Research Press, 1982).

Gant-Britton, Lisabeth. "African Women and Visual Culture: A Sample Syllabus." *Camera Obscura* (Special Issue on Black Women, Spectatorship and Visual Culture), special editor, Deborah R. Grayson, no. 36, 1995, pp. 85-117.

Gardies, A. and P. Haffner. *Regards sur le cinéma nègro-Africain.* (Brussels: OCIC, 1987). Includes synopsis of the films *Kodou* and *Fad'jal*: "Le discours de l'espace: *Kodou*, de Babacar Samb Makharam," (*Kodou* is a film about a young girl who goes mad after being rejected by her community when she is not able to complete a lip tattooing exercise), and "L'ambivalence comme fondement du récit: *Fad'jal* de Safi Faye."

Gaye, Amadou. "Women filmmakers in Morocco." Profiles of Farida Benlyazid, Touda Bouanani, Farida Bourquia, Izza Genini, Imane Mesbahi. *Ecrans d'Afrique*, nos. 5-6, 3rd-4th quarter, 1993, pp. 10-11.

————. Profile of Mouna Fettou, Morocco-Actress. *Ecrans d'Afrique*, no. 3, 1st quarter, 1993, p. 43.

Gibson-Hudson, Gloria J. "The Ties that Bind: Cinematic Representations by Black Women Filmmakers." In: *Black Women Film & Video Artists*, ed., Jacqueline Bobo (New York: Routledge, 1998), pp. 43-66. Includes an analysis of works by Salem Mekuria and Ngozi Onwurah.

Hadj-Moussa, Ratiba. "The Locus of Tension: Gender in Algerian Cinema." *With Open Eyes, Women and African Cinema*, ed., Kenneth W. Harrow. *Matatu* 19, 1997, pp. 45-66.

Haffner, Pierre. "Jean Rouch jugé par six cinéastes d'Afrique noire." *CinémAction* (Special issue: Jean Rouch, un griot gaulois) ed., René Prédal, no. 17, 1982. pp. 63-64. Safi Faye interviewed.

————. "*Petit à petit* en question: le film de Jean Rouch discuté dans deux ciné-clubs d'Afrique noire." *CinémAction* (Special issue: Jean Rouch, un griot gaulois) ed., René Prédal, no. 17, 1982, p. 79. Discusses Safi Faye's role in the film, *Petit à petit* by Jean Rouch.

Hall, Susan. "African Women on Film." *Africa Report* (Special Issue on Women in Africa), January-February 1977, pp. 15-17.

Harding, Frances. "Speaking for Women: Interview with Anne Mungai." *With Open Eyes, Women and African Cinema*, ed., Kenneth W. Harrow. *Matatu* 19, 1997, pp. 81-92.

Harrow, Kenneth W., ed. *With Open Eyes, Women and African Cinema. Matatu* 19, 1997.

Harrow, Kenneth W. "With Open Eyes, Women of Stone and Hammers: The Problematic Encounter between Western Feminism and African Feminist Filmmaking Practice." *With Open Eyes, Women and African Cinema*, ed., Kenneth W. Harrow. *Matatu* 19, 1997, pp. 133-149.

Herzberger-Fofana, Pierrette. "La femme dans l'imaginaire des femmes-ecrivains d'Afrique de l'ouest francophone." *Women and the Media in Africa*. Association of African Women for Research and Development/AAWORD, Occasional Paper Series, no. 6, Dakar, 1992, pp. 176-216.

Houenassou-Houangbe, Kayissan D. "Les femmes des services de la communication au Togo." *Women and the Media in Africa*. Association of African Women for Research and Development/AAWORD, Occasional Paper Series, no. 6, Dakar, 1992, pp. 8-38.

Ikor, Glélé Agboho Roger. Interview with Keita Mama, Mali-Actress. *Amina*, no. 216, April 1988, p. 29.

Ilboudo, Patrick G. *Le FESPACO 1969-1989, Les cinéastes africains et leurs oeuvres.* (Ouagadougou: Editions La Mante, 1988).

Imam, Ayesha. "Ideology, Women and Mass Media: A Case Study in Kano, Nigeria." *Women and the Media in Africa.* Association of African Women for Research and Development/AAWORD, Occasional Paper Series, no. 6, Dakar, 1992, pp. 39-104.

Kabé, Zilma. "Franceline Oubda et Henriette Ilboudo deux figures de la télé burkinabé." *Amina*, no. 232, August 1989, p. 39.

Kaboré, Francis. "Trois actrices à coeur ouvert." Profile of three actresses, veteran and newcomers: Jeanne Dah, Ivory Coast; Zélika Souley, Niger; Djénéba Dao, Burkina Faso. *Amina*, no. 131, May 1983, p. 52.

Kaboré, Françoise. "Female Scoop in Harare." *Ecrans d'Afrique*, nos. 17-18, 3rd-4th quarter, 1996, p. 84.

_____. Interview with Kahena Attia, Tunisia-Chief Film Editor. *Ecrans d'Afrique*, no. 8, 2nd quarter, 1994, p. 67.

_____. Profile of Funmi Osoba, Nigeria-Director. *Ecrans d'Afrique*, no. 2, 3rd quarter, 1992, p. 70.

Kaboré, Françoise and Sakbolé. "Alone: A Film about a Family in Zimbabwe by Tsitsi Dangarembga." *Ecrans d'Afrique*, nos. 13-14, 3rd-4th quarter, 1995, p. 62.

Kaplan, E. Ann. *Looking for the Other: Feminism, Film and the Imperial Gaze.* (New York: Routledge, 1997).

Keita, Alkaly Miriam. "Women's Image in the Niger Mass Media." *Women and the Mass Media in Africa: Case Studies of Sierra Leone, the Niger and Egypt.* African Training and Research Centre for Women/Voluntary Fund for the United Nations Decade for Women. Research Series, Addis Ababa, 1981, pp. 13-19.

Kiba, Simon. "Voix féminines de la télévision privée multi-media du Burkina." Profile of hosts and announcers on the multi-media television of Burkina: Delphine Ouattara, Host-Announcer; Assétou Simporé, Host in Jula language; Ledy Clémentine Yameogo, Host in Moré language; Maryse Balima, Announcer. *Amina*, no. 301, May 1995, p. 34.

_____. Interview with Oumou Sy, Senegal-Costume designer. *Amina*, no. 285, January 1994, p. 20.

_____. "Les femmes journalistes face au haut-conseil audio-visuel." *Amina*, no. 259, November 1991, p. 34.

Kindem, Gorham H. and Martha Steele. "Women in Sembene's Films." *Jump Cut*, May 1991, pp. 52-60.

Kituno, Kusaka. Interview with Amba Elonda, Democratic Republic of Congo-TV Announcer. *Amina*, no. 148, October 1984, p. 18.

Koulibaly, Isaie Biton. "Les speakerines de Canal II." Profile of three announcers at the Ivory Coast television: Marie-Chantal Zouzoua, Marie-Flavie Echene, and Noelle Yor. *Amina*, no. 247, November 1990, p. 12.

_____. Interview with Loulou Akissi Delphine, Ivory Coast-Actress. *Amina*, no. 215, May 1988, p. 85.

_____. Interview with Nadia Sani-Agatta, Benin-Actress. *Amina*, no. 215, May 1988, p. 85.

_____. "Les charmes de la télévision ivoirienne." Profile of five women announcers at the Ivory Coast television: Viviane Sahoa, Marie-José Oulai, Fatou Diagne, Elisabeth Tanoh Amon, and Hortense Koffi Aya. *Amina*, no. 213, March 1988, pp. 40-41.

Ladd, Florence, C. "*Sidet: Forced Exile.*" *Sage* No. 1, Summer, 1990.

Landau, Julia. Portrait of Miriam Patsanza, South Africa-Producer. *Ecrans d'Afrique*, no. 8, 2nd quarter, 1994, p. 30.

Larouche, Michel, ed. *Films d'Afrique.* (Montréal: Guernica, 1991).

Latoundji, Nafissatou. "Conditions d'émergence d'un cinéma au féminin en Afrique noire." In: *L'Afrique et le Centenaire du Cinéma/Africa and the Centenary of Cinema*, Pan-African Federation of Filmmakers. (Paris: Présence Africaine, 1995), pp. 371-372.

Lihamba, Amandina and Penina Mlama. "Women in Communication: Popular Theatre as an Alternative Medium: The Mkambalani Popular Theatre Workshop." *Women and the Media in Africa.* Association of African Women for Research and Development/AAWORD, Occasional Paper Series, no. 6, Dakar, 1992, pp. 105-174.

Liking, Werewere. "An African Woman Speaks Out Against African Filmmakers.*" Black Renaissance/Renaissance Noire*, Fall 1996, pp. 170-.

_____. "Quand l'art se confond avec la vie." In: *Femmes d'Images de l'Afrique Francophone*, ed., Najwa Tlili. (Montreal: Vues d'Afrique, 1994), pp. 91-94.

Mackanga, Bindza. Profile of Sheila Comlan, Niger-Actress. *Amina*, no. 204, August, 1987, p. 17.

MacRae, Suzanne H. "The Mature and Older Women of African Film." *With Open Eyes, Women and African Cinema*, ed., Kenneth W. Harrow. *Matatu* 19, 1997, pp. 17-30.

Maiga, Cheick Kolla. Interview with Hafsa Z. Koudil, Algeria-Director. *Ecrans d'Afrique*, no. 12, 2nd quarter, 1995, p. 12.

_____. Profile of Aminata Zouré, Burkina Faso-Make-up Artist. *Ecrans d'Afrique*, no. 3, 1st quarter, 1993, p. 87.

Maldoror, Sarah. "To Make a Film Means to Take a Position." In: *African Experiences of Cinema*, ed., Imruh Bakari and Mbye Cham (London: British Film Institute, 1996), pp. 45-47.

_____. "Une culture du devenir." In: *L'Afrique et le Centenaire du Cinéma/ Africa and the Centenary of Cinema*, Pan-African Federation of Filmmakers. (Paris: Présence Africaine, 1995), pp. 393-394.

Malkmus, Lizabeth and Roy Armes. *Arab and African Filmmaking.* (London: Zed Press, 1991).

Mamari, K. "Visages de femmes: deux actrices de talent." Profile of Albertine N'Guessan and Carmen Levry, two actresses in the film, *Visages de femmes* by Désiré Ecaré. *Amina*, no. 194, October 1986, p. 16.

_____. Interview with Suzanne Coulibaly, Ivory Coast-Script Supervisor. *Amina*, no. 303, July 1983, p. 18.

Martin, Michael T., ed. *Cinemas of the Black Diaspora: Diversity, Dependence and Oppositionality.* (Detroit: Wayne State University, 1995).

Mendy, Georges. "Quatre communicatrices gabonaises. Leur atout: le réalisme." Profile of four women in the media in Gabon: Angéle Revignet, Videomaker; Laure Makagha, News announcer; Ntsmae Marie-Clarie Obame, Radio technician; Ntsame Eyogho, Video editor. *Amina*, no. 285, January 1994, p. 16.

Mendy, Renee. Interview with Mariama Hima, Niger-Director/Ambassador to France as of 1997. *Amina*, no. 328, August 1997, p. 15.

Miglioli, Corinne. Portrait of Palesa Letlaka-Nkosi, South Africa-Director. *Ecrans d'Afrique*, nos. 21-22, 3rd-4th quarter, 1997, p. 41.

Morganti, Nike. "Anta and Lingère: Portraits of Women." *Ecrans d'Afrique*, no. 24, 2nd quarter, 1998, p. 54.

Mortimer, Mildred. "Nouveau regard, nouvelle parole: le cinéma d'Assia Djebar." *With Open Eyes, Women and African Cinema*, ed., Kenneth W. Harrow. *Matatu* 19, 1997, pp. 93-110.

Mungai, Anne. "Responsibility and Freedom of Expression." In: *African Experiences of Cinema*, ed., Imruh Bakari and Mbye Cham (London: British Film Institute, 1996), pp. 65-66.

_____. "Liberté d'expression et responsabilité." *Presence Africaine* (Special issue on Cinema and Liberty: Cinéma et Libertés: Contribution au thème du FESPACO '93), 1993, pp. 25-28.

Nanji, Simon. Interview with Félicité Wouassi: "African Directors Lack Imagination." *Revue Noire* (Special cinema issue), no. 8, 1993, p. 7.

N'daw, Aly N'Keury. "Zalika: Star of Niger films." *Ecrans d'Afrique*, nos. 5-6, 3rd-4th quarter, 1993, p. 28.

Ngo-Nguidjol, Emile. "Focusing on Women in African Cinema: An Annotated Bibliography." *With Open Eyes, Women and African Cinema*, ed., Kenneth W. Harrow. *Matatu* 19, 1997, pp. 191-218.

Niang, Sada. *Littérature et cinéma en Afrique francophone: Ousmane Sembène et Assia Djebar.* (Paris: L'Harmattan, 1996).

Nichols, Lee. Interview with Tsitsi Dangarembga. *ALA Bulletin* (African Literature Association), Spring, 1997, pp. 11-16.

Nwachukwu, Frank Ukadike. "Reclaiming Images of Women in Film from Africa and the Black Diaspora." In: *African Experiences of Cinema*, ed., Imruh Bakari and Mbye Cham (London: British Film Institute), 1996, pp. 194-208.

Nwachukwu-Agbada, J.O.J. "Women in Igbo Language Films: The Virtuous and the Villainous." *With Open Eyes, Women and African Cinema*, ed., Kenneth W. Harrow. *Matatu* 19 (1997), pp. 67-80.

Ogazuma, Debrah M. "Film, Video and Development in the 1990's: Challenges/Prospects for the African Woman Director/Producer." A Presentation at the Thirty Third Annual Meeting of the African Studies Association. Baltimore, Maryland, USA, November 1990.

Ouedraogo, Hamidou. *Naissance et Evolution du FESPACO, de 1969 à 1973.* Ouagadougou, 1995. Within this detailed chronology of FESPACO, there is the presence of women in the higher echelons of the institution of FESPACO, such as Alimata Salembéré, Odette Sanogoh and Simone Mensah.

Ouedraogo, Noufou. Profile of Dommie Yambo Odotte, Kenya-Director. *Ecrans d'Afrique,* no. 12, 2nd quarter, 1995, p. 18.

Ouedraogo, Oumdouba. Interview with Anne-Laure Folly, Togo-Director. *Amina,* no. 277, May 1993, pp. 76-77.

Petty, Sheila. "Black African Feminist Film-Making?" In: *African Experiences of Cinema,* ed., Imruh Bakari and Mbye Cham (London: British Film Institute, 1996), pp. 185-193.

_____. *"Miseria*: Towards an African Feminist Framework of Analysis." *Iris* (New Discourses of African Cinema/Nouveaux discours du cinéma africain), special editor, N. Frank Ukadike, no. 18, Spring 1995, pp. 137-145.

_____. "La représentation des femmes dans le cinéma africain." In: *Films d'Afrique,* ed., Michel Larouche (Montréal: Guernica, 1991), pp. 127-141.

_____. "La femme dans le cinéma d'Afrique noire." Université de Paris IV, 1988. Ph.D. dissertation on the woman in the cinema of black Africa.

Pfaff, Françoise. *"Sarraounia*: An Epic of Resistance: Interview with Med Hondo." *With Open Eyes, Women and African Cinema,* ed., Kenneth W. Harrow. *Matatu* 19, 1997, pp. 151-158.

_____. "Africa from Within: The Films of Gaston Kaboré and Idrissa Ouédraogo as Anthropological Sources." In: *African Experiences of Cinema,* ed., Imruh Bakari and Mbye Cham (London: British Film Institute), 1996, pp. 223-238.

_____. "Conversation with Ghanaian Filmmaker Kwaw Ansah." *Research in African Literatures* (Special Issue: African Cinema), Fall 1995, pp. 186-193.

_____. "Hollywood's Die-hard Jungle Melodrama." In: *L'Afrique et le Centenaire du Cinéma/Africa and the Centenary of Cinema,* Pan-African Federation of Film-makers (Paris: Présence Africaine, 1995), pp. 194-149.

_____. "Sembene, A Griot of Modern Times." In: *Cinemas of the Black Diaspora: Diversity, Dependence and Oppositionality,* ed. Michael T. Martin (Detroit: Wayne State University, 1995), pp. 118-128.

_____. "Impact de la co-production sur les composantes socioculturelles du cinéma d'Afrique francophone." *Présence Africaine.* Special issue on Cinema and Liberty: Cinéma et Libertés: Contribution au thème du FESPACO '93, 1993, pp. 43-48.

_____. "Eroticism and Sub-Saharan African Films." *Zast: Zeitschrift fur Afrikastudien,* nos. 9-10, 1991, pp. 5-16.

_____. *Twenty-five Black African Filmmakers.* (Westport: Greenwood Press, 1988). Chapters on Safi Faye and Sarah Maldoror, including a filmography and comprehensive bibliography.

_____. *The Cinema of Ousmane Sembene, A Pioneer of African Film.* (Westport: Greenwood Press, 1984).

_____. "Three Faces of Africa: Women in *Xala.*" *Jump Cut,* July 1982, pp. 27-31.

Piétrus, Fabienne. "MCM Africa, première chaîne musicale africaine." Profile of two women at MCM Africa, the first African music channel: Sempé, Host and Seynabou Sy, Director of Programming. *Amina,* no. 336, April 1998, p. 20

Pouya, André-Marie. Interview with Thérèse Sita-Bella. *Amina,* no. 233, September 1989, p. 44.

Rahman, Awataf Abdel. "Women's Image in the Egyptian Mass Media." *Women and the Mass Media in Africa: Case Studies of Sierra Leone, the Niger and Egypt.* African Training and Research Centre for Women/Voluntary Fund for the United Nations Decade for Women. Research Series, Addis Ababa, 1981, pp. 21-28.

Reid, Mark A. "Dialogic Modes of Representing Africa(s): Womanist Film." In: *Cinemas of the Black Diaspora: Diversity, Dependence and Oppositionality,* ed., Michael T. Martin (Detroit: Wayne State University, 1995), pp. 56-69.

_____. "Black Feminism and the Independent Film." In: *Redefining Black Cinema,* Mark A. Reid (Berkeley: University of California Press, 1993) pp. 109-125.

Revue Noire, no. 8, 1993, p. 12. "Fanta Nacro, *Un certain matin.*" (Special cinema issue).

_____, no. 8, 1993, p. 20. "Ngozi Onwurah, *Coffee Coloured Children.*" (Special cinema issue).

_____, no. 8, 1993, p. 10. "Oumou Sy, A Dressmaker's Faith." (Special cinema issue).

Richard, Benon B. Profile of Rosine Yanogo, Burkina Faso-Actress. *Amina,* no. 132, June 1983, p. 23.

Rosati, Luigi. Profile of Hanny Tchelley, Ivory Coast-Actress. *Amina,* no. 224, December 1988, p. 32.

Ruelle, Catherine. "La place de la femme." *L'Afrique Littéraire* (Special number on Sembene Ousmane), ed., Daniel Serceau, no. 76, 1985. pp. 80-83.

Sama, Emmanuel. "Le cinéma au féminin sort ses griffes, 'Un certain matin' avec Régina Fanta Nacro," *Amina,* no. 265, May 1992, pp. 22-21.

_____. "African Cinema in the Feminine: A Difficult Birth Giving." (Summary of the Historical African Women in the Cinema Workshop, FESPACO 1991). *Ecrans d'Afrique,* no. 1, 2nd quarter, 1992, p. 70.

Sarr, Ibrahima. Interview with Safi Faye. *Sud Week-end,* October 1996.

Schmidt, Nancy. "Sub-Saharan African Women Filmmakers: Agendas for Research." *With Open Eyes, Women and African Cinema,* ed., Kenneth W. Harrow. *Matatu* 19, 1997, pp. 163-190. Includes filmography.

Sé, Anne Khady. "Mariam Thinks Positive." Profile of Mariam Kaba, Guinea-Actress. *Ecrans d'Afrique,* no. 20, 2nd quarter, 1997, p. 36.

Sezirahiga, Jadot. Interview with Sarah Maldoror, Guadeloupe-Director. *Ecrans d'Afrique,* no. 12, 2nd quarter, 1995, p. 6.

_____. Profile of Kadiatou Konaté, Mali-Director. *Ecrans d'Afrique*, no. 8, 2nd quarter, 1994, p. 28.

Shohat, Ella and Robert Stam. *Unthinking Eurocentrism: Multiculturalism and the Media*. (London and New York: Routledge, 1994).

Signate, Ibrahima. *Un cinéaste rebelle: Med Hondo*. (Paris: Présence Africaine, 1994). Med Hondo discusses the place of women in Africa and African film: "Les Femmes," pp. 79-80.

Siyolwe, Wabei. "Discovery of a Festival." *Ecrans d'Afrique*, no. 21-22, 1997, p. 55.

_____. "The Variety of African Cultures." *Ecrans d'Afrique*, nos. 21-22, 3rd-4th quarter, 1997, p. 67.

Speciale, Alessandra. Profile of Viola Shafik, Tunisia-Director. *Ecrans d'Afrique*, nos. 9-10, 3rd-4th quarter, 1994, p. 32.

_____. "A Threefold Trial: African, Female and Actress." Portrait of Naky Sy Savane, Ivory Coast and Félicité Wouassi, Cameroon. *Ecrans d'Afrique*, no. 7, 1st quarter, 1994, p. 24.

_____. Interview with Oumou Sy, Senegal-Costume designer. *Ecrans d'Afrique*, no. 2, 3rd quarter, 1992, p. 104.

Stringer, Julian. "On the Rise: The Work of Ngozi Onwurah." *CineAction*, no. 37, 1995, pp. 38-48.

Tanifeani, William. "Gloria Rolando on Slavery." *Ecrans d'Afrique*, no. 23, 1st quarter, 1998, p. 86.

Tapsoba, Clément. "The Women of FESPACO 97: Valérie Kaboré or the filmmaker 'of all trades'." *Ecrans d'Afrique*, no. 19, 1st quarter, 1997, p. 35.

_____. "Aids in the City." Interview with Hanny Brigitte Tchelley, Ivory Coast-Actress/TV Producer. *Ecrans d'Afrique*, nos. 17-18, 3rd-4th quarter, 1996, p. 88.

_____. "When Women Standup, African Cinema Moves." Interview with Martine Ilboudo Condé, Guinea/Burkina Faso-Director. *Ecrans d'Afrique*, nos. 17-18, 3rd-4th quarter, 1996, p. 22.

_____. Profile of Oum Dierryla, Senegal-Actress. *Ecrans d'Afrique*, no. 12, 2nd quarter, 1995, p. 17.

_____. Profile of Sarah Bouyain, Burkina Faso-Assistant Director. *Ecrans d'Afrique*, no. 11, 1st quarter, 1995, p. 18.

_____. Profile of Margaret Fombé Fobé, Cameroon-Director. *Ecrans d'Afrique*, no. 8, 2nd quarter, 1994, p. 27.

_____. Profile of Joyce Makwenda, Zimbabwe-Director. *Ecrans d'Afrique*, nos. 5-6, 3rd-4th quarter, 1993, p. 39.

_____. Profile of Franceline Oubda, Burkina Faso-TV Director. *Ecrans d'Afrique*, nos. 5-6, 3rd-4th quarter, 1993, p. 40.

_____. Profile of Anne-Laure Folly, Togo-Director. *Ecrans d'Afrique*, no. 2, 3rd quarter, 1992, p. 36.

_____. Profile of Maysa Marta, Guinea-Bissau-Actress. *Ecrans d'Afrique*, no. 2, 3rd quarter, 1992, p. 36.

Tiberio, Margaret. "An Interview with Salem Mekuria." *Visions*, Winter 1991.

Tiemtoré, Tiégo. "Forte percée féminine." *Amina*, no. 301, May 1995, p. 38. Summary of FESPACO 1995.

Tlili, Najwa. *Femmes d'Images de l'Afrique Francophone*. Montreal: Vues d'Afrique, 1994. Filmography of African women in francophone regions of Africa.

Vieyra, Paulin Soumanou. 'La femme dans le cinéma africain." In: *Réflexions d'un cinéaste africain.* (Brussels: OCIC, 1990), pp. 82-88. Focus on the woman in African cinema.

Vincent, William A. "The Unreal but Visible Line: Difference and Desire for the Other in *Chocolat*." *With Open Eyes, Women and African Cinema*, ed., Kenneth W. Harrow. *Matatu* 19, 1997, pp. 125-132.

Wilson, Elisabeth. Interview with Franceline Oubda, Burkina Faso-TV Director. *Amina*, no. 279, July 1993, p. 22.

Yeye, Zakaria. Inteview with Hanny Tchelley, Ivory Coast, Actress-Director of Festival International du Court Metrage d'Abidjan FICA. *Amina*, no. 344, December 1998, p. 26.

Zacks, Stephen. "A Problematic Sign of African Difference in *Reassemblage*." *With Open Eyes, Women and African Cinema*, ed., Kenneth W. Harrow. *Matatu* 19, 1997, pp. 3-16.

Zanklan, Bernard G. "Beninoises caméra au poing" Profile of video camerawomen from Benin: Micheline Adjovi, Ayi Corinne, Alapini A. Micheline, Charlotte D'Almeida, Anasthasie Nevis, Alexine Quenum, Leocadie Tohoueho, Laurette Vigouroux, Bintou Yessoufou. *Amina*, no. 266, June, 1992, pp. 52-53.